JOHN PIPER
AND STAINED GLASS

Remembering Myfanwy

JOHN PIPER AND STAINED GLASS

JUNE OSBORNE

SUTTON PUBLISHING

First published in the United Kingdom in 1997 by
Sutton Publishing Limited · Phoenix Mill
Thrupp · Stroud · Gloucestershire · GL5 2BU

British Library Cataloguing in Publication Data

A catalogue record for this book is available from the British Library

ISBN 0 7509 1088 7

Typeset in 10/14 pt Sabon.
Typesetting and origination by
Sutton Publishing Limited.
Printed in Hong Kong by
Midas Printing.

CONTENTS

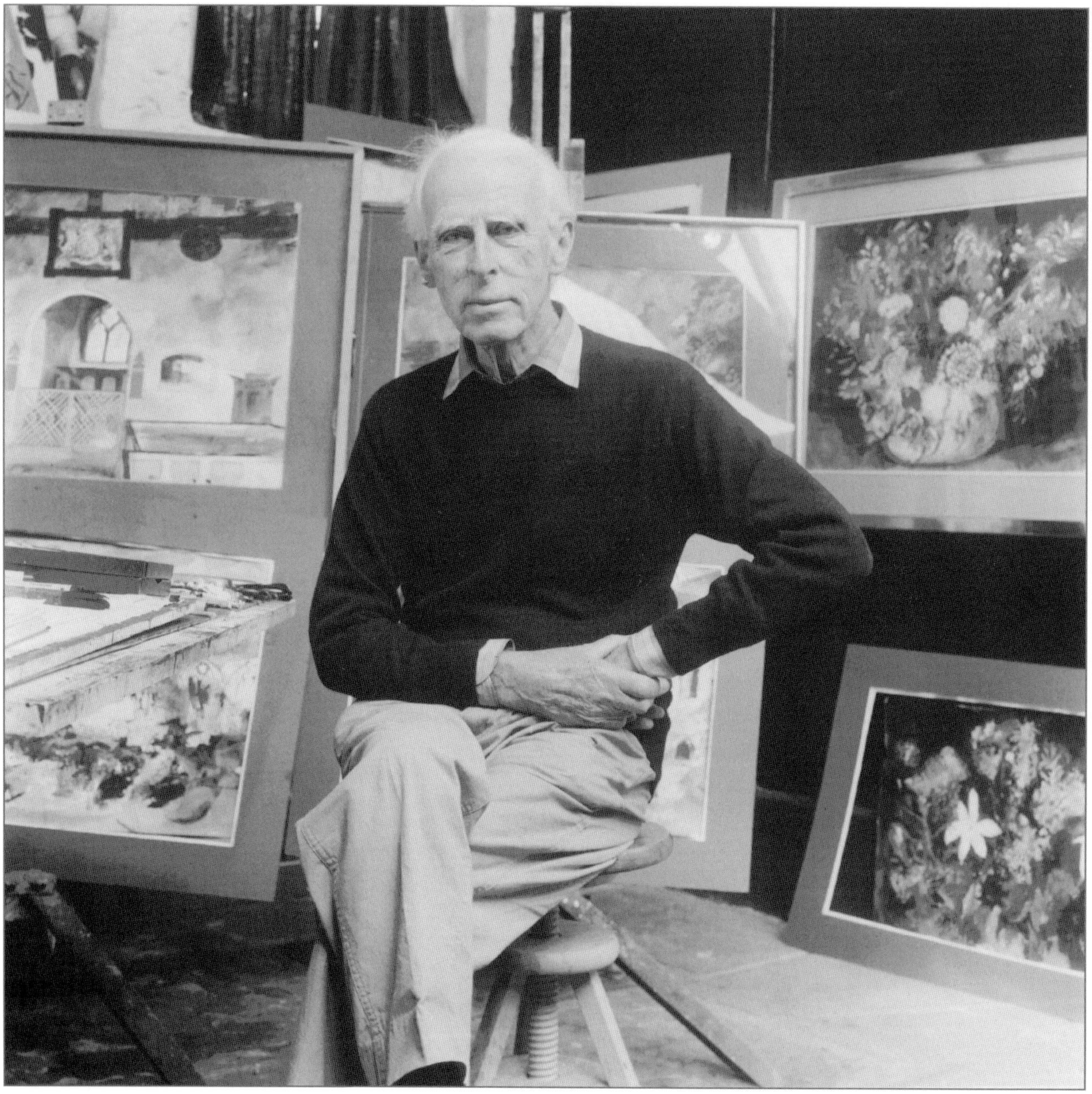

Frontispiece: John Piper, *c.* 1985. (Photo. courtesy of the Piper family)

LIST OF ILLUSTRATIONS

Unless stated otherwise, all photographs were taken by and remain the property of the author.

I know that my mother Myfanwy would want me to thank June Osborne for compiling this book of John Piper's stained glass, and I wish her every success in its publication.

Suzannah Piper (Brooks)

PREFACE AND ACKNOWLEDGEMENTS

What a joy and what a privilege it has been to write this book. A privilege because it breaks new ground; the book is the first to deal with this particular subject, which in the writing of it I have become increasingly convinced is an important one. For it is only between the pages of a book that the range and quality of John Piper's work in this field can be demonstrated. No exhibition can do this, for the windows are happily ensconced in their rightful settings the length and breadth on the county (and, indeed, abroad). Meanwhile, the cartoons on which the windows are based, which are full-size working drawings – or rather, paintings in gouache with collage – are many of them too big to display in a gallery. They are, nevertheless, immensely important. While Burne-Jones, for instance, made only black-and-white designs for windows and left it to William Morris to put in the colour as he thought fit, with Piper the colour was vital and intrinsic to his ideas; and he made it clear to the interpreters who actually made the windows exactly what effects he wanted. Rolled-up pieces of card stacked in a studio can thus be of the greatest significance.

The joy has been in the discovery. The revisiting and reappraisal of windows one already knew (which always turned out to be even more wonderful than one ever believed); the delving into archives to enhance appreciation and give one greater understanding; the challenge of doing one's own photography, which somehow underlines the experience. And then the probing into sources to discover the symbolism of the windows. I may not be a particularly holy person, but I have never read the Bible so much as in the preparation of this book.

Another great joy has been to see for the first time remote windows of astonishing beauty. After waiting two hours for the key of St Peter's, Babraham, the delight when one opened the door to discover the splendid East Window with its strutting cock. Or to go to Thorpe Tilney on a hot midsummer day, and there to see the panels in a garden pavilion by a pool and flanked with beds of old-fashioned roses. Or coming to Farnborough on the Berkshire Downs just after sunset to find the Betjeman Window luminous in the afterglow. And finally to see the Nativity Window, brilliant as never before, in a Norman window embrasure at St Mary's, Iffley (just outside Oxford).

There have been all these delightful experiences and many more. Added to this, there has been the enormous pleasure of meeting people, and the great welcome I received wherever I went, whether into great cathedrals, famous boys' schools, or people's homes. The greatest joy was to visit, and revisit many times, Fawley Bottom Farmhouse – a special place like nowhere else – and to be greeted with such friendliness and hospitality by Myfanwy Piper; to be given the freedom of the place, to be allowed to hunt through sketches and correspondence, to unroll cartoons on the studio floor, even to re-paste a collage butterfly which had become semi-detached from the cartoon for the Betjeman window.

So in making a list of acknowledgements, it is to Myfanwy Piper that I owe the first and greatest debt. Indeed, without her cooperation the book could hardly have been written. I was greatly helped too by David Wasley, who kindly lent me his photographic record of seven years' interpretation of Piper's designs, whether by his own hand or by Patrick Reyntiens, and did much to enlighten me about the workings of the Beaconsfield studio.

My next debt is to Leyland Shawe, who has patiently driven me many miles, and has been most generous of his time in assisting me in my researches.

My four children, Ian, Elizabeth, Jane and Patrick, also their partners, have been supportive and encouraging throughout.

My thanks are due to Martin Harrison for the work he has done on this subject, and for generously leaving me a free field; to Patrick Reyntiens for allowing me to quote from his writings; to Joseph Nuttgens for a measure of his time when he was particularly busy.

I should also like to thank those kind people who share my enthusiasm and who invited me into their homes, in particular Norman Scarfe of Woodbridge; Mr and Mrs Ian Russell of Shulbrede Priory; Mrs Betty Kelaart of Nettlebed; also Irene and Heather Carr for a pleasant overnight stop, and Eily and John Buffone for another one.

I have been encouraged by the interest and helpfulness of the Piper family, especially Suzannah Brooks; also Roger Thorp; Martin Henig; David Jenkins; Caroline Swash; Di Gold; Jennifer Bartlett; Jane Burton; Alan Glencross; Robert Wilkins; Victor Bugg; the Revd Peter Judd of St Mary's, Iffley; Jennifer Patten; Professor Ian McDonald (for information on Christ's College, Christchurch, New Zealand); in addition Professor Christopher Frayling of the Royal College of Art; the Tate Gallery Archive; the Victoria and Albert Museum; Paul Robinson, Curator of Devizes Museum; and the staff of the Bristol City Art Gallery.

I would also like to thank the Provost and Fellows of Eton College and the very helpful members of the staff I met there, in particular Mr Eaton and the Librarian, Penny Hatfield; the Headmaster and staff of Oundle School; the staff of the Hall of the Bakers' Company; the Warden and staff of Robinson College, Cambridge, and the Archivist there, Cdr George Coupe; the administrative staff of Churchill College, Cambridge; the Chaplain of Nuffield College, Oxford; the staff, in particular the Archivist, at Coventry Cathedral; Cathedral House and the archivists at the Metropolitan Cathedral of Christ the King, Liverpool; the Very Revd Patrick Mitchell, Dean of Windsor, together with the staff of the Chapter Office; J.A. Dalberto of the Washington National Cathedral; Christine Reynolds of the Muniment Room at Westminster Abbey (for information on St

Margaret's); Crispin Gill and the Revd Nick McKinner of St Andrew's, Plymouth; the Revd Adrian Alker of St Mark's, Sheffield; Fr Paul Baker of St Paul's, Jarrow; the Revd P.G. Cobb of All Saints, Clifton; the Revd Robert Middlewick of St Mary's, Lamberhurst; the Revd Peter Brown of All Saints, of Laleham-on-Thames.

I am also indebted to the staff of St Lawrence College, Ramsgate; Malsis School, near Keighley; Bradfield College; Cheltenham College; and Ipswich School (in particular Sally Dawson, the Headmaster's Secretary); the staff at Thorpe Tilney; the staff at St John's Hospital, Lichfield; at Charing Cross Hospital; at the Wessex Hotel, Winchester; and the caretaker at No. 52 Berners Street.

In addition to those I have already mentioned, my thanks are due to the incumbents and keyholders of the following: St Peter and St Paul's, Abington; St Peter and St Paul's, Aldeburgh; St Peter's, Firle; All Saints, Misterton; St Peter's, Babraham; St Paul's, Bledlow Ridge; St Mary's, Turville; St Mary's, Fawley; All Saints, Farnborough; Llandaff Cathedral; St Woolo's Cathedral, Newport; St Mary's, Swansea; St Matthew's, Southcote, Reading; St Giles, Totternhoe; St Martin's, Sandford St Martin; St Peter's, Wolvercote; St Bartholomew's, Nettlebed; St Paul's, Pishill; All Hallows, Wellingborough; St Andrew's, Wolverhampton; All Saints, Brightwalton; St Martin's, Eastleach; St Leonard's, Grateley.

Thank you all for letting me come and see your beautiful windows, and for allowing me to photograph them. Without your help, I should never have been able to write this book.

June Osborne
1996

POSTSCRIPT TO AUTHOR'S PREFACE

Myfanwy Piper was consulted at all times throughout the preparation of this book, and had promised to write a foreword for it. 'Don't worry, I haven't forgotten about you' were her last words to me. The foreword may have existed in her head, but unfortunately had never been committed to paper when the sad news came of her death on 18 January 1997.

My intention had been to dedicate this book 'To my children, and theirs'. But under the circumstances (with their permission and the approval of the Piper family), I thought it right to dedicate it instead to Myfanwy's memory – since I am assured it was done with her blessing.

June Osborne
February 1997

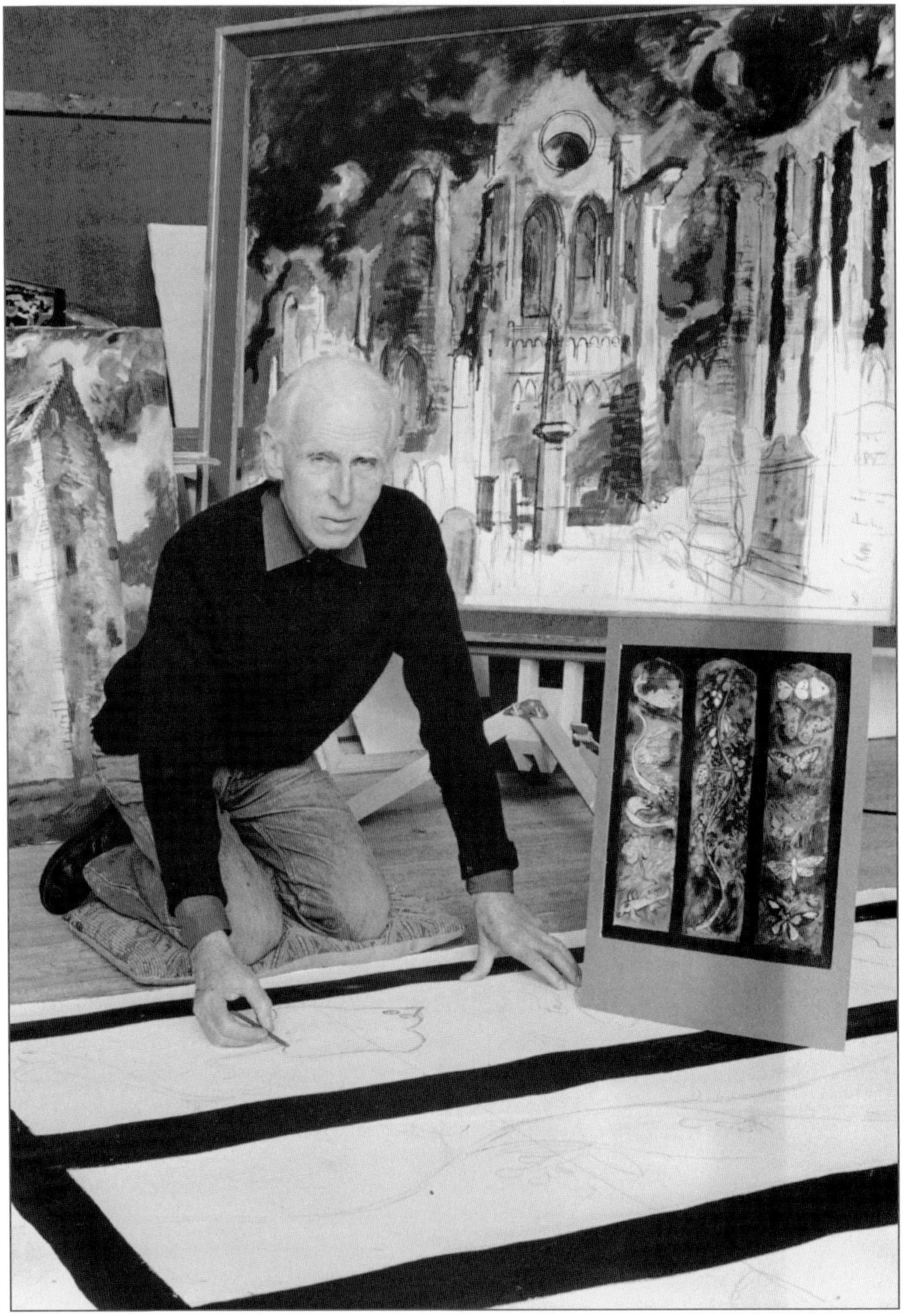

John Piper at work on the cartoon for the John Betjeman Memorial Window (see also pp. 142, 143, 148–9). (Photo. courtesy of the Piper family)

INTRODUCTION

> The One remains, the many change and pass;
> Heaven's light forever shines, Earth's shadows fly;
> Life, like a dome of many-coloured glass
> Stains the white radiance of Eternity.
>
> Adonais, *Percy Bysshe Shelley* (1792–1822)

Colouring the heavens, making a mutation of the sky, that is what stained glass uniquely does. No other medium has this property; painting, sculpture, drawing, these are revealed by the passage of light across them, but with stained glass the movement is through, penetrating to the sky beyond. Consequently it is subject to perpetual change; sun sharpens it, cloud mutes it, twilight softens it. One may look at a window a hundred times but it is never quite the same.

Subject to the vicissitudes of nature, the fluctuations between light and dark, stained glass nevertheless bears the imprint of man. This is the artistry: not the mere filling of the window embrasure with this incredible material, keeping as it does the texture of liquidity, not even the saturation of space with colours – but the balancing of those colours, the juxtapositions, the superimposing sometimes of glass on glass, the modification with brush-line or stippling, and the enhancing of the whole by the emphasis of lead-lines. And the ultimate intent is not, or should not be, simply decoration; stained glass at its best and most profound has something compelling to say.

This above all is what characterizes the windows designed by John Piper. He approached the medium with high seriousness. At the same time, he had a freshness of vision and a range of style that has never been rivalled. Every window he designed has his own personal signature; that is to say, there is some quality about it which makes it instantly recognizable as 'Piper glass'. What an exhibition it would make if all the examples could be gathered into one gallery. Scattered throughout the country and beyond as they are, this is clearly an impossibility: it is to bring them together for the first time that is the primary objective of this book.

In his seminal work *Stained Glass: Art or Anti-Art?* (Studio Vista, 1968; see Appendix A), Piper stressed that it was time that the artist rescued the medium from the artisan, and for that matter, from the archaeologists. He felt that one should look for quality, regardless of age, and criticized the latter for encouraging the belief that everything that was old must necessarily also be good. He considered that this attitude led inevitably to extreme conservatism in design, degenerating ultimately into mere copying. He himself found much to admire in Romanesque and Gothic art, yet felt this was not the way forward. 'Stained glass', he believed, 'would die of undernourishment if left to archaeology.'

In wanting to rescue stained glass from the artisan, Piper was by no means denigrating or shutting out the craftsman on whose skill the interpretation of his concepts depended. He was thinking more of the employee of a commercial firm, working by rote, preoccupied with the day-to-day business of filling spaces, his mind blinkered to the vision that might be lent it by the other arts, or that should indeed have been implicit in the very material. Piper himself, I believe, never disregarded the nature of the medium.

So familiar is glass to us today that it is easy to forget that the material itself is man-made. Silica and alkali are transformed by heat into this wonderful light-transmitting substance. The technique is ancient, the Egyptians knew it, and it is at least as old as the Pyramid of Cheops. Initially it was used for making beads, and small vessels built on a core of sand. With the discovery (in Syria in the first century BC) that glass in its liquid form could be blown as well as moulded, came the making of windows; these adorned the palaces and richer villas of imperial Rome. Generally greenish, they did not, as far as we know, represent anything. There is no evidence of a pictorial element, but the material was left to speak for itself, to repel the weather and to demonstrate the opulence of the patricians who had commissioned it.

Glass-making was, in both senses of the word, a mystery. It was a skilled and secret craft, kept in the family or handed down from master to trusted apprentice; outside this circle it was little understood and much wondered at. Even less understood was how the colour got in: that metallic oxides (cobalt for blue, ferric oxide for yellow/brown, copper for green, copper again but in a reducing or smoky kiln for red) were added while the glass was actually being made, and in its liquid form, at a temperature of about 1,200°C.

It was possible to make window-glass by casting the liquid into a shallow mould, but the method that seems to have been favoured in ancient times (certainly in medieval France) is that which produced 'crown glass'. A 'gather' or blob of the liquid is collected at the end of a glass-blower's pipe and then spun until it forms a disc; when it is cooled, rectangular pieces – often eleven in number – can be cut from it.[1] Because of the way they are made, the pieces will have a distinct whorl pattern.

There is also 'Norman slab' or 'Early English' glass (invented in the nineteenth century), a glass of irregular thickness and texture. A glass bubble is blown into a square mould, and when cooled it is cut along the sides, forming five pieces, much thicker in the centre than at the edges. The glass produced in this manner obviously has an individual quality not found in factory-made glass produced on rollers. But the trouble with both these methods is that the glass has almost too much character, it is too assertive to be assimilated easily into a design. Most stained-glass artists today prefer what is termed 'antique' glass. This is made by blowing an elongated bubble of glass, cutting off one end, splitting the cylinder thus formed, and flattening it into a sheet. When this process is completed, the glass is cooled gently and slowly by being passed through an annealing oven.[2]

Glass made in this way will be fairly regular in thickness, yet it will not have the dead, mechanical flawlessness of commercial glass. It often contains impurities, bubbles, striations, variations in colour, and it is these very imperfections which give it life. It is a material ideally suited to the interpretation of ideas.

Since the colour normally runs right the way through each piece of glass (this is known as 'pot-metal'), rather than being applied to the surface, it follows that wherever a different colour is wanted, a different piece of glass must be used. There are exceptions (notably, as was discovered in the fourteenth century, glass may be stained yellow by the use of silver nitrate), but this was the rule. Hence the need for leading. The leads come in the form of flexible H-shaped calms, which make a secure junction between one piece of glass and the next. Before leading up, any detailing or shading will have been carried out in iron-oxide paint applied to the surface of each piece and then fired to make it permanent. There are other methods of putting windows together – such as *dalles-de-verre* (thick slabs of glass embedded in concrete, which may be used architecturally), and the use of fibreglass – but leading is the traditional way, and the way in which most of Piper's designs were interpreted. If leading, then, is going to be part of the physical structure of the window, it follows that it should be taken into account during the process of design. Indeed, it should be considered not as a limitation, but as a way of giving emphasis to that design, and integrating it with its setting.

Stained glass is inextricably bound up with architecture – there are those who would like to see it regarded as part of it. John Piper in his *Stained Glass: Art or Anti-Art?* quotes Alfred Manessier (in *Le Vitrail Français*): 'I believe less and less in stained-glass window designing; more and more in the simultaneous creation of a light-filled architectural unit, thought out and created by the painter at one go.' There is nothing very new in this view – the Ste Chapelle in Paris was designed on this principle in the thirteenth century – but it presupposes that the building and its windows are both conceived at the same time. More often the stained-glass designer is called upon to create something within an architectural framework that is already in existence. Without being daunted or dominated by the setting, he should be aware of it. Piper, for instance, when he designed his first two windows for Eton College Chapel (The Raising of Lazarus and The Light under a Bushel; see pp. 49–62) had the problem not only of integrating them with the elegant Gothic lines of the architecture, but also of making them fitting companions for the great Evie Hone East Window (Fig. 14, p. 28) which they flank – a window of power and solemnity, which Piper much admired. He solved this by surrounding the main compositions with borders, abstract in conception and pinpointed with specks of colour echoing the dominant hues found in the central themes; and though the borders are far from neutral in colour, they make a subtle transition between these and the mullions.

Of all such niceties, the stained-glass artist should be aware. There have been those, like Ervin Bossanyi[3] and many of the members of the Arts and Crafts Movement, who have insisted that the person who designs the window and the person who brings it into physical being should be one and the same. Certainly this helps ensure an innate knowledge of the qualities of the medium, though there may perhaps be a danger that the craft may sometimes overshadow the art. And surely it becomes very time-consuming when the designer must also be responsible for the cutting, painting and leading of the glass, and its installation within the window-embrasure. This is all good, honest craftsmanship and much of it involves the highest degree of skill and artistry. As far as we know, the designers of medieval windows were in general glaziers. When John Thornton of Coventry was commissioned to create the Great East Window of York Minster (1405–8), he was required to take a hand in the painting, although one cannot believe he was involved in all the processes. In this century, Bossanyi, though he used assistants in making the magnificent 'Peace' and 'Salvation' windows in Canterbury Cathedral, liked to be involved in every stage of their creation. Yet this approach must inevitably cut down on the number of windows an artist can create within his lifetime. The range and diversity of glass designed by Piper is quite astounding, especially if one considers all the other media he was working in at the same time; but how could it have been so great if he had had also to stop and make it?

The interpretation of Piper's ideas into the medium of stained glass was a matter of extreme sensitivity and complexity.[4] Unlike any other artist one can think of who designed for the medium without being involved in the actual making, Piper produced full-scale cartoons in colour. Essentially painterly works, these are executed in gouache, often with the addition of collage to emphasize details. So his interpreter would be left in no doubt as to the colours of glass needed to approximate to these designs. From first looking at the cartoon, he would with his experience be able to judge whether to order English, German or French glass; for instance, for Thorpe Tilney (see pp. 117–20) a great deal of 'flashed' glass[5] was needed, and this was ordered straight away from Germany, because only there did they have the appropriate colours.

Even so, it was often impossible to obtain a good match for Piper's colours from any one piece of glass. Therefore the interpreter had to employ 'plating', that is, superimposing one layer of glass on another, in order to create these subtle nuances. Frequently the whole window would be plated in this way (as had never been done before to this extent), with anything from two to four pieces of glass superimposed one over the other to achieve the correct shade. Indeed, the interpreter with an eye for these things would sometimes introduce more variations in hue than were actually dictated by the cartoon, in order to create texture and interest in areas of the window which might otherwise have seemed a little empty. The positioning of the lead-lines was also left to the interpreter. Initially, before the window was made up, their position would be indicated by painting them in black while the glass was still on the easel.

However carefully the colours of the glass were matched with the colours of Piper's cartoon, this was seldom enough in itself to reproduce the complex textures. Therefore the glass would have to be etched with hydrofluoric acid. Every piece of glass would then be painted with iron-oxide paint, a brownish-black when fired, darkening and modifying the colours. This was brushed on *alla prima* (at first stroke), first to establish the principal tones, then to delineate and develop further subtleties. The additional techniques of enamelling, and staining with silver nitrate (which produces a yellow colour), might then be applied in places. The processes would if possible be done in parallel, because each needed to be fired to fix the effect, and the structure of the glass could be weakened by too many firings.

John Piper would always visit the stained glass studios at the beginning of a project to discuss how his design should be interpreted, then sometimes again before the window was leaded up. He was never shown the cartoon alongside the panel, for the work in glass could never be an exact replica. He realized this; he was aware that it was a very different medium, the result a parallel, not an equivalent.

Piper was full of admiration for those who interpreted his ideas, like – first and foremost – Patrick Reyntiens, and later David Wasley and Joseph Nuttgens. Had it not been for people such as these, there would be no such thing as 'Piper glass'. But for his part, Piper found that he worked more creatively if he kept himself most of the time away from their busy workshops and stayed slightly remote. 'The big problems of painting and sculpture', he wrote (*Stained Glass: Art or Anti-Art?*), 'are still best tackled in isolation'. That, as far as he was concerned, went also for designing stained glass, and Piper found his own creative isolation in the congenial surroundings of Fawley Bottom Farmhouse.

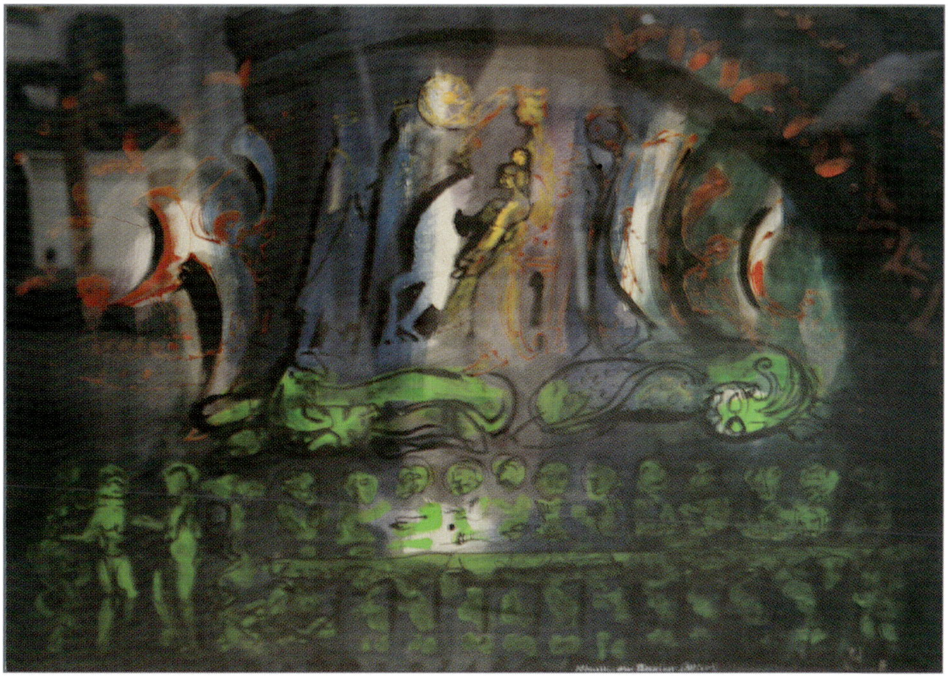

Fig. 1: Tympanum at Neuilly-en-Donjon. Painting by John Piper, *c.* 1969 (see pp. 92, 129, 131, 132)

With his profound knowledge of architecture, and his incomparable awareness about it – he had that kind of inner vision which Gerard Manley Hopkins called 'inscape' – the windows Piper designed were never at variance with their settings, yet embellished them in a wholly original way. And while he usually kept himself aloof from the actual process of making (once the cartoon had left his studio, he sometimes did not see the resulting window until it was almost finished), he nevertheless understood what the medium was about. He put his faith in his interpreters to do justice to his ideas.

Although from his youth he had been deeply interested in the subject, it was not until he was in mid-career that Piper came to design stained glass. He had already proved himself in many fields – in draughtsmanship, painting (see Fig. 1, p. xix), collages, print-making, book-illustration, making constructions, writing guide-books and other works, photography, designing sets for theatre, ballet and opera – yet there was no stained glass before the 1950s. This was in a way an advantage; when Piper did come to design for this medium, he brought with him a wealth of experience and understanding. There were many cross-references that he could make; he could work with the courage born of maturity. In his book *Stained Glass: Art or Anti-Art?*, Piper quoted Marcel Arland, 'It is not certain that every great painter could become a great stained-glass designer, but there is a chance. . . .'

Piper's first commission for stained glass was for three tall windows of three lights each to illumine the apse of Oundle School Chapel (see pp. 39–44). For these he devised nine powerful figures symbolizing the different aspects of Christ. Their limbs are clothed in flame-like sweeps of yellow, plum-red, sea-blue, salmon, leaf-green; their heads are mask-like, enigmatic, and crowned in gold. Boldly conceived, they emerge from a dark background flickering with points of colour. They are striking in their modernity and originality, yet one can perceive that they have their roots in the art of Romanesque and Gothic France.

When they were first displayed in the Grocers' Hall in London, Piper's life-long friend Sir John Betjeman went to see them, and wrote to him at once, hailing them 'your masterpiece to date'.[6] There would be many more masterpieces to come, establishing his significant place in the whole history of stained glass.

CHAPTER ONE

A PASSION FOR TRADITION: JOHN PIPER AND MEDIEVAL GLASS

'A fusion of a life-long search for a contemporary idiom with a passion for tradition.'

Stephen Spender[1]

Stephen Spender's definition of the artistic achievement of John Piper is particularly apposite with regard to his work with stained glass. Piper's interest in the subject long antedated his designing for it. As a boy he delighted in going off on his bicycle and exploring old churches, noting down his discoveries in the form of guidebooks. In 1929, when he was scarcely more than a student, he made a detailed study in water-colour of 'The Stoning of Stephen', a panel of thirteenth-century glass in St Leonard's Church, Grateley, Hampshire (Fig. 2, overleaf). 'On the whole I learnt more about using colours doing this copy than I have ever learned before or since,' Piper wrote nearly forty years later.[2]

It is a square panel, set diamond-wise; in the corners are trefoil designs set against red, and the main field in the centre is a roundel where against a blue ground three figures enact the story of the martyrdom. The two tormentors, gesticulating wildly, are shown in profile, caricatured as was customary to denote wickedness. Their faces are brownish, their clothes subdued in hue, except for the legs of the left-hand figure, which are wearing bright red stockings (which balances the red on the other side of the composition) – the drama is intensified by the way one of his feet breaks into the border of the roundel. St Stephen is shown in the act of going down on his knees; he extends his hands in prayer. His face is composed and resigned; set against a green halo (green the colour of hope and resurrection), it is red with the blood of martyrdom. Piper notes that it 'is represented on a piece of "flashed" glass shaded in deepening red in an abstract impression of his bleeding to death as he kneels'.

The panel was not original to Grateley, but came from Salisbury Cathedral. It was rescued after the almost total destruction of the Cathedral's medieval glass towards the end of the eighteenth century. One shudders to think how many precious and delightful windows were shovelled into the town ditch, to be beaten to pieces by plumbers for the lead. The vogue at that time was for

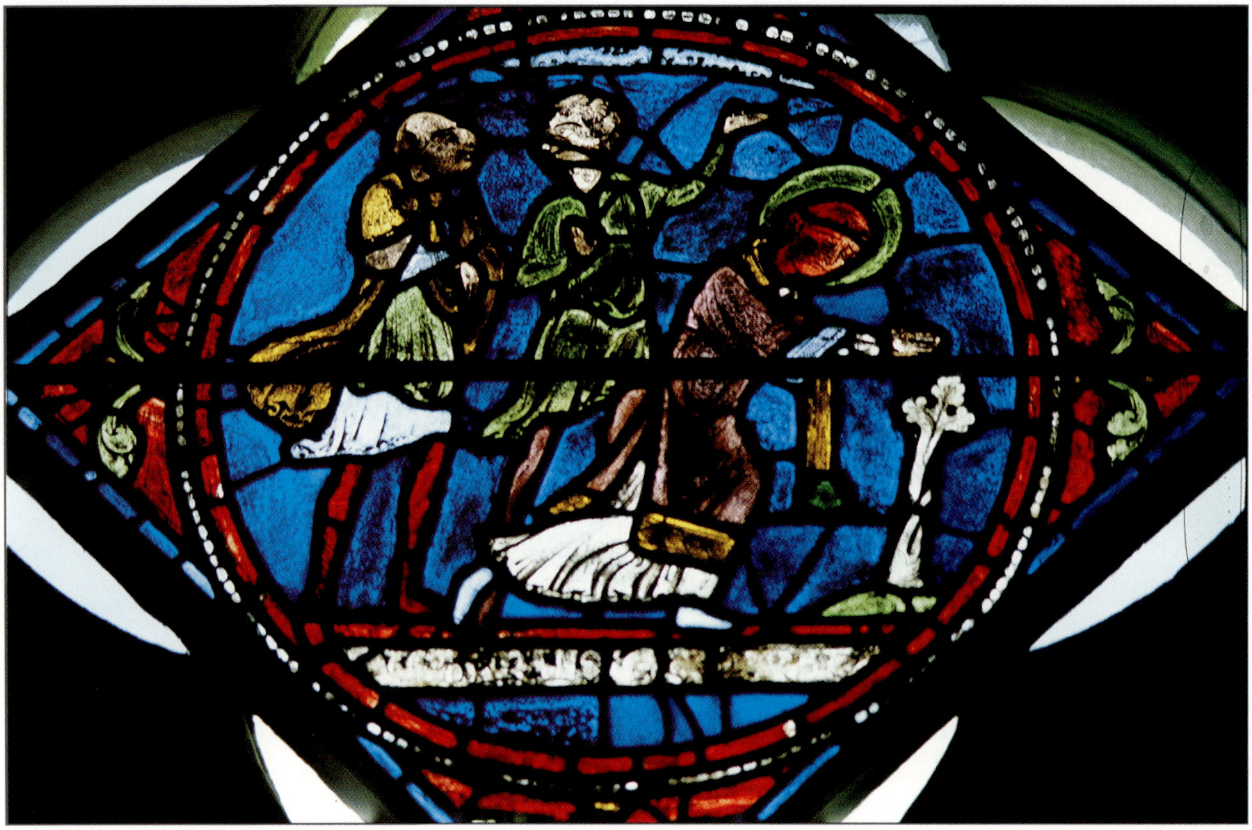

Fig. 2: Grateley, St Leonard's. The Stoning of Stephen

enamelled glass; Gothic was a term of abuse, and the medieval was out of fashion.

Out of fashion too, one suspects, was the intensity of religious belief that had inspired the making of such a panel as 'The Stoning of Stephen', and the filling of whole cathedrals with a symphony of coloured glass. But for Piper this was a living thing; and it was with this ancient tradition of the art as an expression of faith, rather than with the bland rhetoric that characterizes eighteenth-century glass, that his affinity lay. So his own work can best be appreciated in context, not only of his contemporaries, but of his forebears in the past. As he was aware, stained glass is an art of great antiquity.

St Gregory of Tours (539–94), who was elected Bishop of Tours in 573, rebuilt the Cathedral there as well as refurbishing St Martin's Church. In his writings there is the earliest mention I have been able to find of the use of coloured window-glass in churches. Certain it is that stained-glass making must have been well established in France when a century later (AD 680), Benedict Biscop, Abbot of Jarrow and Monkwearmouth, sent messengers there with instructions to bring glaziers back with them to England.[3] We know this from the Venerable Bede's *Lives of the Abbots of Wearmouth and Jarrow*. Benedict Biscop imported the glaziers 'so that by a craft until then unknown in Britain, they might glaze the windows of the church, the cloister and the refectory. They came and this was done, and they not only did the work required of them, but also taught English folk their mystery.' In the eighth century the two monasteries were laid waste by the Danes and the art died out again.

For many centuries Bede's account had to be taken on trust. Then, in fairly recent years, excavations took place at these sites, under the direction of Dr Rosemary Cramp, and many examples of cylinder-blown soda glass[4] were discovered, exhibiting a fine range of colour. While they do not appear to bear any trace of iron-oxide paint, on further investigation it was found that some of them could be reconstructed into a small, abstract, circular window (to be seen at St Paul's Church, Jarrow), and other pieces, all from the same site, could be made up convincingly into a standing figure. These, together with other Saxon fragments, are the earliest examples of stained glass that are known to date. Yet since the art came to England from the Continent, and it is extremely unlikely that Benedict Biscop's messengers removed from France all the glaziers they could find, there may well be discoveries yet to be made.

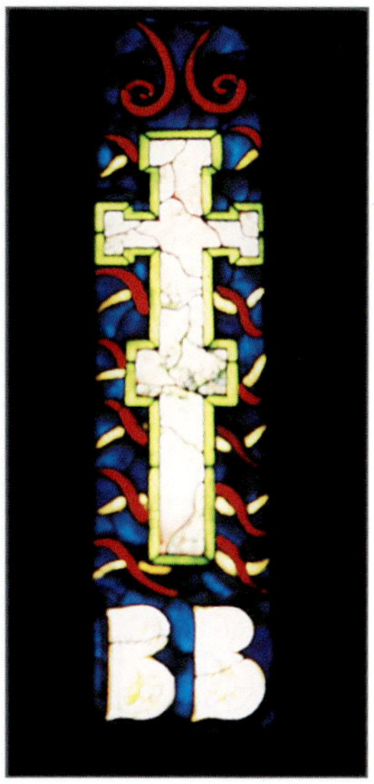

Fig. 3: Jarrow, St Paul's. Benedict Biscop Window, designed by Piper (see pp. 133, 136)

When we hurl our unwanted glass into bottle-banks, we are unlikely to remember that to medieval eyes this would be the equivalent of throwing away sapphires and rubies. The substance was infinitely rare and precious (few people would have it in their houses, and if they saw it at all it would probably be in church); it was held to be the stuff of miracles. Here was the basest of materials, earth or sand, converted by heat into a wonderful translucent form. Glass was in itself a thing of wonder.

It is a matter of supposition whether glass of Merovingian or Saxon times was used to depict anything, but it seems likely that it was. As well as importing glaziers, Benedict Biscop (a most enterprising and adventurous man, who travelled five times from Northumbria to Rome) brought back not only masons to work in the classical style he admired, not only choristers to sing the liturgy, but also books, relics, and a number of religious paintings to adorn his church:

> a painting of the Mother of God, the Blessed Mary Ever-Virgin, and one of each of the twelve apostles which he fixed round the central arch on a wooden entablature reaching from wall to wall: pictures of incidents in the gospels with which he decorated the south wall, and scenes from St John's vision of the Apocalypse for the north wall.[5]

All these he introduced to enlighten the people and strengthen their belief. It would be reasonable to think that stained glass was put in for the same purpose. There was obviously no doubt in his mind that it was right and proper to adorn the house of God with such embellishments; they, together with their making, were a expression of faith.

What was accepted without question in the seventh century was a matter of debate in the twelfth. On the one hand there was St Bernard of Clairvaux (1090–1153), eminent in the Cistercian Order, who believed that too much decoration in churches distracted men's minds from spiritual matters:

> Their eyes are feasted with relics cased in gold, and their purse-strings are loosed. They are shown a most comely image of some saint, whom they think all the more saintly that he is the more gaudily painted . . . there is more admiration for his comeliness than veneration for his sanctity. Hence the church is adorned with gemmed crowns of light – nay, with lustres like cart-wheels, girt all round with lamps, but no less brilliant than with the precious stones that stud them. The church is resplendent in her walls, beggarly in her poor, she clothes her stones in gold, and leaves her sons naked.

Cistercian monks wore habits of undyed wool and practised self-denial and solitude. Their churches and abbeys are almost as austere as their lives. They have great purity and clarity of line, and on this they depend for their effect; there was little place in them for stained glass.[6]

St Bernard's contemporary, the Abbé Suger (1081–1151) strongly disagreed. While he did not undervalue spirituality, he believed that it could find expression in the creation and contemplation of beautiful things:

> The loveliness of the many-coloured gems has called me away from external cares, and worthy meditation has induced me to reflect, transferring what is material to that which is immaterial, on the diversity of the sacred virtues; then it seems to me that I see myself dwelling, as it were, in some strange region of the universe which neither exists entirely in the slime of the earth nor entirely in the purity of heaven; and that, by the grace of God, can be transported from this inferior to that higher world . . . to me, I confess, one thing has always seemed pre-eminently fitting: that every costlier or costliest thing should serve, first and foremost, for the admission of the Holy Eucharist.[7]

The Abbé Suger, who, though of humble origins, enjoyed the patronage of Louis VI of France, rebuilt the Abbey of St Denis on the northern outskirts of Paris. He was elected Abbot in 1122, and the choir of the building is still largely glazed with the windows he commissioned. Sometimes he had himself portrayed as donor (Fig. 4); in the corner of a twelfth-century 'Jesse Tree' window (expressing the human genealogy of Christ) is a tiny figure of the Abbot holding up a miniature version of it. His tenet was that all man's finest talents should be used to adorn the house of God; the making of beautiful things, such as the designing and creating of stained-glass windows, he held to be in itself a form of worship.

This is the medium used not superficially, as extraneous decoration, but with genuine profundity of intent. And wherever he designed for ecclesiastical settings, the same might be said of the work of John Piper. He owed a tremendous debt to the art of the past, particularly medieval, particularly French. In his *Stained Glass: Art or Anti-Art?* he listed four windows which he considered absolutely outstanding; 'The Ascension' at Le Mans, 'The Crucifixion' at Poitiers, 'The

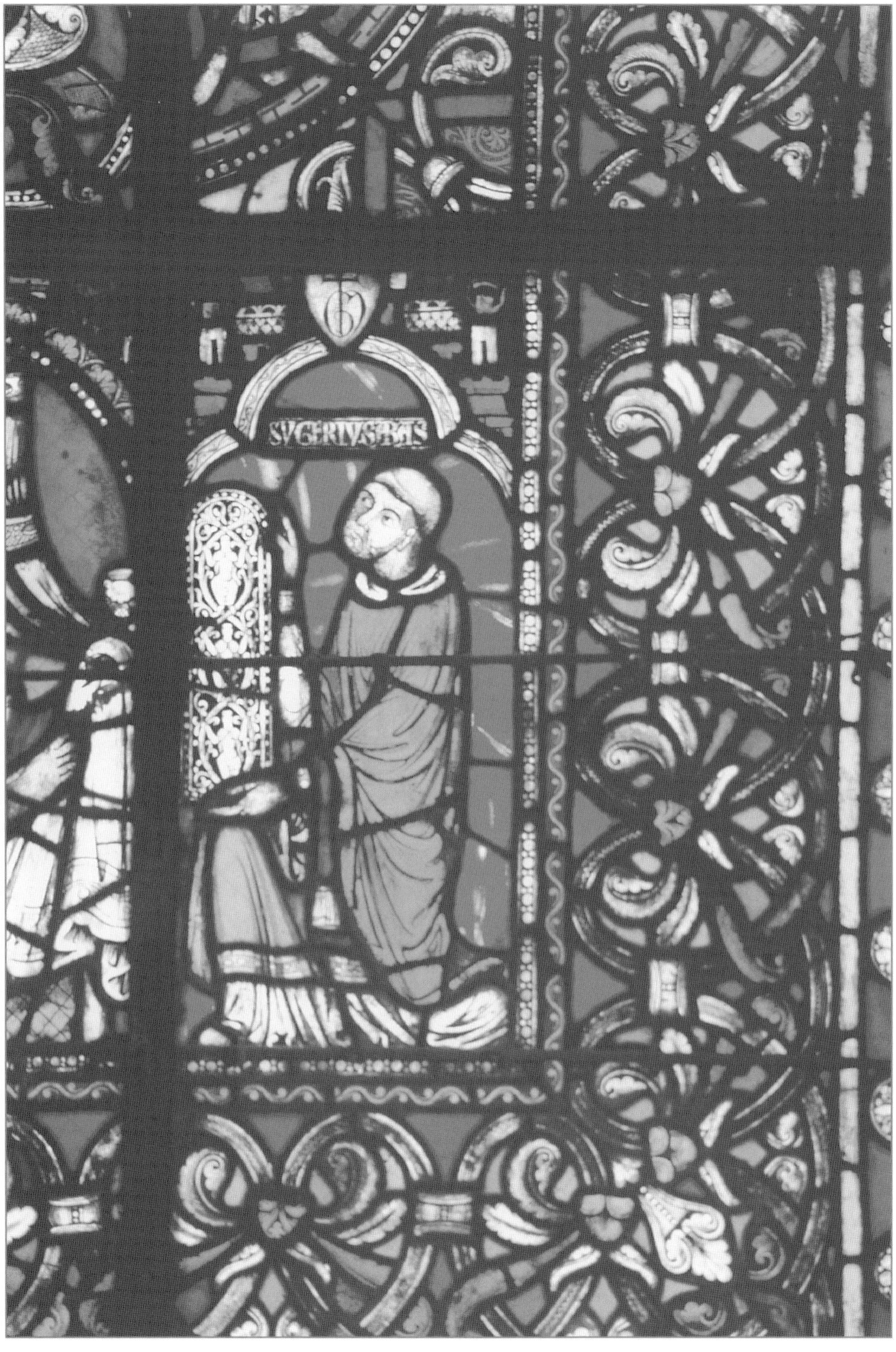

Fig. 4: St Denis. The Abbé Suger giving his window

Virgin and Child' at Vendôme, and 'Notre Dame de la Belle Verrière' at Chartres. These, he said, are not only 'the best, the gems, the prizes of their period; they are masterpieces in their own right, and by obvious leaders.'

All four windows are to be found in France, all date from the twelfth century, and in the case of none of them do we know the identity of the artist. For their

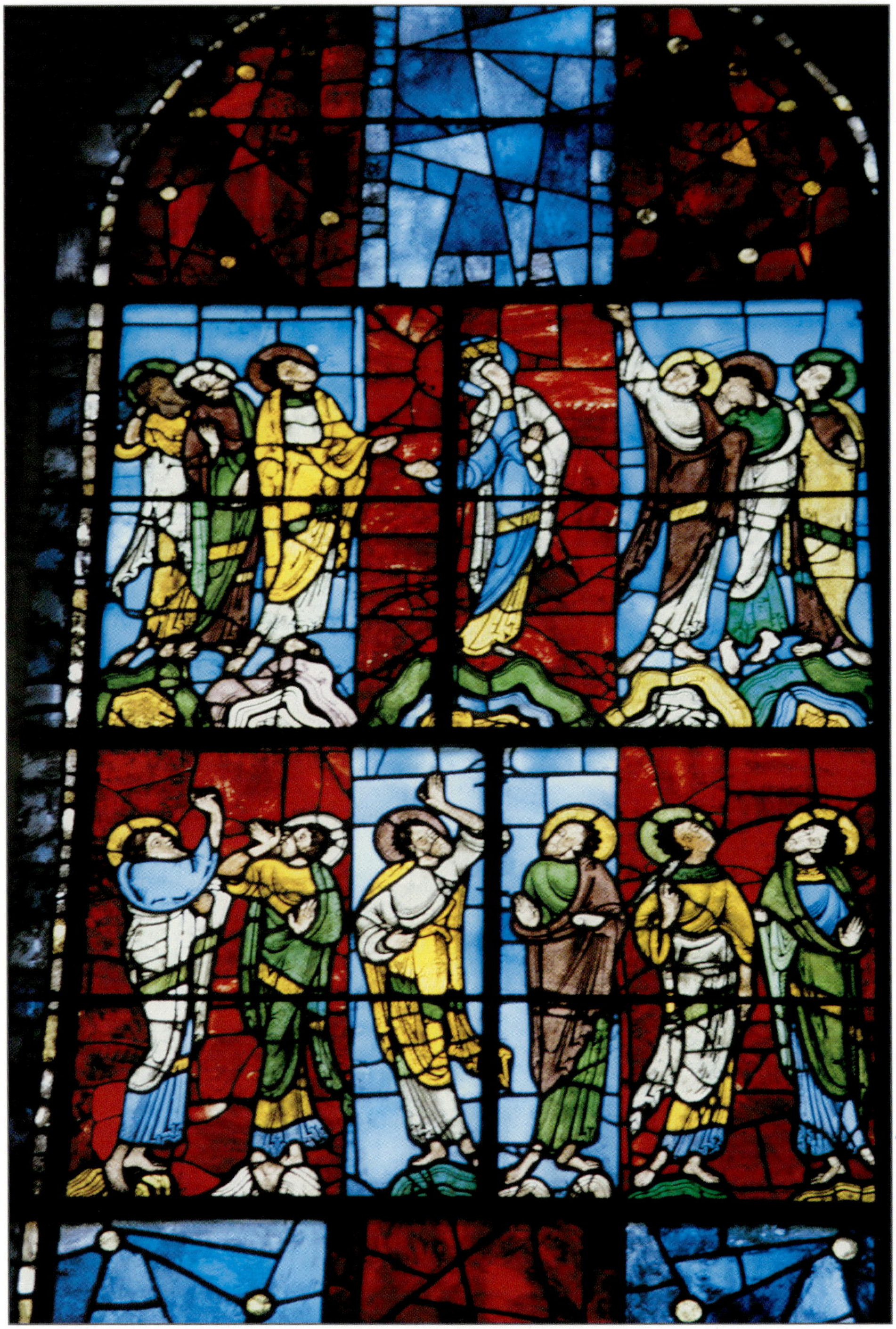

Fig. 5: Le Mans. Cathedral of St Julien. Window of the Ascension

own sake, and in this context because Piper singled them out as being of exceptional merit, each deserves to be looked at in some detail.

The Cathedral of St Julien at Le Mans, its apse crowned with a double row of flying buttresses, overlooks the market-place far below; it is Gothic architecture at its most soaring and delicate. But entering at the west end, we have a totally different impression; we find a nave that is solemn, processional, Romanesque. A number of the windows retain their original glazing, dating from the twelfth century, mainly of *c.* 1165. They include a window of 'The Life of St Gervase', one with two angels supporting the Cross, and a delightful roundel showing the body of the martyred St Stephen guarded by wild animals and birds; but one's eye is drawn above all to a window of even earlier date. This is 'The Ascension' (Fig. 5); it compels the viewer not because of its size (it is quite small) but because of its intensity. The colour is vibrant; a chequer of red and blue grounds form a framework for the animated figures. The apostles are dressed mainly in yellows and greens; they gesticulate and look upwards to where one might expect to see Christ, or perhaps (in the medieval manner) just His feet, disappearing into the heavens; but this panel is missing. Although smaller in scale than the others, most striking of all is the figure of the Virgin; she is shown elongated, swaying, ethereal, as if she might be caught in some heavenly wind and rise up from the mountain top. She wears a crown, a white veil, a blue robe over a yellow under-dress; her head is ringed with a blue halo, and she is shown against a sky of startling red.

Piper commented in his book on the 'masculinity' of the Le Mans glass, with its bold juxtapositions. And although he did not detail *why* he considered this particular window so outstanding, it must surely have been to do with its dramatic impact and its extraordinary use of colour, symbolic rather than representational.

Symbolic and unexpected use of colour is what we find also in the very much larger East Window of 'The Crucifixion' at Poitiers (Fig. 7, overleaf). It was made slightly later than 'The Ascension' at Le Mans, and dates from between 1162 and 1189. It was given to the Cathedral by Henry II (of England) and his wife, Eleanor of Aquitaine.[8]

The figures in the window vary in size according to their importance in the theme represented. Dominating the whole composition is an enormous cross, red against blue, on which is outstretched the figure of Christ, who, despite the giant proportions, appears gentle and sorrowing. His body droops sideways, and his hair is, surprisingly, blue. The Cross is outlined with borders, separating it from the rest of the composition. Beneath its arms, and little more than half the size of Christ, are the *mouvementé* figures of the soldier with a spear and the curiously hunched man with a sop of wine on a stick. Beside them, almost holding themselves aloof from the action, are the slender sorrowing figures of the Virgin and St John. The background for all four figures is red. Above the arms of the Cross, against a blue background, stand small figures of the disciples pointing and looking upwards towards the Ascension, where the potent figure of the Risen Christ appears in a mandorla. (A mandorla is more special than a halo; almond-shaped, it signified initially the cloud on which Christ ascended to heaven.) Below the foot of the Cross is a quatrefoil of the Deposition, flanked by the Three Maries coming to the tomb. The whole is contained within a richly patterned border. The predominating colours are red and blue – the red of the Passion and the blue of heaven – and the predominating theme the power of the Cross.

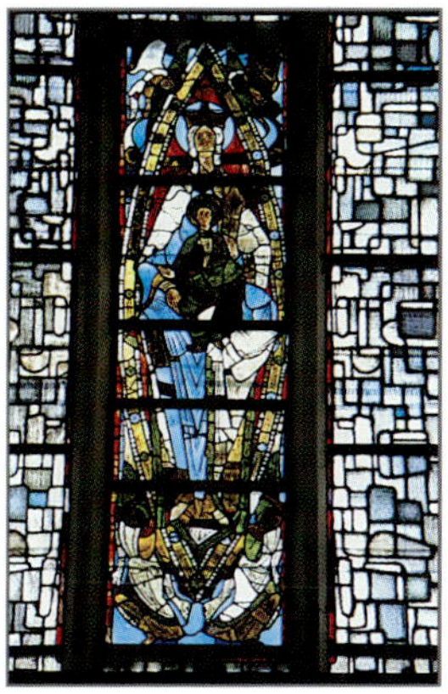

Fig. 6: Vendôme. The Virgin and Child

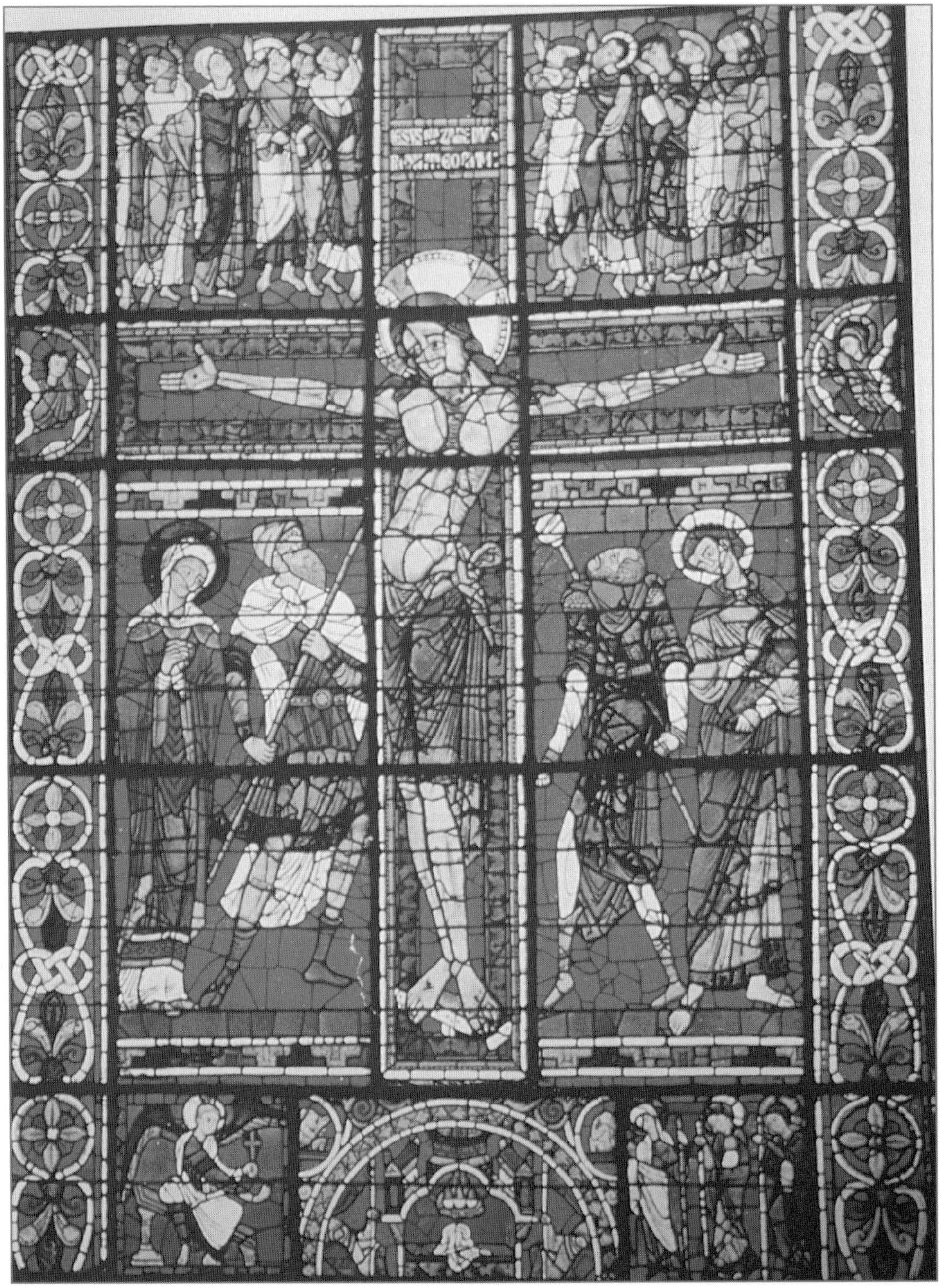

Fig. 7: Poitiers Cathedral. East Window of the Crucifixion

The other two windows singled out by Piper portray the Virgin and Child. That at Vendôme seems on stylistic grounds to be the more ancient. Indeed, it has been claimed (at least in Vendôme) that this is the earliest image of the Virgin to be seen in stained glass anywhere. The window is to be found in the Abbey Church of La Trinité (Fig. 6, p. 7). One enters the church through the early sixteenth-century west façade, a tour-de-force by Jean de Beauce in the flamboyant style of late Gothic, and it is not until one reaches the easternmost chapel of the ambulatory that the window of 'The Virgin and Child' is to be seen. The surrounding architecture in this part of the church being late thirteenth century, the panel is not *in situ*, but set within a larger pointed-arched window embrasure, the surrounds filled with modern bluish-grey *dalles-de-verre*. (The latter do not, in my opinion, make a wholly successful foil for it; their lighter tones tend to diminish its impact. One has to concentrate on the panel and disregard its setting.) The Virgin is seated within a mandorla, which, in the context of the Virgin, symbolized her Assumption and in general the glory that surrounds her. Within the shape of this framework, her figure is extraordinarily elongated. Staring straight ahead, she balances on her knee the Christ Child, but He appears not as a child but as a miniaturized adult, pin-headed. The Virgin is crowned, as the Queen of Heaven, a blue halo behind her head. She is dressed in blue, with a white veil; the Child is in deep green. Behind the figures the background is rich red, within the gold of the mandorla.

The Virgin of Vendôme has nothing to do with naturalism; she is pure symbol, an icon, hieratic and remote. The Virgin and Child of Chartres, that is, the most famous depiction of the Virgin there, known as 'Notre Dame de la Belle Verrière' (Fig. 8, overleaf), is different in character. The cult of the Virgin in this city was a very ancient one; indeed it is thought that there was a druid cult of virgin birth there, and that this was taken over by Christianity. From the ninth century, Chartres was guardian of a very precious relic: the Virgin's tunic or veil[9] – a piece of silk about 5 metres long – which was given by Charles the Bald (823–77). The Virgin was said to have worn it while giving birth. The relic was held to have special powers, and to be effective in repelling pagan invaders, and curing 'St Anthony's Fire' or ergotism.

St Bernard of Clairvaux encouraged the cult of the Virgin, who was seen as a mediator for the human race, 'The Son shall answer the prayers of his Mother, and the Father shall answer the prayers of his Son', and Chartres became a great centre of pilgrimage.

The Cathedral was repeatedly ravaged by fire, in AD 962, 1020, 1134, and most severely in 1194, when almost the whole building was destroyed. It was possible to save only the crypt, the two west towers together with the tall Romanesque windows between them, and (which was thought miraculous) the Virgin's veil and 'Notre Dame de la Belle Verrière'. Consequently, the stained-glass panel was held in almost as much reverence as the relic. In the thirteenth century a new surround was made for it, with adoring angels on either side, and the window was installed in the newly constructed choir.

While one's feeling about the window today is somewhat swayed by the fact that the Virgin was given a new face in the nineteenth century (a face probably different in character from the original one), the general impression is of a Virgin who, while Queen of Heaven (censers swing above her head, and over her veil she wears an ornate and heavy-looking crown), is not remote from humanity. Her shoulders and arms have palpable solidity. Between her knees sits, or rather, half-stands, the Child – a mysterious figure in brown, his small

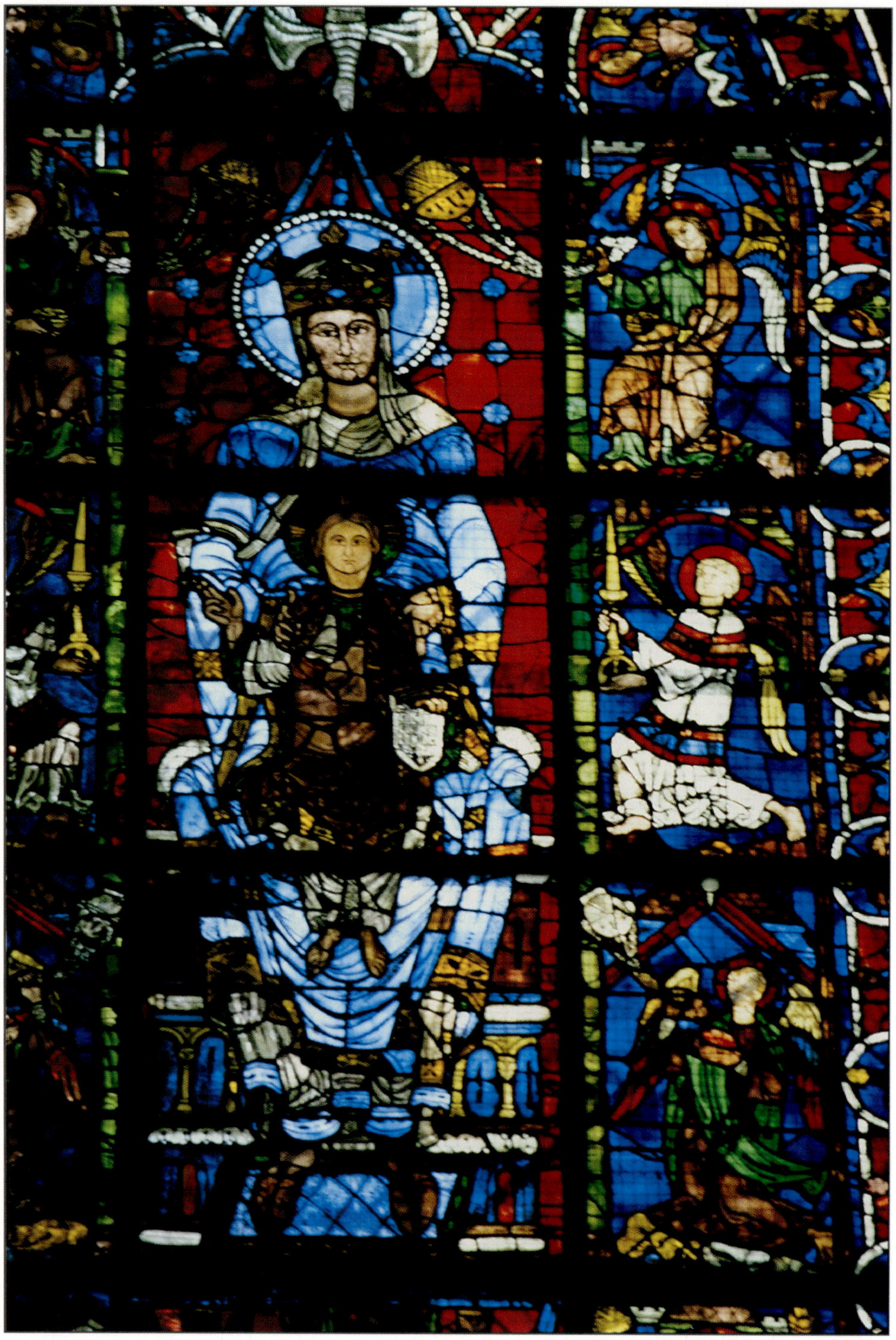

Fig. 8: Chartres Cathedral. Notre Dame de la Belle Verrière

adult face gazing straight ahead. It is above all the colour of the window which is so memorable: the rich variety of ruby reds that surround the two figures, and the ethereal ice-blue of the Virgin's robe and halo. This is a hue which, if not unique to the twelfth-century glass of Chartres, is especially associated with it, and may have largely accounted for the esteem in which the 'Belle Verrière' was held.

John Piper being, as he said, a 'fairly new and fervent convert to Romanesque', described graphically and with passion his impressions of Chartres Cathedral as a whole: 'What we admire at Chartres today is the overall effect of iridescence, flame and fantasy coruscating in the near darkness.' He wrote about how it appeared on a February day:

> The predominant blues blazed deeply out of what seemed like great areas of black in the windows; the black looked scrawled or poured, apparently at random. Figures, and the geometrical pattern of panels in the whole design, even at close range, looked purely incidental. Reds gashed themselves across the blue like wounds, and the mollifying yellows and greens and whites trilled and piped and warbled in between, but there were very few of them, and they seemed very small in the area of rich, but barely illuminated, wall. One felt surrounded by cliffs of stone with coloured perforations; the windows seemed to give onto tunnels with light only at the far end of them.

CHAPTER TWO

'A GREAT LEADER-ASTRAY': DEVIATION AND REDISCOVERY

'Stained glass is a great
leader-astray for anyone who works at it.'

John Piper

John Piper summed up the continuing history of medieval stained glass thus: 'the thirteenth century was the age of the coloured wall of glass; the fourteenth of the coloured perspective; the fifteenth century of the transparent wall with fancy interruptions'.[1] 'Perspective' may seem at first sight an odd description of fourteenth-century stained glass, if the word is interpreted as the diminishing of sight-lines as they recede from the viewer, but probably Piper was using it in its literal sense of something which is seen through. In any case, Piper's summary suggests a progressive trivialization of the medium. If this was, broadly speaking, the truth, there were historical and architectural reasons for it.

It was believed that the commissioning of windows was a way of saving one's soul, of buying oneself a desirable place in the next world:

Wouldst thou glaze the gable, and grave therein thy name,
Secure should thy soul be for to dwell in heaven.

William Langland, *Piers Plowman*

So it was with this intention in mind that William of Wykeham commissioned extensive schemes from Thomas Glazier of Oxford for the chapels of Winchester College and New College, Oxford, not omitting the exhortation to the viewer, '*Orate pro anima*' – to pray for his soul. And at Tewkesbury Abbey, Eleanor de Clare presented the windows of the Choir, to save not only her own soul, but also the souls of various male members of her family. They are shown in full armour and heraldic dress (so the Almighty could not mistake who they were), ranged on either side of the Last Judgement; Eleanor meanwhile kneels in her shift. The Great East Window of Gloucester Cathedral was commissioned partly to commemorate the Battle of Crécy, but partly also to salve the royal conscience over the highly unpleasant death of Edward II in Berkeley Castle. Piper quoted Herbert Read about its appearance: 'this wide, radiant triptych, gleaming rather like crystals of snow than flames of fire'.[2] Against alternating fields of red and blue, and under elaborate canopies, are set predominantly white figures, resembling sculpture set in coloured niches.

By the fifteenth century churches were growing in size and decoration. Windows were taller, wider, admitted more light; consequently more and more glass was needed to fill them. The finest quality coloured glass was generally imported from France; with the Hundred Years' War, however, the supply obviously became uncertain. The increasing use of white (clear) glass was not only fashionable but a necessity; and it cost only half as much as coloured glass. Moreover, the technique had been discovered (in the early fourteenth century, but used increasingly in the fifteenth) of staining glass yellow by means of silver nitrate; this enabled, for instance, an angel's face, hair and halo all to be depicted on one piece of glass. 'The churches in the wool countries such as Suffolk and the Cotswolds', wrote Piper, 'glow with gold and light from yellow-stained windows with delicately-drawn angels with outspread wings.'[3]

It was now possible to obtain quite rich effects at much less expense. Instead of being basically a mosaic of coloured pieces, as it has been in the earlier Middle Ages, stained glass became what Piper called 'a transparent wall with fancy interruptions'. It was more linear, more akin to the new-found discoveries of printing and engraving.

The rot set in, Piper believed, when instead of being treated as an art in its own right, stained glass began to imitate the other arts, and in particular painting. This was the impact of the Renaissance, and was, in Piper's opinion, its 'undoing'.

Flemish glaziers, refugees from the extreme Protestantism, and indeed iconoclasm, rife in their native country, were encouraged by Henry VII to settle in England. And they prospered; to the disgust of the English glaziers, who had banded themselves into guilds, and were still working in the late Gothic style, it was nearly always the Flemish who were given the plum commissions (royal commissions especially). They, rather than the indigenous craftsmen, were entrusted with the glazing of the Chapel of the Vyne in Hampshire, and their guiding hand is to be seen in the elaborate schemes not only of Fairford in Gloucestershire, but in the Chapel of King's College, Cambridge, itself. With them they brought the Renaissance style. It was not just that they treated the medium in a more pictorial way, that their windows come to include perspective and landscape, and that compositions run across from one light to another; some of the designs were taken directly from recognizable works of graphic art. In King's College Chapel, for instance, we find the window of 'The Temptation of Christ', based on a German engraving, 'The Fall of Ananias', derived from Raphael's cartoon, and a female figure in 'The Massacre of the Innocents' reflects the same master's 'Fire in the Borgo' in the Vatican *Stanze*.

Piper allowed the magnificence of such windows, 'Where would we be without them?' One cannot help being impressed by the sixteenth-century glass (from Herckenrode Abbey, near Liège) in the Lady Chapel of Lichfield Cathedral, or the windows (similar in period) of St Mary Magdalene, Christ and his Disciples, and 'The Calling of St Peter' at Vendôme; we are captivated by

Satan and his devils at St Mary's, Fairford, and the astonishing achievement at King's College, Cambridge, fills us with awe. Yet the leading-astray was already happening; stained glass was becoming one of the minor arts, subjugated to painting.

In the seventeenth century, when the supply of pot-metal virtually dried up, the art of making coloured glass windows almost disappeared, and would have done so altogether if it had not been for the technique of enamelling. This involved the painting of the design on the surface of clear glass, and then fixing it by firing. (The Van Linge brothers, whose work is mainly to be seen in Oxford, did this to considerable effect.) This technique meant that the colour was no longer integral, nor was leading a necessary part of the window. The effect was very much that of a picture seen through a grid. During the eighteenth century enamelling was preferred and developed, by such glaziers as William Peckitt, to great technical perfection. Windows were frequently based on existing paintings. Thomas Jervais set up an exhibition of panels based on such unlikely subjects as 'A Sleeping Cupid' by Guido Reni, 'A Smith's Forge' by Wright of Derby, and 'Cows' by Paul Potter. Glaziers advertized their wares in the public press. Perhaps the most notorious example of eighteenth-century enamelled glass is the West Window of the Antechapel of New College, Oxford. Beneath a brown and smudgy night-scene of the Nativity, based on Correggio, vaporous beauties represent the Virtues. These were designed by Sir Joshua Reynolds and executed by Jervais. What one deplores is the destruction of medieval glass that was done to make way for such windows; yet if this were in its turn to be taken out, it would, as Piper remarked, be 'sadly missed'. It is, after all, redolent of its period, but it is in the wrong setting. Piper did indeed praise the best of Georgian glass when it was sympathetically housed in chapels and colleges of the same period; an example would be Great Witley in Worcestershire, where the glass is very much part of the whole conception. It accords perfectly with Classical proportions, decorative plasterwork, and the music of Handel.

Reverting to the New College glass, one might think, superficially, that there was a parallel to be drawn between Piper and Reynolds. Here were two major artists, established as painters, undertaking important commissions to design windows, which they did not themselves physically make. But there the resemblance ends. The difference is that while Piper had a genuine love and understanding of the medium, Reynolds did not. For him it was just a means of reproducing paintings; for Piper it was infinitely more.

While the Gothic Revival sought to restore the popularity of the medieval, it tended to be the mock-medieval rather than the real thing. In relation to ancient glass it was, Piper wrote, 'the bright inner arc of a double rainbow in relation to the great dim arc of real Gothic'.[4] Indeed, where genuine old windows had fallen into disrepair, there was a tendency to replace them with copies. In new work there was a deplorable vogue for suave enamelled saints under canopies. Only occasionally were works of real verve and passion produced, as Pugin in collaboration with Hardman did for Milton Abbey in Dorset (south window of south transept, 1847).

The large commercial firms of Victorian times tended to flourish, as Piper observed, 'in inverse ratio to the beauty of their goods'. In any case, until it was rediscovered how to make good pot-metal glass, there were severe limitations on what could be achieved.

The great name in connection with this rediscovery is that of Charles Winston (1814–64). By profession Winston was a barrister, but his main preoccupation was surely stained glass. He wrote analytically on the subject, and in 1847 published his *Enquiry into the difference of style observable in ancient glass-paintings, especially in England, with hints on glass-painting, by an amateur*. He was an amateur in the best sense, in that he loved his subject, and was very much aware of how it had gone astray in the previous century or so.

'Glass paintings', he wrote, 'did not cease to be glass-paintings until the "new manner" in oils was so imbibed by the glass painters that they strove to over-finish and to *imitate the effect of oil*; in which they necessarily failed', and he looked upon most glaziers of the time as 'mere tradesmen at best', over-zealous in their pursuit of naturalism. He was much concerned with the problem of designing appropriate glass for medieval churches. But in order for windows to be made which would look right, it was necessary to have good pot-metal colours. He got together with his friend Dr Medlock of the Royal College of Chemistry to discover, by trial and error, how the colours in medieval glass had been obtained. They found, for instance, that the wonderful range of blues were derived not from lapis-lazuli, as they had imagined, but from cobalt.

The range of colour they made possible was produced commercially by the firm of Powell's of Whitefriars, and further developed by Chance Brothers of Smethwick. At last artists and craftsmen had at their disposal the means to make stained-glass windows in the traditional way, a mosaic of true and luminous colour.

Perhaps it went to their heads a little. The St Frideswide Window[5] in Christ Church Cathedral, Oxford, has a wonderful colour range, but compositionally it works better in sections than as a whole. Some of the windows made at this time (around 1860) have a rather raw, what Piper called 'unfledged' quality. He cited two examples of this description: the windows in the dining-hall at Bradfield College, Berkshire, and the Wroughton Window in the church of All Saints, Brightwalton, in the same county. The Bradfield College glass (Fig. 9) was designed by Edward Burne-Jones (1833–98) for Powell & Sons. It displays a fresh and astonishing range of colour and the minimum of shading. It might perhaps be called strident, and the composition is in places confused (the designer was after all very young, not yet out of his twenties); yet after the dark winter that the art had been suffering, it sings with the colours of spring.

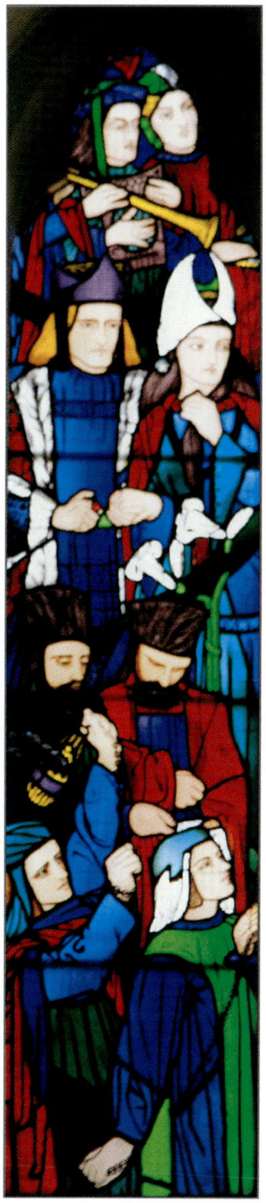

Fig. 9: Bradfield College. Burne-Jones, Dining-hall Window

The Brightwalton window (Fig. 10, overleaf) is equally stunning, and has perhaps greater coherence of design.[6] There have been various attempts to attribute it. Dating from about 1860 it is too early to be Morris glass, and it is held to have been made by Lavers, Barraud and Westlake (who established their

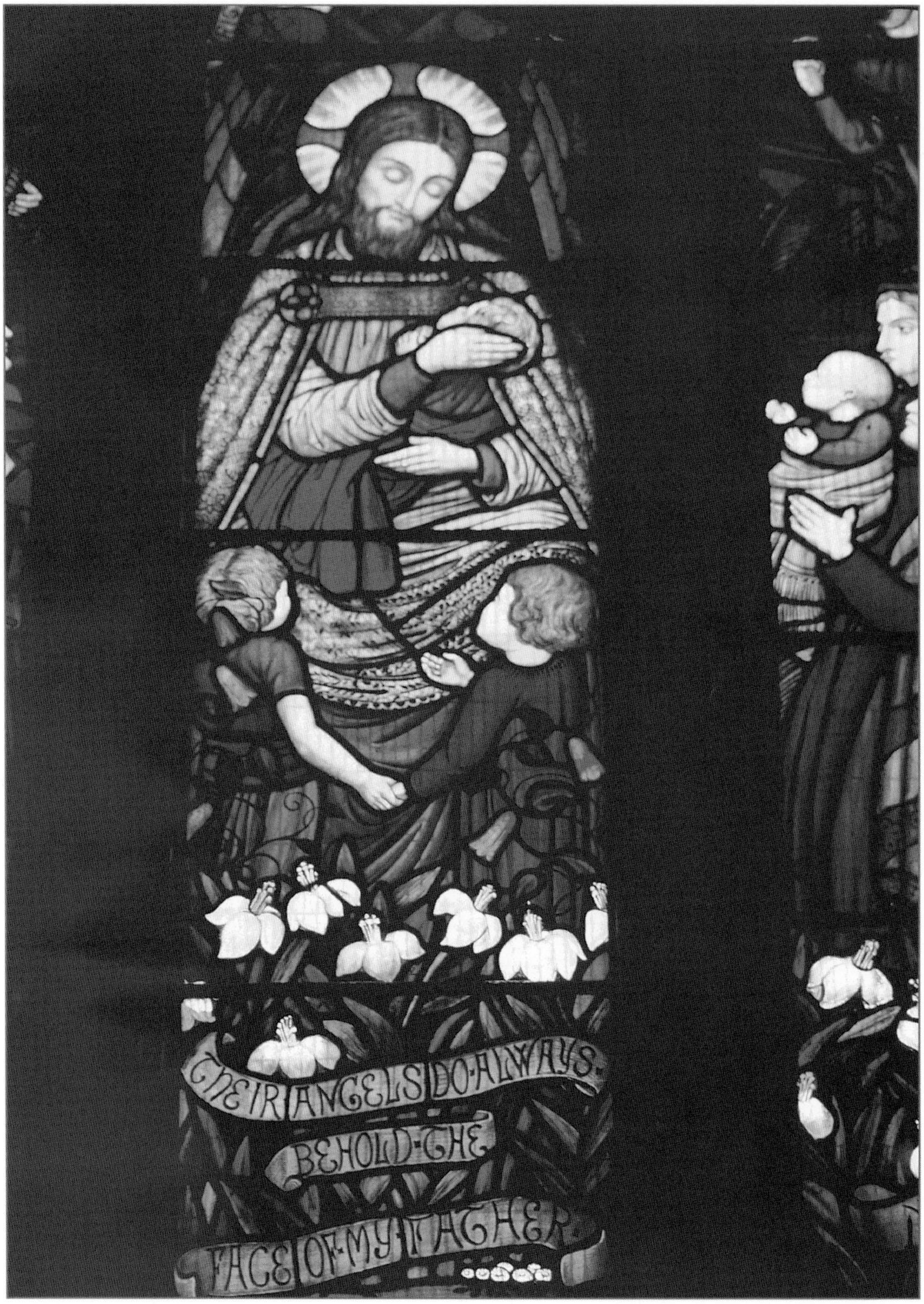

Fig. 10: Brightwalton, All Saints. Wroughton Window

firm in Covent Garden in 1855). According to expertise from the William Morris Gallery, the designer is Michael Halliday (1822–69), who worked in association with John Everett Millais.

The subject is Christ welcoming the little children, 'for of such is the kingdom of heaven'. As well as the colour, we are aware of the intensity, the way that all is focused towards the centre, the rapt expressions of the worshippers, the swinging forms of the censing angels. The only slight anticlimax is that the portrayal of Christ is a little pedestrian.

Windows such as these are the precursors, but the great flowering of the art, the bringing it back after so long to the true path, came with William Morris and the circle of artists who surrounded him.

> The artist who undertakes to practise glass-painting should bear in mind that he is dealing with a material essentially different from any with which he has hitherto been familiar; and his first object should be to obtain a thorough knowledge of the peculiarities and of the extent of the available means of his art; of the excellencies which ought to be developed, and the defects which should be concealed.

The words are Charles Winston's, the precepts could well have been Morris's, or, indeed, John Piper's. By glass-painting, Winston pointed out that he did not mean painting *on* glass, which he felt the artist should keep to a minimum in order not to muddy the colours, but painting *with* glass, creating a translucent mosaic, letting the material speak for itself.

Piper regarded Morris as 'a real reformer and a real prophet'. Here at last was a man who brought back stained glass, after centuries of deviation, to the true path. The artists gathered into the Morris circle would, in Piper's opinion, be valued in the future less for their painting than for their contributions to the applied arts, including stained glass. Eminent among them was Edward Burne-Jones.

Morris had met Burne-Jones when they were both undergraduates at Exeter College, Oxford, reading theology – a course which, though neither of them completed it, was obviously relevant to their work later on. Added to this, they shared an interest in mythology, art and poetry. They were much influenced by the writings of Ruskin, the idea that art should be the 'expression of man's joy in labour'. Morris decided to train as an architect, under George Edmund Street, Burne-Jones as a painter, under Rossetti. Although, again, Morris did not complete the course, the influence of Street was beneficial; for Street believed that architects should not work in isolation, but should have a knowledge of related crafts, especially stained glass, embroidery and metalwork.

It was in Street's office that Morris met Philip Webb, the architect who designed the Red House for him in Bexleyheath, and who worked for many years with his company. Morris was fortunate in having a private income, providing capital for the firm, which was in fact founded largely because it had proved impossible to buy furnishings to suit the newly constructed Red House; they had had to fall back on 'turkey-red cotton and dark blue serge'. The firm was at first called Morris, Marshall, Faulkner and Company and was started in 1861. The original members were Burne-Jones, Rossetti, Ford Madox Brown, Philip Webb, C.J. Faulkner, P.P. Marshall and Morris himself. To begin with, each of the seven contributed £1.00 (fortunately those finances were rapidly augmented), and their workshop was in Red Lion Square, Holborn; four years later they moved to larger premises at 26 Queen's Square, Bloomsbury.[7] Stained glass was one of their chief concerns from the very beginning; initially, several of the artists took a hand in it – Rossetti, Madox Brown, Burne-Jones and Morris himself – though from the mid-seventies the designing was done exclusively by Burne-Jones. What was special about the stained glass produced by the undertaking, which Morris himself described as 'the only artistic firm of the kind',[8] was above all Morris's guiding hand in the whole process of creation. Whoever did the designing, the interpretation was essentially his. When the cartoons were completed, he went to the stock of pot-metal glass, chose which colours were to be used, and then oversaw the process of the painting on of details in iron-oxide paint, making sure that not too much shading was put in and that the colours were allowed to speak for themselves. Once the window was put together in the workshop, Morris scrutinized it to make sure that the whole effect of colour, tone and design was what he wanted it to be. Finally, if it was a work of some importance, he would go and inspect it again after it was installed.

The personal concern that Morris took in the products of his workshop was quite exceptional. In Piper's words, it swam 'against the stream of commerce'. It was only to be expected that, as well as the fluctuating nature of the market for stained glass, they met with competition and even opposition from established firms. When the designer and writer on stained glass Lewis F. Day joined Lavers and Barraud in 1866, he was warned about this 'set of amateurs who are going to teach us our trade'.

The earliest Morris glass commissioned for ecclesiastical settings was for three new churches designed by G.F. Bodley: St Michael and All Angels, Brighton, St Martin's, Scarborough, and the church of All Saints, Selsley (just outside Stroud). The stained glass at Selsley largely forms a frieze running part way up across the windows which were otherwise left plain and unadorned; an idea which surely stemmed from the medieval glass at Merton College. Had such strong colour been used for the entire glazing scheme, the effect would have been too dark, too intense. One of the arts was knowing when to stop. Piper remarked 'To this day it is quite common for artists and designers to be asked to provide one window for a church that may well be better off without it; a church that perhaps needs all the light it can get, or that has plenty of stained glass already.'[9]

Piper particularly admired the lyrical beauty of Morris glass that came just after this early period, when they were still rather feeling their way, more of the time 1865 to 1875. The designs became bolder, more assured, and yet they did not lose the quality of freshness. One can sense that they were made with a particular idea in mind, for a particular window, in a particular church; and we know enough about the company's working methods to be sure that this was so.

Morris preferred on the whole to work for new buildings, so that the glass was part of their original conception. Fortunately, the third quarter of the nineteenth century was an extremely active period for building Anglican churches. We are informed[10] that between 1840 and 1876 no less than 1,727 Church of England churches were erected, so there was plenty of work available. But after this came the vogue for medieval churches to be restored – which really

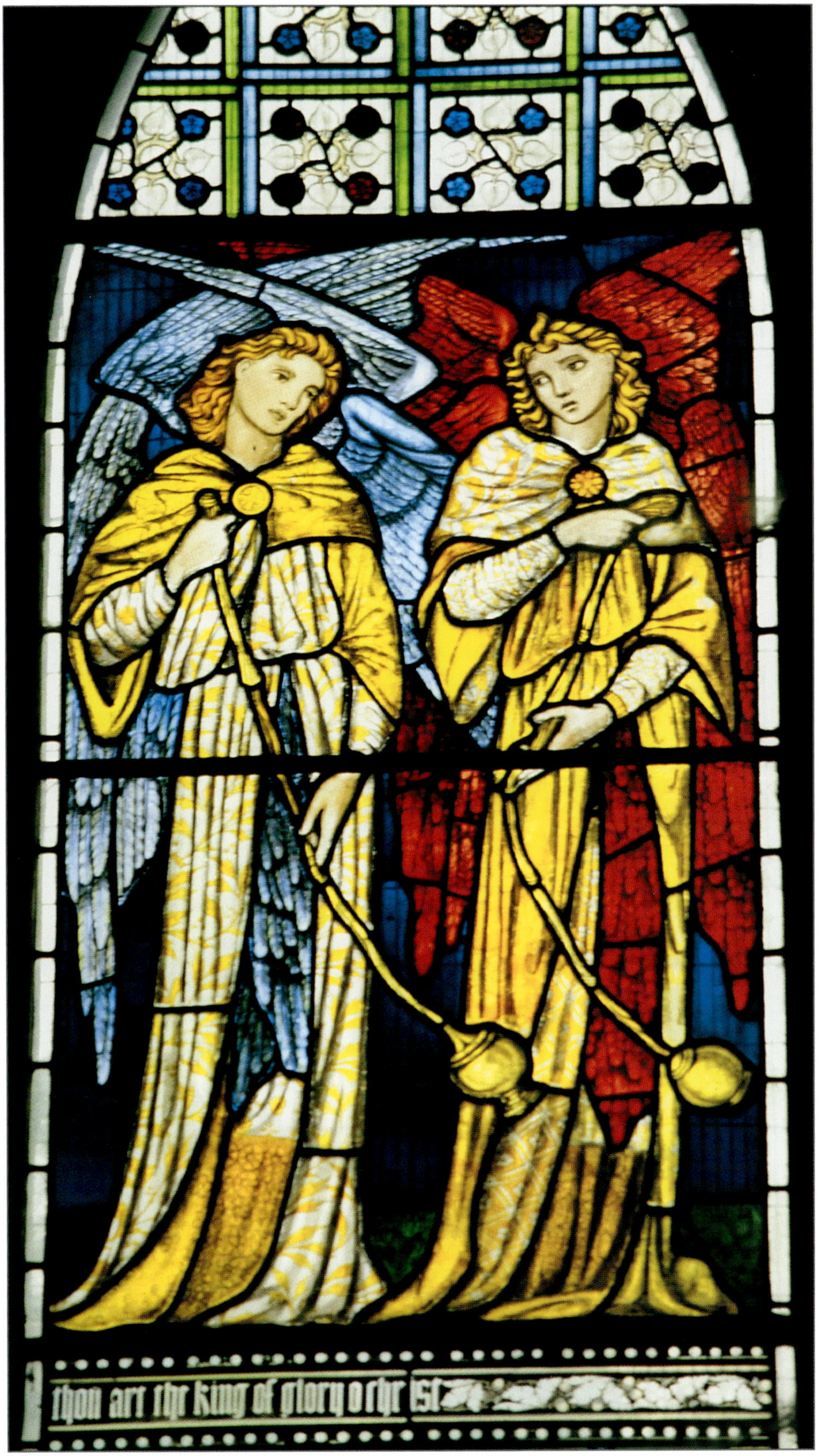

Fig. 11: Bromham, St Nicholas. Two Angels. Burne-Jones/Morris, 1870

meant stripping and replacing the walls and furnishings. Morris protested vigorously, and wrote a manifesto for the Society for the Protection of Ancient Buildings (or Anti-Scrape) entreating all people who had responsibility for their care not to destroy, not to replace the fabric, but to conserve it. With Morris holding these principles (with which Piper a century later would fervently agree), the firm's production of new stained glass was bound to be affected. He did not impose a complete ban on making windows for medieval churches, but in 1877 declared that he would no longer supply them for such churches if they were being submitted to so-called 'restoration' or 'scrape'.

Unfortunately, a small group of idealists could do little to stop the process. The fearful result of all this activity was later to be satirized in John Betjeman's *Hymn*,

> The Church's Restoration
> In eighteen-eighty-three
> Has left for contemplation
> Not what there used to be.
> How well the ancient woodwork
> Looks round the Rect'ry hall
> Memorial of the good work
> Of him who planned at all.

However, until his death in 1896, Morris kept true to his principles, and although there was towards the end rather less impetus, rather more re-using of designs, his influence continued. In Piper's words, 'He was a precedent, to act on and to quote'. Morris wrote a commentary or manifesto to accompany the company's stained glass exhibits in the Boston Foreign Fair of 1883, and the principles he laid down still hold good:

> Glass-painting differs from oil and fresco, mostly in the translucency of the material and the strength, amounting to absolute blackness, of the outlines. . . . These, then, are the first conditions of good glass-painting as we perceive them – well-balanced and shapely figures, pure and simple drawing, and a minimum of light and shade. There is a reason for this. Shading is a dulling of the glass; it is therefore inconsistent with the use of a material which was chosen for its brightness. After these we ask for beautiful colour. There may be more of it, or less; but it is only rational and becoming that the light we stain should not be changed to dirt or ugliness. Colour, pure and sweet, is the least you should ask for in a painted window.

CHAPTER THREE

GREAT WINDOWS OF MODERN TIMES

'The great windows of modern times are all the
work of artists working with collaborative craftsmen.'

John Piper[1]

When Morris died in 1896, his obituary (by 'A.L.B.') appeared in *The Art Journal*:

> The principles which Morris advocated, both by his theories and his practices, have become part of our Art Creed; and his many imitators have learned that a share of his success can only be earned by working as far as possible in accordance with his methods.

Two years later, Burne-Jones also died, and although the firm of Morris & Co. continued until well into the twentieth century, the principles on which it was founded could no longer be maintained to the full. And, as Lewis F. Day complained in an article in the same volume of *The Art Journal*, when the ornamentation of a church was contemplated the clergy were now in the habit of turning not to an artist but to a church furnisher; designs would be chosen from catalogues. Very occasionally it was otherwise, as when Walter Crane was commissioned to design glass for the Church of the Good Shepherd, Stamford Hill. Executed by V.S. Sparrow, his windows are an expression of pure Art Nouveau, sinuous, ecstatic, and sometimes doom-laden. Occasionally too there are flashes of bold originality in the field of secular glass, for instance the metal and glass dome, more than 30 metres in diameter, over the staircase in the Galeries Lafayette in Paris (1890–1903).

To find the true heirs of William Morris, however, we have to turn to the Arts and Crafts Movement, and first and foremost to Christopher Whall. Whall had trained initially as a painter, but in the 1880s he set out to discover every stage in the making of a stained-glass window. Whall showed his 'Fire' and 'Water' in the inaugural exhibition of the Arts and Crafts Exhibition Society in 1888. He joined the Art Workers' Guild and wrote for its *Journal*, and he published his *Stained Glass Work* in 1905. In 1898, invited by Walter Crane, he had joined the staff of the Royal College of Art. Whall's great masterpiece is the glazing of the Lady Chapel of Gloucester Cathedral. The building, with its delicate lines, is truly a lantern of glass; it dates from the second half of the fifteenth century. When it was being restored at the end of the nineteenth century, new stained glass was contemplated; it was thought (according to an article in *The Builder*) that this would be an enhancement, 'provided the stained glass is really modern art-work, and not mere ecclesiastical shop-production'.

'Let your colours *sing*', Whall instructed his pupils. He was very fortunate that the firm of E.S. Prior had just begun to produce their 'Norman slab' or 'Early English' glass; this was of uneven thickness, chunky, with many bubbles and striations, sometimes streaky, and it had a range of colour ideal for Whall's requirements. Especially lovely were the purples, reds, violets, and a rich hyacinth blue of which he was especially fond. Dramatic too was Whall's use of white glass. In his work, white is not just an absence of colour but a very positive statement; in the window of 'The Annunciation', for instance, rays shoot diagonally across three lights, from above the archangel's head, and seem to pierce the kneeling figure of the Virgin.

Whall had numerous pupils and assistants, and was later helped by his daughter Veronica, but it was he who chose every piece of glass. He understood too the importance of leading as part of the design, to be used to emphasize that design, and not apologetically.

There is something splendidly idealistic about Christopher Whall. Funds available for the Lady Chapel windows would only allow for 30*s* a square foot; Whall decided to make no charge for his work, and persuaded his pupils and assistants while employed on this project, to take a voluntary cut in their wages.

With Mary Lowndes and Alfred Drury, Whall set up the Glass House in Fulham in 1906, and this became a centre for the Arts and Crafts Movement. Whall lived until 1924, by which time he had established quite a dynasty. Eminent among his followers were Louis Davis and Karl Parsons, both artists very much aware of the colour and texture of the material for which they designed. Karl Parsons made windows of a gentle intensity; he developed the technique of acid etching to add a distinctive sparkle to his designs. Davis's work is to be found at its most dramatic in the fine windows he did for Cheltenham College Chapel: Prospero, and Galahad, and Mercy dropping as the gentle rain from heaven, all seen in terms of glass.

On very rare occasions an artist not connected with the craft of glazing was commissioned to design windows. Sir Frank Brangwyn, for instance, was sometimes asked to do so. There is a window of his in Elvedon in Suffolk, but the composition is crowded and has not really been thought out in terms of stained glass. Piper commented that Brangwyn's glass reflected 'his own painterly mannerisms too strongly'. A far more telling instance is to be found at St Mary's, Slough. In 1915 Alfred Wolmark was invited by Ellerman (of Ellerman's Embrocation) to design for the tall lancets at the west end of the church. It was stipulated that they should be totally abstract, and the windows are a mosaic of coloured pieces, including orange and sunflower yellow, set among darker tones of crimson, ultramarine and emerald. Piper called this a 'landmark, because it is an artist's window clearly related to a contemporary movement', that is to say, Vorticism. But it was an isolated landmark; it stands alone, without anything else (at least, in this country) related to it.

On the outskirts of Paris, near the Porte des Lilas, stands the concrete church of Notre Dame de Raincy, completed in 1922. The architect was Auguste Perret, and the stained glass was designed principally by Marguerite Huré. Above her windows are figurative panels by Maurice Denis, but Huré's work is entirely abstract: Piper compared its effect to 'the first modern parallel to the Romanesque transformation scene'. The glass is set in small panels of geometric shapes, in each bay of the church the base colour of the glass is either blue, green, red or purple. The pin-pricks of light coalesce to illumine the otherwise gloomy interior, in the same way that, as Piper remarked, the windows of Chartres do on a dark February day.

Meanwhile in the British Isles, the Arts and Crafts Movement, and indeed the whole development of stained glass, was given an infusion of new life by the Irish glaziers. Their art, in Piper's words, 'pressed on strongly against the tide of browns and mauves and plentiful dirty whites', so that 'positive constructive relations were again established between stained glass and painting'.[2] It is remarkable how this progress was caused by a mere handful of people.

Unlike England and France, Ireland had virtually no legacy at all of medieval glass. In the eighteenth and nineteenth centuries there had been a few Irish-born glaziers (Thomas Jervais, James Pearson, Michael O'Connor) but they tended to settle in England where there was more prospect of commissions. Meanwhile in Ireland at the turn of the century the art was at a low ebb. The writer George Moore exclaimed in disgust, 'All modern stained glass is so utterly bad and so beastly ugly, that it is simply throwing away money trying to improve it – in fact, the sooner it dies the better'.[3] Equally forceful but in the end, rather more constructive criticism was levelled by the playwright Edward Martyn.[4] Since Catholic Emancipation, a greater number of churches were being erected in Ireland, but too often the commissions went to commercial firms (like Mayers of Munich), represented by trade salesmen 'with an oily tongue and an ever-ready kiln', firms which offered competitive prices but paid no regard to what was needed for any particular commission. Windows were chosen from catalogues. With this deplorable state of affairs, and the lack of any tradition of good stained glass in Ireland, Martyn turned for advice to Christopher Whall. He could hardly have chosen better. Though Whall himself was too involved with his London-based work to remain long in Ireland, he introduced his friend Selwyn Image. Image designed the first Arts and Crafts windows to be seen in Ireland (for Edward Martyn, at Ardrahan, Co. Galway), and set up classes in stained glass at Dublin Metropolitan School of Art. Whall sent over his 'favourite pupil', Alfred Ernest Child, to be instructor. Then together with Sarah Purser – initially a painter, she was to find herself increasingly involved in administrative work – Martyn set up his romantically named 'An Túr Gloine', 'The Tower of Glass'.

The site was 24 Upper Pembroke Street, Dublin, and it was opened on 1 January 1903. Far from romantic, it was in a fact a functional sort of building. Essentially a co-operative stained glass workshop, it contained a studio, glaziers' workshop, gas-fired furnace and a small office. Sarah Purser laid down the highest principles. 'Each window is the work of one artist who makes the sketch and cartoon and selects and paints every morsel of glass him or herself.' A stained-glass window was to be 'a work of free art as much as any painting or picture'. Among the first to learn his trade at 'An Túr Gloine' was Michael Healy (1873–1941). A profoundly religious man, Healy was a consummate draughtsman, and his windows demonstrate a perfection of line; he worked in glass very slowly and painstakingly, and made much use of aciding. He remained at 'An Túr Gloine' until his death. Fine artist though he was, his work was little known outside Ireland and was therefore less influential than that of the three Irish artists Piper singled out for special mention, Wilhelmina Geddes, Harry Clarke and Evie Hone.

Wilhelmina Geddes (1887–1955) came from Northern Ireland; her father was a railway engineer. She trained at Belfast Art School, and then under Orpen at the Metropolitan School of Art in Dublin. She had a great flair for graphic art, and the sense of design in her illustration 'Cinderella and an Ugly Sister', shown at the Fourth Exhibition of the Arts and Crafts Society, impressed Sarah Purser so much that she suggested Geddes should take up stained glass. Her first panel was made in 1911 at the Belfast Art School; then she won a travelling scholarship to London, where she spent much time studying artefacts at the British Museum. On her return she remained at 'An Túr Gloine' until 1922, and only left because of ill health. She moved to London in 1925, and worked in a studio at the Fulham Glass House.

What especially characterizes Geddes's work is her magnificent sense of line, her attention to detail (she chose each piece of glass herself), and above all her profound spirituality. These qualities are shown to the full in her richly coloured window of St Christopher with St Eustace and St Cecilia[5] at Laleham-on-Thames (near Staines, Surrey) (Fig. 12). It was made in 1926, shortly after she came to work in England. With its muscular figure at St Christopher almost pushing for space between the borders of the central light, it is a design of tremendous power, yet combined with control.

In 1921 the poet W.B. Yeats declared in a speech on the arts and industry:

> About twenty years ago . . . the stained glass made in Ireland was the worst in the world. Now some of the best glass in the world is turned out in Dublin. Then the maker of the worst glass in the world was a Dublin man named Clarke; now the acknowledged best glass in the world is made by his son Harry Clarke.

As was only to be expected, Harry Clarke[6] sprang to the defence of his father, Joshua. He could not deny that the art had been in a poor state generally, but it had been in the family ecclesiastical decorating business, at 33 North Frederick Street, Dublin, that Harry had learnt his trade. He extended his vision by attending night-classes at the Metropolitan School of Art in the city, and also briefly in London; then he won a scholarship which enabled him to study full-time in Dublin (1911–13), under A.E. Child. For three years running Clarke won a national competition Gold Medal. His entry in 1913 was the Judas panel; Judas is dressed in saffron yellow, his robe studded with the thirty pieces of silver

Fig. 12: Laleham-on-Thames, All Saints. Wilhelmina Geddes, St Christopher Window

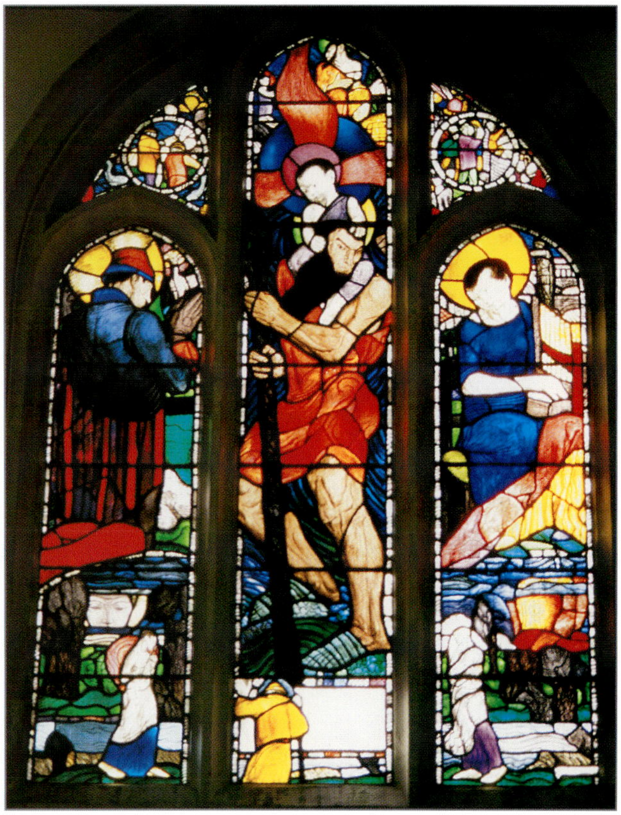

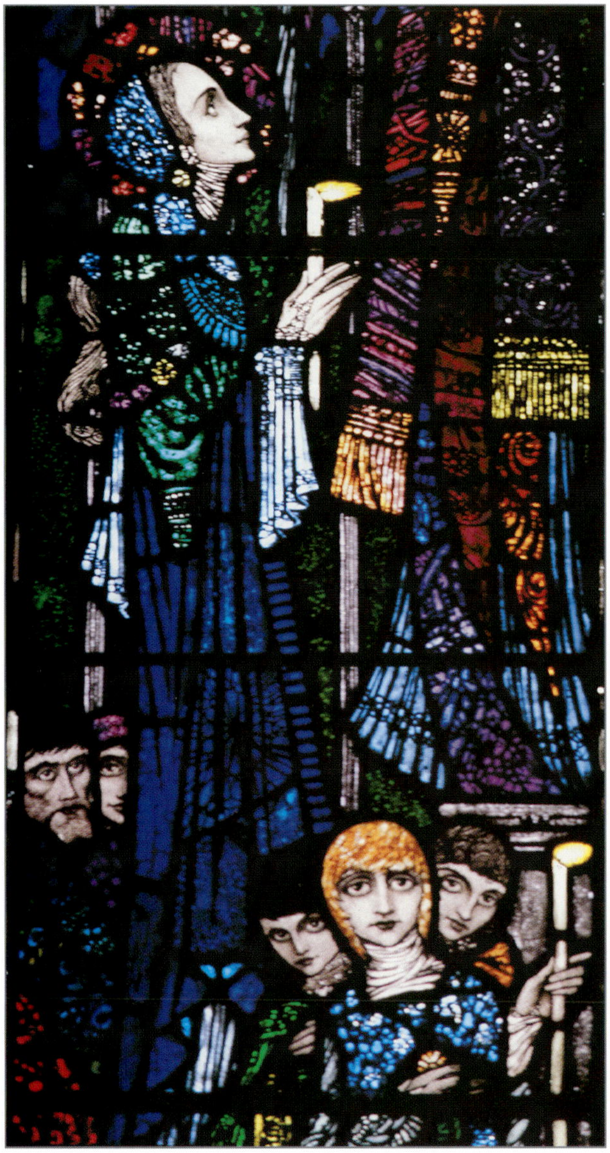

Fig. 13: Ashdown Park Hotel. Harry Clarke, detail of Presentation of Our Lady Window

that were the price of his betrayal. The rope with which he hanged himself is like a slipped halo round his neck; above, angels transport his redeemed soul to heaven. The panel is intricately made with a very positive use of leadwork, which wriggles between the jewel-like colours.[7]

This helped to establish Clarke's reputation and he received his first public commission, for the Honan Chapel in Cork, for which he was ultimately to design eleven breathtaking windows; these were completed in 1915–17. Mainly on the theme of Irish saints, they combine figures of great power and drama with exquisitely detailed backgrounds rich in symbolism.

As well as designing stained glass, Clarke was a graphic artist and did a good deal of book illustration, including fairy stories and, very forcefully, the works of Edgar Allan Poe. Allied to this are his miniature stained-glass panels of literary subjects, such as Keat's 'Eve of St Agnes', haunting and exquisite. In Britain Clarke's work is rare, but his extraordinary artistry is well represented in the windows of the life of the Virgin in the apse of the former convent, now Ashdown Park Hotel, near East Grinstead, Sussex (Fig. 13, p. 25), also by the three-light window in St Mary's, Sturminster Newton, Dorset. Dating from 1921, the latter has a standing figure in each light: the Virgin and Child, flanked by St Elizabeth of Hungary and St Barbara; the haunting faces gaze from a tapestry of streaky colour (reminiscent of Bakst's settings for the Ballets Russes). To achieve such richness, Clarke used painstaking techniques: for instance, plating blue 'flashed' glass on top of red 'flashed' glass, and then painting, staining and aciding. It is almost impossible to put into words the quality of Harry Clarke's glass; George (A.E.) Russell probably came nearest when he commented in 1925:

> I imagine that if one scraped a little the subconscious mind of the artist you would let in a flood of rich colour out of some inner luminous aether, where the fire is more brilliant than the eye can see, and the only way he could recreate that colour for us was by the art he practises. There is not a square inch in these windows which is not invented. Everywhere one looks one sees the creative faculty at work. . . .

Harry Clarke, however, was never strong physically. His constitution was probably affected by overwork – he drove himself unmercifully, as his diaries testify – together with chain-smoking, and the frequent use of aciding, which he employed to achieve his effects. He died of tuberculosis in a Swiss sanatorium, aged only forty-one.

Born slightly later than Harry Clarke, and outliving him by more than twenty years, was Evie Hone (1894–1955). She too was a Dubliner; her father was a Director of the Bank of Ireland, so hers was a relatively affluent background. When she was eleven she contracted poliomylitis, and this left her permanently disabled. Despite this handicap, she travelled to Europe; she studied in London under Byam Shaw, with Meninsky, and briefly with Walter Sickert. Then in 1920 she went to study in Paris, where her work was influenced by, on the one hand, Cubism, on the other, the art of the Middle Ages.

In the 1930s Hone turned away from abstract painting, and looking perhaps for a vehicle in which she could express her deeply held faith (at one time she had joined a community of Anglican nuns; later she was converted to Roman Catholicism), she decided to take up stained glass. She applied to 'An Túr Gloine', and on being turned down, went to London to work under Wilhelmina Geddes. Finally accepted by 'An Túr Gloine' in 1935, she worked there until 1943. Because of her disability, it was scarcely possible for her to create a window through all its stages from start to finish, and her designs were interpreted by the glazier Thomas Kinsella. Nevertheless, Hone had a very clear idea about the potential of the medium; she welcomed the return to traditional techniques of making stained-glass windows as they had been in the early Middle Ages, and stressed that 'The material used should be employed in accordance with its nature and capacity'; the aim was not verisimilitude but arranging colour and form to 'produce an effect of beauty, a living organism with rhythm and balance'.

Influences on Hone's work were as diverse as Irish stone-carving, Byzantine mosaics, and the paintings of Rouault. In the excellent *Gazetteer of Irish Stained Glass*,[8] Nicola Gordon Bowe describes Hone as 'a true Expressionist in her treatment of glass, providing a singular link between the early medieval painters and Modernism'. Her work is dignified and emphatic; in Piper's words, she designed 'painter's windows conceived in terms of glass'. Much of Hone's glass is in Ireland, notably the series of five windows for Tullabeg, Co. Offaly (1946); but her most famous achievement is the great nine-light East Window for Eton College Chapel (Fig. 14, overleaf). The power and scale of this conception, dominated above by the Crucifixion, and below by the Last Supper, must have impressed Piper enormously when he was called upon to design the windows that flank it. A lesser artist would have found the challenge daunting.

'There *is* good stained glass,' wrote John Piper, '*but only a little*.'[9] Hoping that he might bring about a similar movement in Britain – which in fact he not only inspired but created – he described the renaissance of the art on the Continent after the Second World War. To some extent this took place in Germany – Piper mentioned the work of Jan Thorn-Prikker and Carl Schmidt Rotluff – but above all he dealt with developments in France. Parts of that country had been subjected to utter devastation; whole cities, such as Caen, Rouen and Reims had been virtually razed. With amazing vision, the Ministère des Beaux Arts, who assisted the Ministère des Bâtiments Anciens in looking after the cathedrals and larger churches of France, approached the most celebrated artists of the time to design new windows. 'It is not certain', wrote Piper, quoting Marcel Arland, 'that every great painter could be a great stained glass designer, but there is a chance. . . .' In France, at least, the opportunities were there; and, with the exception of Picasso, the artists agreed to try their hand at what was to many of them an unknown medium. The result was an extraordinary freshness of approach.

The Cathedral of St Maximin at Metz came to be adorned with windows by Marc Chagall, Julius Bissière, and very dramatically by Jacques Villon. Villon's windows in the Chapelle du St Sacrement are conceived in great sweeps of

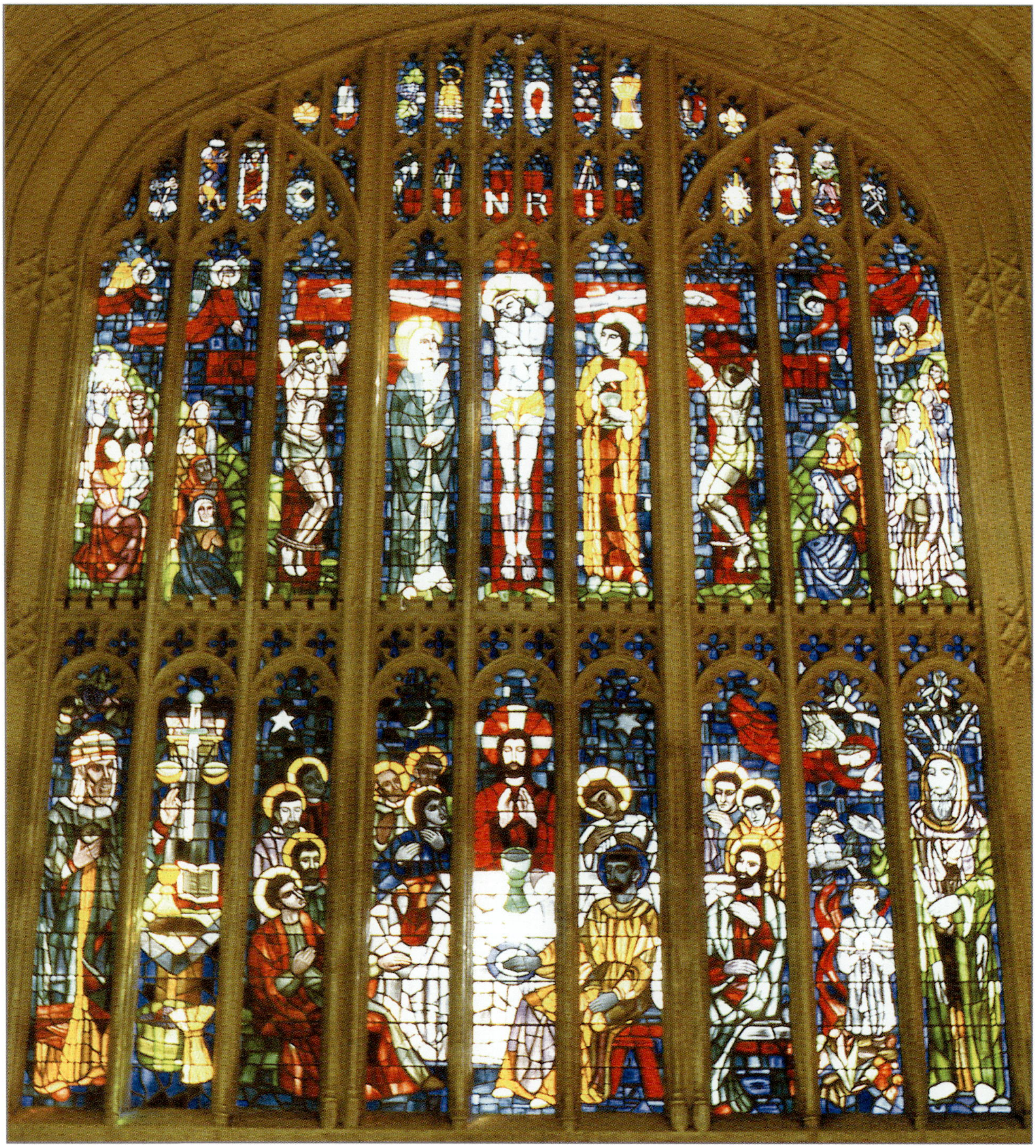

Fig. 14: Eton College Chapel. Evie Hone, East Window

colour, such as a mass of blues in the top left corner and a concentration of reds in the bottom right; and it is only after the initial impact of the colours has receded that one becomes aware of the delineation of figures within them.

At Amiens and Beauvais the cathedrals were enriched with windows by Paul Bony and Jean Barillet. (Barillet's work is to be seen also in England in the church of All Hallows, Wellingborough.) Both of them were essentially stained-glass artists already, and as well as executing their own windows, they, together with Charles Marq of Reims, interpreted the designs by painters who could not otherwise have ventured into the medium. Thus we get the fruitful collaborations of Léger with Jean Barillet, Braque and Matisse with Paul Bony, Chagall with Charles Marq; in the same way, Piper was to work first and foremost with Patrick Reyntiens, later with David Wasley and Joseph Nuttgens.

Fernand Léger (1881–1955), who was of Norman peasant origin, worked frequently on a large scale, whether it was in the Cubist style he favoured in his youth, tending towards violence and full of machine images, or in the more ordered Classical style he was later to adopt. In the early 1920s he did several sets for the Swedish Ballet, notably 'La Création du Monde' (1923) with its bold patterning of blockish forms. Throughout he was a highly disciplined artist, and much concerned with formal values. When he came to design for stained glass, as at Audincourt near Belfort (1950), he chose to be interpreted (by Barillet) in the difficult medium of *dalles-de-verre*. Piper called Léger's windows 'masterpieces of a different kind, symbolic and heraldic; designed by a man of such conviction and strength that they are, as it were, "signed all over"'.

Dalles-de-verre were also chosen by Alfred Manessier to interpret his ideas at the church of Ste Therèse at Hempempont, near Lille in north-east France. The windows are, again, executed by Barillet. As well as being a painter, Manessier designed for tapestries at the famous centres of Aubusson and Gobelins. When it came to stained glass, his preference was to use the medium as part of the concept of the building as a whole, what he termed 'the simultaneous creation of a light-filled architectural unit'.[10] *Dalles-de-verre* has obvious limitations as regards figurative work, but has advantages in other respects – which Piper listed, 'its capacity for hardening an already bold design, for giving full point to white areas among rich colours' – and he described this work by Manessier as 'original and influential'.

The windows designed by Henri Matisse (1869–1954) at Vence were very much part of a 'light-filled architectural unit'; indeed his advice was taken in the planning of the whole chapel. In his youth, Matisse (like Piper) abandoned the legal profession in order to study art; one of his tutors was Moreau. His grasp of form developed through his understanding of the work of Cézanne, and led to increasing simplification of colour, line and composition. In 1914 Matisse settled on the Riveria. By this time he was employing in his painting a fluid calligraphic line (as in his 'Bonheur de Vivre', 1907); avoiding any sort of chiaroscuro, he became a master of patterning.

The quality of patterning is very evident at Vence. Matisse had gone there in order to convalesce in a convent run by Dominican nuns, and at their request designed them a new chapel. It was to be his last major work. With the use of gouache and *papiers collés* (which Piper was also to employ in his cartoons), he devised compositions of leaf or tulip forms, leaving the glass unpainted to speak for itself. Although his designs were realized by Paul Bony, Matisse selected the exact colours to be used, and was meticulous in his choice. The whole effect, glass integrated with architecture, is one of stunning simplicity. It is, of course, the art that conceals art; Piper commented: 'What nobody can see today is how to be simple. Only Matisse. He bought up the whole rights of the twentieth century for simplicity!'

While some artists designing for stained glass thought of it in terms of architecture, for others it was more an extension of painting. Such an artist was Georges Rouault (1871–1958). He knew the medium from his youth; he had been apprenticed for five years in his teens as a stained glass designer, only then turning to painting, which he studied under Gustave Moreau, one of his fellow-pupils being Matisse. Encouraged by the dealer Vollard, he turned also to print-making and illustration; he also worked for the Diaghilev Ballet and designed tapestry. His characteristic technique as a painter is distinguished by the luminosity and brilliance of his colour, emphasized by the black lines that surround it. The concept of stained glass is never far away. In the late 1940s six of his paintings were interpreted in glass for the little church of Assy, Haute Savoie, the realization being the work of Paul Bony, and they are entirely at home in the medium. They are small windows, seemingly ingenuous, but colour and composition are balanced to perfection, and they have a haunting quality.

In the post-war years, Marc Chagall designed for many of the greater churches and cathedrals of France – and further afield too. His windows are to be found, for instance, in Zurich and Jerusalem. His collaborator was Charles Marq. Chagall's work is often trance-like in conception, and it has a painterly quality, perhaps because he undertook some of the painting on glass himself. The first of his windows to be seen in England was at Tudeley in Kent, 3 miles east of Tonbridge:[11] a memorial window to Sarah d'Avigdor Goldsmid, a girl who was drowned (Fig. 15). It dates from 1967, and its theme is the personal resurrection of the girl. At the bottom of the window she is shown drowning in a dark and heaving sea, while at the side her mother weeps; then we see her raised up towards the crucified Christ. Piper said of Chagall, that in this window, 'his message may become more real and urgent, and acceptable'; and he concluded, 'the windows he produces are a real contribution to the medium, not a mere extension of painting'.

This is a generous enough assessment, but Piper had little to learn from Chagall; he had himself been designing stained glass for some years when this window was made. An artist he rated especially highly was Georges Braque (1882–1963), whom he met as early as 1927, at Jim Ede's house in Hampstead. Born at Argenteuil, Braque worked as a decorator before going on to study painting in Paris. Originally a Fauvist, he was much influenced by Picasso's 'Les Demoiselles d'Avignon', which redirected him towards Cubism. He worked frequently in collage, and, especially in his paintings of still-life, he was

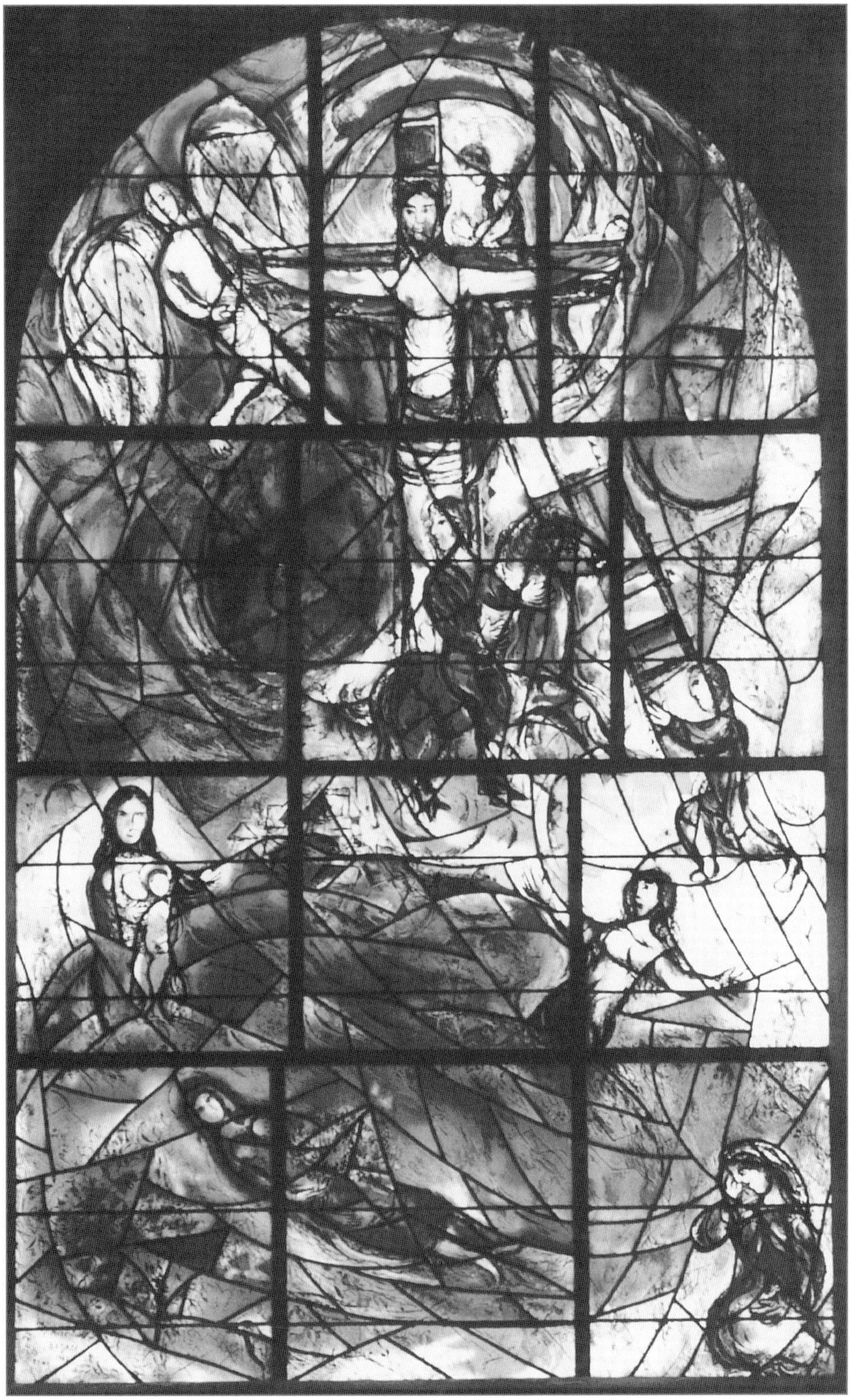

Fig. 15: Tudeley. Marc Chagall, East Window. A memorial window to Sarah d'Avigdor Goldsmid

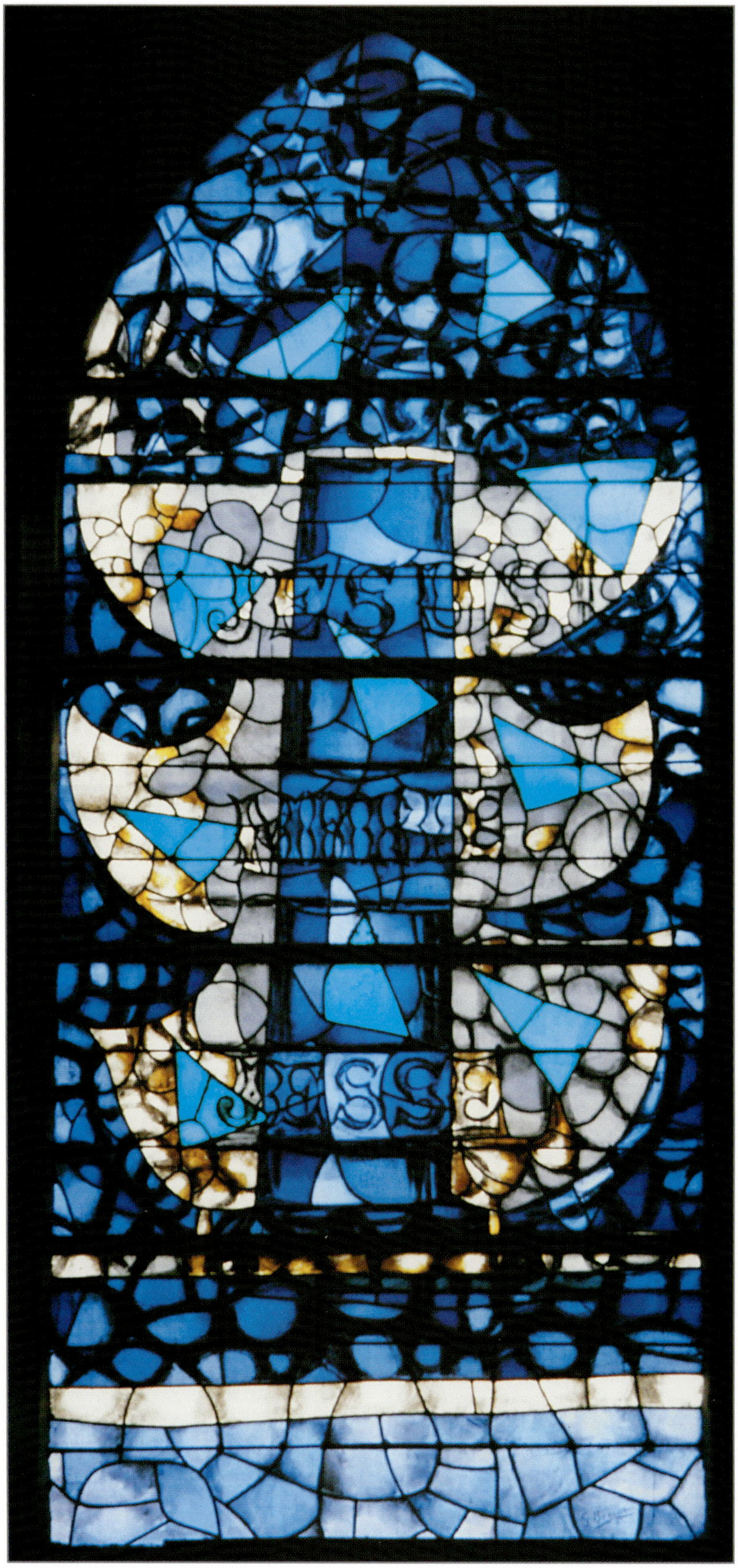

Fig. 16: Varengeville. Jesse Tree Window, designed by Georges Braque

preoccupied with shifting illusions of reality. Stained glass was his swan-song. At the end of his life he had a studio in Varengeville-sur-Mer near Dieppe, and for the churches in this village he designed glass which was brought into being by Paul Bony. During the 1950s Braque designed eight windows for the parish church, including a rose window of floating shapes in gold and russet brown against a blue ground; while for the Romanesque church on the top of the cliff, he designed his own interpretation of the ancient theme of a Jesse Tree window (Fig. 16).

The significance of the Jesse Tree was to illustrate the genealogy, and therefore the humanity, of Christ. In medieval art, it generally shows Old Testament kings and prophets seated among the branches of a vine which has its roots in the sleeping figure of Jesse himself. But Braque's window contains no figures. The ground is a mass of blue forms, like sea-tossed pebbles; against them is placed the simple and stalwart form of the stem, also blue, and from this project fan-like shapes of paler colour curving upwards like the branches of a tree. Across these and the stem are written, as an integral part of the design, the words 'JESUS ARBRE JESSE'. It is a reticent window, subtle rather than showy: a statement of personal faith whose image remains in the mind long after leaving the church. Piper's collaborator, Patrick Reyntiens, went so far as to call this window at Varengeville 'the best stained glass of the twentieth century'.[12]

Such judgements are subjective; it may be invidious to talk about 'the best'. But on the Continent there had undoubtedly happened what John Piper called an 'eleventh-hour rescue' of the art. His book *Stained Glass: Art or Anti-Art?* was written with the idea of prompting a similar renaissance on the other side of the Channel.

The renaissance happened; its progenitor, and leader, was Piper himself.

CHAPTER FOUR

THOUGHTS ON RESTORATION AND THE FIRST WINDOWS

'The trouble is, stained glass is not too "difficult"
to do, as people think; but too "easy", too easily effective.'
John Piper[1]

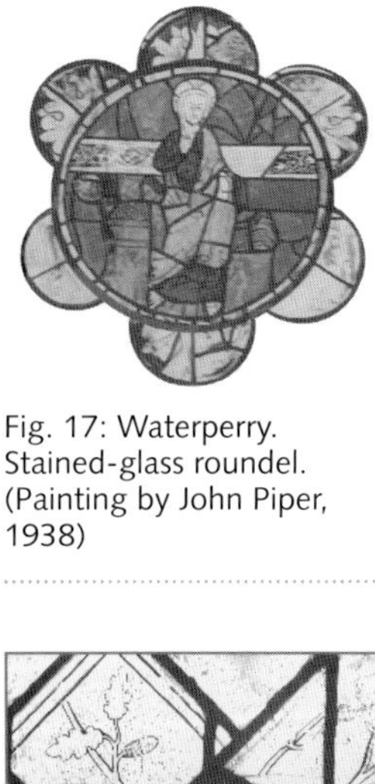

Fig. 17: Waterperry. Stained-glass roundel. (Painting by John Piper, 1938)

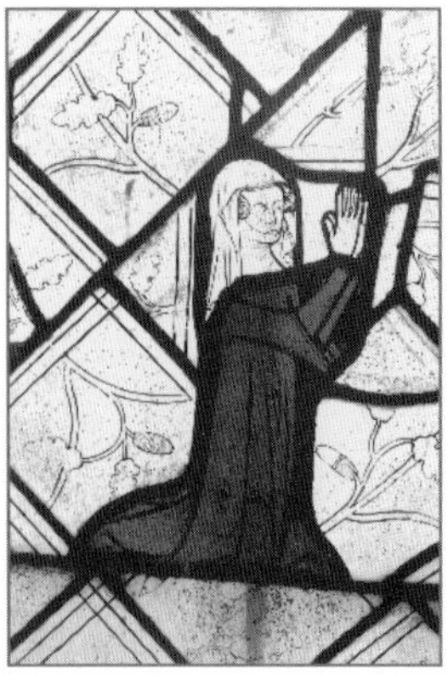

Fig. 18: Waterperry, St Mary's. Fourteenth-century donor. (Photo. by John Piper)

Even at the age of twelve, John Piper was fascinated by stained glass. In his autobiography,[2] his father recalled how the boy took the family around the Surrey countryside 'showing us all sorts of interesting places which otherwise we should never have visited'; and young John would stop to make drawings of architectural features, including the stained-glass windows. This was a habit which never left him. Even during the 1930s, a period when he was creating abstract paintings and constructions, he still went exploring old churches, making architectural drawings, photographing and tracing stained glass.

It was not always the obvious things that took Piper's eye: he would look up at the tracery lights, as in the Beauchamp Chapel, St Mary's, Warwick, to note the music-making angels; he would detect an affinity between a twelfth-century head of a saint at Wilton and a head of a girl by Picasso; he would stop and photograph (his photographs were always in black and white) a fourteenth-century donor figure at Waterperry in Oxfordshire (Fig. 18). But where he took pains to draw or copy a panel of old glass in water-colour – as he did at Grateley (see pp. 1–2) – this suggests a more lingering attachment. It is likely that Piper also stopped to do drawings in order to elucidate, where the glass was too decayed or obscure to come out well in a photograph. This seems to have been the case with a drawing he made in Brightwell Baldwin (Oxfordshire) of 'The Angel of the Annunciation'. There is very little colour in the actual glass: a touch of yellow stain on the angel's feathered legs and in his hair, and the effect of the figure relies on the fluidity of the drawn lines – barely decipherable now, so pitted and corroded is the surface. At Eastleach St Martin in Gloucestershire, Piper made a drawing of the head of a female saint: a shadowed yet expressive face with raised eyebrows and a speaking look. (The drawing is in the Ashmolean Museum, Oxford.) When I visited the church I had great difficulty in locating the panel, mainly because it is extremely small, barely the size of one's hand. There is no colour in it, just iron-oxide paint, and texture due mainly to age and decay.

In an article entitled 'Buildings in English Art',[3] Piper wrote:

> I know perfectly well that I would rather paint a ruined abbey half-covered with ivy and standing among long grass than I would paint it after it has been taken over by the Office of Works, when they have taken all the ivy off and mown the grass with an Atco.

And he had much the same feelings about stained glass: 'Time and the action of weather surely give unity and this look of purpose and organization to stained glass, good or bad, as they do to buildings good or bad', and 'Here in England medieval stained glass panels and fragments are to be found in quantity, small symbols of man's informal relationship with the past. . . . Restoration is their great enemy.'

This last observation brings one up with a jolt. It all depends upon the meaning and interpretation of the word, and this, I suspect, has shifted a good deal over the years. Most people now would probably equate 'restoration' with 'conservation', the process that has revealed an ancient panel of St Michael in Dalbury (Derbyshire), and rescued the twelfth-century glass of Canterbury Cathedral before it corroded away into nothingness.[4] The techniques now used constitute a very delicate science; it is a matter of preserving the ancient glass, removing corrosion, and revealing as far as possible the original colour. The age of each individual piece of glass is recorded, and every scrap that belonged to the original window scrupulously preserved.

It was not always so. In the nineteenth century, Viollet-le-Duc dealt ruthlessly with the windows of St Denis; where we should see nothing but twelfth-century glass, in fact we see largely replacements. Lewis F. Day, who was in every sense a stained glass man, wrote in his book *Windows* (1909) that the 'arch-enemy' of ancient windows 'is the restorer. He is the thief who has robbed so much old glass of its glory, and a most impenitent one; there are times when anyone who cares for glass could find it in his heart to wish he were crucified.'

At the time when Day was writing, the choice was either to leave the glass in whatever state it happened to be, or to replace it with new, and newly painted, glass; no other techniques had been devised. So if this is what the restoration of medieval windows meant, it was rightly to be condemned. In Piper's words, 'Preservation, maybe re-leading, is all they need'.

In 1927 Piper transferred from the Richmond School of Art to the Royal College of Art, where he remained for two years. At the Royal College, stained glass was taught, together with lithography, by Francis Spear; so he will have gained some practical experience of the subject. His interest in it, of course, always remained. Meanwhile, his main concerns during the next ten years were (more or less in this order) graphic work; landscape painting often in gouache and collage;[5] abstract work whether pictures or constructions; writing and broadcasting on art; designing posters and advertisements. He assisted Myfanwy Evans, whom he had met in 1934, in setting up the art magazine *Axis*. Then he became involved in theatre design, in which he worked alongside musicians such as Benjamin Britten, and writers including Christopher Isherwood and Stephen Spender. Already he had got to know such artists as Ivon Hitchens, Paul Nash and Frances Hodgkins – artists who preferred to work as individuals rather than be part of a group and issue manifestos (which was the current vogue).

Then in 1936 Piper met John Betjeman, who in the following year commissioned him to write the *Shell Guide to Oxfordshire*. This was the beginning of a firm and lasting friendship, and it was through Betjeman and his wife, Penelope, that Piper was to obtain his first commission to design stained glass.

Meanwhile, on the domestic front, in 1937 Piper divorced his first wife, Eileen Holding (they had been fellow-students at Richmond College of Art), and married Myfanwy Evans. They had met some three years earlier. Myfanwy relates how it happened.[6] She had been invited down to Suffolk to stay for the weekend with Ivon Hitchens, who had rented a cottage on the beach at Sizewell (before the days of nuclear energy); he wanted to make some drawings of her. John Piper, who was already a friend of Hitchens, although ten years his junior, was already staying there, and he came to meet her off the train at Saxmundham. Together they walked along the beach, stopping to swim and, to Ivon Hitchens's annoyance, arriving late for supper.

The following year John and Myfanwy set up home together – but where? The problem lay in finding a place which was in the country, which Piper loved, yet not too far from London. The couple solved it by using a pair of compasses, and finally a pin. The pin stuck in the map at Fawley Bottom, where miraculously, there was a farmhouse to let. At that time it was not what a house-agent would call a desirable property, having neither mains water nor electricity; but it was a house with which they had perfect empathy, and it was to be their home together for nearly sixty years. Myfanwy went on living there until her death in January 1997. They identified so much with the place, and the farmhouse with them, that

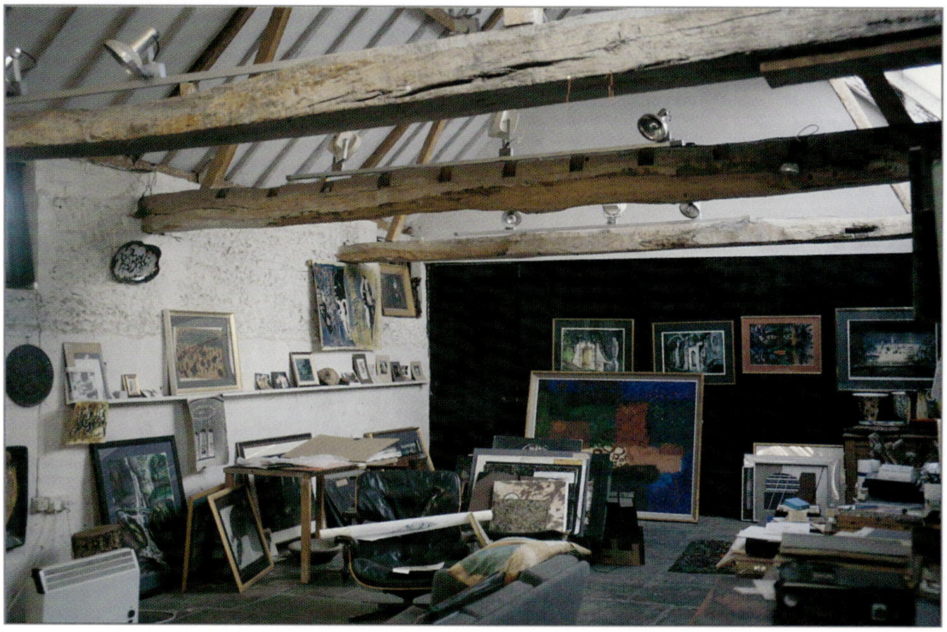

Fig. 19: Fawley Bottom. The original studio

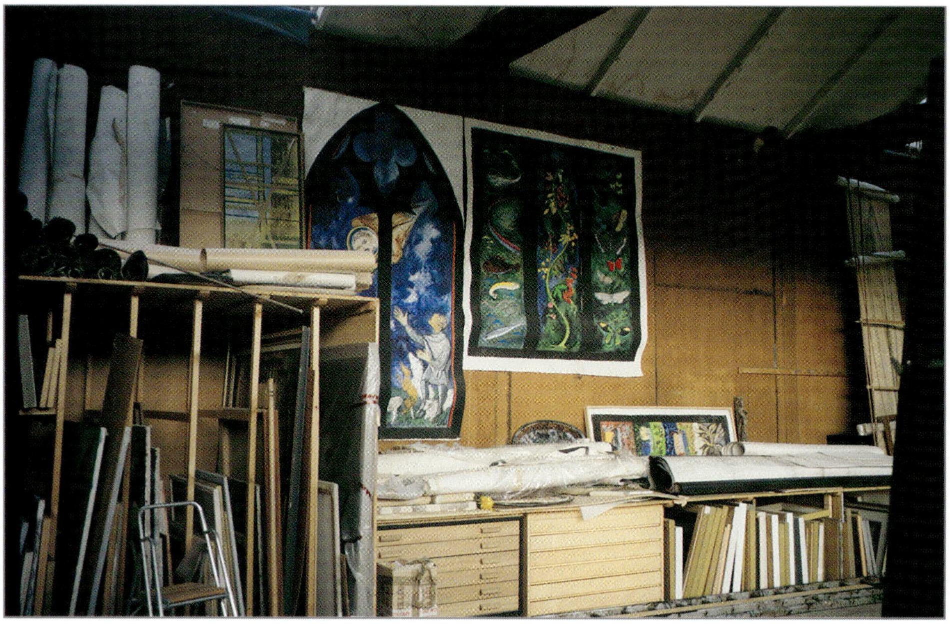

Fig. 20: Fawley Bottom. Piper's large studio, with cartoons

it is impossible to consider the work of either of them without reference to the setting in which it was produced.

Fawley Bottom Farmhouse dates from the 1830s. It is constructed largely of flint, with brick surrounds to the doors and windows, an unpretentious building. It sits low in a wooded valley, the exterior giving little indication of the treasures within. The roofline is broken by high dormers which light up the original studio. This is approached through the generous farmhouse kitchen. The ceiling here goes right up to the rafters, supported by massive and irregular beams. Around the room is pottery made by Piper, and rugs designed by him, his brushes still in a jar by the window, two ancient stone gargoyles, umbrellas in a stand, volumes on Picasso, a sculptured head of Myfanwy, a marmalade cat, and everywhere are Piper's paintings, his prints, his photographs, and – dare one say it? – his presence.

In the words of David Piper, 'the home is also the workshop' (Fig. 19).[7] Across the grass is another workshop, a larger studio converted from a barn (Fig. 20). This is where all the sizeable stained-glass projects were designed, from Coventry Cathedral onwards.

But in all probability there would have been no windows at all if it had not been for Patrick Reyntiens.

Reyntiens had newly graduated from Edinburgh School of Art; after a short period of unemployment, he found a niche for himself working in the studio of J.E. ('Eddie') Nuttgens (Fig. 23, overleaf). Nuttgens was a stained glass designer who had grown up in the Arts and Crafts tradition. He was an extremely fine craftsman, and Reyntiens judged him 'the finest painter of stained glass through three generations'. He had a roomy studio, rather like an Italian Renaissance 'bottega', at Piggotts Hill near High Wycombe,[8] and this is where Reyntiens came

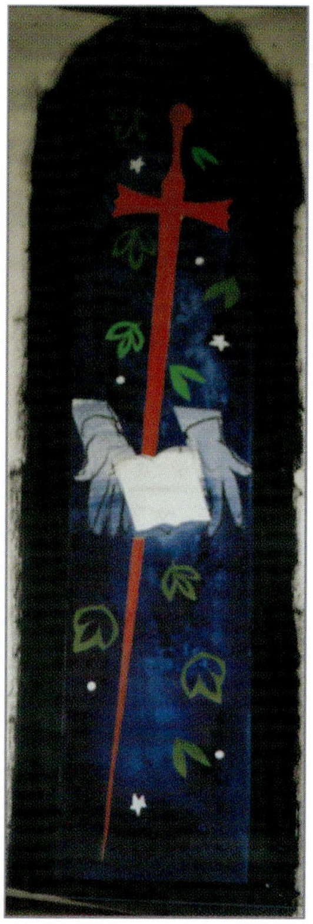

Fig. 21: Detail from the cartoon for St Paul's, Pishill, photographed at Fawley Bottom studio (see p. 100)

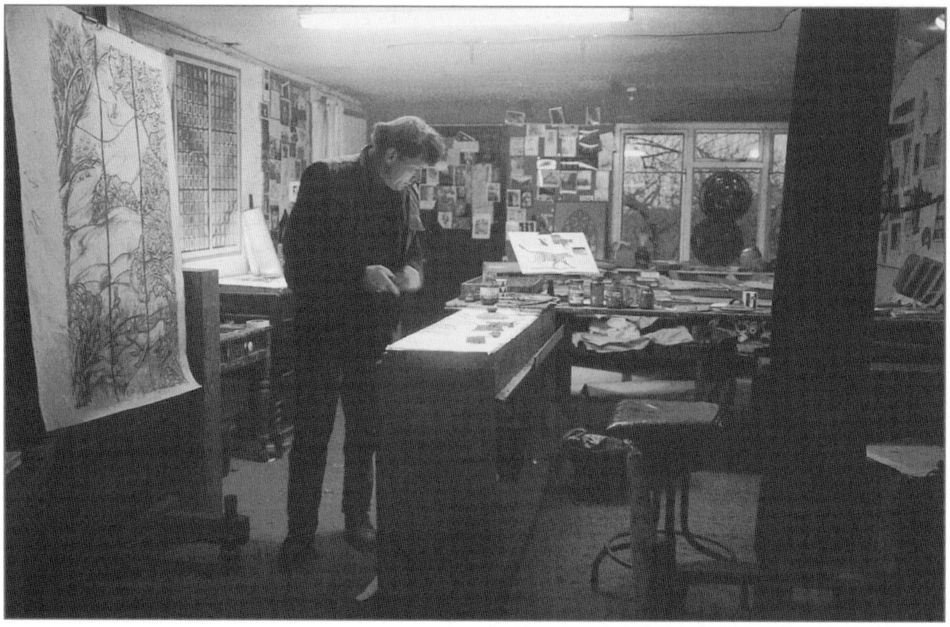

Fig. 22: Joseph Nuttgens in the studio he inherited from his father, Eddie Nuttgens

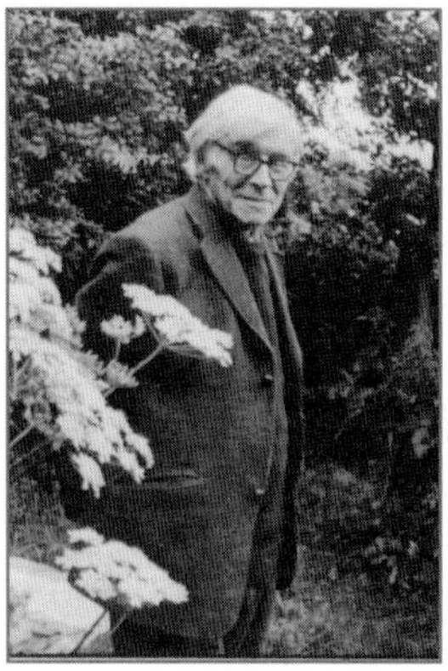

Fig. 23: J.E. (Eddie) Nuttgens, 1977. (Photo. courtesy of Jessie Matthews)

to be versed in all the techniques involved in the medium. In 1953 he married the artist Anne Bruce (Fig. 24), acquired a house and renovated it. He and John Piper first met in the late spring of 1954; it was through Penelope Betjeman. She happened to remark to the Pipers that she had met in Nuttgens's studio a young man who had actually heard of Matisse (a rare distinction). This prompted the Pipers to invite him to lunch at Fawley Bottom; he rode there on a Vespa.

Piper had already been approached to design glass for the Chapel of Oundle School. The commission came from Major L.M.E. Dent, a trustee of the Sanderson Memorial Fund administered by the Grocers' Company, who paid for it. Major Dent was a friend of John and Penelope Betjeman; through them he was introduced to John Piper, and he invited him to undertake the project.

Major Dent has left a much fuller account (held in the Tate Gallery Archive) of how Piper came to be commissioned. The commissioning of the new East Windows was part of the celebrations for the four hundredth anniversary of the founding of the school. The Headmaster, Graham Stainforth, had originally wanted Hugh Easton to design the new windows, as he had already done the small windows in the ambulatory. However, Easton eventually dropped out. Other names put forward included Francis Spear of Reigate (who had work in Glasgow Cathedral), Ervin Bossanyi (then known for his window in the Tate – the Canterbury glass came later), and Peter White of Ealing. John Piper's name was first suggested by Keith Harrison, despite the fact that he had not designed for the medium before. The approach was made via Betjeman, but not until May 1953 as it was known that Piper was busy designing sets for Britten's opera *Gloriana*, celebrating the coronation of Elizabeth II. Then Dent wrote to him, enclosing photographs of the chapel. Piper replied 'It is an exciting possibility!'. His first idea was to make the windows himself at the Royal College of Art, but

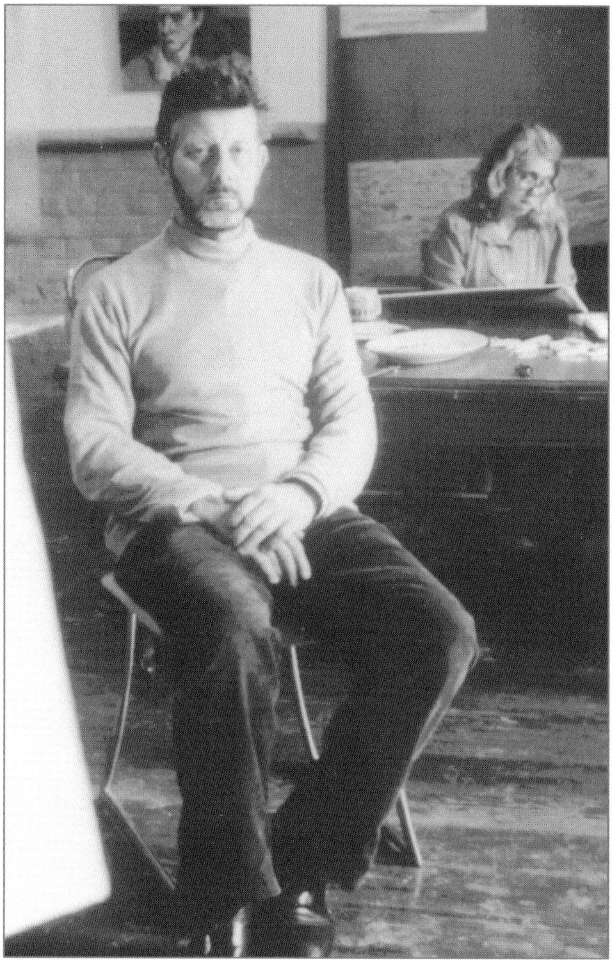

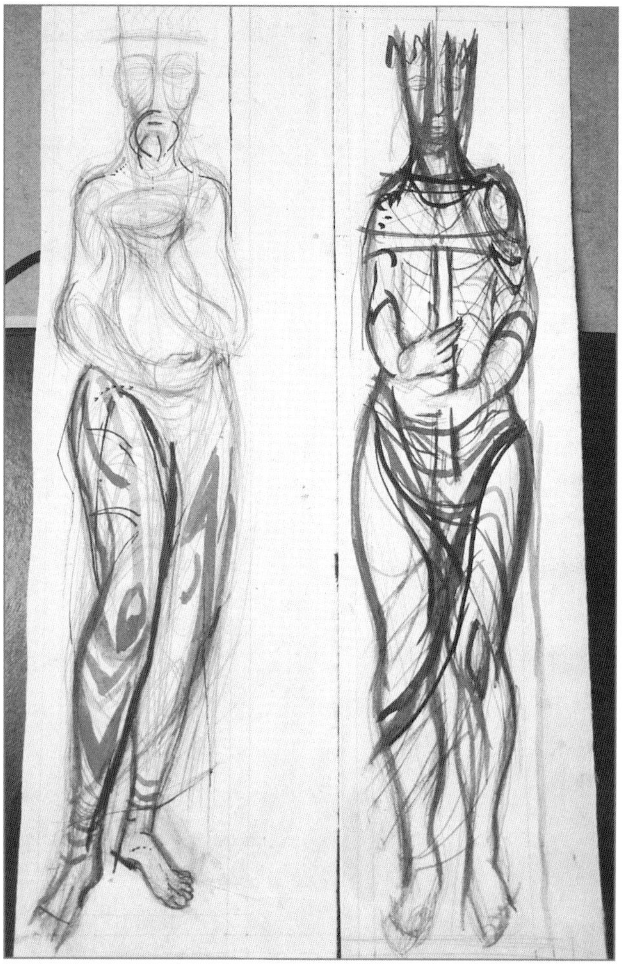

Left: Fig. 24: Patrick Reyntiens and his wife, Anne Bruce. (Photo. courtesy of David Wasley)
Right: Fig. 25: Drawings for Oundle glass

Betjeman persuaded him that this was scarcely practical. So the introduction to Reyntiens was a godsend.

In the first place, Piper prepared preliminary sketches, and not full-scale cartoons (Figs 25, 29 (p. 44), 30 and 31 (p. 45)). He showed these to Reyntiens, who grasped at once their potential as stained-glass designs, while at the same time guessing at the difficulties he would have in interpreting them.

As a trial piece, rather than embark straight away on the Oundle windows, they decided that Reyntiens should take back with him to Eddie Nuttgens's studio a gouache drawing of two crowned and mask-like heads. There were part of a series derived from medieval sculpture and roof-bosses, including foliate heads,[9] which Piper was working on at the time. (I remember seeing some of these myself, when I first came to Fawley Bottom in the fifties.) Reyntiens was to see how this drawing would translate into the medium. 'The experience was so vivifying and beautiful', Reyntiens recalled, 'that the drawing *had* to be interpreted into glass; love would find a way.'

Six weeks later Reyntiens returned in triumph with the completed panel balanced precariously on the back of his Vespa. Piper was delighted, and this very first

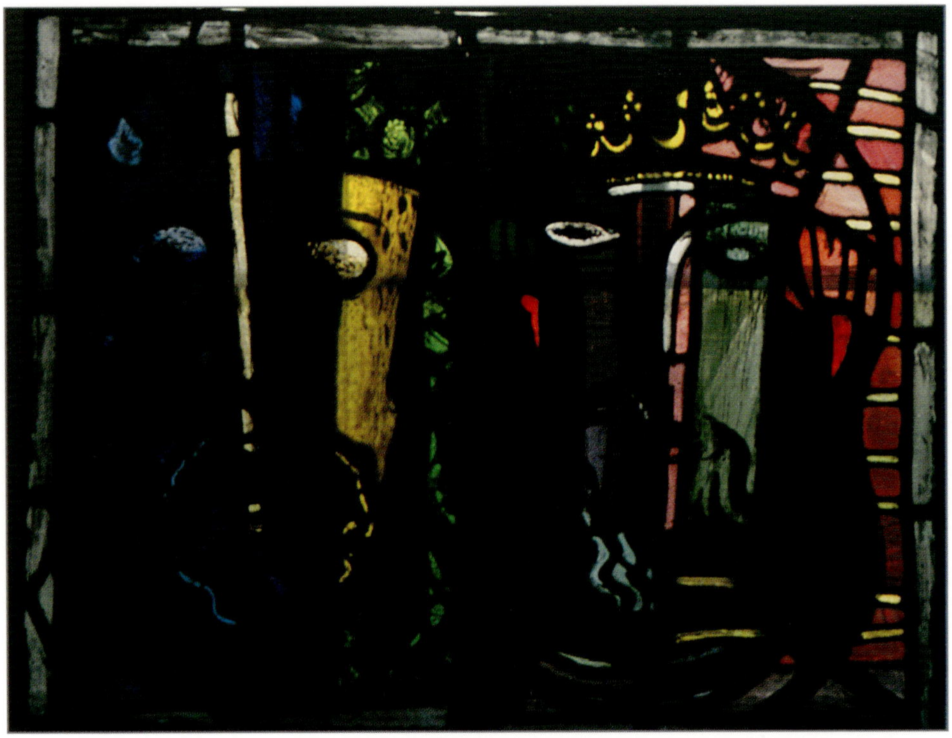

Fig. 26: Two Heads (see pp. 39, 44, 81). (Coll. Myfanwy Piper)

window is still kept in the farmhouse at Fawley Bottom (Fig. 26).[10] The two heads, one darkest blue with yellow, the other red, pink and grey, both heightened with slashes of white, stare inscrutably ahead, their eyes set beneath glittering crowns.

The Oundle windows represent nine different aspects of Christ, a theme suggested by the Revd V.E.G. Kenna, who was a friend of Piper. Dent relates that Piper brought to his house gouache paintings of the nine figures, and pinned them up on the wall of his office. Then they were displayed, rather secretly, at the end of a long passage in the cellars of the Grocers' Hall; they were shown only to a select few. Although he was venturing into what was for him new ground, Piper was very determined about he wanted, and would not enter into discussions about the designs with the Headmaster (who had suggested that the faces should look inwards). Dent wrote to the latter (10 December 1953):

> the only three people whose aesthetic judgement he really respects are his wife, Kenneth Clark and Betjeman, and I at least know that the last two are greatly impressed by these heads. He thinks that what he has done is the right answer, and being a person of great artistic integrity and some reputation he is not going to compromise.

At the cost of about £200 it was agreed to have a trial panel made of one of the figures ('The Good Shepherd'), and this was displayed in the Grocers' Hall, in the passage by the first-floor dining-room.

When Betjeman first saw the panel, shortly before it went on public exhibition, he wrote to his friend in great excitement:

22 May 1954
5th Sunday after Easter

The Mead,
Wantage
Berkshire

Dear Mr Piper,

The more I think of that window, the more the beauty of its colour and the strength of its great figure – particularly the hands and arms – haunt me. It is your masterpiece to date.

The Major telephoned to me yesterday to ask me what I thought of it. My dear, he was *most* enthusiastic. He thought that you as an artist, Reyntiens as executant and interpreter in glass, and Nuttgens with his experience, were an ideal combination. He was full of enthusiasm for the design and for the raspberries and for the colour. So I don't think we need worry about him. He thinks it best that it should be displayed to the Grocers somewhere in London. He wonders if you could get it displayed at the R(oyal) C(ollege of) A(rt) Schools in South Ken(sington) as they would impress the Grocers. I said I would ask you. Failing that the V(ictoria) and A(lbert Museum). Or, I suggest, the B(ritish) M(useum) if Tom Kendrick can fix it. He does not think there is anywhere in Grocers' Hall big enough and light enough behind, to do it justice.

The *Little Guide to Bed(ford)s(hire)* is excellent, particularly the architectural preface. The county is full of treasures.

Love to Goldilegz.[11]

J.B.

The trial panel having been so successful, Piper was commissioned to design the rest of the windows for Oundle. There are three windows of three lights each. They represent: the Way, the Truth and the Life; the True Vine, the Living Bread and the Water of Life (Fig. 27, overleaf); and Christ the Judge, the Teacher, and the Good Shepherd.

In the left-hand window, the Way is a mysterious figure in prussian blue and dark red; the Truth, whose pale limbs in white and green scintillate against crimson, holds a tau cross; the Life is an enigmatic figure clothed mainly in green, supporting a shield. In the central window the colours are sharper and more brilliant: the True Vine is dressed in gleaming gold and salmon pink, and carries wine in a silver chalice; the Living Bread is in different shades of blue and turquoise, shot with a shaft of yellow; The Water of Life has fluid forms of green and blue, heightened with white. The basic tones are darker again in the right-hand window. In the figure of Christ the Judge we find an inverted 'V' of gold, yellow features and crown set against deep blue; the Teacher is a sinuous figure in mauves and reds with a cloak of aquamarine; the Good Shepherd, holding a crook diagonally against him, appears in warm, earthly colours with lines of red and discs of gold. The faces of all are remote, enigmatic, formalized almost into abstraction.

Piper had recently visited Chartres and Bourges, and the images of thirteenth-century French glass must have been much in his mind: richness of colour, flecks of light penetrating the gloom. Yet it is difficult to find any direct derivation from stained glass. In the north transept at Chartres are the imposing figures of David, Solomon, Aaron and Melchisadek, their eyes ringed with lead rather than delineated

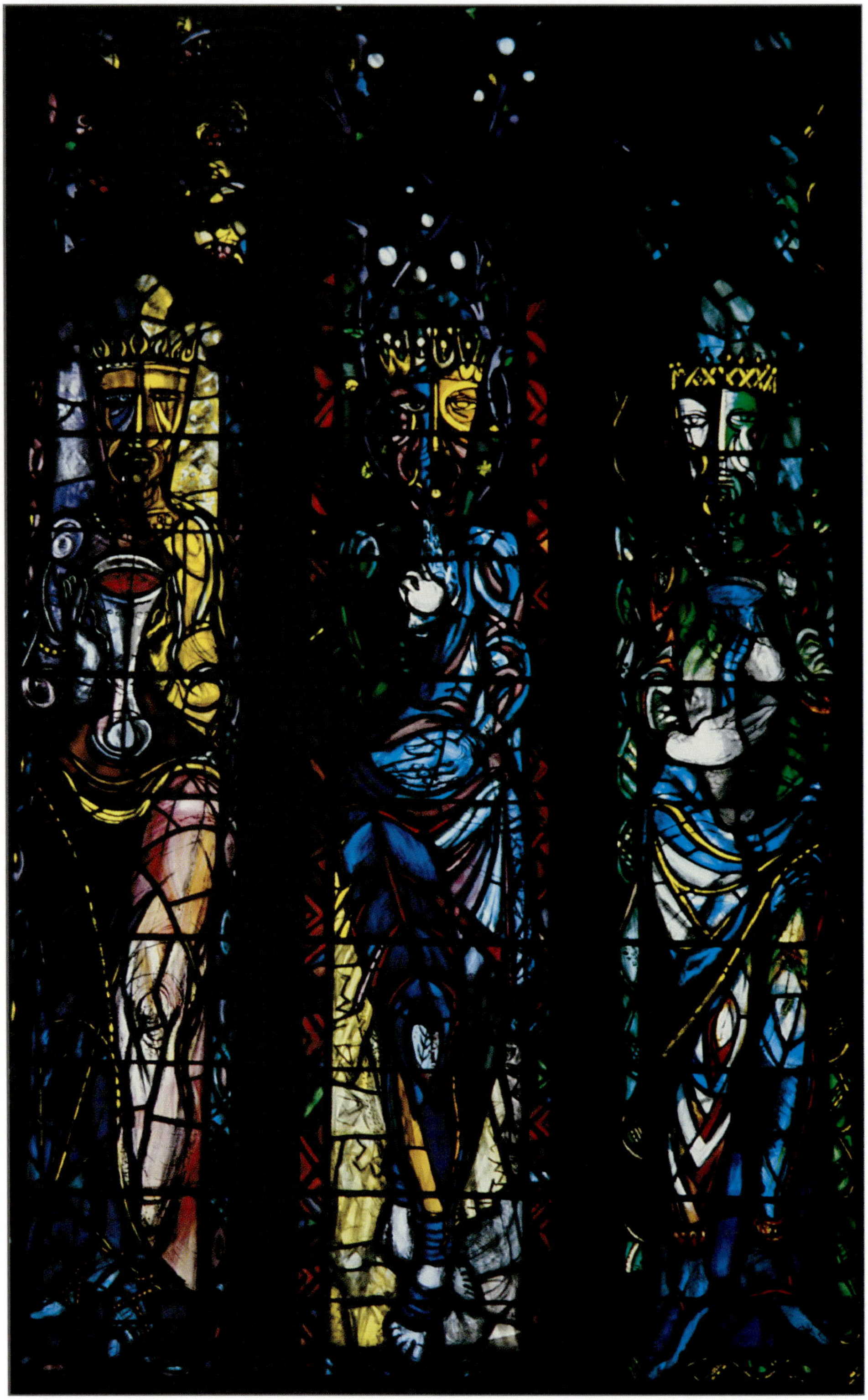

Fig. 27: Oundle School Chapel. The Vine, the Bread, the Water

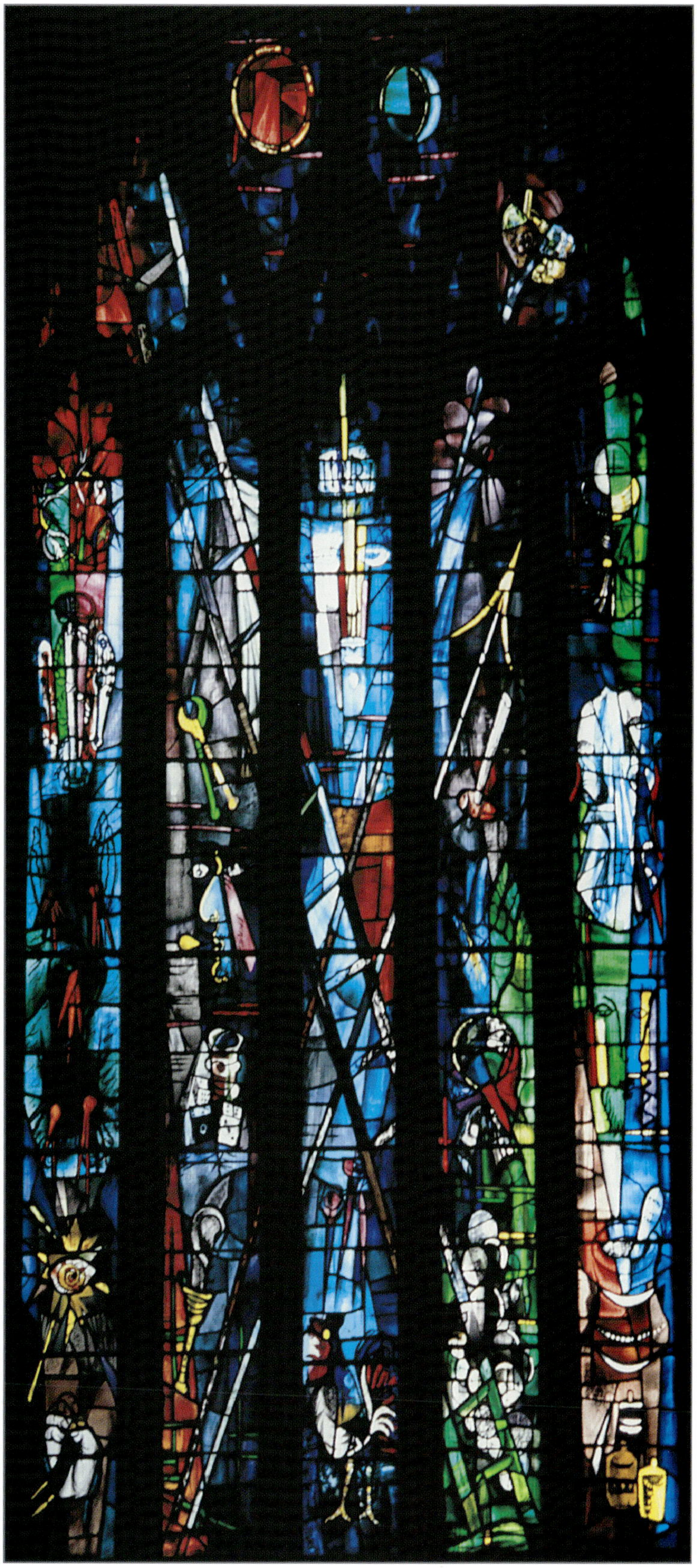

Fig. 28: Plymouth, St Andrew. The Instruments of the Passion and the Cross of St Andrew. The William Waldorf, 2nd Viscount Astor Memorial Window (see p. 45)

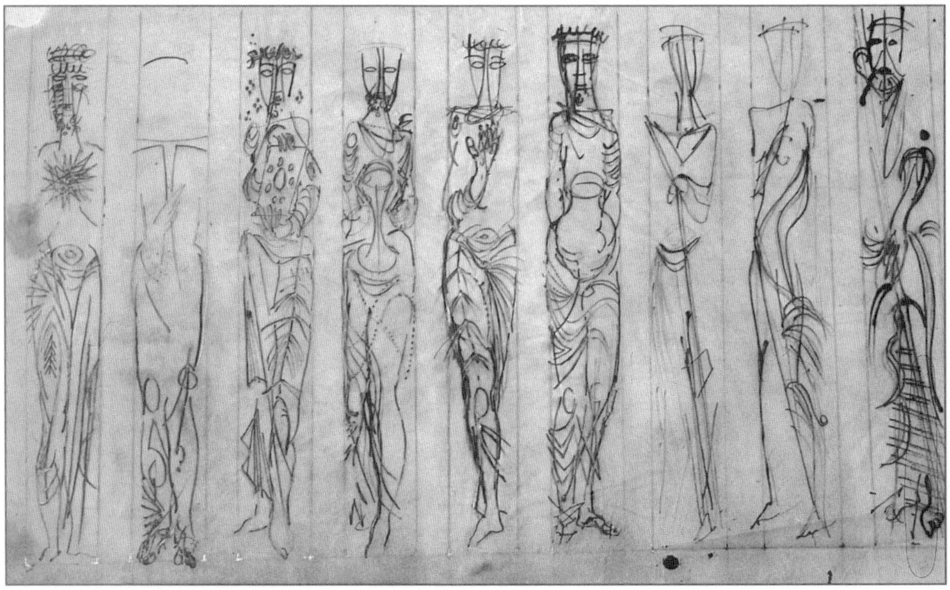

Fig. 29: Drawing on tracing paper, preliminary to Oundle cartoons

with paint. In the Choir at Bourges we find the prophets, such as Amos, Ezekiel, Micah, Nahum, Malachi – imposing again, yet the faces of several of them look sideways, and in general they seem more humanized, less hieratic. It seems that Piper's figures, with their remote and attenuated quality, owe at least as much to sculpture, such as the elongated figures grouped around the Portail Royal and the North Portal of Chartres, or the sinuous forms at Moissac (on the River Garonne in southern France; see Fig. 31, opposite). At the same time, the heads in particular remind us of modern French art of the interwar years, the Cubist paintings of Picasso and Braque.

It took Reyntiens fifteen months to complete the windows (Dent commented on the skill and sensitivity with which he did it), so the project was not finished until 1956. Meanwhile, during the year in which it was initiated (1954), Piper designed scenery for Bizet's opera *The Pearl Fishers*, and both scenery and costumes for Britten's *The Turn of the Screw*, libretto by Myfanwy Piper (based on the story by Henry James), and produced by Basil Coleman; it was staged at the Fenice Theatre, Venice.

The following year (1955) Piper and Reyntiens put on an exhibition at the Aldeburgh Festival, 'A Small Anthology of Stained Glass'. This included their first experimental panel, 'Two Heads' (Fig. 26, p. 40).

The Oundle windows were dedicated by the Bishop of Fulham on 26 May 1956; the ceremony was attended by the Queen Mother. Reyntiens wrote to Dent, 'What a great triumph for John it was, and a wonderful ending to so much work'. When Betjeman had seen the very first figure to be completed, he had called Piper's design 'awe-inspiring, reverent and magnificent', and now declared that Oundle School Chapel deserved to become a place of pilgrimage. The windows demonstrated a new and vital approach to stained glass, and met with well-deserved acclaim. In consequence, Piper received his next commission, to design the first of his windows for the then devastated Church of St Andrew, Plymouth.

Plymouth had suffered heavily from bombing raids during the Second World War. When Nikolaus Pevsner described it in the first edition of *South Devon* in the 'Buildings of England' series (1952), he observed 'at the time of writing, its centre is not a picture to be described in terms of architecture, but of dust and mud and rubble and weirdly shaped fragments of walls'. St Andrew's, the fourteenth-century parish church drastically restored in 1824, had been bombed in 1941, and virtually all its former stained glass was destroyed. Thus Piper had, as it were, a 'clean sheet'. It was perhaps in consequence that in most of his windows for St Andrew's he decided to let his design flow across the lights, rather than be made to fit their shape.

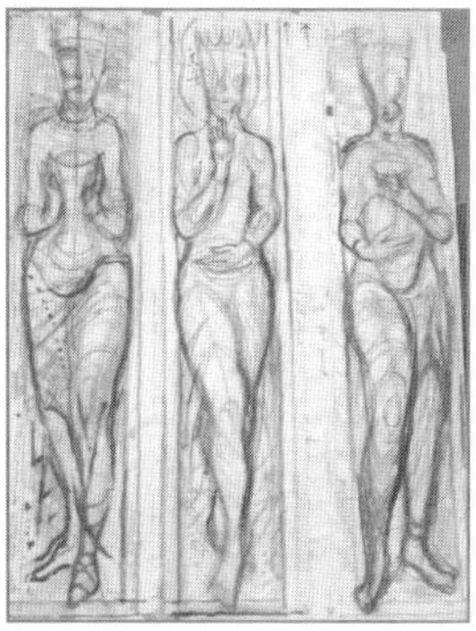

Fig. 30: Drawing for Oundle windows (see pp. 38–44)

The first window (Fig. 28, p. 43) is situated in the church tower, and commemorates William Waldorf, 2nd Viscount Astor, who had died in 1952; it was paid for by the Astor family. The colours gleam out of the dark in a way that reminds one of Piper's paintings of blitzed buildings that he did when he was a war artist. Dealing in the language of symbols, the window displays the Instruments of the Passion. Although this subject frequently appeared on the walls of fifteenth-century West Country churches (in sculpture, for instance), it was a new concept in stained glass. In this medium, the custom always had been to show the Passion and Crucifixion pictorially.

The window consists of five lights. In the first we find the Crown of Thorns, the Pillar and Scourges of the Flagellation, the Five Wounds, the Lantern of Betrayal, and the Hand plucking Hair; in the second, the Pincers, Spitting Jew, the Dice, and Malchus's Ear; in the third, and central, light, Saint Veronica's Handkerchief (which was said to bear the impression of Christ's face), the Nails and the Crowing Cock. Then in the fourth, the Hammer (that drove in the nails), the Smiting Hand, Christ's Loin Cloth and the Thirty Pieces of Silver (the amount paid to Judas for the betrayal); then in the fifth, extreme right-hand light, are the Chalice, the Seamless Robe, the Kiss of Judas, Pestle, Mortar and Spice Boxes. But the symbolism goes further: the ladder, reed and spear are arranged in the form of the Cross of St Andrew, the apostle to whom the church is dedicated.

This is a large and complex window and although it was started in 1957, it was not completed until 1962. In 1957 Piper visited Audincourt to see Léger's stained glass, and Ronchamp to see the work of Corbusier. He was still much involved in theatre design, including sets for the ballet *The Prince of the Pagodas*, with music by Benjamin Britten and choreography by John Cranko. He had already received the commission to design the Baptistry Window for Coventry Cathedral, and although he did not start work on this project immediately, the large barn to the side of the farmhouse was converted with it in mind.

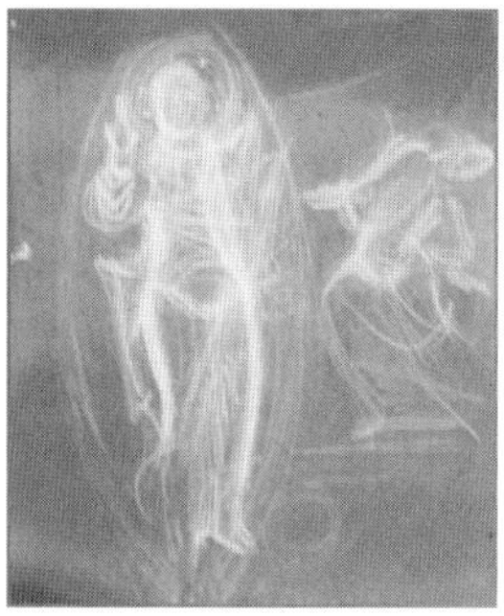

Fig. 31: Drawing of sculpted figure, Moissac. (This could be a point of inspiration for the Oundle windows; see pp. 38–44)

The second of the Plymouth windows (Fig. 32, overleaf) was made in 1963. It was commissioned as a memorial to Lady Nancy Astor, Britain's first woman MP; she was the member for Plymouth from 1919 to 1945. This central East Window of six lights is on the theme of the Four Elements: Water, Earth, Fire, and Air. It was bold to the extent of revolutionary to use this subject for an east window, traditionally reserved for the Passion and Crucifixion, but these themes had already been treated in the other Astor window in the tower. The East Window is

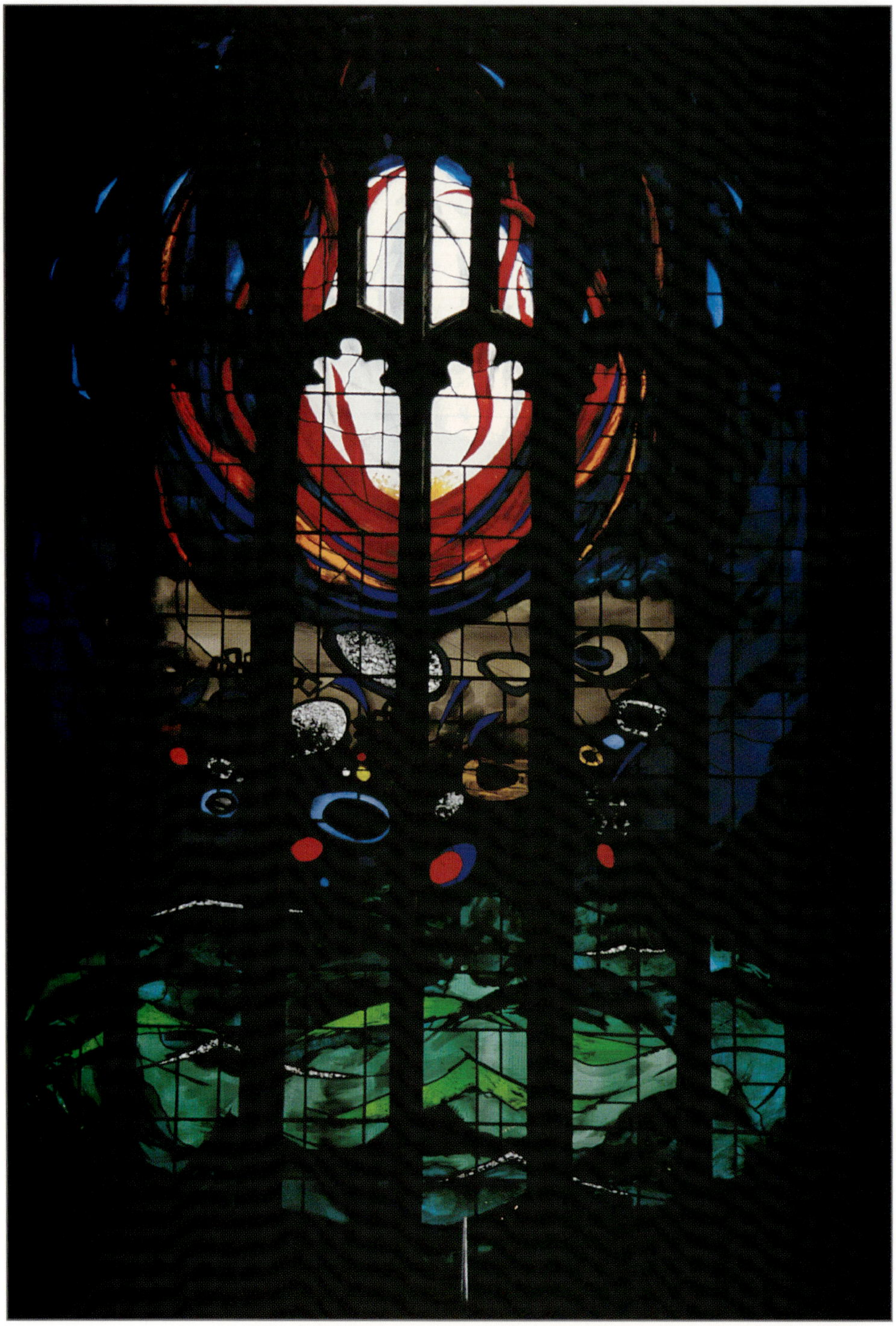

Fig. 32: Plymouth, St Andrew's. The Four Elements. The Lady Nancy Astor Memorial Window (see p. 45)

Fig. 33: Plymouth, St Andrew's. The Dr Moreton Memorial Window (see p. 48)

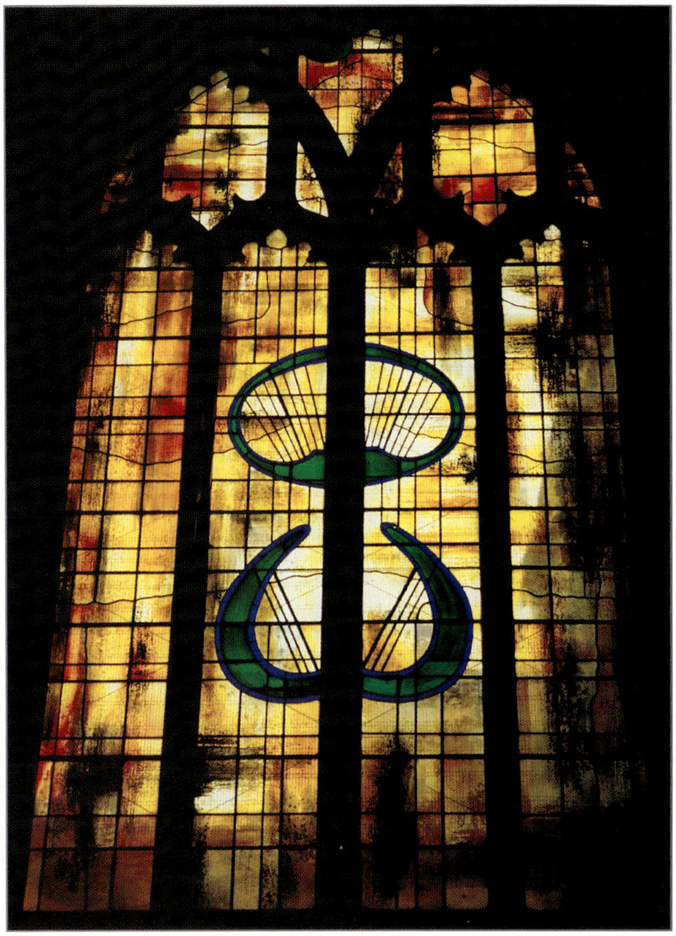

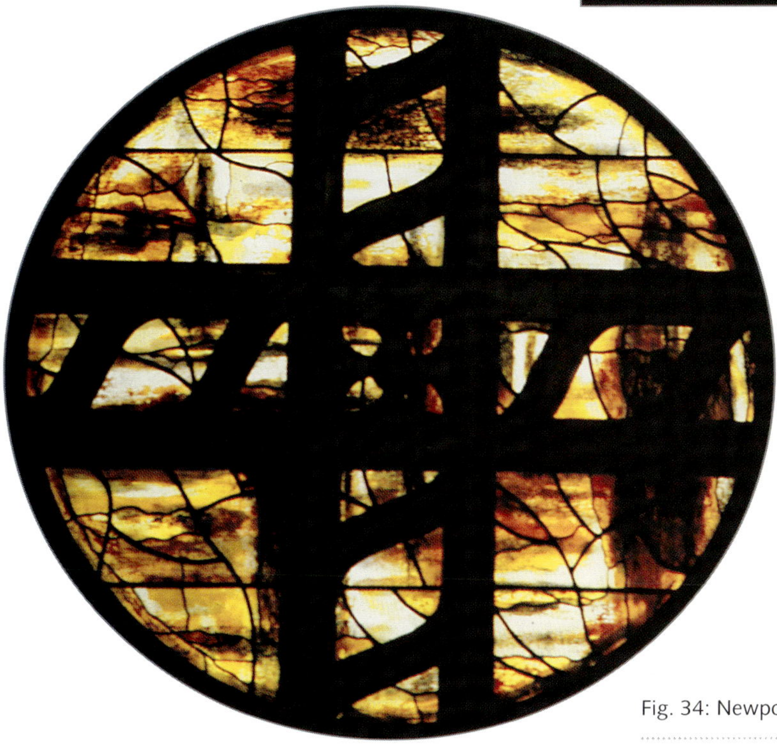

Fig. 34: Newport, St Woolo's Cathedral. Rose Window (see p. 77)

almost, but not quite, abstract. It is concerned with the symbolic use of colour, and nothing like it had been seen in this country before. The bottom section (Water) is a turbulent sea of different shades of green, predominantly viridian; above that is Earth, a pebbled beach (such as Piper was later to portray in his 'Brittany Beach' panels); above again is Fire, red flames licking upwards around a mandorla of white heat; and all around is the deep ultramarine of Air, towards the top flecked with dashes of paler colour, and at the base deepening to purple.

During 1965–6 the two other East Windows were added: in the Lady Chapel of the north aisle, and the St Catherine's Chapel of the south aisle. The former is based on the Litany of Loreto (the different titles or attributes of the Virgin Mary) and added to these are the Burning Bush of Moses, and the Flowering Rod of Aaron. All these symbols are shown in detached form against a ground of varying shades of blue. The St Catherine window has greater unity. It is dominated by the wheel, symbol of St Catherine of Alexandria, and interlaced with the wheel is the blue diagonal Cross of St Andrew. The ground is in shades of purple, mulberry and pink, and at the corners are dramatically shown the four symbols of the evangelists, linked with a serpentine design of fronds.

The last two windows for St Andrew's date from 1968: the south transept window, symbolizing the Creation and the Trinity, and the north transept window, in memory of Dr Harry Moreton (Fig. 33, p. 47). The south transept window is full of curving lines, designed right across the verticals of the mullions. In the centre is shown the Hand of God, while around leap and soar fishes and birds. They are reminiscent in a way of the Creation as seen in early fifteenth-century glass in the Great East Window of York Minster, except that here the colour is kept very cool, almost wholly confined to green, blue and white. The north transept window, on the other hand, is in different shades of yellow and gold, achieved with silver nitrate stain. For this reason the leading is much less important here, mostly it is just an open grid. Dr Moreton, whom the window commemorates, was organist and choirmaster at St Andrew's from 1885 to 1961 – a total of seventy-three years. Appropriately enough, therefore, the theme of the window is music and inspiration. Hanging in the air in the centre of the window, and crossing the line of the mullion, are two harps; they are said to be based on the earliest drawings of the instrument that are known.

Covering as they do a span of eleven years, it will be seen how varied are the windows at St Andrew's. Despite designs crossing mullions, the windows all accord with the church as a building – note, for example, how in the transept windows warmer colours have been used in the north and cooler ones in the south – and yet each window has been conceived separately, each has its own particular vision. Bold new ideas have been tried out, especially in Dr Harry Moreton's golden window, and in the totally original East Window of the four elements.

It seemed best to consider all the Plymouth windows together and yet, long before they were completed, Piper was receiving other very important commissions. The first of these was for Eton College.

CHAPTER FIVE

THE ETON WINDOWS

'It is the *idea* that is such a committing sort of undertaking!'

John Piper[1]

It is no use a stained glass designer being inhibited by architecture, not even Perpendicular architecture.

The foundation stone of Eton College Chapel was laid in 1441 by Henry VI, and the building of it, together with the rest of the school, was begun two years later. Thomas Gray (1716–71) wrote of the 'distant spires' and 'antique towers' of Eton, and indeed it is striking enough. Yet, although the general impression is one of loftiness, splendour and coherence, the original plan was for a very much larger chapel still. This defies imagination. As it is, each of the windows is about 35 feet (10 metres) high, the side windows 15 feet (nearly 5 metres) in width, and the East Window wider than that. When they were all blown out during the Second World War, it was not, it seems, to the least regret of the staff of the time. The original glass had been destroyed long since and had been replaced by Victorian windows of, it appears, insufferable dreariness. The post-war organist was instructed to play *fortissimo* in order to bring down any remaining fragments, which the masters delighted in grinding under their heels. So there could be no question of restoring the nineteenth-century glass and in February 1949 a committee was set up by Lord Crawford & Balcarres with Dr Milner White, Dean of York, and Sir Kenneth Clark, to advise on a new East Window.

Lord Crawford was enthusiastic about the work of Evie Hone (although the Dean of York was not keen), and in June of that year she was invited to submit cartoons. In November 1949 she was given a firm commission for her great window of the Last Supper and the Crucifixion. This caused a furore. The college architects, Seeley and Paget, promptly resigned, but the project went forward. Hone's work was defended vigorously by Sir Kenneth Clark ('Either you have something which is architecturally right and dead, or architecturally wrong and alive'), and the window was installed in 1952 (Fig. 14, p. 28).

What Evie Hone produced was a design of utter conviction. In the top half, the Crucifixion, the figures are set against a rich blue ground. Christ is shown against a red cross, each of his long arms extended across two lights. (Perhaps this disregard of tracery is the least satisfactory part of the composition.) The figures are shown in varying size, according to their importance in the iconography; the Virgin and St John are larger than the contorted bodies of the two thieves, which are larger in turn than the subsidiary groups on either side. In the lower lights, below the transom, the principal subject is the Last Supper. The

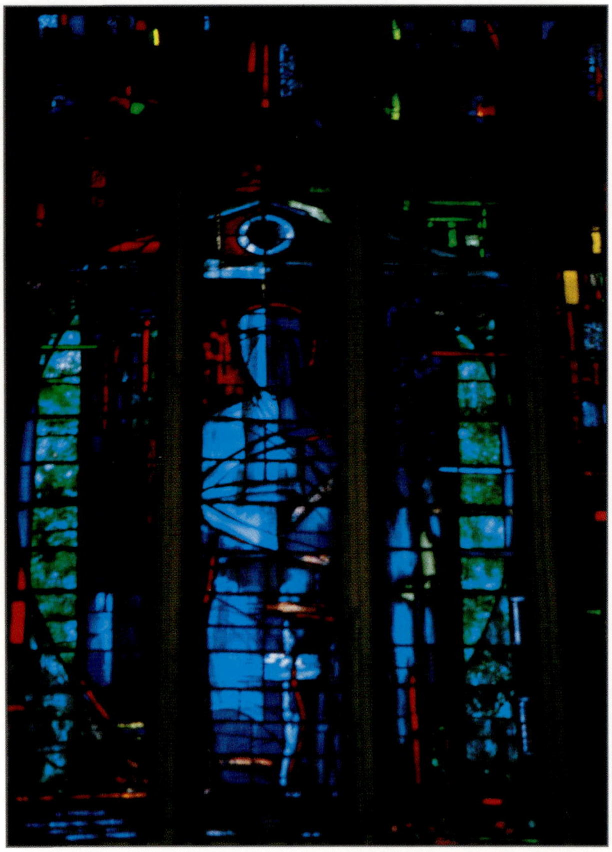

Fig. 35: Eton College Chapel. The Raising of Lazarus (upper half) (see pp. 57–8)

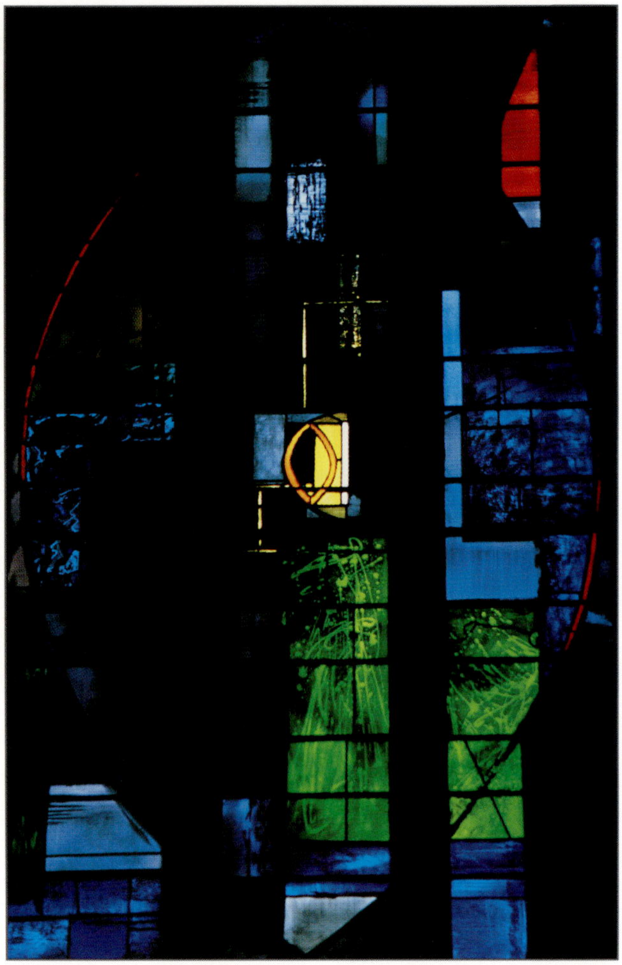

Fig. 36: Eton College Chapel. The Light under a Bushel (lower half) (see p. 58)

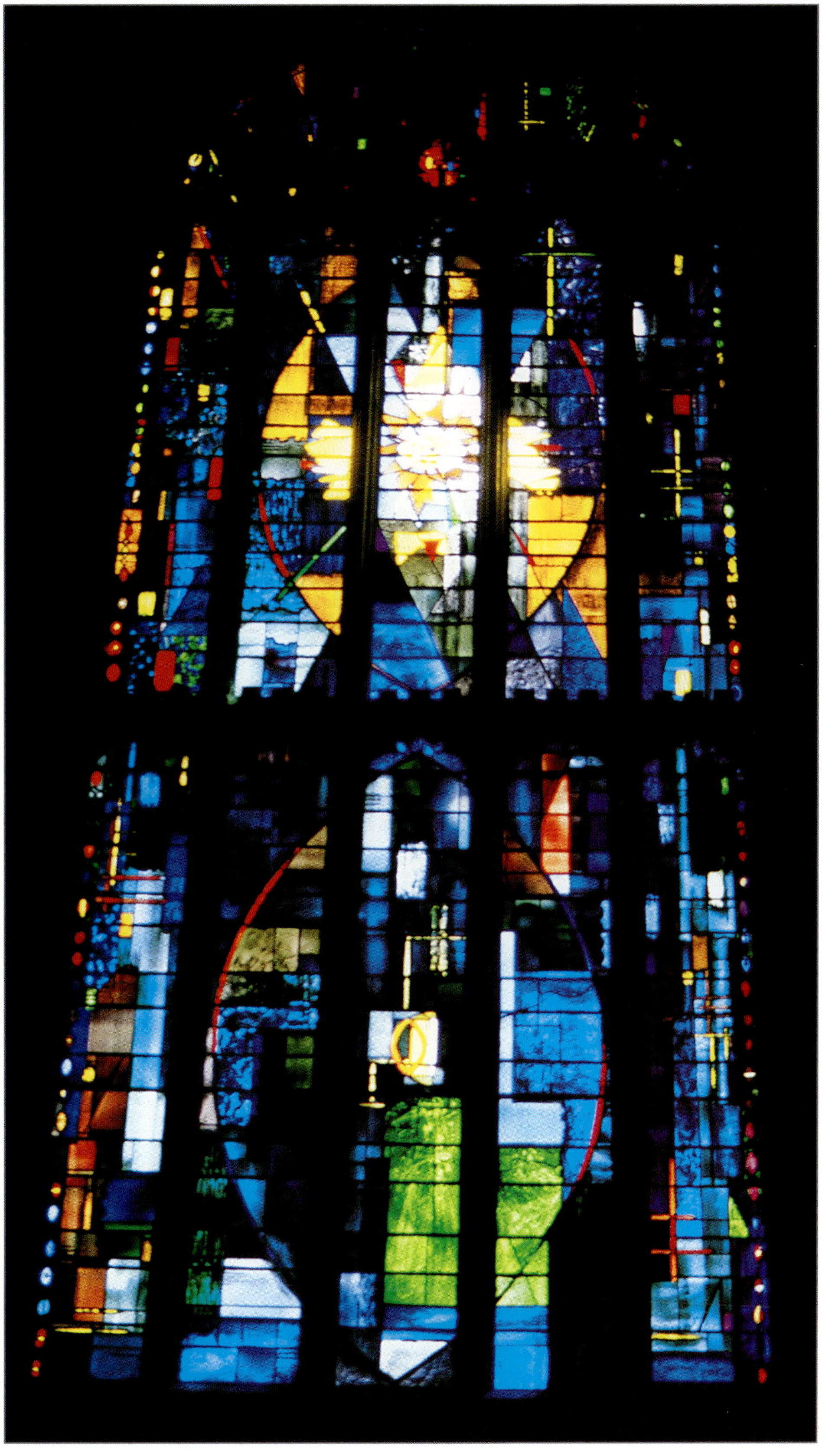

Fig. 37: Eton College Chapel. The Light under a Bushel (see p. 58)

disciples are grouped around an apparently oval table; they are dark figures, their heads nimbed in gold. The white cloth on the table catches the eye; behind is the solemn Christ with hands upraised in prayer, and in front of him an emerald chalice (green being the colour of rebirth). On either side are Old Testament figures: Melchisadek to the left, Abraham and Isaac to the right, the offered sacrifice of the son prefiguring the Crucifixion. The whole effect is one of compressed power, a kind of Byzantine rigidity, and unshakeable faith.

It must be one of the most dominant windows ever made. The problem was then how to design glass that would not only grace a fifteenth-century chapel, but also stand alongside Evie Hone's creation. She was not even sure herself how to do it. She was commissioned to design for the two flanking windows but, dissatisfied with her first sketches, she went on to make further designs. At the same time, it was noticeable that her health, never robust, was rapidly declining, and she died early in 1953.

Even if Hone's designs had been completed and were available (they seemed to have disappeared, and by July 1956 were nowhere to be found), it was felt that it would be unsatisfactory to have the easternmost side windows designed by one artist and the rest by another. In 1955 various names were put forward, including Piper's, to take on the commission: Rosemary Rutherford and Kitty O'Brien of Dublin, both fine, sensitive glaziers, but perhaps lacking in power for such an immense project; Patrick Reyntiens also asked to be considered, as an independent artist, informing the Provost that he and Piper had already received the commission for the Baptistry Window of the new Coventry Cathedral.

Meanwhile another serious problem had been detected in the chapel. Cleaners had for some time been sweeping up the bodies of insects, but it was not until June 1956 that it was officially revealed that the timber roof (not original to the building, but dating from 1669) was riddled with death-watch beetle. It was decided that the roof was irreparable, and, rather than attempting restoration, that it should be replaced. Sir William Holford was the architect in charge, and he daringly designed a fan vault. Visually, this was based on that of King's College Chapel, Cambridge, but it was in fact to be constructed of steel and concrete. 'All art is make-believe', Holford defended himself to his critics; and it is indeed quite extraordinary how convincingly Perpendicular the finished vault appears. It was completed in 1959.

Meanwhile, back in 1955–6, the problem of who was to design the north and south windows was still not resolved. Piper's name was suggested by Oliver Van Oss, who was described as 'the master most widely cultivated in the arts'. Holford was doubtful, and wondered whether Piper 'had sufficient experience of this difficult medium';[2] would he really want to do it? Lord Crawford, however, was impressed with Piper's work: 'we went to Piper's studio and saw some of his works and in particular a window which he had nearly finished for Oundle Chapel, which is very striking'.[3]

Piper was invited to come to Eton and to submit sketches for the two windows adjoining the East Window. It was put to him, delicately, that Evie Hone's intention had been to make these subsidiary to it. Although they should doubtless be rich and use some of the same colours, she had thought of them as being largely abstract in design.

Piper went back to Fawley Bottom to ponder the problem. There were, of course, his other commitments to consider. In 1956, as well as stained-glass projects for St Andrew's, Plymouth, and for Llandaff Cathedral, and the big window under discussion for Coventry, he was doing a good deal of theatre work. He designed the scenery for John Cranko's revue *Cranks* at St Martin's Theatre, and both scenery and costumes (with Alix Stone) for a production of Mozart's *The Magic Flute* at the Royal Opera House. In the following year, he designed scenery for the ballet *The Prince of the Pagodas*, and a play by Derek Monsey, *Less than Kind*, put on at the Arts Theatre Club. At Fawley Bottom, there was also the matter of converting the barn into a studio so that he could make full-size cartoons.

On 6 March 1957, Piper sent to Eton his first scheme for the two windows nearest to the east. Like his window for the tower at St Andrew's, Plymouth, commemorating Lord Astor, it was a carefully worked-out concept based on symbols. The two windows, he suggested, should be on the theme of Sacred and Profane Love, or, otherwise expressed, the Heart of God and the Heart of the World. Obviously he had been thinking about it long and hard, and he exclaimed in his letter on the fourteenth of the same month, 'it is the *idea* that is such a committing sort of undertaking!'

However, this initial idea did not meet with much enthusiasm, and since it was some time before he produced another, by November 1957 doubts began to be raised as to whether he was the right man for the job; should they not continue in their search for other artists? The Dean of Lincoln suggested Harry Stammers[4], or a certain young glazier called W. Wilkins. The name of Lawrence Lee was also mentioned. The opinion was sought of Robin Darwin, Principal of the Royal College of Art; he was unimpressed by Piper's work – 'For all his charm and scholarship and delicacy as a person, I find his work rather coarse and brutal' – but then he did not care for Evie Hone's work either.

John Piper was naturally upset by the suggestion that other artists might be considered for the project, although he candidly admitted in his letter of 26 November 1957, 'I do not yet know in the least what I shall be able to produce'. As well as his having, as usual, many other concerns demanding his attention, the fact was that his ideas were taking time to mature.

Then the following February (1958), Piper produced an alternative scheme based on the Miracles and Parables. This met with far more approval, and was the turning-point of the whole affair.

On 20 March 1958 the Provost (Sir Claude Elliott) and Fellows visited Piper's studio and were 'much struck by the richness of his colour'. The point was made by the Provost that if Piper were to do the windows, they should ask him without delay, before he became too preoccupied with Coventry.

Sir William Holford had by now forgotten his initial misgivings about Piper. On meeting him he found him to be 'a man of great intelligence and in some ways quite a considerable scholar', and he wrote to the Provost:

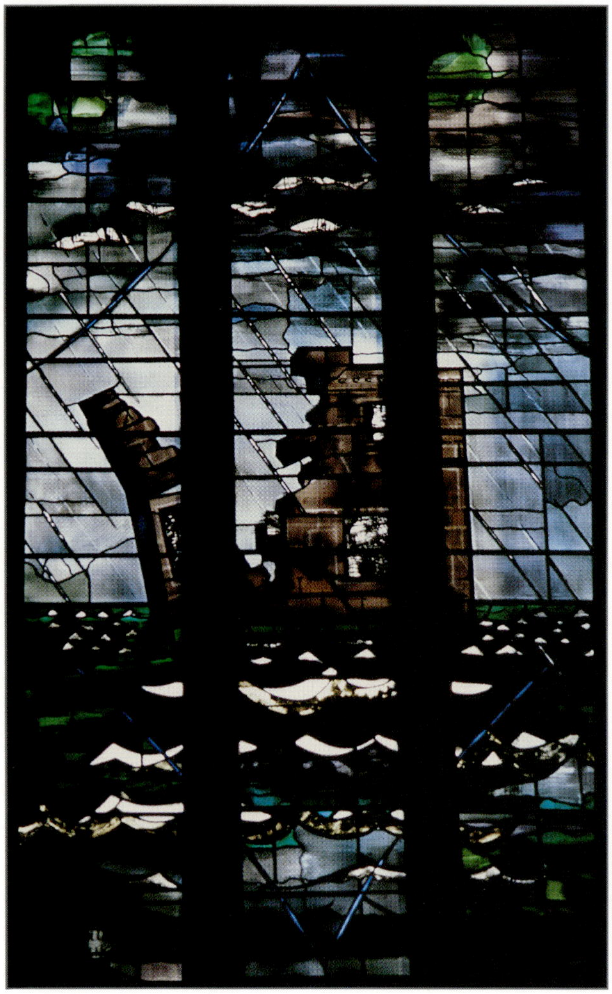

Fig. 38: Eton College Chapel. The House built on Rock (lower half) (see pp. 58–9)

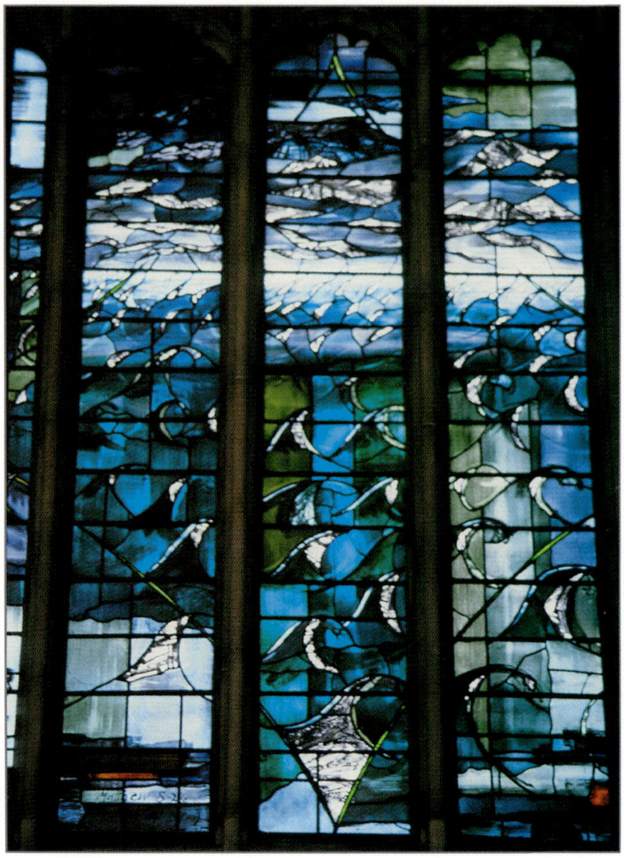

Fig. 39: Eton College Chapel. The Stilling of the Waters (lower half) (see p. 59)

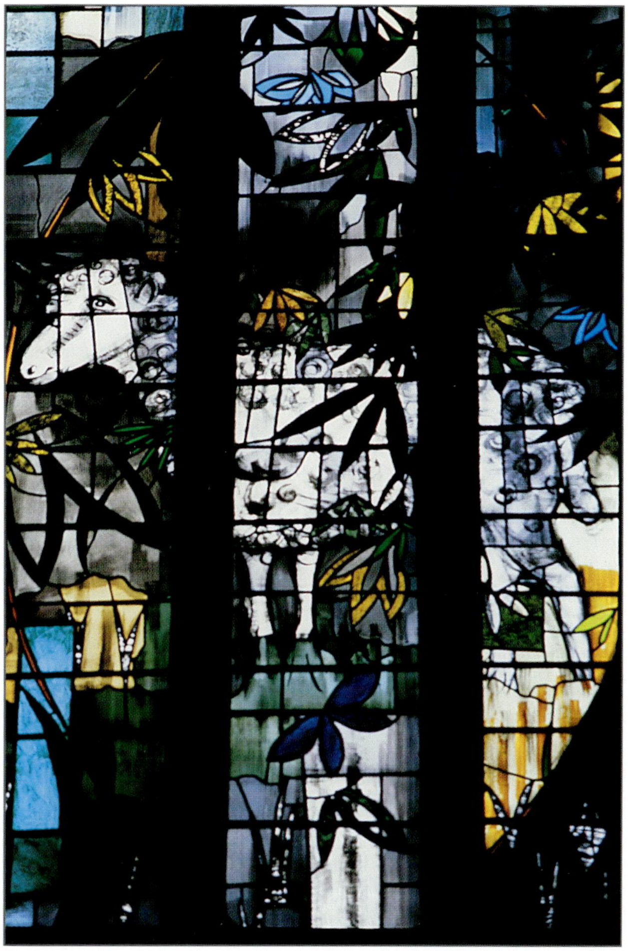

Fig. 40: Eton College Chapel. The Lost Sheep (lower half) (see pp. 59–60)

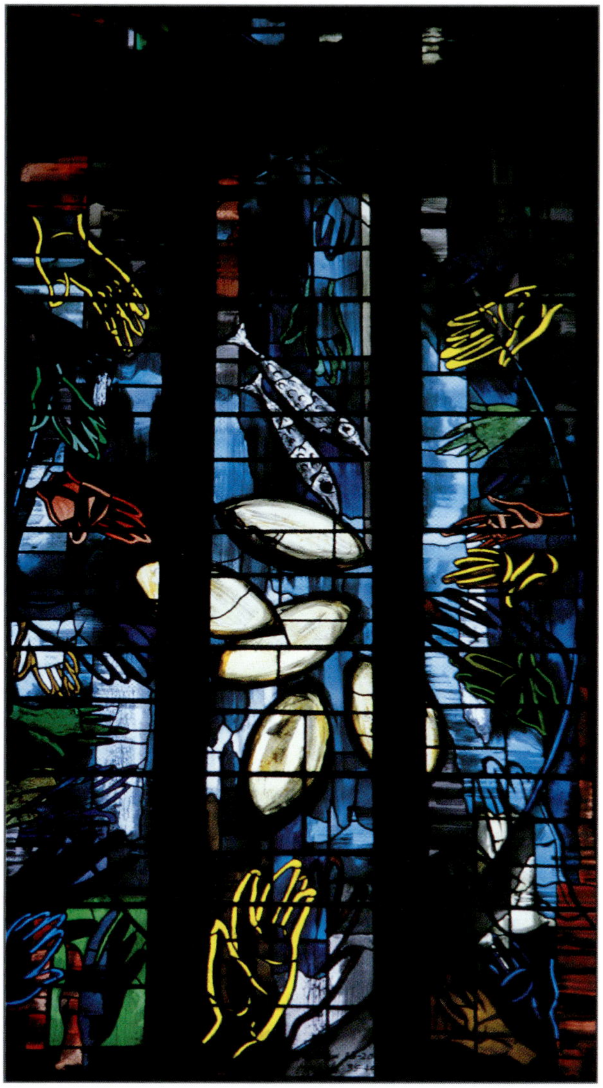

Fig. 41: Eton College Chapel. The Feeding of the Five Thousand (lower half) (see p. 61)

> My feeling about Piper is not based on any new enthusiasm for his work in stained glass but purely on his capacity as a man of great skill to produce something which will be a real contribution to the art of his time, no matter what the medium.[5]

The Provost replied the following day: 'I am most interested by what you say about Piper, and I am very glad that you approve of the suggestion that we should get Piper to submit designs.'

Meanwhile, the preliminary designs had been approved, the Provost and Fellows expressing a preference for the Miracles and Parables, rather than the symbols of Sacred and Profane Love. It was decided to let Piper go ahead in the first place with designing the two easterly windows, and see how they looked, rather than commit themselves at this stage about the others.

However, on 6 June Piper was indeed asked to go ahead with all eight windows. He was offered £1,000 for each window, a separate contract to be drawn up with Reyntiens, who was to make them.[6] It was proposed that they should comply with the following schedule:

Year ending 1 August 1959	1 window
Year ending 1 August 1960	2 windows
Year ending 1 August 1961	2 windows
Year ending 1 August 1962	3 windows

The final sketches for each window were to be submitted to the Provost and Fellows before its construction was started.

It was, as Piper had remarked earlier, 'the *idea* that [was] such a committing sort of undertaking'. The content of the windows was a subject he could discuss with the Headmaster, Robert Birley,[7] with whom he seems to have had a good relationship. They decided it would be better if the windows did not contain any angels; neither of them really believed in angels, so they could not expect the boys to either. And on the whole, Piper thought it advisable here to avoid the human figure; there are birds, fish, a sheep, the Hand of God, the rather classical head of the Shepherd, the hands of the multitude outstretched for bread, but the only thing approaching a human figure is the grave-wrapped Lazarus. Yet the windows do not deal principally in abstractions, but in symbols. At the same time, the vision is kept wide, and the treatment dramatic. On the north side are the four Miracle windows, to the south the Parables. The windows are divided by transoms, the 'problem' shown below, and its resolution above. The colours are paler to the west, where they abut grisaille glass, and deeper and richer in the more easterly windows. Thus not only do they make a fitting foil to the Evie Hone Last Supper and Crucifixion – in fact, they are much more than that – they seem to process towards it with a growing sense of climax.

The first two windows to be made were those adjoining the East Window. (Biblical references are quoted at the bottom of each window, listing the chapters and verses of the different gospels in which the theme appears; however, for the

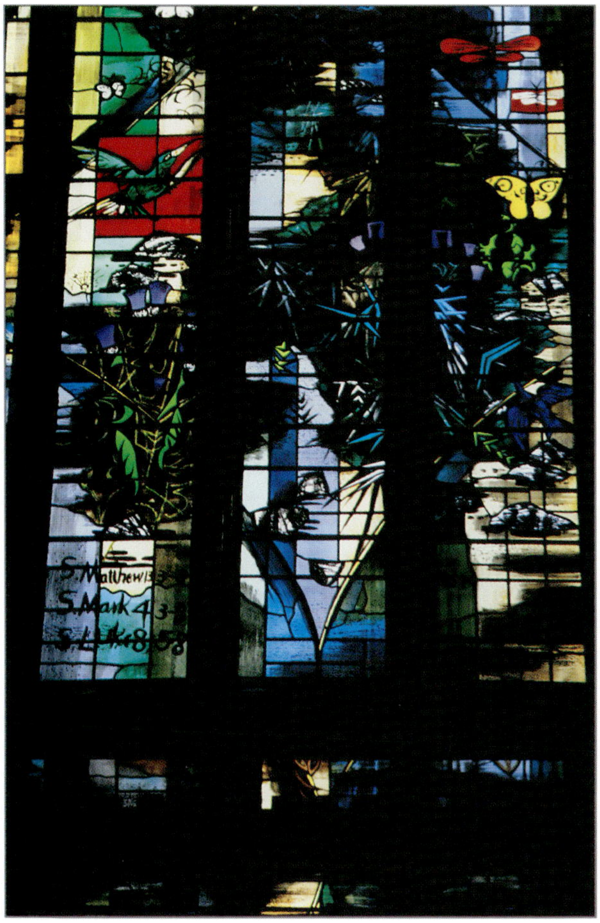

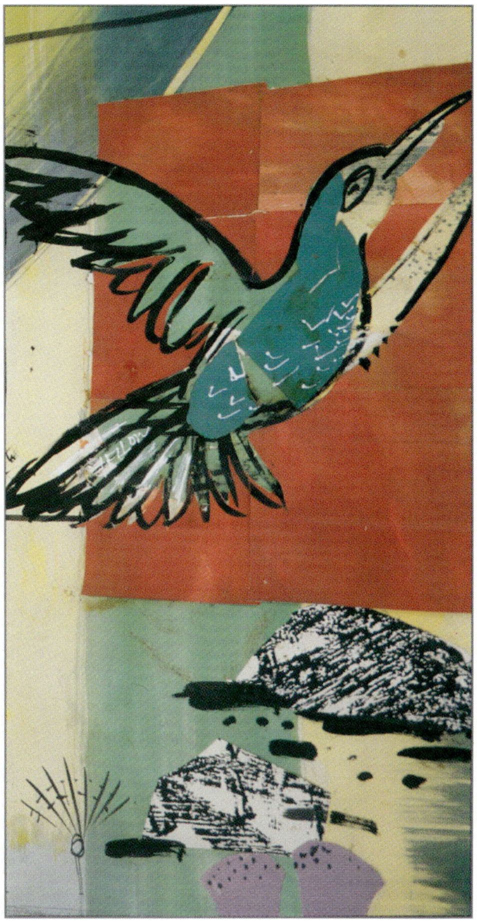

Left: Fig. 42: Eton College Chapel. Detail from The Wheat and the Tares. *Right*: Fig. 43: Detail from the cartoon for The Wheat and the Tares, photographed at Fawley Bottom studio (see pp. 61–2)

sake of clarity only one source for each is given here. Bible passages are quoted from the Authorized version.) On the north side, we find the 'Raising of Lazarus'. The story is related in John's Gospel, chapter 11. Lazarus was the brother of Martha and Mary; Jesus had been told he was very ill:

> [v. 17] Then when Jesus came, he found that he had lain in the grave four days already.
>
> [v. 21] Then said Martha unto Jesus (v. 21) Lord, if thou hadst been here, my brother had not died.
>
> [vv. 23–5] Jesus saith unto her, Thy brother shall rise again.
>
> Martha saith unto him, I know that he shall rise again in the resurrection at the last day.
>
> Jesus said unto her, I am the resurrection, and the life; he that believeth in me, though he were dead, yet shall he live.

Martha's sister Mary had gone to the grave to weep. Jesus came too, and commanded that the stone covering it should be moved away; then having given up a prayer to God:

> [vv. 43–4] . . . he cried with a loud voice, Lazarus, come forth.
> And he that was dead came forth, bound hand and foot with graveclothes; and his face was bound about with a napkin. Jesus saith unto them, Loose him, and let him go.

Piper has given the theme a most dramatic treatment. The borders are done in a rich abstract mosaic of colour, from which crosses emerge. In the lower half of the window (Fig. 35, p. 50) is the doorway of the tomb; against a field of red, or rather, any number of reds, is shown the hand of God pointing upwards. If one looks carefully, one can see the line of a mandorla, symbol of resurrection. This line is repeated in the upper half, where the shadowy figure of Lazarus, still swathed in his grave-clothes, emerges from a haze of blues and turquoises.

It is a concept of tremendous power, and it might have been thought impossible to match it with anything of similar force on the south side. Amazingly, this is just what Piper has achieved. The theme is the 'Light under a Bushel' (Fig. 37, p. 51). We read in Matthew 5: 14–16:

> Ye are the light of the world. A city that is set on a hill cannot be hid.
> Neither do men light a candle, and put it under a bushel, but on a candlestick; and it giveth light unto all that are in the house.
> Let your light so shine before men, that they may see your good works, and glorify your Father which is in heaven.

Piper's design again has abstract patterning in the borders, and again a mandorla in both sections. The lower half (Fig. 36, p. 50) is mainly in blocks of deepest blue; against them is set the streaky green of the bushel, and almost obscured by the surrounding shadow is the incandescent shape of the candle-flame, a miniature mandorla in itself. The upper part of a window is a sunburst of light against darkness – 'let your light so shine before men'.

Piper's achievement is such that it is difficult to imagine how the extraordinary problem of flanking the Evie Hone glass could have been better solved. Although he now had the commission to design all eight windows, he realized the subtleties of juxtaposition, how each should be a separately entity and yet complement those on either side. He and Reyntiens worked gradually, from east to west.

The parable of the 'House built on Rock' is the subject adjoining the 'Light under a Bushel'. We find the text in Matthew 7: 24–7:

> Therefore whosoever heareth these sayings of mine, and doeth them, I will liken him unto a wise man, which built his house upon a rock:
> And the rain descended, and the floods came, and the winds blew, and beat upon that house; and it fell not: for it was founded upon a rock.
> And every one that heareth these sayings of mine, and doeth them not, shall be likened unto a foolish man, which built his house upon the sand:
> And the rain descended, and the floods came, and the winds blew, and beat upon that house; and it fell: and great was the fall of it.

In the lower half of the window (Fig. 38, p. 54) we find a house crumbling away, lashed by the fury of the storm; the rain is shown in sharp diagonals and the waters seethe below. In the top half the tempest is raging with equal fury, but the house stands foursquare and erect. The colouring throughout the window is kept cool; greys and slatey blues predominate, with the occasional flash of green or turquoise, and white crestings on the waves.

In a way the Miracle window opposite has a similar theme; it is related also in colour. It shows the 'Stilling of the Waters' – Christ's power over the elements – which we find in Matthew 8: 23–7:

> And when he was entered into a ship, his disciples followed him.
>
> And behold, there arose a great tempest in the sea, insomuch that the ship was covered with the waves: but he was asleep
>
> And his disciples came to him, and awoke him, saying, Lord, save us: we perish.
>
> And he saith unto them, Why are ye fearful, O ye of little faith? Then he arose, and rebuked the winds and the sea; and there was a great calm.
>
> But the men marvelled, saying, What manner of man is this, that even the winds and the sea obey him!

In the lower part of the window is shown the storm – the jagged sea and the troubled sky, the waves lashed into sharp points by the fury of the wind (Fig. 39, p. 54). The colours in the upper part are much the same, a range of blues and greens with turquoise predominating, but here all is shown in horizontals, expressing perfectly the great and sudden calm.

Magnificent as the windows are, Piper and Reyntiens were finding it impossible to keep up with the schedule that had been outlined in the contract. Piper wrote to the Provost on 26 May 1961 expressing his regret that they were a little behind with the windows – by this time they were also busy with the Coventry project – 'but' he added hopefully, 'the situation is not, I think, desperate'. The following month, however, the Provost was complaining of the slow progress.

Next on the Parable side (south) is the story of the 'Lost Sheep'. This can be found in Luke 15: 4–7:

> What man of you, having an hundred sheep, if he lose one of them, doth not leave the ninety and nine in the wilderness, and go after that which is lost, until he find it?
>
> And when he hath found it, he layeth it on his shoulders, rejoicing.
>
> And when he cometh home, he calleth together his friends and neighbours, saying unto them, Rejoice with me; for I have found my sheep which was lost.
>
> I say unto you, that likewise joy shall be in heaven over one sinner that repenteth, more than over ninety and nine just persons, which needeth no repentance.

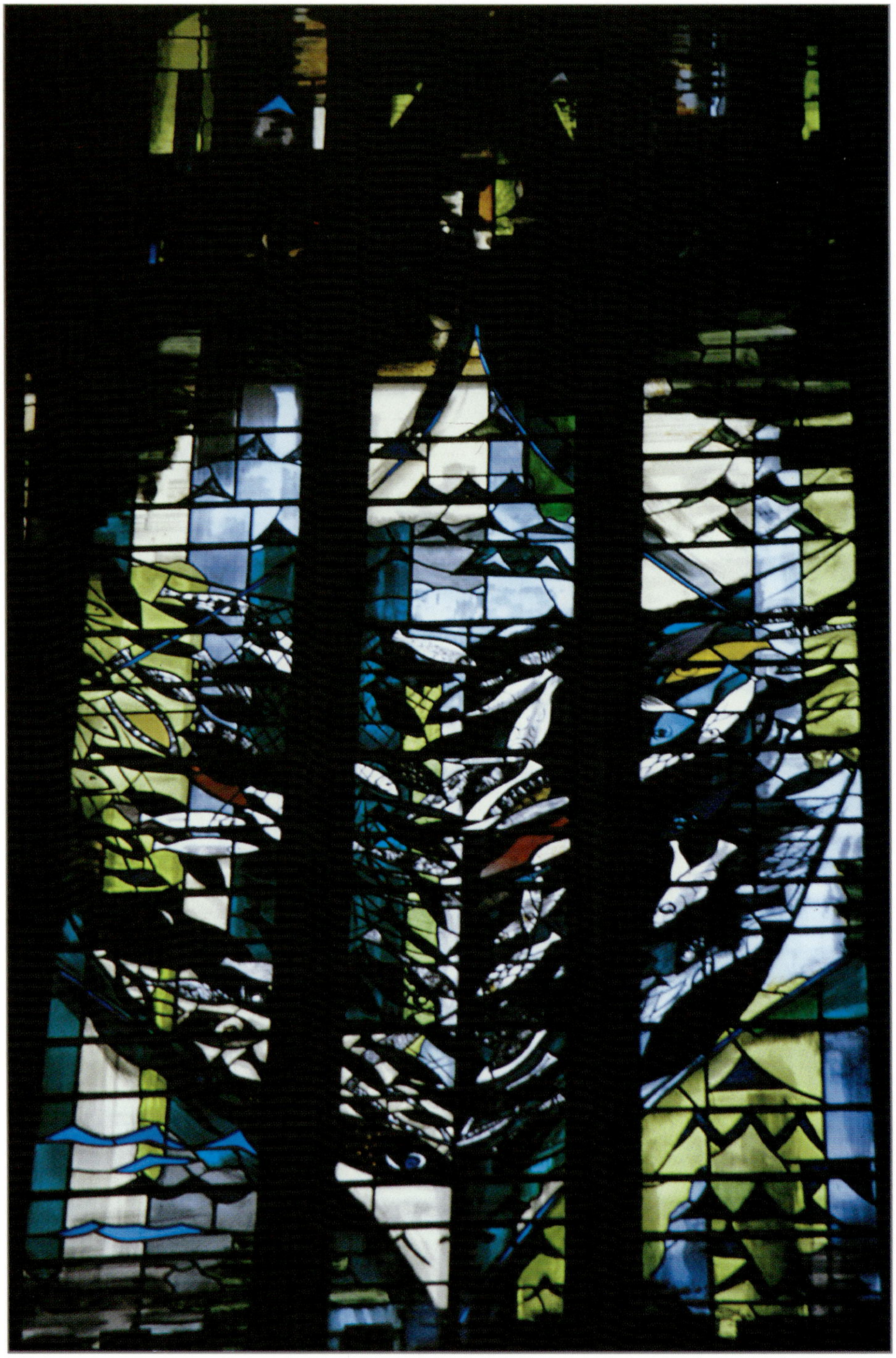

Fig. 44: Eton College Chapel. The Miraculous Draught of Fishes (upper half) (see p. 62)

Below the transom of the window we see the bewildered sheep caught in a tangle of leaves and brushwood (Fig. 40, p. 55); above, it is being brought back by a weary-looking shepherd whose head is like that of a classical statue. Colour is reticent and used only around the edges; sheep and shepherd are in black and white only. Although the windows were appearing later than the schedule ordered – after all, it was one thing for Piper to design the cartoon, and quite another for Reyntiens to complete the transformation into glass – they were meeting with approval and delight. This window won a special mention from the Provost: 'I am glad the sheep looks a complete moron, and quite unlike any of the really hardy mountain sheep of Scotland or Cumberland who always know where they are anywhere.'

Opposite the 'Lost Sheep', on the north side, we find the 'Feeding of the Five Thousand'. The story is in all four gospels; this is a summary of the account in John's Gospel, chapter 6. Jesus had crossed the Sea of Galilee, and because of the miracles he had performed he was followed by a great number of people, in all some five thousand. Jesus turned to Philip and asked him (in order to prove him) where they should buy bread to feed so many. Philip answered that two hundred pennyworth would not be enough. Then Andrew, brother of Simon Peter, said, 'There is a lad here, which hath five barley loaves, and two small fishes; but what are they among so many?' But Jesus miraculously transformed the food so that it was enough to feed everybody, and twelve baskets were filled with the fragments of barley loaves left over.

Piper's interpretation of the story portrays, in the lower half of the window, many hands of different colours outstretched, and in the centre of a mandorla is the simple food, five loaves and two small fishes (Fig. 41, p. 55). Apart from the richly fragmented borders, which some of the hands cross, the background is in rather quiet blue. Again we find the double mandorla shape. In the top half of the window all is static, and there in the centre are the baskets of food left over. Like the 'Stilling of the Waters' this window depicts a powerfully dramatic contrast between turbulent action and ultimate resolution: the motion of the outstretched hands counterbalanced by the many horizontal shapes in the upper half.

The westernmost window on the south side shows the parable of the 'Wheat and the Tares' (Fig. 42, p. 57). This is the account in Matthew 13: 36–40.

> . . . his disciples came unto him, saying, Declare unto us the parable of the tares of the field.
>
> He answered and said unto them, He that soweth the good seed is the Son of man;
>
> The field is the world; the good seed are the children of the kingdom; but the tares are the children of the wicked one;
>
> The enemy that sowed them is the devil; the harvest is the end of the world; and the reapers are the angels.
>
> As therefore the tares are gathered and burned in the fire; so shall it be in the end of this world.

Against an outlined diamond-shape we find in the lower half the spiky forms of the tares, dark in themselves although set against a lighter ground. From them rises up a brightly coloured bird, and also butterflies. (I was able to inspect the cartoon of this part. It is an emerald green bird, set against a square of red (Fig. 43, p. 57). In the cartoon the bird's tail feathers are pale green, but Piper has written across them 'yellow', and yellow they are in the glass.) Butterflies again appear, and more of them, in the upper part of the window, floating around a sheaf of luxuriant golden wheat. There is a wonderful autumnal glow about this, rich warm colours set against the shimmering verticals of the air.

Finally on the north side is the 'Miraculous Draught of Fishes' (Fig. 44, p. 60). The subject of this window is perhaps one of the best known of the miracles. This is the account given in Luke's Gospel, chapter 5, vv. 3–10. Jesus saw two fishing boats anchored in the Lake of Gennesaret, but the fishermen were ashore, washing their nets:

> And he entered into one of the ships, which was Simon's, and prayed him that he would thrust out a little from the land. And he sat down, and taught the people out of the ship.
>
> Now when he had left speaking, he said unto Simon, Launch out into the deep, and let down your nets for a draught.
>
> And Simon answering said unto him, Master, we have toiled all night, and have taken nothing: nevertheless at thy word I will let down the net.
>
> And when they had this done, they inclosed a multitude of fishes: and their net brake.
>
> And they beckoned unto their partners, which were in the other ship, that they should come and help them. And they came, and filled both ships . . .
>
> . . . And Jesus said unto Simon, Fear not; from henceforth thou shalt catch men.

Since the next window after this is of grisaille (there is also heraldic glass in the west), it was suggested to Piper that he should use rather lighter colours than he had first intended for this window. Piper wrote to the Provost: 'I am sure you are right about the tendency to darkness in this cartoon, and we will be certain, in the making of the glass, to remember the transition to the grisaille windows.'

The ground colour is mainly white and lemon yellow. Across this is spread a tracery of forms: in the lower half, the drooping shapes of the empty nets, black and turquoise, and a dogstooth pattern of little wavelets; in the upper part, the profile of a broadbeamed boat, crammed to the gunwales with glittering fish.[8]

The project had been a tremendous undertaking, designing a dramatic yet coherent scheme for the glazing of eight great windows. When they were all completed, in February 1964, the Fellows congratulated Piper on his success, and Piper wrote to the Provost: 'I have enormously enjoyed working on the College Chapel windows. . . . I hope they will give pleasure to many people – and to some of the boys!'

They had constituted, without doubt, one of his greatest achievements.

CHAPTER SIX

ABSTRACTIONS, SACRED AND PROFANE: BRITTANY BEACH, BERNERS STREET AND COVENTRY

'Abstraction is a luxury, a luxury that
has been left to the present day to exploit.'

John Piper

Thus wrote John Piper in his article 'Abstraction on the Beach'.[1] He goes on to describe how, when you come to look at it, an apparently empty beach is not empty at all:

> Louring clouds that belong to romantic painting hanging over a bare beach that might have been made for Courbet. At the edge of the sea, sand. Then, unwashed by the waves at low tide, grey-blue shingle against the warm brown sand: an intense contradiction in colour, in the same tone, on the same plane. Fringing this, dark seaweed, an irregular litter of it, with a jagged edge towards the sea broken here and there by washed-up objects; boxes, tins, waterlogged sand shoes, banana skins, starfish, cuttle fish, dead seagulls, sides of boxes with THIS SIDE UP on them, fragments of sea-chewed linoleum with a washed-out pattern. This line of magnificent wreckage vanishes out of sight in the distance, but it is a continuous line that girdles England, and can be seen reappearing on the skyline in the other direction along this flat beach. Behind this rich constricting belt against the sand dunes there is drier sand, sparser shingle, unwashed even at high tides, with dirty banana skins now and sides of boxes with THIS SIDE UP almost unreadable. That, in whatever direction you look, is a subject worthy of contemporary painting. Pure abstraction is undernourished. It should at least be allowed to feed on a bare beach with tins and broken bottles.

Although Piper primarily had painting in mind when he wrote this, and it was to be nearly twenty years before he was to design for stained glass, the description is evocative of the panels he was to make in the early 1960s on the theme of 'Brittany Beach'. There are three of these, two in the studio at Fawley Bottom, and one at the Victoria & Albert Museum (Fig. 45, overleaf). The colours in these are quiet, almost subdued, and the designs are based on

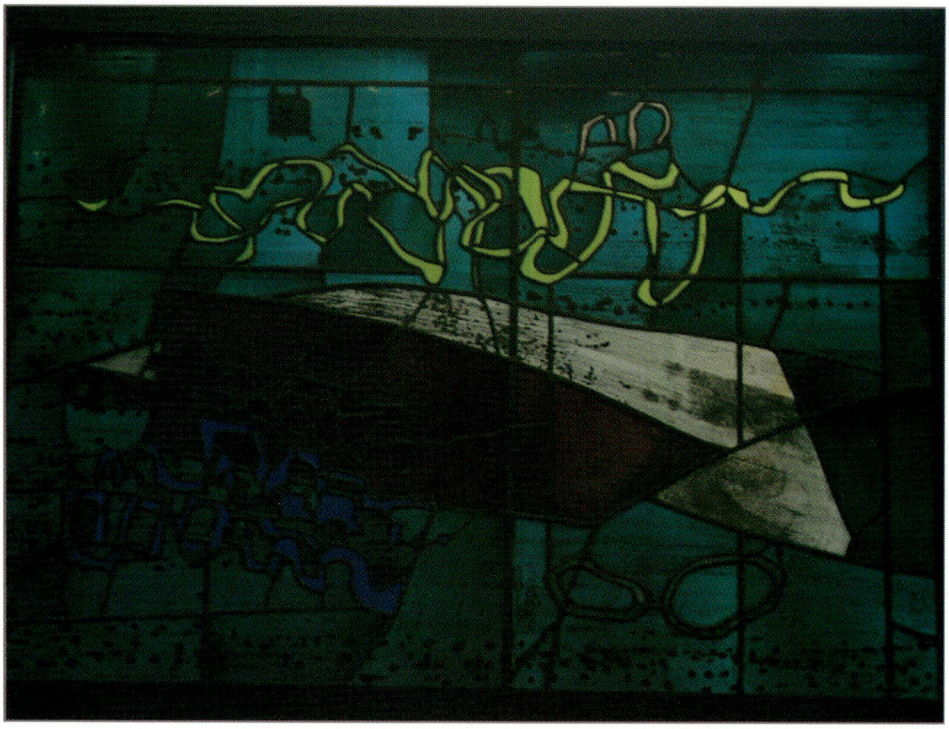

Fig. 45: Brittany Beach scene, 1961. (Victoria & Albert Museum)

landscapes in gouache and collage; he was doing similar landscapes of Welsh scenes at the same time. Although the panels may appear at first sight totally abstract, yet they contain between them almost all the elements that Piper listed, the driftwood, seaweed, pebbles and all sorts of detritus – doubtless the beaches of Brittany were at the time no tidier than the beaches of Britain.

In all three panels Piper's design is interpreted in the medium of glass by Patrick Reyntiens, an exercise demanding considerable artistry, especially here, where texture is all-important.

Reyntiens was also responsible for the realization of Piper's first major commission for secular glass. This came in 1959 from Ivan Sanderson, of Arthur Sanderson & Sons Ltd, in connection with the new showrooms he was having built in Berners Street, in order to display wallpaper and curtain fabrics alongside each other. It seems that in the first place Sandersons had invited Sir Jacob Epstein to make a sculpture for the hall of the new building; but Epstein declined the commission, on the grounds that he was too old. (More likely he was not really interested. He was then involved with the great figure of St Michael for Coventry Cathedral.) The structure of the showrooms was not yet complete, and with the promised cooperation of Piper and Reyntiens, it was re-designed to incorporate a wall of stained glass (Fig. 46). This was to measure 32 feet (9.75 metres) across and 21 feet (6.40 metres) high. A staircase runs diagonally across it, and there are landings so that it can be seen from different levels. It was to be lit artificially; in fact, one of the dangers was that lights put in for other purposes might have diminished its effectiveness. (This can of course be equally

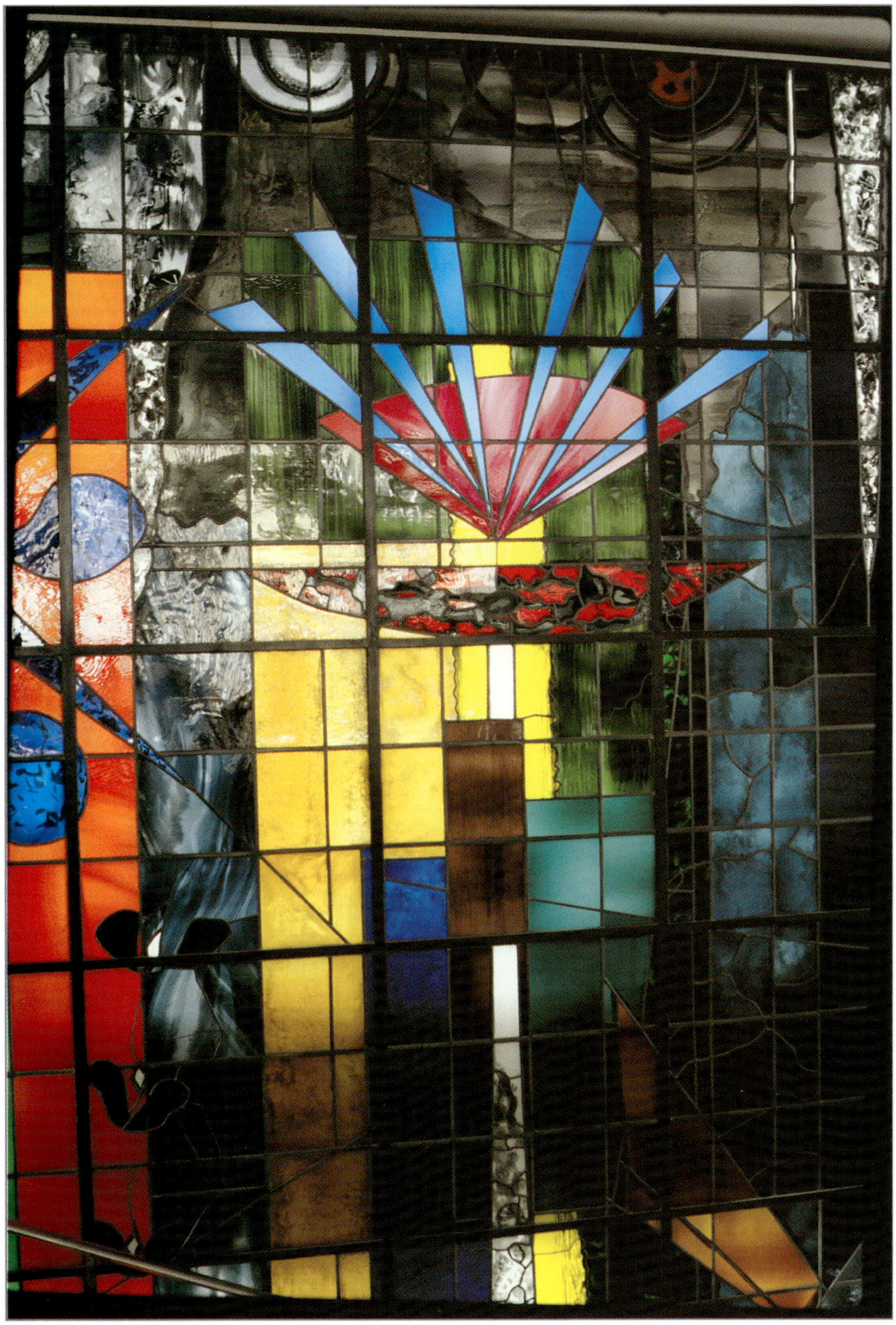

Fig. 46: London, No. 52 Berners Street. Abstract Composition of Biomorphic Forms. Detail from the glass wall

true of stained glass in ecclesiastical settings; the difference is that here it was a known hazard, and it likely that Piper bore it in mind while designing the glass.) Piper's first design was in water-colours with collage of marbled papers, but for the final version stronger contrasts were chosen.

Ivan Sanderson left the choice of subject to Piper. Unlike Eton, there is no precise iconography. The title of the glass, if it may be said to have one, is 'Abstract Composition of Biomorphic Forms', that is to say, forms that have their origins in the natural world. The general feeling is one of upward growth, vertical motifs set against the horizontal shape of the glass wall. Although they are derived from plants, some resembling lilies, some bursting out into the shape of a carnation or a fan, they are rigid and formalized, rather in the Art Deco style. They are set against blocks of colour which are carefully juxtaposed, reminiscent of the abstract paintings and constructions Piper had been making in the 1930s.[2]

In a sense, Piper had a free hand; and yet at the same time, it was necessary to create a wall of glass appropriate to a building whose purpose was the sale of wallpaper and fabrics. Intensity would have been out of place. This is a lighthearted design, a *jeu d'esprit*, just as he was to make three years later (1962), when he devised a fibreglass mural for the North Thames Gas Board. When art serves commerce, the emotions are unlikely to be deeply involved. But within its field, the Berners Street glass is undeniably successful and a joy to the eye.

Designing glass for a new cathedral, as he was invited to do at Coventry, was bound to be a different matter altogether. And yet the two enterprises have this in common: the stained glass is indissolubly part of the architecture. This is both a virtue and a limitation.

During the Second World War Piper worked as an Official War Artist. This meant that he was sometimes asked to paint such unlikely and perhaps rather mundane subjects as air-raid precaution control rooms (May 1940). Far more moving are Piper's paintings of the blitzed ruins of churches. The very first of these he did in Coventry in November 1940, immediately after the devastation of the old Cathedral. It was based on sketches he made of the smoking ruins the morning after the raid.[3] Both this picture, and even more so the other oil painting he did of Coventry Cathedral (Fig. 47; now in the City Art Gallery, Manchester) are strangely evocative of stained glass. Masses of rich, luminous colour are emphasized by the black calligraphy of the burnt-out tracery, in the same way as the colours of glass are emphasized by the pattern of lead-lines.

The destruction of the medieval Coventry Cathedral took place during the night of 14 November 1940. The events are vividly described by R.T. Howard,[4] who was Provost at the time, and was on duty at the Cathedral that night. He and his three colleagues were able to deal with the first incendiary bombs, smothering them with sand; but then more fell, especially on the roof of the Girdlers' or Children's Chapel. Since they could not deal with the blaze, the Provost and his colleagues could only hope for the arrival of the fire brigade, and meanwhile set to work rescuing what treasures they could. But the whole city was on fire; all the engines had already been called out and some were trapped between one crater and the next. Eventually, the fire brigade from Solihull arrived; but they were powerless to fight the blaze as the water-main was shattered. Virtually the whole cathedral was alight, and there was nothing that Howard and his colleagues could do but watch its rapid and dreadful

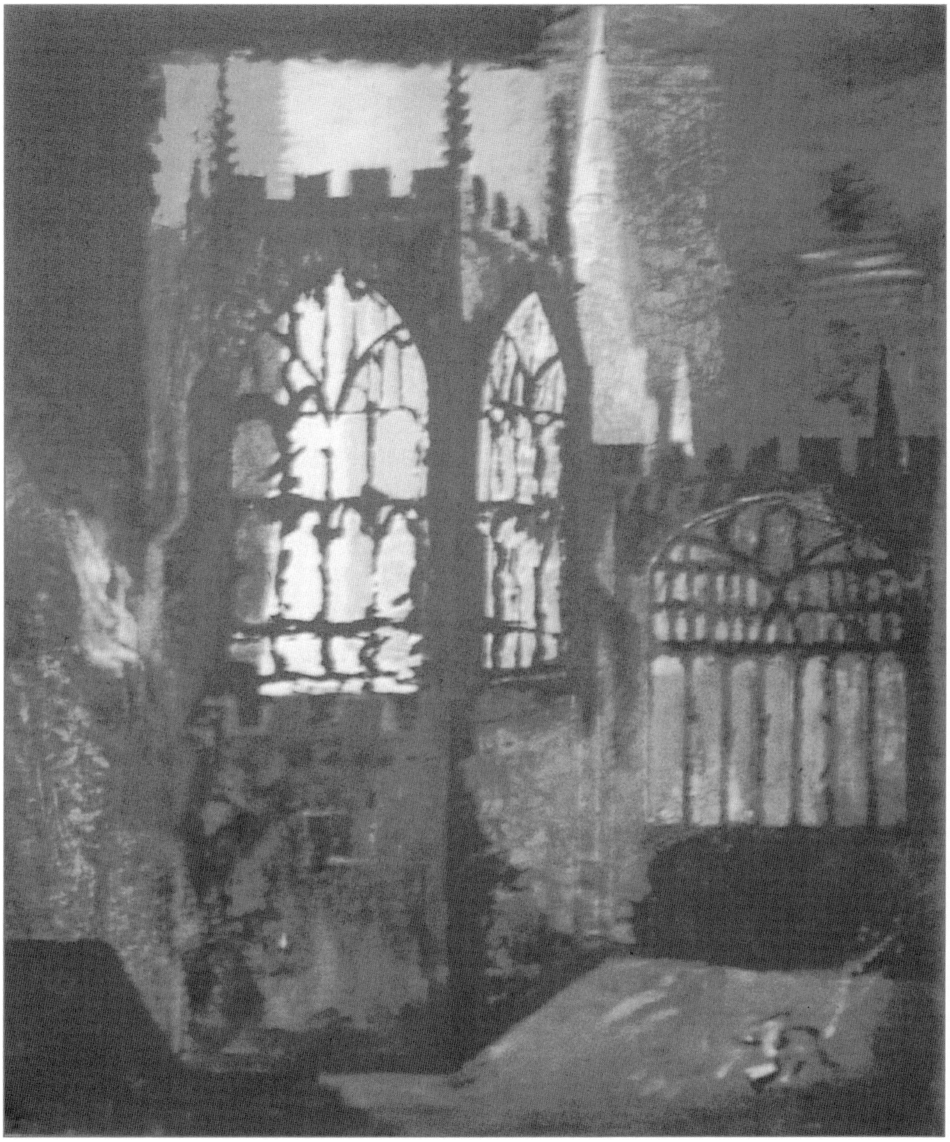

Fig. 47: Coventry Cathedral, from a painting by Piper. (© Manchester City Art Galleries)

destruction. By morning the roofs, pillars, arcades, the eighteenth-century organ, and all the carved medieval woodwork had been destroyed. Nothing remained above ground but the south porch, the tower and spire, and the circling walls; in the centre, an expanse of smoking debris.

The Provost was as moved as if he had been witnessing the Crucifixion, and two months later he ordered the stone-mason Jock Forbes to build an altar of rubble. This, with a cross of charred timber over it, was set up on the site of the original high altar. A cross was made from nails picked up among the ashes. These became symbols of the continuing faith, which was to express itself in the building of a new cathedral.

A Rebuilding Commission was set up, consisting of twelve members of the Cathedral Council. Initially it was proposed that the new building should be on the same site, retaining the outer walls, and therefore Gothic in style. Sir Giles Gilbert Scott, architect of the Anglican Cathedral of Liverpool, was invited to submit designs. However, these did not find favour with the Fine Art Commission, and in 1947 he resigned. A new commission, later to be known as the Reconstruction Committee, was then formed, consisting of eminent men in public life,[5] and an architectural competition organized. It was realized that the outer curtain walls had so deteriorated that they could no longer be incorporated into the new building; however, the Committee still clung to the notion of adhering to the Gothic style, until it was pointed out that if this were made a condition, many eminent architects would be deterred from entering the competition.

It was stipulated that the Cathedral should seat comfortably 1,200 people, and if filled to capacity 1,750; the altar should be placed at the liturgical east end, and there should be no screen between chancel and nave. A place should be found within the precincts for the Charred Cross, the Cross of Nails, and the Altar of Rubble. Together with other conditions, it was laid down that entries should be submitted anonymously, and no perspective drawings should be enclosed with them. While there was no absolute rule about building materials, it was pointed out that there were still available adequate supplies of a pink-grey sandstone, which would make the new building blend in with the nearby Holy Trinity Church and the fourteenth-/fifteenth-century St Mary's Hall. Entries had to be received by 2 July 1951. Drawings were submitted by 219 different architects, and were exhibited in King Henry VIII School, Coventry, later that month.

Among the entries the assessors found one which they deemed to be of 'outstanding excellence'. This was the design of the Scottish architect, Mr (later Sir) Basil Spence. Since the stained glass, and indeed all other art work commissioned for it, had to at least blend in with, and to some extent be subordinated to, his architectural conception, it is relevant to quote from his own description:

> THE IDEA. As the Cathedral stands now, it is an eloquent memorial to the courage of the people of Coventry. It is felt that the ruin should be preserved as a garden of rest . . . and the new Cathedral should grow from the old and be incomplete without it. . . .
>
> The tower and spire of the old Cathedral were retained to fulfil the same function in the new one. The ruins, with the Sanctuary, Altar of Rubble, Charred Cross, and Cross of Nails, were preserved as a memorial 'garden of rest' and as a forecourt and approach to the new Cathedral.
>
> The new Cathedral was to be built out from the old Cathedral on lower ground to the north, and constructed in pink-grey sandstone throughout.
>
> The West wall would contain a very large glass screen . . . engraved with the figures of saints and angels. . . .
>
> Within the Cathedral the altar would be visible from practically every part of the building.

> On the east wall, behind the altar, there would be a great tapestry. . . .
>
> The font would be inside the door on the right, with a conical canopy reaching nearly to the roof, lit by a great baptistry window of 195 lights. . . .
>
> The windows of the nave would be in five pairs, set at an angle, rising from ground to roof level, throwing the light in waves up the Cathedral towards the altar. They would be filled with stained glass, in significant colours and figures, symbolizing the pathway of human life from childhood through adolescence to middle age and old age, and on to the After Life.

Sir Basil Spence summed up his ideas: 'The author of this design does not see the building as a planning problem, but as an opportunity to create a Shrine to the Glory of God.'

Dominating the whole east end is the great tapestry of Christ in Glory, designed by Graham Sutherland, and made by Pinton Frères of Aubusson in France. It is only from this end of the Cathedral that one can appreciate the tall stained-glass nave windows, set as they are in the angled bastions. They were commissioned by Sir Basil Spence from the Royal College of Art, and they were made in 1952–6. The stained glass department was under the professorship of Lawrence Lee, and he and his then students Geoffrey Clarke and Keith New (now well-known names in the field) designed and made them at the College. They were exhibited at the Victoria & Albert Museum before being installed in the Cathedral.

The windows are broadly abstract, although some figurative work can be found in them. They symbolize the different ages of human life – childhood, manhood, middle age, old age and the after-life – on the north side the human aspect of these themes, and on the south side the divine. Starting from the west, the first pair of windows (childhood) is predominantly green and was made by Keith New; the second pair (manhood) mainly red, by Lawrence Lee; the third pair (middle age) multi-coloured, by Keith New and Geoffrey Clarke; the fourth (old age) mainly purple, by Geoffrey Clarke; and the easternmost windows (after-life) in gold and pale colours, by Geoffrey Clarke and Lawrence Lee. The symbolism is a little hard to grasp, because the architecture makes it impossible to experience them in this order; they are totally obscured when the building is viewed from the west. Yet they are an impressive sequence seen from the east: a procession of colour almost Gothic in its splendour.

The west end is entirely taken up by an engraved glass screen, the work of John Hutton, and filled with saints, angels and Old Testament figures. It forms a link between the old and new cathedrals, and brings in a great deal of light – Piper had to bear this in mind when designing the window next to it.

This was one of the two major commissions that were to follow, both initiated in 1955: the sculpture of the winged St Michael overcoming the Devil, by Sir Jacob Epstein, for the exterior of the south wall, and adjoining this the great Baptistry Window (Fig. 49, p. 72).

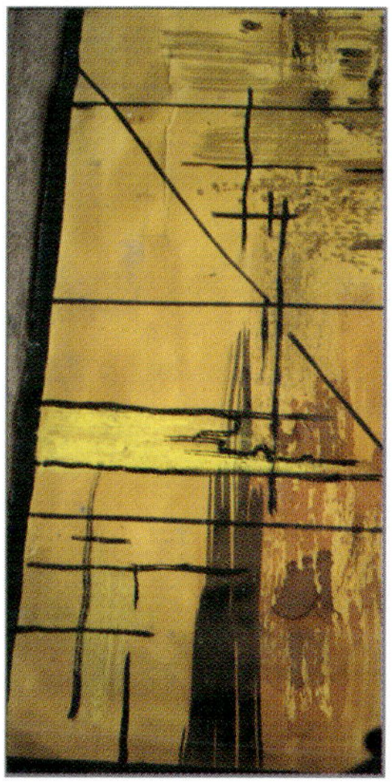

Fig. 48: Cartoon for one panel of Coventry Cathdedral Baptistry Window (see p. 71)

The choice of an artist capable of designing this window was by no means easy. It is colossal, 85 feet (21.9 metres) in height, 56 feet (about 18 metres) in width; it is slightly bowed in shape, and the 195 (or, as some say, 250) glass lights are recessed behind stone mullions which jut out at right angles into the interior of the church. Sir Basil Spence was hard-pressed to find any British artist capable of taking up such a challenge; that is, until he saw the Oundle windows, and visited Piper's studio.

A visit to Fawley Bottom Farmhouse is almost always inspiring. The Provost also went, and after he had seen Piper's work there, he wrote to the artist (21 October 1955),[6] 'It gave me a very strong and enjoyable sense of confidence in what you may be able to do for our Cathedral'. Four days later, Sir Basil asked Piper to supply a rough estimate for the cost of the work.

Meanwhile, Piper was giving much thought as to how the window should be treated in terms of design. He jotted down his first idea:

ARK (salvation) mainly green	SINAI (discipline) red
BAPTISM (gift of the Spirit of Jesus) yellow	PENTECOST (gift of the Spirit of the Church) blue

He discussed with Reyntiens, who was to be responsible for making it, the costing of the window, and on 31 October 1955 he wrote giving a rough estimate on the basis of £15 per square foot; for the 1,712 square feet concerned this worked out at a total of £25,680, excluding fitting.

At this stage there was a slight lull as far as the Coventry Commission was concerned; John Piper had in any case other demands on his time. Myfanwy wrote on 15 January 1956 to explain that he was up in London every day working on settings for *The Magic Flute* at Convent Garden (it opened on the nineteenth of that month), and was getting back too late and too tired to be letter-writing. However, he travelled again to Coventry; he was offered a cheque to cover his expenses for this, but returned it as a donation to the Reconstruction Fund (1 March 1956). On the twenty-sixth of that month he wrote to Sir Basil, raising the estimate for the Baptistry Window to £27,000. This worked out at just under £16 per square foot, which was more expensive than the Royal College of Art windows (these cost only £10 10*s* per square foot); but, as Piper explained, the higher rate was necessary 'if I am to give it constant attention for four years'. He explained that he and Reyntiens worked separately, 'and therefore cannot hope to compete with a low designer-maker's price'. He said he hoped to have the window finished by 1961, and added that with their increased experience 'I am sure we could make a fine thing of it'. The Secretary of the Reconstruction Committee then wrote to Piper confirming the commission and accepting the price.

Meanwhile, Piper was giving serious thought about the way in which the window should be treated. He wrote to the Provost on 14 May:

> I wonder how much detail of a *subject* we shall read (as it were) across all that stonework?. . . I think that it may be that we shall have to be more abstract than we first imagined – a pattern of colour rather than one of line or form as a basis of the whole design.

On the same day he wrote to the Secretary of the Reconstruction Committee, saying how pleased he was to have the 'go-ahead', and saying that Reyntiens ought to be present at any detailed discussion of the contract. The latter was drafted on 20 September. Piper was to get £4,750 in instalments, mainly of £120 a month.[7] He was to make his basic design or sketch by 30 November 1957. He was to supervise, jointly with the architect, the work of Patrick Reyntiens in the making of the window. Reyntiens, who had a separate contract, was to 'work under the general supervision of Mr Piper and the Architect'.

Piper's sketch was approved, various problems about the contract were sorted out, Reyntiens obtained funds of approximately £2,000 for the purchase of glass to be imported from France and Germany, and the work went forward.

This year too the barn at Fawley Bottom had been converted into a studio large enough to take full-size cartoons for most windows, the cartoons being spread out on the floor (Fig. 48, p. 69). But the Coventry window was another matter. The sketch was a pencil, chalk, water-colour and gouache drawing, over which was superimposed a black card template with cut-outs (made by Piper's son, Edward), to suggest what the glass would look like when seen in its architectural context. In this design the bottom panels are shown as red, whereas in the finished window they are multi-coloured, mainly pale blue-green.

Clearly it was impossible to make, and house, a full-scale cartoon for the whole window, so Reyntiens suggested that a scale model should be made in glass inside a wooden frame.[8] This measures 12 feet by 7 feet 8 inches (336 × 229 cm) and was supported vertically. In making his cartoons, one for each of the many panels, Piper could refer constantly to this, as well as to the sketch, to ensure the colour gradations were exactly as he wanted. He would make about ten cartoons of similar colour at a time, and then send them to Reyntiens to be interpreted in glass. The panels vary in length, being longer at the very top, and also at the bottom, than in the centre. Reyntiens relates that in making the window, 'we preferred to start at the top and work down, since, because it was so gigantic a task, we wanted to make all our starting mistakes at the top where they would be far off.'

What mistakes? one may ask. Gazing at this magnificent window (Fig. 49, overleaf), mistakes are the last thing on one's mind. Piper kept the colours very rich because of the proximity of Hutton's transparent screen; the Baptistry Window had to make a positive statement. In the end he dismissed all thoughts of figurative glass or complex symbolism. The mullions, and the chequer pattern of the masonry made it necessary to keep the concept simple. Above the font,

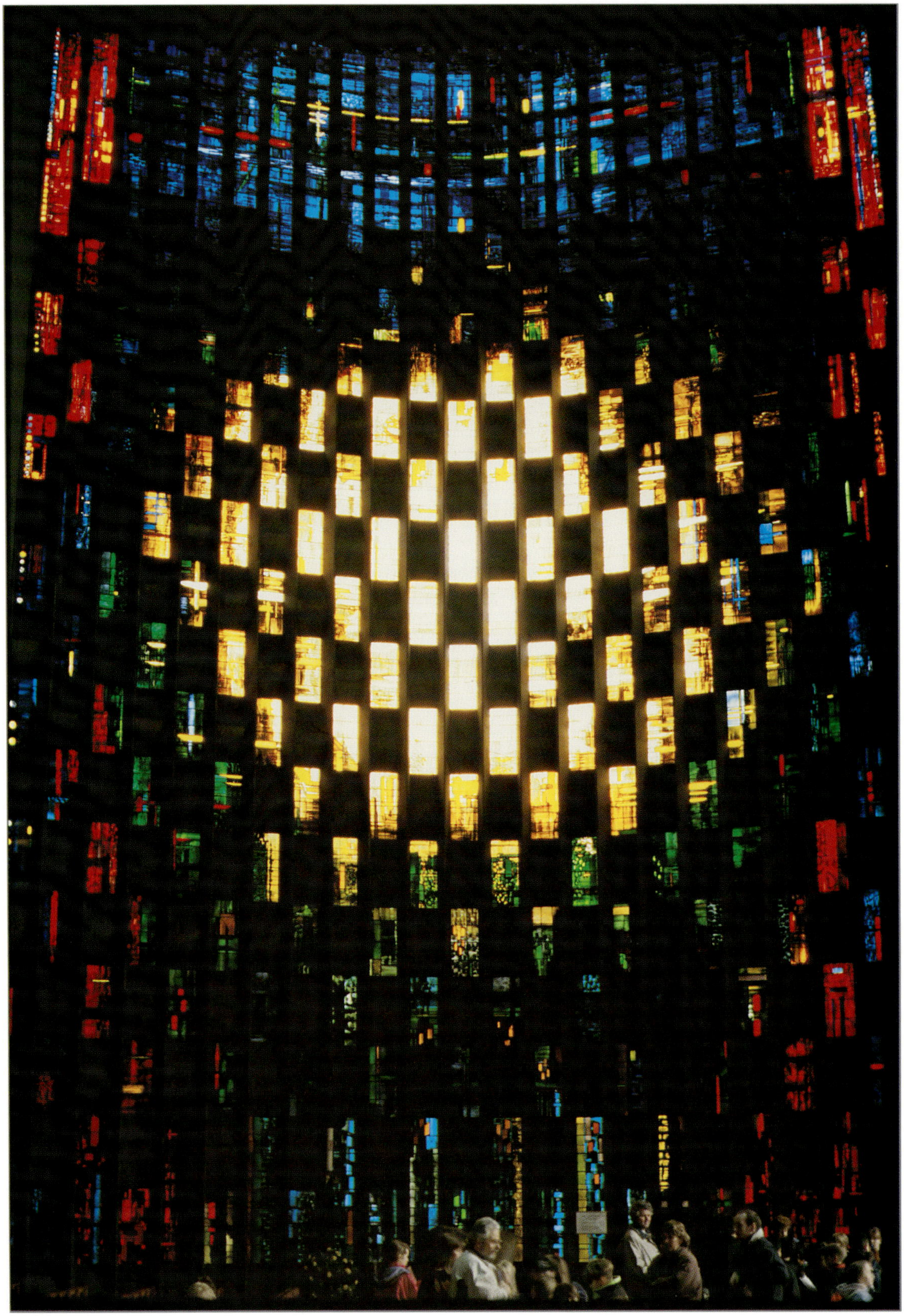

which is a boulder from the hillside at Bethlehem, the window has just one theme to express – the Light of the Holy Spirit. All is subordinated to that; and yet with what artistry it is done. Along the outside edges, circles of different colours shine from a dark ground (he used a similar device at Eton); this makes a border as in medieval glass, and ensures that the colours within lose none of their intensity. The head of the window is a multiplicity of different blues; Reyntiens relates that the strongly coloured pieces were plated on to thinner blue-green glass, so that while there is diversity, there is also unity. On either side, next to the border, the panels that run down the full length of the window are predominantly red; they curve round and broaden out at the base, until in the centre we find multi-coloured sections with a high proportion of blue. The curve of the red section merges above into panels predominantly green, while all this serves to frame a sunburst of gold and yellow, lightening almost to white in the very centre. These are the main areas of colour, yet one spills over into another: in the section mainly blue we find flashes of yellow, red and green; the red panels are often streaked with blue; there are flecks of orange and green in glass which is mainly turquoise. All this helps to unify the window and to make it pulsate with life. And just as on the beach Piper could perceive a wealth of detailed forms so that it was no longer wholly an abstraction, so it is here. Against the green, and green to yellow panels, there is a suggestion of leaf-forms; and in some of the yellow-white panels of the very centre we can half-imagine landscapes.

The window was completed in 1962. It had been a stupendous undertaking; but how right Piper had been in his confident prediction, 'I am sure we could make a fine thing of it'.

Opposite: Fig. 49: Coventry Cathedral. Baptistry Window. (Reproduced with permission from The Bursar, Coventry Cathedral)

CHAPTER SEVEN

SYMBOLS, SACRED AND PROFANE

MORE WORK OF THE EARLY 1960S, INCLUDING WELLINGBOROUGH AND NUFFIELD COLLEGE, OXFORD; INTRODUCTION OF THE GREEN MAN (WINCHESTER)

'After an abstract period – what a release one feels!'

John Piper[1]

As far as stained glass is concerned, it is difficult to speak of any one period of Piper's work as being wholly abstract; it is rather that sometimes one style was appropriate, sometimes another. At the same time, the language of symbols was to him a natural means of expression.

Together with Myfanwy, John Piper had joined the Church of England shortly after the outbreak of the Second World War; it was a mature decision, consequently a significant one. Peter Pears, who, like Benjamin Britten, knew him well, wrote, 'Nature and religion are the most profound ingredients in John Piper's art'.[2]

In the 1960s Piper designed three windows for the parish church of All Hallows, Wellingborough. The first was the Helena Wells Chapman Memorial Window of 1961 (gift of Millicent and Constance Chapman in memory of their sister). In common with all the windows until late in Piper's career, it was made by Patrick Reyntiens. As at Eton, Piper had to design glass to stand alongside that of Evie Hone. Admittedly there is not quite the same proximity, but something of the same intensity of colour was required.

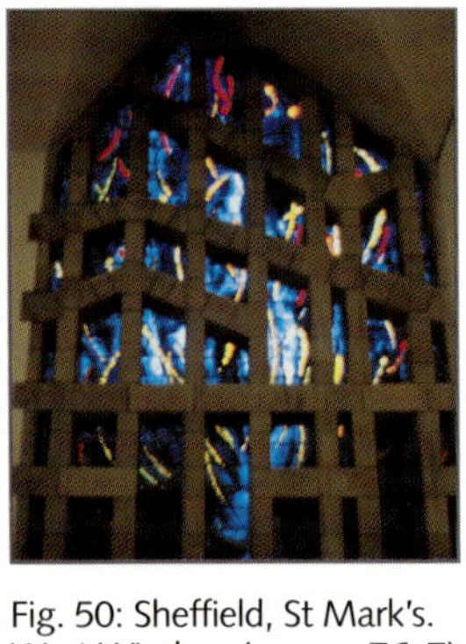

Fig. 50: Sheffield, St Mark's. West Window (see pp. 76–7)

Hone's window dates from 1955. It glows quietly and is close-packed with symbolism. In the centre light, under the Star of David, is the Lamb of God, below that are the five loaves and two fishes (reference to the miraculous feeding of the five thousand), below that the Chalice. In the left-hand light we find the Ark and Rainbow, the Tablets of the Law and the Seven-branched Candlestick; then in the right-hand light, the Dove of the Holy Spirit, the Tongues of Fire (Pentecost), and the Keys and Ship of Peter (relating to the founding of the Church, and the saying that the disciples would become fishers of men). This window is on the south side of the west wall; the Helena Wells Chapman window in the same wall to the north.

Less static than the Hone window, Piper's work is equally rich in colour, but flashes rather than glows. It symbolizes the four gospels and is sometimes known

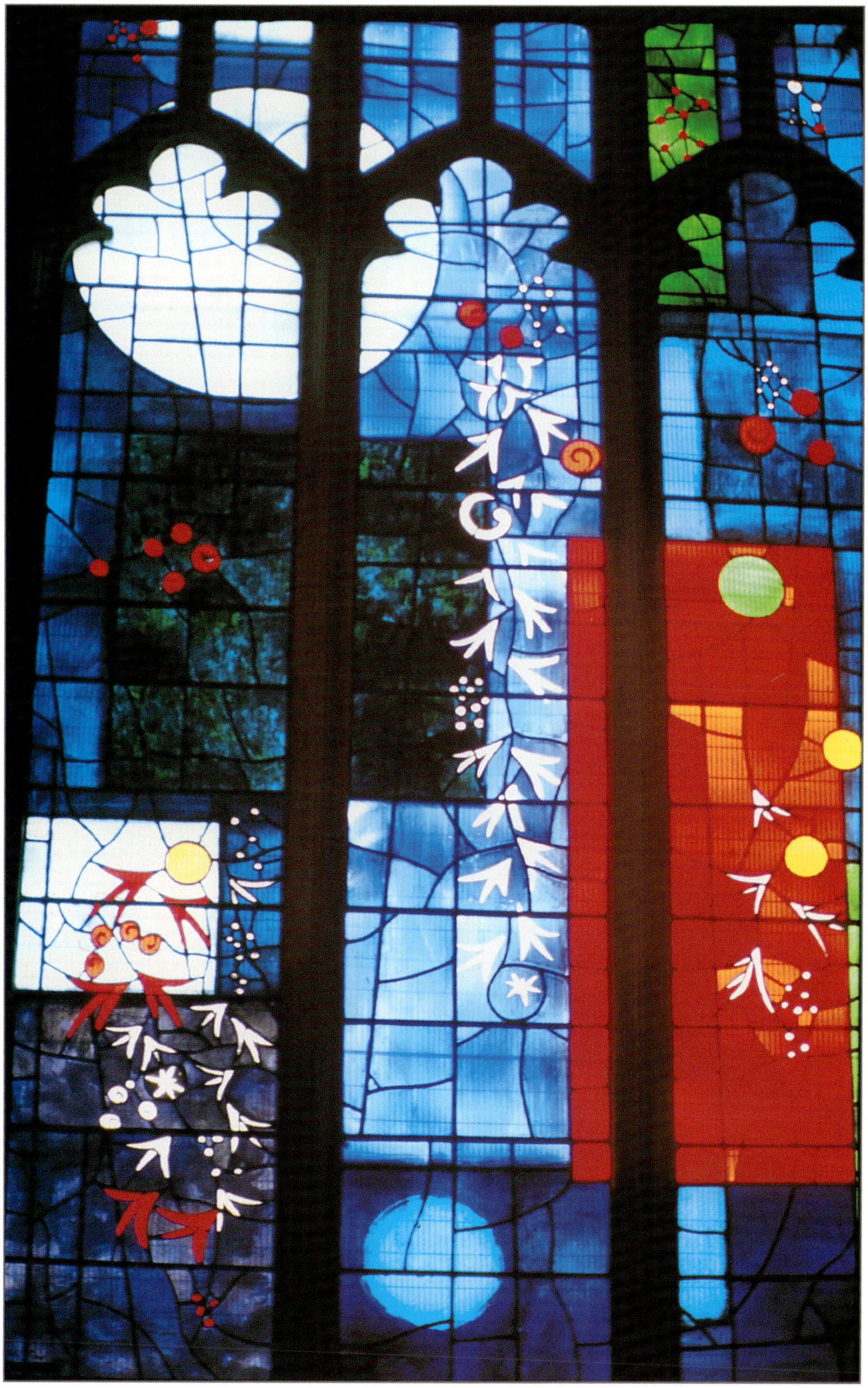

Fig. 51: Wellingborough, All Hallows. The Constance Elizabeth Chapman Memorial Window (see p. 76)

as the 'Beasts of the Evangelists'. Appropriately, it is a window of four main lights. On the extreme left, the St Matthew panel; the evangelist is symbolized by an angel, and the subject concerns Christ as the second Moses bringing new law into human life. To the right of this, the St Mark panel; the saint is symbolized by his lion ('Judah' is written below – the Lion of Judah), and for the rest the theme is Christ as the True Vine – vine leaves are shown in the top tracery – symbolizing strength with sweetness. To the right of the central mullion the theme of the glass is St Luke. He is symbolized by a bull, denoting the power of the Christian message; below is, we are told, the almond tree, or it may be the topmost branch of the Tree of Jesse which illustrates the human lineage of Christ. Finally, the extreme right-hand light shows at the top a rather contemplative Eagle of St John;[3] and below that, Elijah's Chariot of Fire – wheels, flames (which are repeated in the tracery), and his mantle which fell upon Elisha, who was to continue the teaching initiated by Elijah.

While modern in design, the window illustrates the very old concept of typology; that the events and ideas of the Old Testament prefigure those of the new. This was a theme often to be found in medieval glass, and in fact goes right back to the Saxons and Benedict Biscop. It may be thought that the symbolism is a little obscure for people today. Three or four years later, Piper was designing the tapestry to go behind the High Altar in Chichester Cathedral. Here he used symbols with great courage, denoting the Trinity and the Four Evangelists; symbolic too was his use of colour, giving the tapestry rather greater impact than the 'Beasts of the Evangelists' window.

Also at the west end of the church is a Piper/Reyntiens rose window of bold simplicity. It dates from 1964, and was paid for by the Arts Council of Great Britain and the Contemporary Art Society. Against a ground of varying shades of blue there is a star-like form, with a rose in the centre and radiating leaf-like forms. So while one's first impression may be that it is abstract, it is understood to symbolize Our Lady of the Mystic Rose.

The third, and latest, Piper/Reyntiens window at Wellingborough is in the South or Lady Chapel. Near it is Jean Barillet's richly figurative window of St Crispin/Crispinian (1962). Contrasting with this rather busy composition, Piper designed a window of sublime tranquility. It is in memory of Constance Elizabeth Chapman and dates from 1969 (Fig. 51, p. 75). Almost but not quite abstract, it has been called the 'All Things Bright and Beautiful' window or, in Piper's own words, 'It is what you make it to be'. The predominant colour is blue, though there are panels of red and olive green. Set against the tracery on the left-hand side is a large pale disc which suggests the moon, and scattered across all three main lights are cascades of flowers, white and occasionally red. It is a most cheerful, ingenuous and uplifting window, using motifs which Piper also employed at Bledlow Ridge (Fig. 74, p. 102), and later at Wolverhampton (Fig. 90, p. 115).

The glass he designed for St Mark's, Sheffield, on the other hand, is far more akin to his great window at Coventry Cathedral; much the same factors influenced it. The original St Mark's, a Victorian church, was destroyed by incendiary bombs during the night of 12 December 1940. The tower and spire were preserved, and the new church, by G.G. Pace, was constructed alongside. It dates from the 1950s, and is made of reinforced concrete. From the main entrance on the site of the north porch of the original church, a long passage runs down the full length of the building. But the main problem in designing stained glass for this church was the emphatic and angular tracery.

The East Window is by Harry Stammers, and its main theme is '*Te Deum Laudamus*' – We Praise Thee, O God. Although Stammers put in a great deal of figurative detail, it does tend to get lost among the masonry – a problem that Piper was careful to avoid when designing his Baptistry Window at Coventry. Here in Sheffield too, where he was commissioned to design the West Window of the Narthex (Fig. 50, p. 74; it dates from 1963–4), he wisely decided to keep it simple. He wrote in the church guide:

> The flames, yellow on blue, with their sparks and tongues of red and orange, provide an abstract pattern which I hope will unite and contrast happily with the design of Mr Pace's geometrical tracery . . . We worked on eight windows for Eton College Chapel . . . and the big task of the Baptistry Window at Coventry Cathedral. This took about four years; and it has clearly influenced my design at St Mark's in its simplicity and directness of approach. Patrick Reyntiens in his interpretation has also used a technique which was also much influenced by his other masterly interpretations of my cartoons. I hope the rich colour may give pleasure and inspiration. We have both greatly enjoyed working on it.

It was much at this time that Piper designed glass for three different churches in Wales: Llandaff Cathedral in 1961–2, St Woolo's Cathedral, Newport (Fig. 34, p. 47), in 1964, and finally St Mary's, Swansea (Fig. 52, overleaf), in 1965–6. Of the three, only the window at Llandaff has figurative glass. It represents the Supper at Emmaus, and is set high in the chancel arch. It must be confessed that from floor level it is difficult to appreciate the subject of the window – one longs for scaffolding so that one might appreciate it properly. One is left with the impression of brilliant colour, and a general sense that one is missing something.

For the ancient and fascinating Cathedral Church of St Woolo in Newport, Piper decided to keep his concept very simple. Here he designed for the modern Sanctuary not only a round window (Fig. 34, p. 47) but also the reredos in which it is set. The latter looks like marble, but is in fact marbling painted on canvas; it rises in a tall arch which echoes the Norman architecture at the west end of the church. The window is set at the head of the reredos; the tracery in it forms the shape of a double cross. Piper restricted the colours to gold and yellow, and Reyntiens interpreted them in silver stain.[4] This technique made possible a very light reticulation of leadwork, which enhances the airiness of the window.

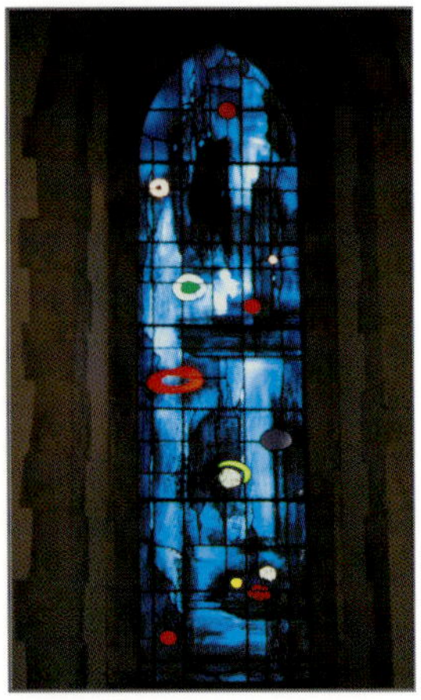

Fig. 52: Swansea, St Mary's. Left-hand East Window, Lady Chapel

The church of St Mary, Swansea, is a veritable treasure-house of modern glass. Most of the Chancel windows are by J. Powell of Whitefriars, and are of a similar date to the Piper/Reyntiens glass of 1965–6. Since that time, there have been added two windows by Catrin Jones (1982, to celebrate, wryly it now seems, the marriage of the Prince and Princess of Wales), two delicately delineated windows by Kuni Kajiwara, and an almost monochrome Falklands War window by Rodney Bender. The glass designed by Piper is found in the Lady Chapel (Fig. 52). There are two abstract windows, one on each side of the altar. The reredos is also by him, marbled painting on a blue ground within a recessed Gothic-arched niche. The stained glass is abstract in style. Both windows have a streaky blue as their ground, varying in hue from deep navy, through prussian, to almost white. Against this, dots and rings of brilliant colour seem to hang in space, the red in particular appearing as if on a different plane, with the blue receding behind.

It occasionally happened that Piper was involved in the design of a whole interior, as well as the stained glass that it housed. So it was in the case of the Chapel at Nuffield College, Oxford, which was executed in 1965–6.[5] It is in an upper room in the tower, and a complete departure from traditional Oxford college chapels with their inverted T-shape of antechapel and choir. The creation of the Chapel was at the instigation of Margery Petham (1895–1982), a pioneer in African Studies and for forty-three years a Fellow of the College. The entrance is through an ordinary door. The interior is predominantly white, with narrow black lines emphasizing the horizontals; pews and altar were designed by John Piper. Fifteen years earlier (1950) he had brought out his delightful King Penguin book on Romney Marsh; this includes a water-colour illustration of the interior of Fairfield Church, with its white box-pews edged in black in exactly the same way. This then, rather than stone mullions, is the setting for the stained glass,

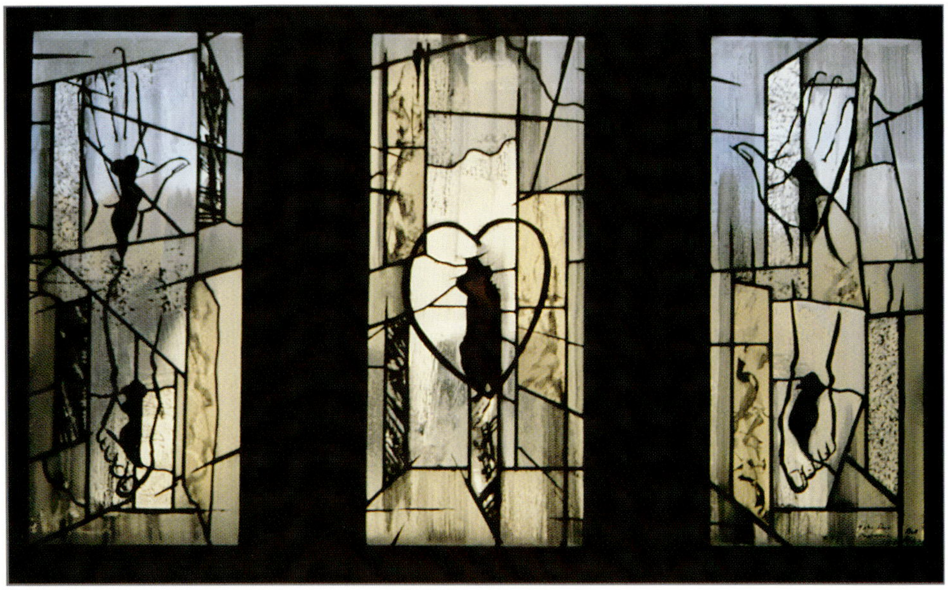

Fig. 53: Oxford, Nuffield College. The Five Wounds of Christ

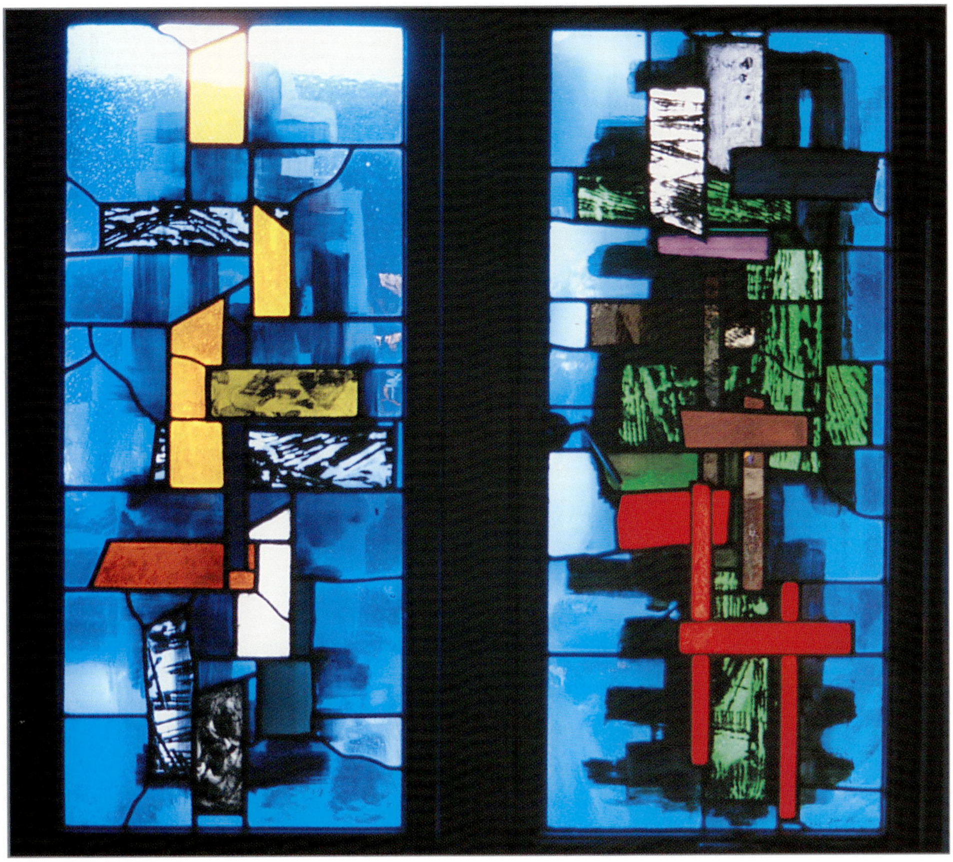

Fig. 54: Oxford, Nuffield College. South window

which is contained in ordinary rectilinear casement windows, some of which may be opened.

The principal window is in the (liturgical) west, and symbolizes the Five Wounds of Christ (Fig. 53). Here the colour in all three lights is kept very quiet, subtle rather than brilliant, restricted to beige and a cold pale blue. On the side panels are seen the wounds to the hands and feet, in the centre to the heart. The wounds themselves are shown in black, and agony is suggested by the angularity of the lead-lines. The rest of the windows are, or appear to be, abstract, and are reminiscent of the paintings and constructions Piper was doing in that style in the 1930s. They vary very much in tone and colour. Of the side windows on either side of the altar, one is in the same cold, pale tones as the three west lights, the other is in deeper, warmer, earthy colours. The side windows towards the west are far more colourful, the most brilliant being on the south side – red, orange and streaky green shapes set against blue (Fig. 54). Opposite we find shapes no less brightly coloured in themselves, but set against a smudgy brown, resembling stonework. The placing of horizontals against verticals in these windows may perhaps not accidentally suggest crosses.

The stained glass inside this little chapel needs to be seen as part of the whole interior. Piper may well have felt limited by the prosaic shape and small size of the windows, especially as at the side they are so deep-set as to be invisible in an oblique view. Perhaps his scope for self-expression was restricted. But since he was also responsible for the design of most of the rest of the interior, the glass should not be considered in isolation, and judged as a whole, the Chapel has both consistency and atmosphere. The stained glass serves as a handmaiden in this tranquil, contemplative place.

Such self-abnegation is not to be pursued indefinitely. It is far more in the nature of stained glass to be focal. Sometimes Piper found in a commission for secular glass a freedom of choice not always to be realized in ecclesiastical settings. If Piper may be said ever to have doodled (and even Leonardo da Vinci doodled), then he doodled Green Men. Or to put it another way, the Green Man was his *leitmotif*.

In *Green Man*,[6] his searching study of the subject, William Anderson recognizes three main types: a mask of leaves in the shape of a man's head; a male head disgorging leaves and branches from his mouth, also sometimes from his eyes and ears; and a head, which may be male or female, appearing as the fruit or flower of vegetation (there is a link here with lily crucifixes). The Green Man may be regarded as a life-force, a symbol of renewal and rebirth; it epitomizes man's oneness with nature. And, especially in the form of a face disgorging vegetation, it may be said to denote inspiration.

The Green Man is an extremely ancient concept, linked with the Greek god Dionysos, the Roman god Vertumnus and the Celtic Cerunnus; it may be that one of the prototypes is the famous roundel, usually known as Medusa, on the pediment of the Temple of Sulis Minerva at Bath.[7] Although pre-Christian in origin, the Green Man is not necessarily pagan, and mostly occurs carved in stone or wood inside or outside medieval churches. The earliest known Christian example of him disgorging vegetation occurs on the tomb of St Arbre (appropriately) at St Hilaire-le-Grand, Poitiers (AD 400). Another early one (*c.* 1000) is on a capital in the crypt at Dijon; and there is a fine group of three on the south portal of Chartres Cathedral, one disgorging vine-leaves, one acanthus and the other oak. In the *Sketchbook* of Villard de Honnecourt (early thirteenth-century), one of the most creative draughtsman of the Middle Ages, are to be found different examples of Green Men, both the disgorging or moustached variety, and the leaf-mask.

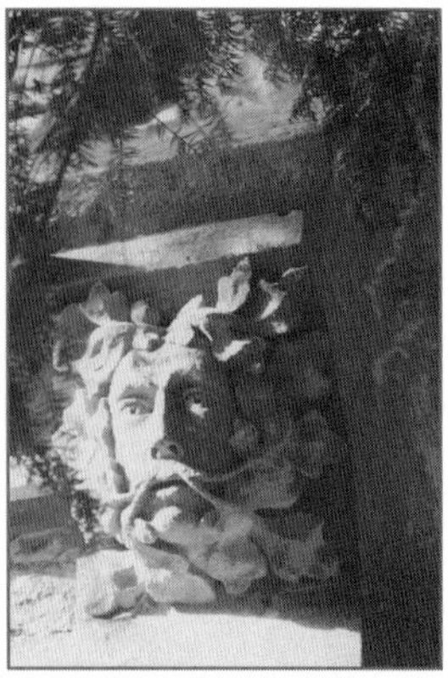

Fig. 55: Sutton Benger. Green Man

England, as well as France and Germany, can produce a wealth of examples. There is an early one, not at first noticeable among all the interlacing, on the right-hand capital at the entrance to the ancient church of Kilpeck (Hereford & Worcs.); this dates from about 1130. They abound in later medieval art. We find them, for instance, on the Choir stalls in the Latin Chapel of Christ Church Cathedral, Oxford. Exeter Cathedral is especially rich; the Green Man is to be seen among the roof-bosses of the nave (early fourteenth century), and very interestingly in a corbel in the Choir, where he supports on his head tiny figures of the Virgin and Child – epitomizing the link between religion and the world of nature. There is a lovely early fifteenth-century example in the east cloister at Norwich; the face peers out nervously from a circle of golden leaves. And it is not just in the great cathedrals that the Green Man is found. In the village church of Sutton Benger in Wiltshire he appears both on the outside of the building (Fig. 55) and in a carving at the west end of the south aisle, a sensitive, suffering face almost engulfed in vegetation.

Thus there is no reason why Piper should not have introduced the Green Man into ecclesiastical settings – no reason except perhaps the timidity of the clergy and the fear that the image might be misunderstood. Piper started making drawings on this theme, often referred to as 'foliate heads', in 1953 (I remember seeing them when I first visited Fawley Bottom in the fifties). A number of them were exhibited in February 1955 in New York, at the Curt Valentin Gallery. In 1956 foliate heads appear in elongated form in Piper's set for John Cranko's revue, *Cranks* (at St Martin's Theatre, Cambridge Circus, London). They made a similar appearance on curtain material he designed for David Whitehead fabrics (Fig. 57). Later they were to appear on screen-prints (Fig. 56; in association with Chris Prater in 1966), and later still on tapestries and ceramics.

The first appearance of foliate heads in stained glass (if we are to discount the first experimental panel of 'Two Heads' (Fig. 26, p. 40) as being not necessarily foliate) was in 1964: a screen for the Wessex Hotel, Winchester (Fig. 59, overleaf). Since this is an internal screen, it is normally seen by artificial light, which invests it with a golden glow, and perhaps gives it a

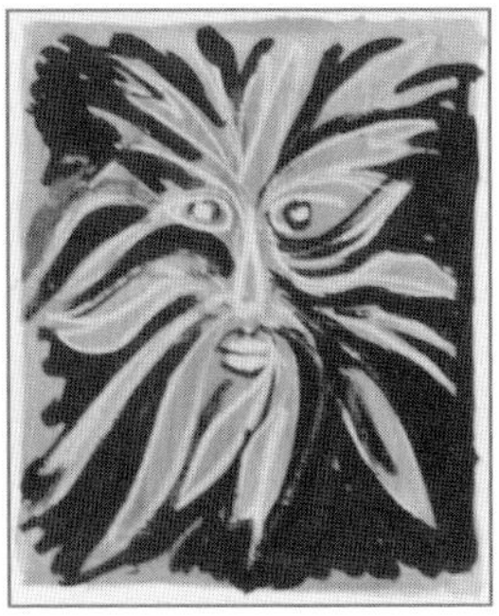

Fig. 56: Foliate head screen-print, designed by John Piper in association with Chris Prater, 1966

Fig. 57: Curtain fabric, designed by John Piper and manufactured by David Whitehead, 1950s

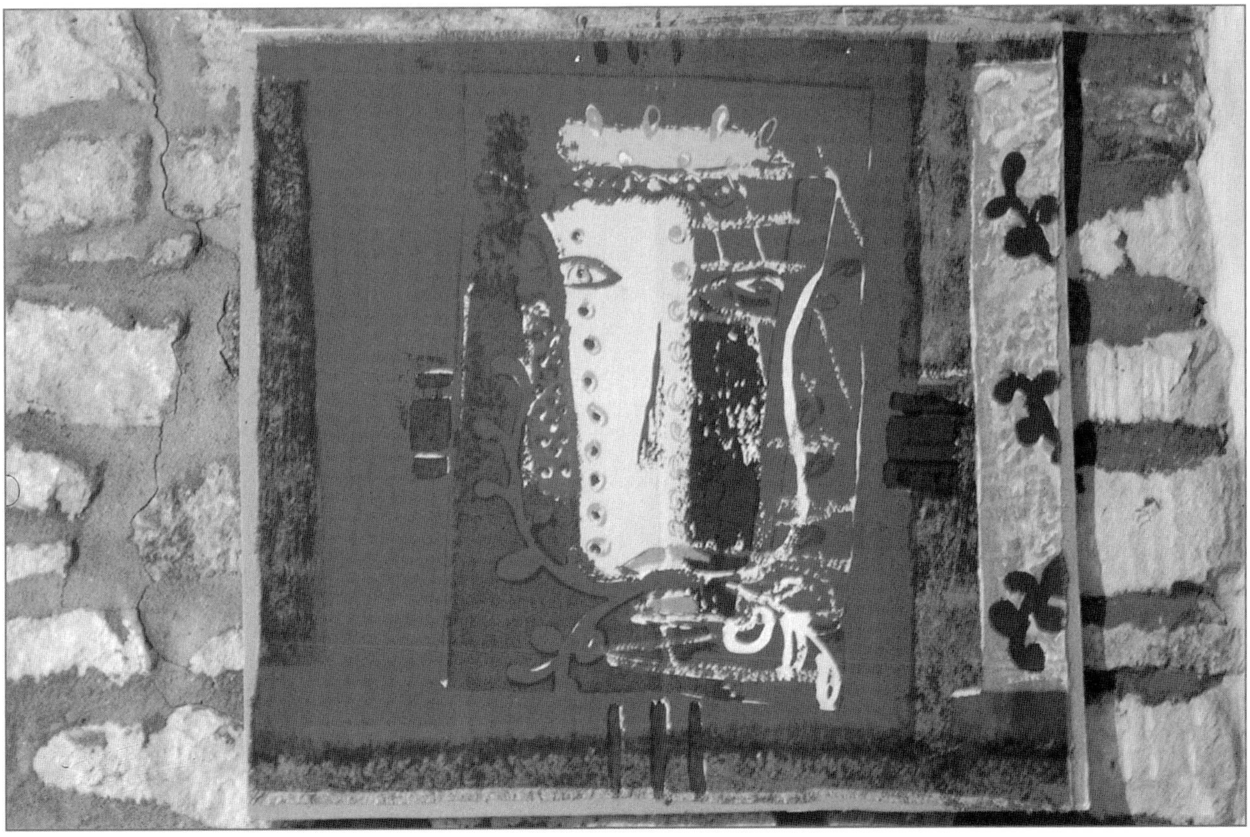

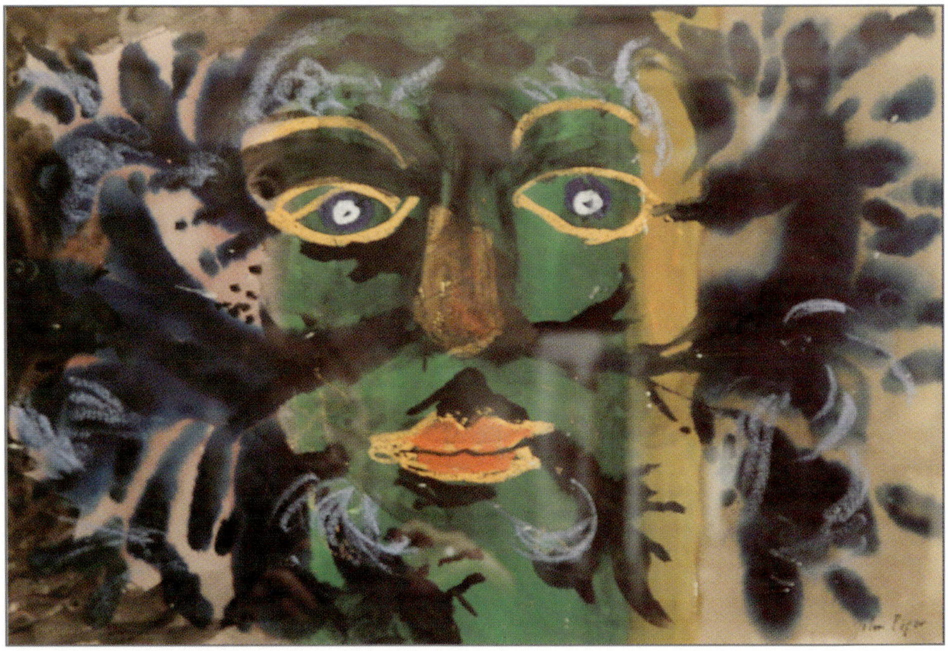

Fig. 58: Gouache with foliate head, by John Piper

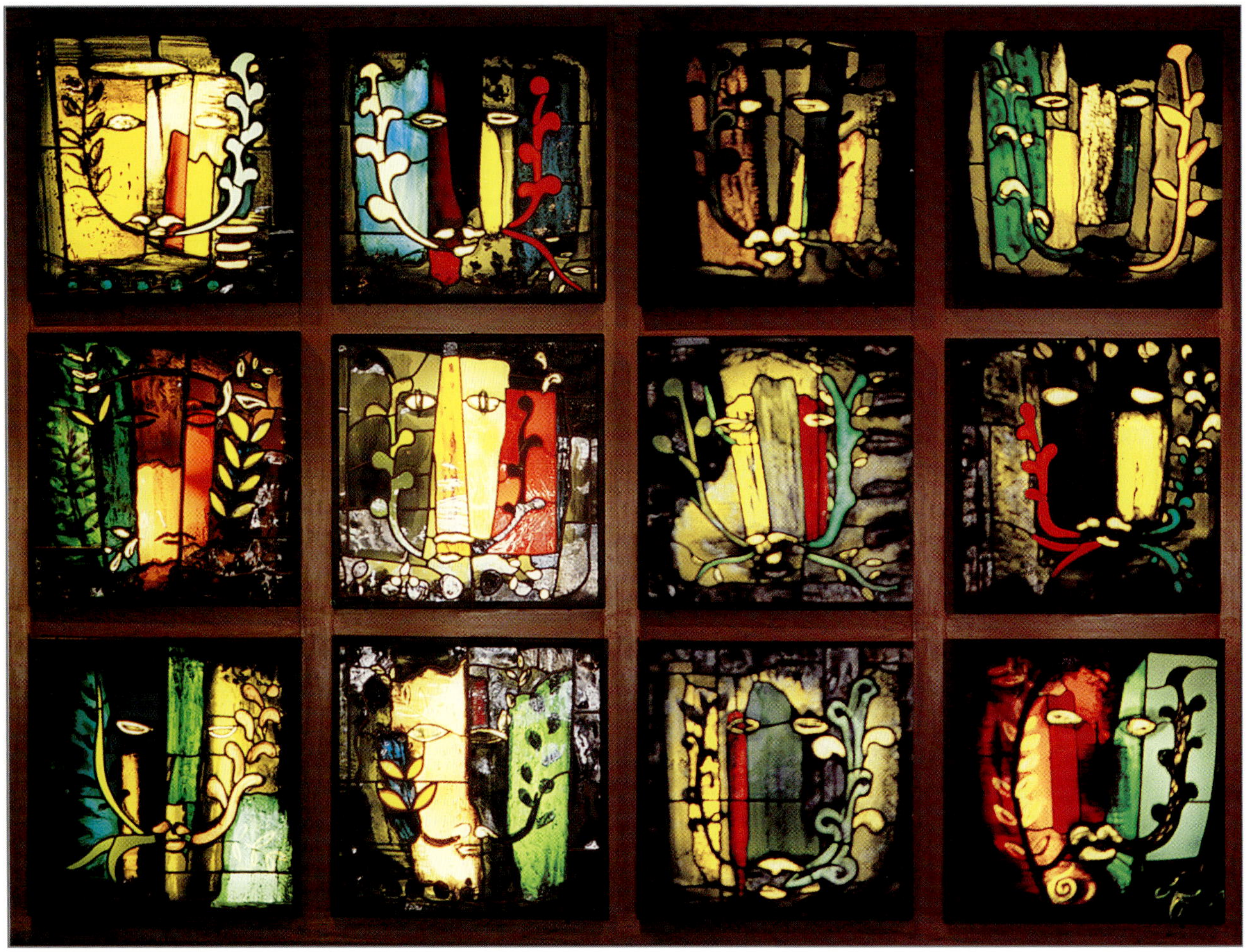

Fig. 59: Winchester, Wessex Hotel. Screen of twelve foliate heads

greater sense of unity. There are twelve different heads in it, suggesting possibly the twelve months of the year; later Piper was to use images of the Green Man to denote the four seasons (Figs 106–9, p. 127). They are elongated, mask-like faces, several of them divided lengthwise into dark and light zones. Vegetation cradles each one in a U-shape. Is it too far-flung to see an affinity between the Green Man and the Tree of Jesse, which links with its branches the divine being at the top and the earthly ones below? Nature and religion being, as Peter Pears observed, not only the profoundest elements in Piper's art, but also elements very closely linked.

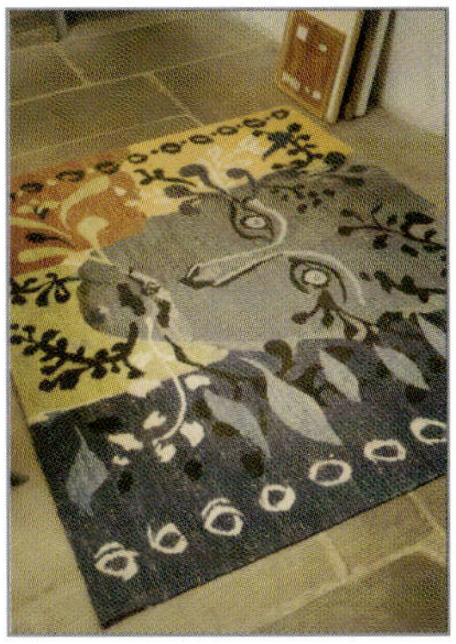

Fig. 60: Mat with foliate head, designed by John Piper and photographed at Fawley Bottom Farmhouse

CHAPTER EIGHT

EXPERIMENTAL TECHNIQUES: TOWER LANTERN OF THE METROPOLITAN CATHEDRAL OF CHRIST THE KING, LIVERPOOL, AND WORK IN FIBREGLASS

John Piper had to endure some criticism in the early 1960s from those who maintained that he was not sufficiently avant-garde. He had been a Trustee of the Tate Gallery since 1944, but resigned from the Board in 1961 after being attacked in the *Times Literary Supplement* for being a defector from abstractionism. The following year he was castigated in an Arts Council publication for having made 'a nostalgic retreat into insular sensibilities'. Such criticism, however misjudged, can be hurtful. He had in fact followed his own path, rather than adhere to the track of whatever style was currently in vogue. In the decorative arts in the fifties the fashionable style was the so-called Contemporary, based on the triangle and the wedge-shape; painting, sculpture, graphic arts and the rest were expected to fit in with this or be labelled old-fashioned. Since Piper's designs for stained glass varied so much – according to the ideas he had in mind and also according to the spirit of the place for which they were commissioned – it sometimes happened that fashion caught up with him and he was in vogue again.

He was not averse to trying new techniques when the occasion demanded. He wrote in *Stained Glass: Art or Anti-Art?* about the use of coloured resins poured on to fibreglass. This enabled windows to be made in large sections, without the use of leads even when there was a change of colour; fibreglass would not to the same extent need the support of saddlebars, and was a good deal less expensive than the traditional way of making windows. Piper commented:

> There is a prejudice against it at present; it is thought to look too synthetic or 'plastic', at any rate for churches. But as good artists use the medium more and more, there is no doubt it will gain ground. In view of the richness of colour and variety, there is probably quite a future for it.

In 1968, the same year as he wrote the book, he designed two diamond-shaped fibreglass windows for St Matthew's, Southcote, Reading. This was a new church, and all the emphasis is on its architectural form. It must be admitted that the windows, with their designs of stylized wings, seem something of an afterthought. Nor do they exploit the material's potential for colour.

Piper's work for the Church of All Saints, Clifton, Bristol (1967) is much more interesting. The original church had been bombed during the Second World War, and only fragments including a side chapel were left standing. A new church, entirely modern in design, was planned to adjoin the chapel. There was financial provision for new windows as the War Damage Commission had made an allowance of £10,500 for the glass in the bombed church. On 26 September 1962 the Parochial Church Council approved the suggestion of the architect (Robert Potter) that John Piper should be invited to design the windows. In March 1964 he travelled to Clifton and discussed with the vicar the themes for the window, notably the Tree of Life and the River of Life. Sketches and slides were shown to the Diocesan Advisory Council, but they were rather unconvinced, and arranged that a sub-committee should be set up to advise on the matter. To this sub-committee Piper explained the technique to be used; he said that it would be rather like painting on canvas, not something that could be prefabricated in a studio. He succeeded in convincing them; they pronounced themselves 'entirely happy to let the artist build up his canvas in situ'. David Gillespie Associates of Farnham made the 3,480 square feet of fibreglass, and Piper received a fee of £2,000 from the funds of the War Damage Commission for his work.

He kept everything bold and simple (Fig. 61, overleaf). For the side of the Lady Chapel, which is triangular, and also for the window opposite, he used nothing but blue, although there is a variation in texture and density of colour. His main design was kept for the very tall West, or Baptistry, Window which goes right up to the roof; pin-points of colour make a border along the top. The centre is all in blue, with strong vertical emphasis; on the left we see the sinuous golden form of the River of Life, on the right the Tree of Life with its branches curving upwards, studded with red and gold fruits.

Piper had in a sense more than the customary amount of freedom; apart from David Gillespie, who made the fibreglass, he did not have to use any intermediary. It was more akin to a theatre set or a mural; he worked in the church, primarily as a painter. Although, apart from St Matthew's, Reading, he did not repeat the experiment in any other church, here as part of the modern architecture at All Saints, it works extremely well, and bathes the interior with coloured light.

'I see no reason', wrote Sir Frank Gibberd, architect of the Roman Catholic Cathedral in Liverpool, 'why the manufacturing process should not be changed from a craft to an industrial technique.'[1] And indeed, an industrial technique was the only way in which the glazing of the Cathedral's enormous Tower Lantern could have been achieved.

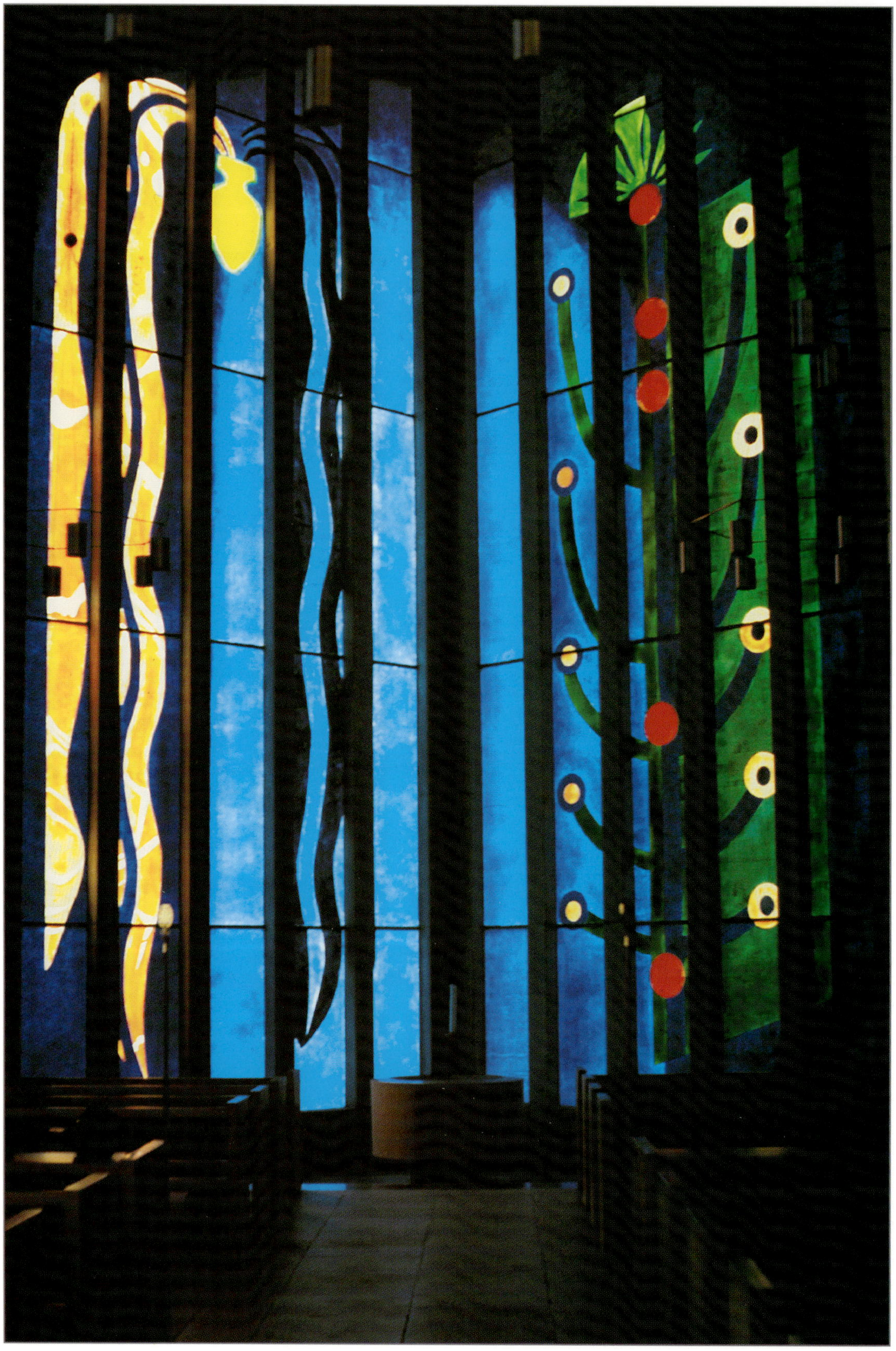

Opposite: Fig. 61: Bristol, All Saints, Clifton. The Tree and the River of Life

The Roman Catholic Diocese of Liverpool was already in the habit of planning on a large scale. The first cathedral was begun in the Gothic style at Everton in 1853, the architect being Augustus Pugin, but only the Lady Chapel was completed. In 1930 it was determined to build a cathedral of phenomenal size and magnificence, to be designed by Sir Edwin Lutyens. He planned a building 680 feet long, 400 feet wide, with a dome 168 feet in diameter (it would have been the largest ever), the height to the top of the dome to be 510 feet. It would have been bigger than St Paul's Cathedral in London, and not dissimilar in style. Construction was begun in 1933, but only the crypt had been finished when work on the project ceased in 1940. Quite apart from the war putting a stop to any such enterprise, it was obvious that it was too large and grandiose a plan ever to be completed.

In 1959 therefore a competition was held, one of the problems for the competitors being that the roof of Lutyens's solid and imposing crypt, which stood 12 feet above ground level, somehow had to be incorporated. The judges were Dr Heenan, Archbishop of Liverpool, Sir Basil Spence (who had made his name as the architect of the new Anglican Cathedral at Coventry), and David Stokes, architect of a number of Roman Catholic churches. After they had selected a winning design, the endorsement of their choice was sought of the Royal Fine Art Commission.

The winner of the competition, chosen out of 298 entries, was Sir Frederick Gibberd. He had already won two awards in connection with the 1951 Festival of Britain. For the Liverpool project he related, 'I shut myself up for three weeks and drew and drew, and the thing just grew'. Gibberd's design was for a centrally planned church – a circle of 194 feet diameter, which would accommodate 3,000 people all within 70 feet of the central sanctuary. It was to be set on a podium formed by the roof of the crypt, with an area for open-air services at the side.

Structurally, the new Cathedral has a reinforced concrete frame; around its vertical walls, sixteen boomerang-shaped trusses converge over a conical roof of aluminium sheeting, and are brought together into a ring of reinforced concrete at the base of the Lantern Tower. There are sixteen external radiating chapels and porches.[2] Above the Tower, delicate pinnacles rise to a height of over 300 feet (Fig. 62, overleaf); they are like a coronet, appropriate since the Cathedral is dedicated to Christ the King. Around the central nave, between the trusses are tall panels of glass, 70 feet high. The glass is predominantly blue – it helps to unify the building visually, and to draw the eye upwards. It was designed by Piper and Reyntiens. A massive High Altar of white marble stands in the centre of the Cathedral, and above it a circular canopy of tubes, designed by Gibberd, which Pevsner describes as a 'doubtful blessing' – it does tend to run counter to the pervading simplicity of the rest.

Both internally and externally, the Tower Lantern is the climax of the whole building. It is, as Gibberd pointed out, 'not an arbitrary architectural form, it is an extension of the sanctuary, the two being inseparable'. The glazing of it was thus a crucial matter. It has a very exposed position; not only because the Cathedral itself stands on high ground at the top of Mount Pleasant, but because much of the Tower is over 130 feet above ground. Added to which, the very extent of the glass, some 12,500 square feet, posed a problem.

Fig. 62: Liverpool, Roman Catholic Cathedral of Christ the King

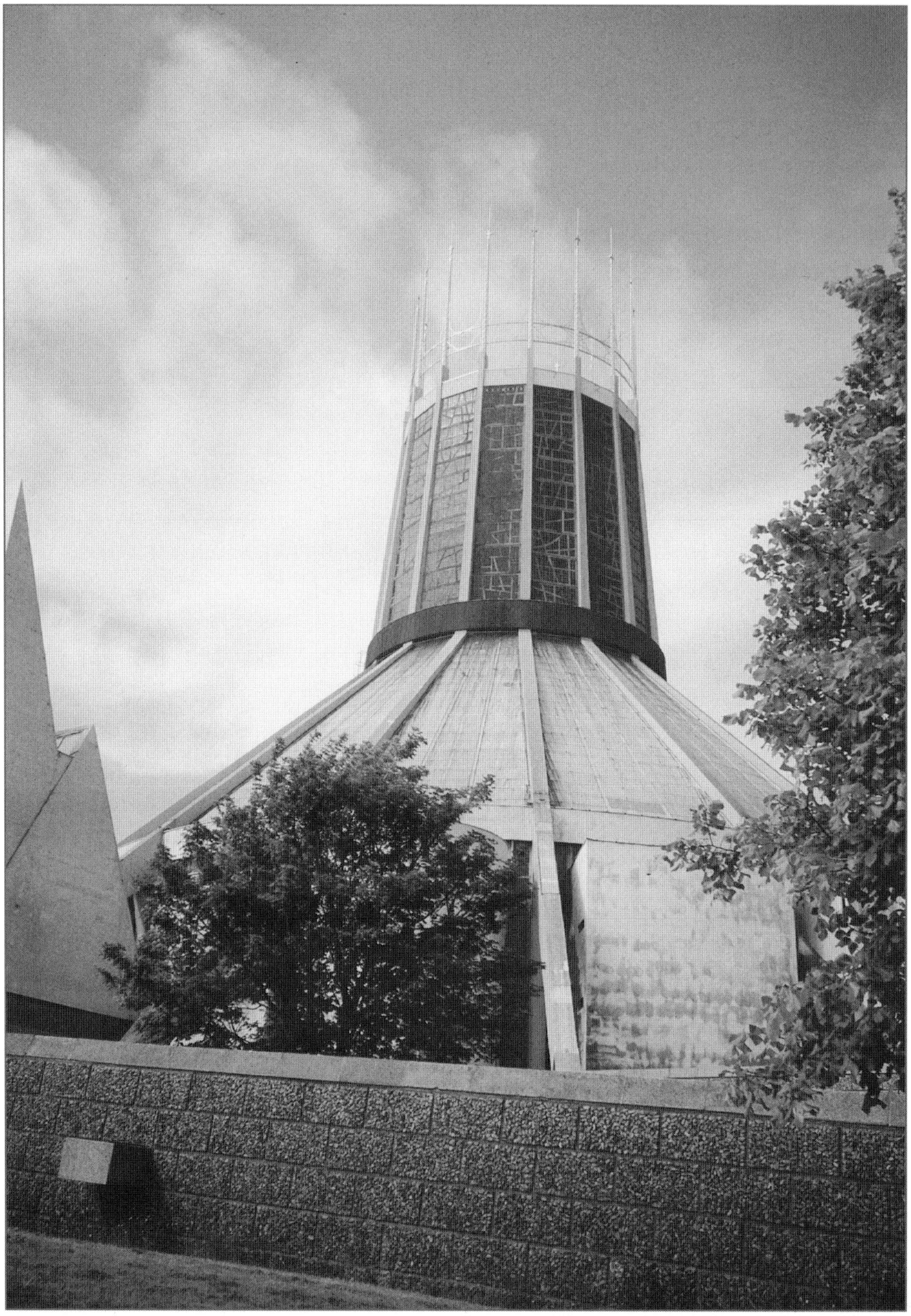

The architect briefly considered the idea of white glass, and then rejected it:

Plain obscure glass gives a very cold light and can transmit a most uncomfortable glare . . . Some churches are whitewashed and flooded with hard light of immaculate austerity; but the people of Liverpool are not Cistercian monks and such an environment seemed to me inappropriate.

Therefore stained glass was decided upon. However, it was realized that the traditional technique of using comparatively small and thin pieces of glass held together with lead cames would not be the answer. It was too delicate in every sense, detailed work would not be seen at such a height, and it would be too expensive – Gibberd estimated that 'superb glass and superb design can cost anything between £13 and £30 a square foot' (1960s prices). The only form of stained glass which would have the necessary toughness, allied with brilliance and dramatic impact, seemed to be *dalles-de-verre.*

Dalles-de-verre had been used to effect in France, especially by Léger and Manessier, but not to much extent in Britain. There was already in existence the Church of Our Lady of Fatima in Harlow New Town, Essex. Here there are whole walls of glass, of dramatic colour in a prevailing grid-design; the *dalles-de-verre* are set in concrete with plain glass outside for protection. It was designed by Gerard Goalen and executed by the monks of Buckfast Abbey. Cardinal Heenan visited this, as well as Coventry, where he was much impressed by the Baptistry Window. Even though it was made using traditional techniques, it encouraged him to share Basil Spence's confidence that those responsible for that endeavour would have the vision to undertake the Tower Lantern at Liverpool.

John Piper undertook this commission jointly with Patrick Reyntiens; they were both involved in the design, and were assisted in the construction by David Kirby. The theme is the Holy Trinity, symbolized by bursts of light within areas of the three primary colours, red, blue and yellow (Figs 63 and 64, overleaf). The first design was a painting measuring about 12 × 4 feet. The next step was to make full-scale cartoons. One cartoon was made for each of the sixteen bays (the Tower being divided into the same components as the rest of the building). Each cartoon was 12 feet wide, but tapering very slightly towards the top,[3] and nearly 70 feet long. Then Taylor-Woodrow, the firm in charge of the construction work on the Cathedral, made a specially designed studio at Loudwater, measuring 70 × 40 feet. It was oil-heated to maintain an even temperature while the panels were being made, it had large folding doors at the end, and an overhead transporter to move the completed panels. There were in all 156 panels; of the sixteen bays, twelve contained nine panels each, and four contained twelve – the extra divisions in every fourth bay giving added strength. Each panel contains about a hundred pieces of glass. Each of these (the *dalles-de-verre*) was cut from a rectangle measuring about 12 × 8 inches and 1 inch thick, which had been made in a mould. The glass was imported from France and Germany. The total weight of the glass in the Tower Lantern is said to be about 70 tons.[4]

Meanwhile, a contract had been drawn up, dated 3 February 1964, and the agreed price for the Tower Lantern glass, including materials, was calculated at £84,500 (the glass costing £21,760 of this). A separate contract was drawn up for the Nave windows, costed at £30,895, including £10,250 for the glass.

The perimeter moulds for each panel, made of reinforced concrete, were delivered to the studio Taylor-Woodrow had built. Each panel was further

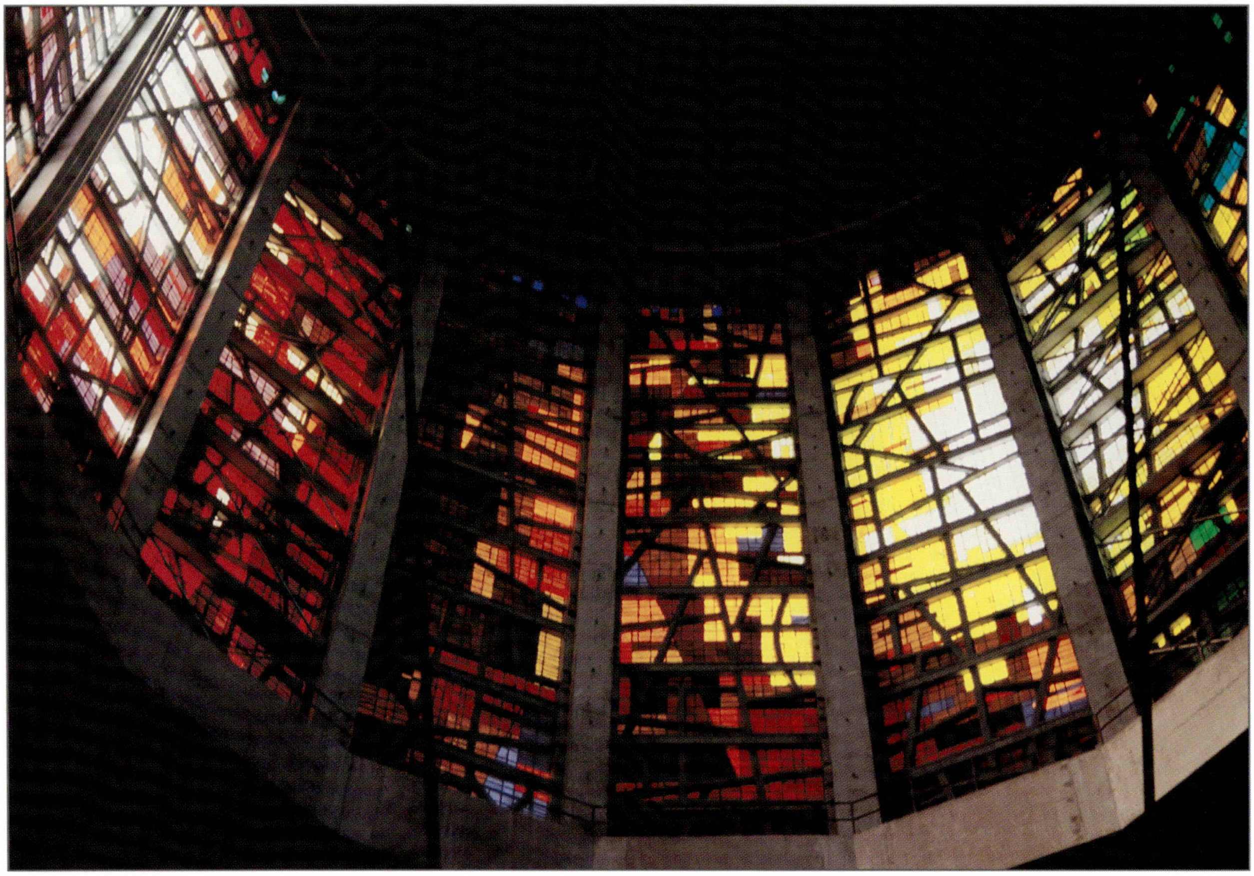

Above and opposite: Figs 63 and 64: Liverpool, RC Cathedral. The Tower Lantern

subdivided into ten or twelve irregular shapes – irregular so as to avoid dull uniformity and give liveliness to the whole effect. The *dalles-de-verre* were placed in position on paper templates backed with polystyrene. Then an epoxy resin (specially made for the purpose by the Plastics Laboratories of the Shell Petroleum Company) was squeezed out from a polythene bag to fill the gaps between the glass. Strands of fibreglass were laid along the fissures, to reinforce the joints, and more resin was applied over the top. After a few hours the resin had hardened sufficiently for the template to be peeled off. The completed panels were stored until they were transported to the site and hoisted up to be installed in the lantern. Thus was completed the largest commission in stained glass ever undertaken.[5]

So much for the means, but what of the effect? It is, quite simply, stunning. While the glass for the Tower had in its making to conform with the structure of the building, in its design it exercises its own freedom – or rather, it follows its own rules. At the very top there are little squares of light in colours contrasting with, or complementary to, the main areas of colour; that is to say, green or yellow at the head of the red section, red above the yellow, red again above the blue. These details give an edge to the glass, prevent it from disappearing into nothingness at the top.

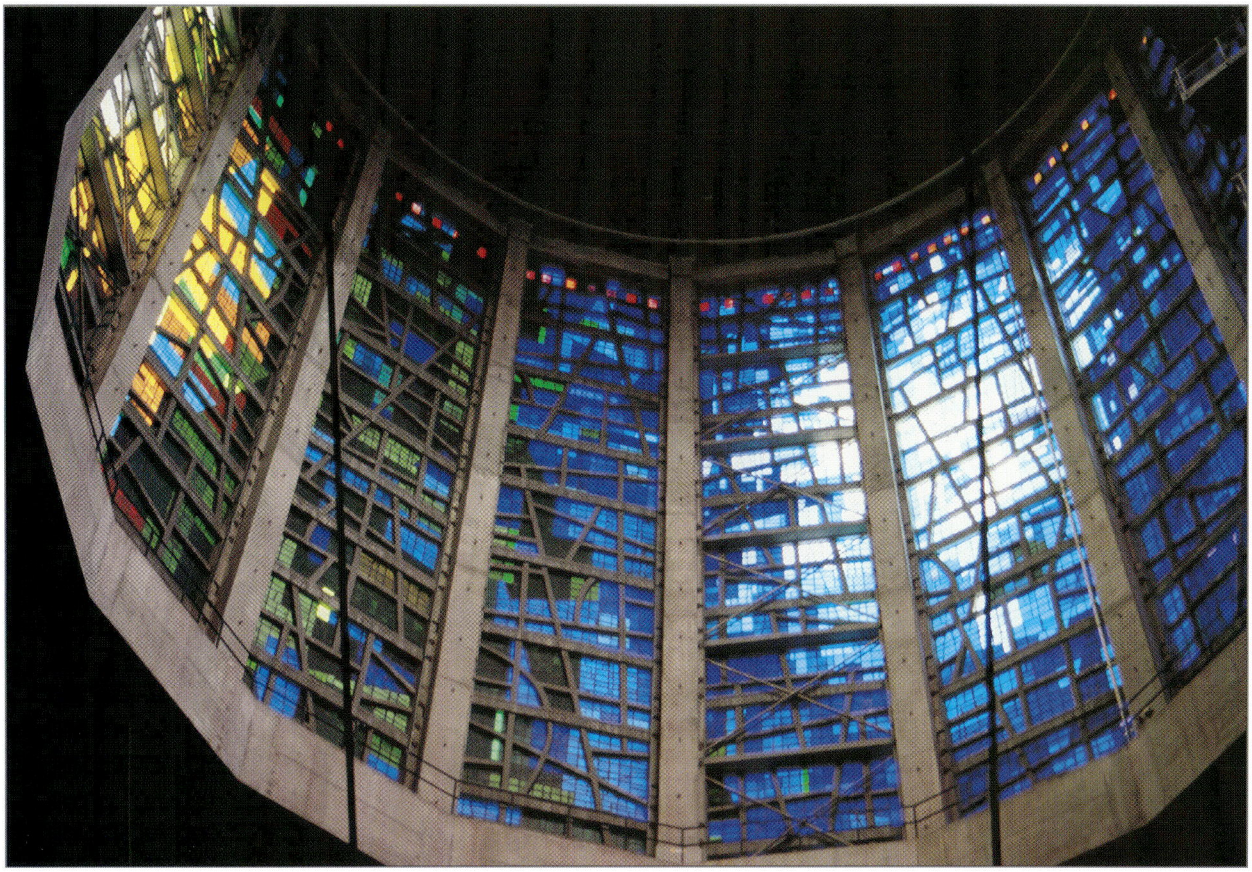

The main colour areas are splashed bravely right across the structural divisions. And while there are three principal zones, red to the south-west, yellow to the north (liturgically the east), and blue to the south-east, and each of these zones blanches to white in the centre, yet it is more complex than that. The yellow has small quantities of browns and greens in it; the red has a touch of blue at the base, and pale orange and mauve to enhance the central burst of white; the blue has one or two squares of mauve, and a tiny touch of green as well as a seemingly infinite variety of shades of the prevailing colour. And while the general trend is for the colours to lighten in tone towards the white, this lightening is not uniform and bland; there are dark surprises.

The glass of the Tower Lantern has a sense of life about it. Visually and emotionally, it is the focal point of the whole interior, and, however abstract, invests it with a spiritual quality.

It had been a commission of enormous magnitude – according to Reyntiens, the biggest commission for stained glass ever undertaken. More significant than this superlative was the success of the enterprise. As far as Piper was concerned, it silenced his critics. No one could now accuse him of being insular or idiosyncratic. He had shown himself to be an artist of power and vision, and had won international acclaim. He must have found his new celebrity quite exhilarating.

CHAPTER NINE

INCREASING VERSATILITY: MORE WINDOWS OF THE LATER 1960S

'Working in stained glass Piper was continually faced with the problem of handling transparent colour masses, almost the antithesis of the painter's normal business with opaque reflecting surfaces.'

Anthony West[1]

The success of the Liverpool glass, both artistically and in terms of cultural acclaim, had a considerable effect on Piper's work. Even if he were never again to face quite the same sort of challenge, it gave him new confidence, having revealed his ability to handle great areas of colour. From now on his painting was also to reflect this: blocks of strong colour not necessarily related to form, and over the colour detail might be superimposed. He worked with new courage and an increasing breadth of vision.

Indeed, some of his paintings from the later sixties have a dramatic quality that makes one think immediately of stained glass; for example, a painting in water-colour and mixed media of the Romanesque tympanum on the outside of the village church at Neuilly-en-Donjon, Allier, dating from about 1969 (Fig. 1, p. xix and Fig. 113, p. 132). Although the subject is taken from a piece of sculpted stone, where if the painting were naturalistic one would expect earth colours, yet Piper's vision of it is predominantly rich ultramarine blue, against which are flashes of white, red, violet, and patches of glowing emerald green. It suggests, and indeed anticipates stained glass; but at this time the taste of those who commissioned windows would not necessarily be ready for anything so bold, nor would the sites necessarily be appropriate. It was not for another ten years or so that the sketch would find its ultimate transformation (at Robinson College, Cambridge) into stained glass.[2]

Meanwhile, commissions came thick and fast, each one with its own set of requirements as to site, its own problems, and possibilities as to treatment. Although Piper's personal preference, other things being equal, may have been to relinquish abstractionism – and he had virtually abandoned it in his painting – yet in the field of stained glass other things never *were* equal. Sometimes it seemed the only appropriate style to use.

This was the case with the Chapel at Malsis School, near Keighley, Yorkshire.

Fig. 65: Malsis School Chapel. Detail from the south window

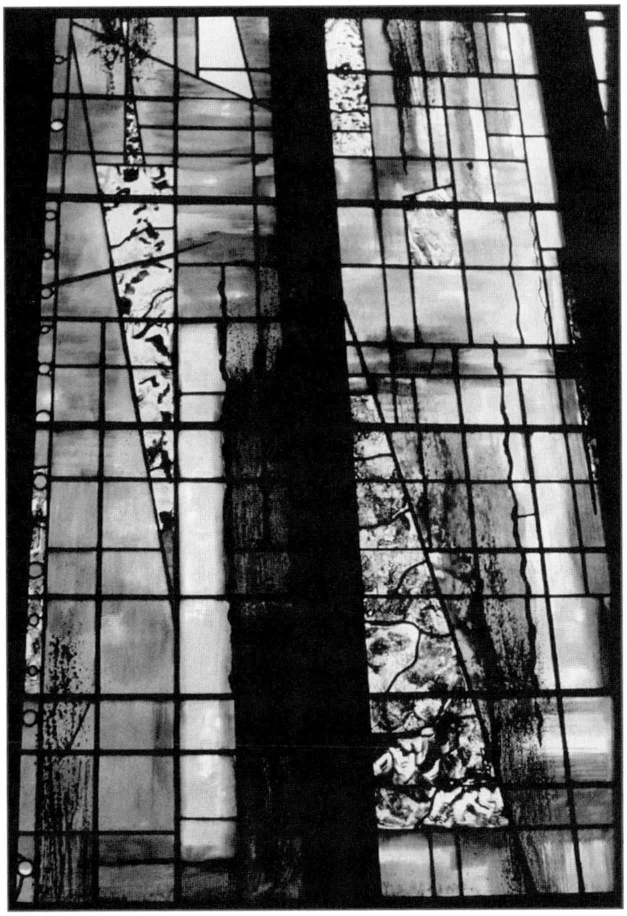

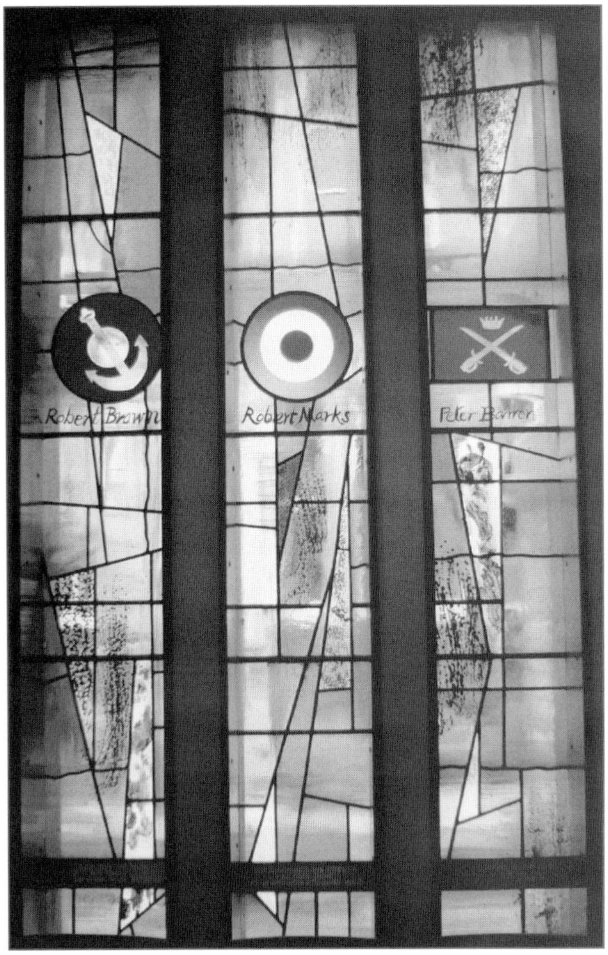

Fig. 66: Westminster, St Margaret's; window under repair in 1982. (Photo. courtesy of David Wasley)

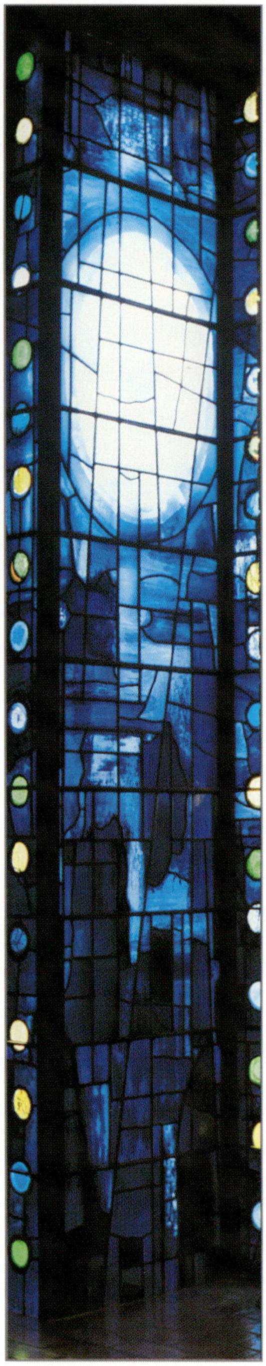

Fig. 67: Cambridge, Churchill College Chapel. Third window from left (see p. 96)

In 1965–7 Piper was called upon to design glass for the tall, narrow lights on both north and south sides (Fig. 65, p. 93), seventeen in all. They commemorate former pupils and staff of the school who were killed in the Second World War, one light for each of them. On each is the name of the young man and the badge of the branch of the armed services in which he served. That is as far as they are individualized; for the rest the glass is in sharp-edged abstract patterns of grey, blue, green and yellow – all in pale tones, so that no lack of light is admitted to the Chapel.

In 1967–8 Piper designed in a similar style, although on a much larger scale, for eight south aisle windows in St Margaret's Church, Westminster (Fig. 66, p. 93). The Victorian glass with which they had been filled had been destroyed by bomb blast during the Second World War (1941), not it seems to any great regret since they had made the church extremely dark. Temporarily, white opaque 'bathroom' glass had been used to fill the gap; then the sum of £3,700 was made available by the War Damage Commission for the purpose of replacing this with stained glass. It was realized that this sum was scarcely adequate; still, Piper, whose work at Coventry, Eton and Liverpool had brought him great renown, was invited to design the glass – it being the opinion of Canon Michael Stancliffe, the then incumbent, that 'only the best is good enough for St Margaret's'.

Piper himself relates what happened:

> We met in the church and I asked which window he proposed for the new

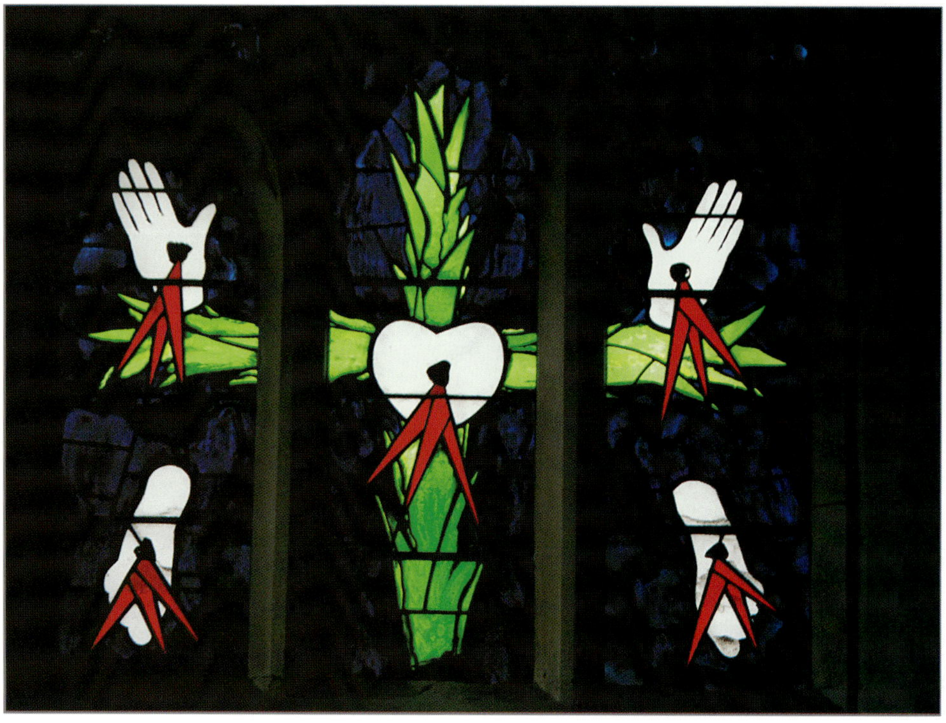

Fig. 68: Misterton, All Saints. The Symbols of the Stigmata (see p. 97)

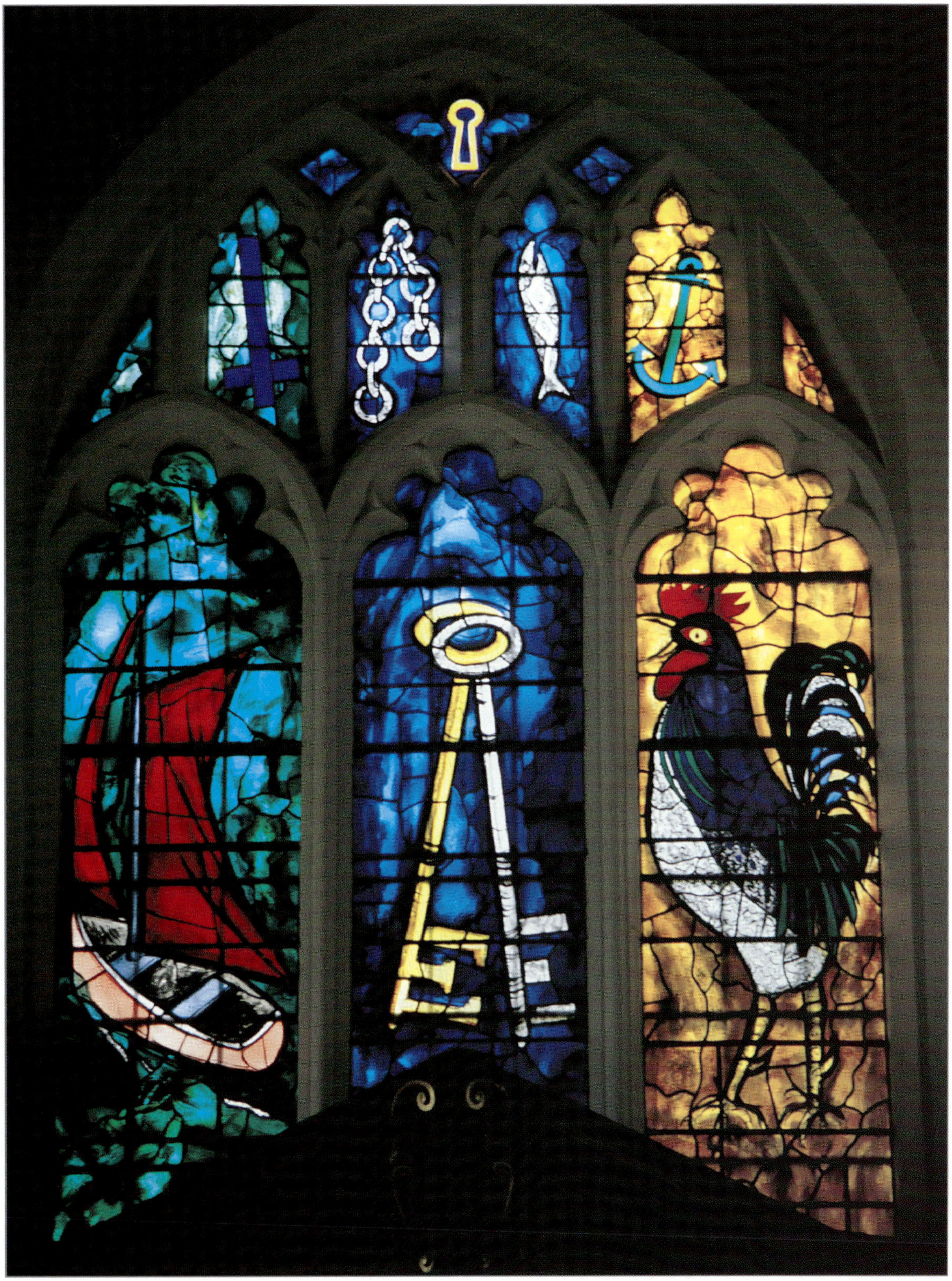

Fig. 69: Babraham, St Peter's. The Emblems of St Peter (see pp. 97–100)

> glass. He said 'any of those in the South Aisle'. There was just about enough money for one window. But it seemed to me unwise, even foolish, to put in this by itself, when it would have to compete with the glorious glass at the East end of the church, made in Flanders in 1501 to commemorate the marriage of Catherine of Aragon (aged fifteen) to Arthur, Prince of Wales. But if more money could be raised it might be possible to provide a complete glazing scheme for the South aisle, not with 'pictorial' glass but with carefully designed, tinted and delicately painted glass in a series of abstract patterns. A limited appeal was raised by Canon Stancliffe, who saw the point of this, and before long a considerable sum was added to the legacy. . . . I consulted Patrick Reyntiens, who has always interpreted my designs for stained glass since we began working together at Oundle in the early nineteen fifties. We decided to work with predominantly light-coloured glass (green, grey-green, pale yellow and near-white). The aim was to provide an unaggressive screen or filter for the daylight on the south side of the church, which would be agreeable in itself and would in no way affect the grand vista eastward in the church. A full-sized cartoon was made for each window, varying the shapes and placing of the interlocking colours.[3]

Some commissions required the maximum of tact. When he was working for Malsis School, it cannot have been an easy assignment to design windows to commemorate a number of young men he had never met; to make a memorial for a monarch was perhaps more difficult still. In 1969 Piper was commissioned to design for the George VI Memorial Chapel at Windsor. Here he used much stronger colours (deep blues with patches of red and occasional circles of yellow), especially towards the altar, though paler towards the edges. His design won royal approval. 'I showed this picture both to the Queen and Queen Elizabeth', it was reported in a letter from the Deanery, Windsor Castle, 'and they are really awfully pleased with them. They particularly liked the light blue variations towards the outside of the principal windows.'

The common factor in all the abstract glass that Piper was designing at this time was that it was done to accord with the architecture. In 1970 he received a commission to design eight windows for the Chapel of Churchill College, Cambridge. They are very closely integrated with the structure; indeed with all its bare brick, the interior would be very stark without them. They are tall, narrow windows, dark purple in the west, green and yellow along both north and south walls; the climax is at the east, where on either side there are more complex windows, Z-shaped in profile, of brilliant blues ranging from ultramarine to almost white, with borders of light-coloured dots (Fig. 67, p. 94).

In all these windows, however successful they are in context, one senses that Piper had felt constrained by one or more factors: by the nature of the commission, by the architecture, and in the case of St Margaret's by not wishing to vie with existing glass that he admired. Hence he used the abstract style; but meanwhile, there were other projects for which he could use the language of symbols and express himself more freely.

In 1966 he was working for All Saints, Misterton, in Nottinghamshire. Here he designed an East Window for the north chapel, on the theme of the Stigmata, the Five Wounds of Christ (Fig. 63, p. 94). It will be remembered that he had used the theme before, in the west window of Nuffield College Chapel, but here the treatment is far more dramatic. The white shapes of the hands, feet and heart, from which blood spurts in an angular form suggesting rays of light, are set against the bright green of a foliate cross – the whole given extra impact by the extreme dark of the surrounding glass.

In the same year he designed an East Window for the parish church of Babraham in Cambridgeshire (Fig. 69, p. 95).[4] It is a charming little medieval church, largely thirteenth century, and the dedication is to St Peter. It was therefore apposite that the theme of the window should be emblems representing the life and significance of that saint. In the main central light are the Keys (Fig. 70, overleaf), referred to in St Matthew's Gospel, chapter 16:

> Thou art Peter, and upon this rock I will build my church. . . .
> And I will give unto thee the keys of the kingdom of heaven.

The Keys, gold and silver-white, swing against a field of deepest blue. Above them in the tracery lights, also against blue, are the Chains, referring to Peter's imprisonment (Acts 12: 7), and the Fish, symbol of the Miraculous Draught and Christ's saying to Peter 'Fear not; from henceforth thou shalt catch men' (Luke 5: 10). In the very top light is the keyhole. To the left of the Keys is Peter's Boat (Fig. 71, overleaf), which relates to his calling as a fisherman and also to his walking on the water (referred to in Matthew 14: 22–33). The Boat is a lively sailing-dinghy, seen from above, its crimson sails brilliant against a troubled green sea.

But of all the symbols of St Peter perhaps the most vivid is the crowing Cock (Fig. 72, p. 99), emblem of his denial. We read in Matthew 26: 34, 'Jesus said unto him, Verily I say unto thee, that this night, before the cock crow, thou shalt deny me thrice'.

Both the saint's failing to keep faith, and at the same time his redemption are implied here. But what a wonderful piece of work this Cock is, strutting in the golden morning light, its neck of indigo, its curling tail-feathers white and viridian, its scarlet comb and wattles, and its beak open in mid-cry. How wonderful that here, as early as 1966 (the Liverpool glass not yet completed), Piper should be designing with such confidence and bravura.

In November 1967 Piper was commissioned by the Court of the Bakers' Company in the City of London to design three windows in their Hall. The Bakers are an extremely ancient confraternity, and in the Middle Ages were a very powerful one, the making and selling of bread being subject to strict

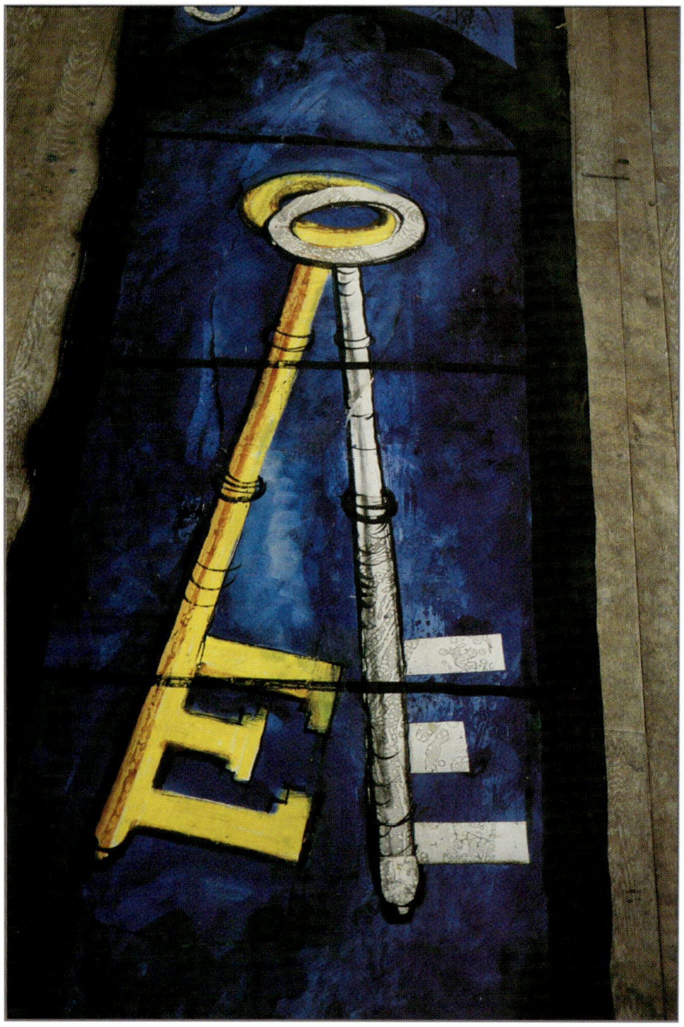

Fig. 70: Babraham. St Peter's. The Emblems of St Peter. Cartoon showing detail of keys

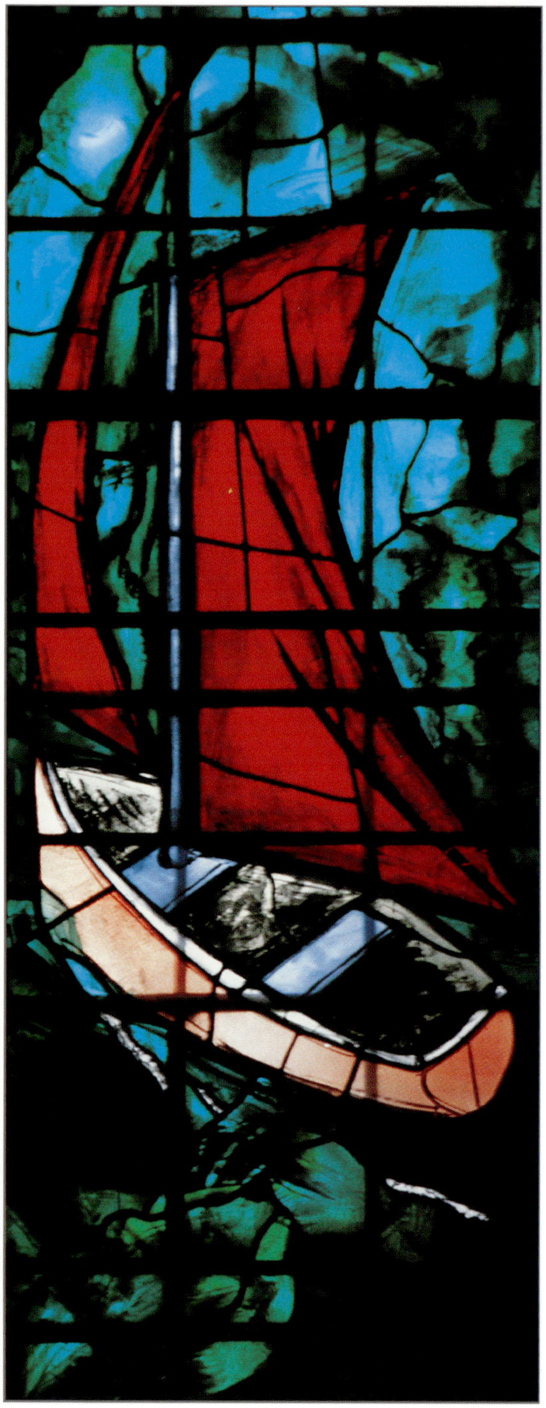

Fig. 71: Babraham, St Peter's. The Emblems of St Peter: the Boat

Fig. 72: Babraham, St Peter's. The Emblems of St Peter: the Cock (see p. 97)

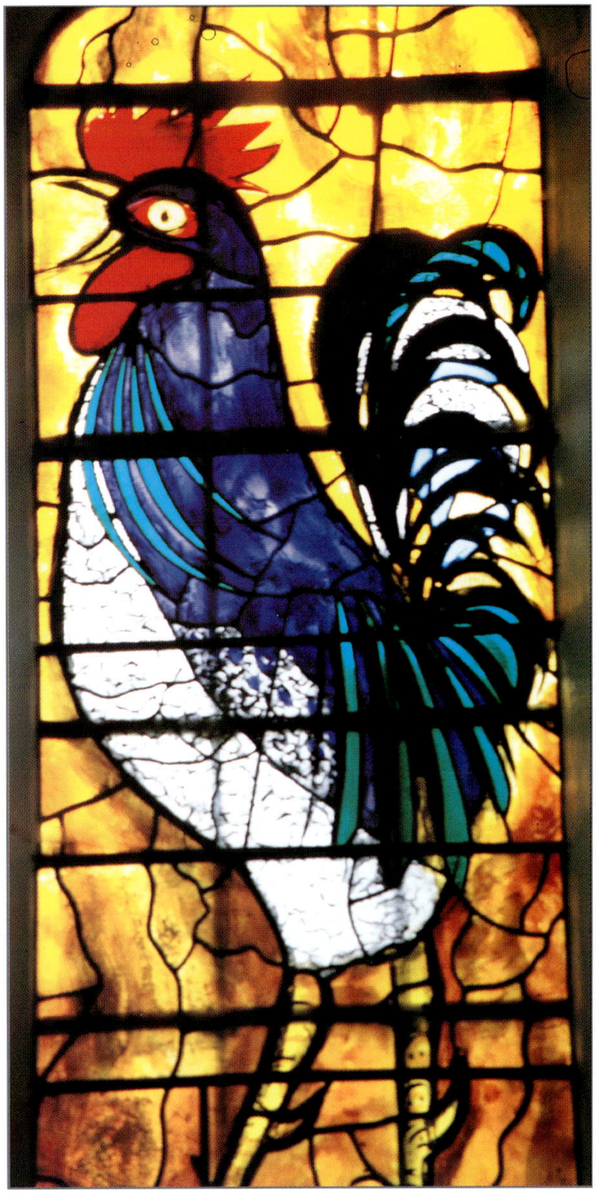

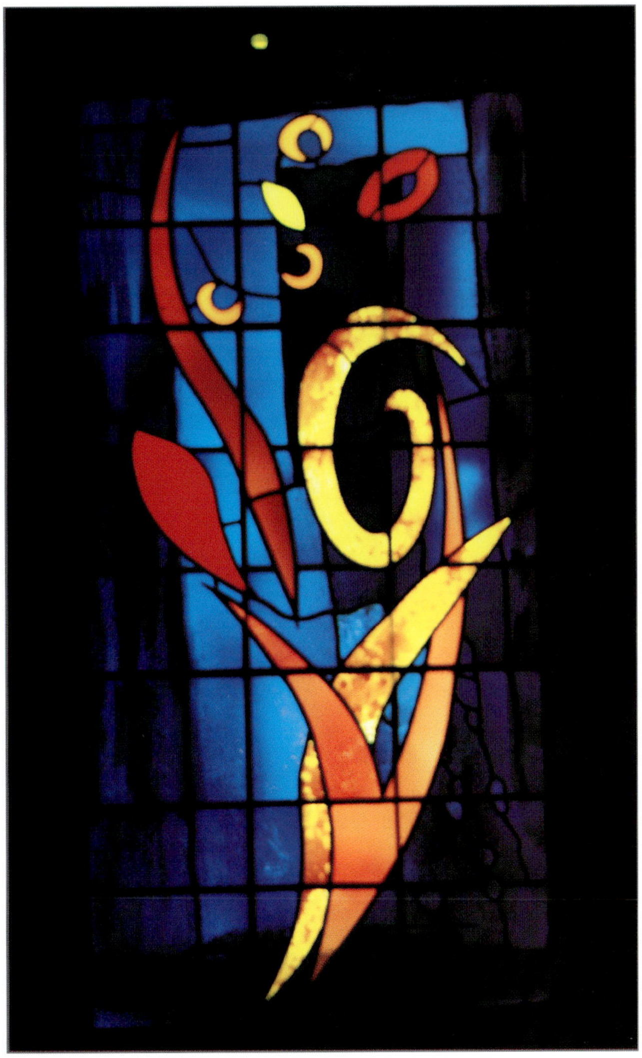

Fig. 73: London, Bakers' Hall. Window three, the Blitz of 1940

controls. Questions of the weight of loaves and the nature of flour to be used were always a matter of concern, and in 1302 London bakers were forbidden to sell their wares in shops and houses, but had to bring them to the open market in Bread Street.

The first idea that Piper submitted for the three windows (each of which measures 7 feet 6 inches high and 3 feet 3½ inches wide) was to base them on symbols connected with the art of baking: a pair of scales, a loaf-shape and perhaps a cornfield. But the Company rejected this – and it must be admitted that the subjects, being all much the same colour, might have been difficult to treat pictorially. However, by the following March Piper had a second idea which met with far greater approval.

The Hall of the Bakers' Company on its present site in Harp Lane[5] had been destroyed three times by fire: first in the Great Fire of London in September 1666; then again by a fire that started in Thames Street in 1715; and finally during the Blitz in the Second World War. This provided Piper with a subject – not so much that one fire could be differentiated from the other, but the general idea of flames licking upwards. All three have rich blue grounds. The Great Fire window has a red, tear-shaped heart from which emerge yellow tongues of fire; the 1715 fire starts from a golden whorl, from which pinky-red flames rise; the third window (Fig. 73, p. 99: the Blitz) has an orange-gold sheaf-shape with red tongues of flame. All three have in the upper part little rings and crescents like sparks ascending.

The Bakers' Company were highly pleased, and expressed to Piper their 'absolute satisfaction and delight' with his designs.

The work for the Bakers' Hall was completed in 1969, and in that year there was a commission to design a lancet for St Paul's Church in the village of Pishill, near Nettlebed in Oxfordshire.[6] Piper did not attempt to depict St Paul as a figure, but (as with Babraham, but on a much smaller scale) he thought of symbols which would best characterize the saint (Fig. 21, p. 37). The usual emblems of St Paul are a sword and a book; he was said to have been beheaded with a sword, and he was a great writer of epistles. Piper's window shows both symbols, but the book is shown held open by two hands, in front of the weapon – signifying the pen to be greater than the sword. The deep blue ground is dotted with stars and falling leaves.

The West Window of St Paul's, Bledlow Ridge, Buckinghamshire (1968), seems to be a fusion of many of Piper's ideas. It has an affinity with some of his paintings. Back in 1951 he did an oil painting, 'Shobdon Folly – Romanesque Fragments', in which white cow-parsley is silhouetted in the foreground. In the same way, the Bledlow Ridge window has silhouetted white and sometimes black plant-forms (Fig. 74, p. 102). It is a window of three main lights, with three quatrefoils in the tracery above; and just as in the 'All Things Bright and Beautiful' window at Wellingborough of 1969 (Fig. 51, p. 75), he has let his design run right across the mullions from one light to another. It is a rhapsody in many shades of blue. There are two pale discs like moons, one larger, one smaller, in the central and right-hand lights, and a black semi-circular shape (the dark side of the moon?) at the bottom of the left-hand light. An outlined form in white – is it plant or human? – appears towards the bottom of the right light, where the blue is deepest. Above float little spirals of brilliant red, seeming to stand proud of the blue and at the same time enhancing it. It is a window of great loveliness, and its subject, if it may be said to have one, is Heaven.

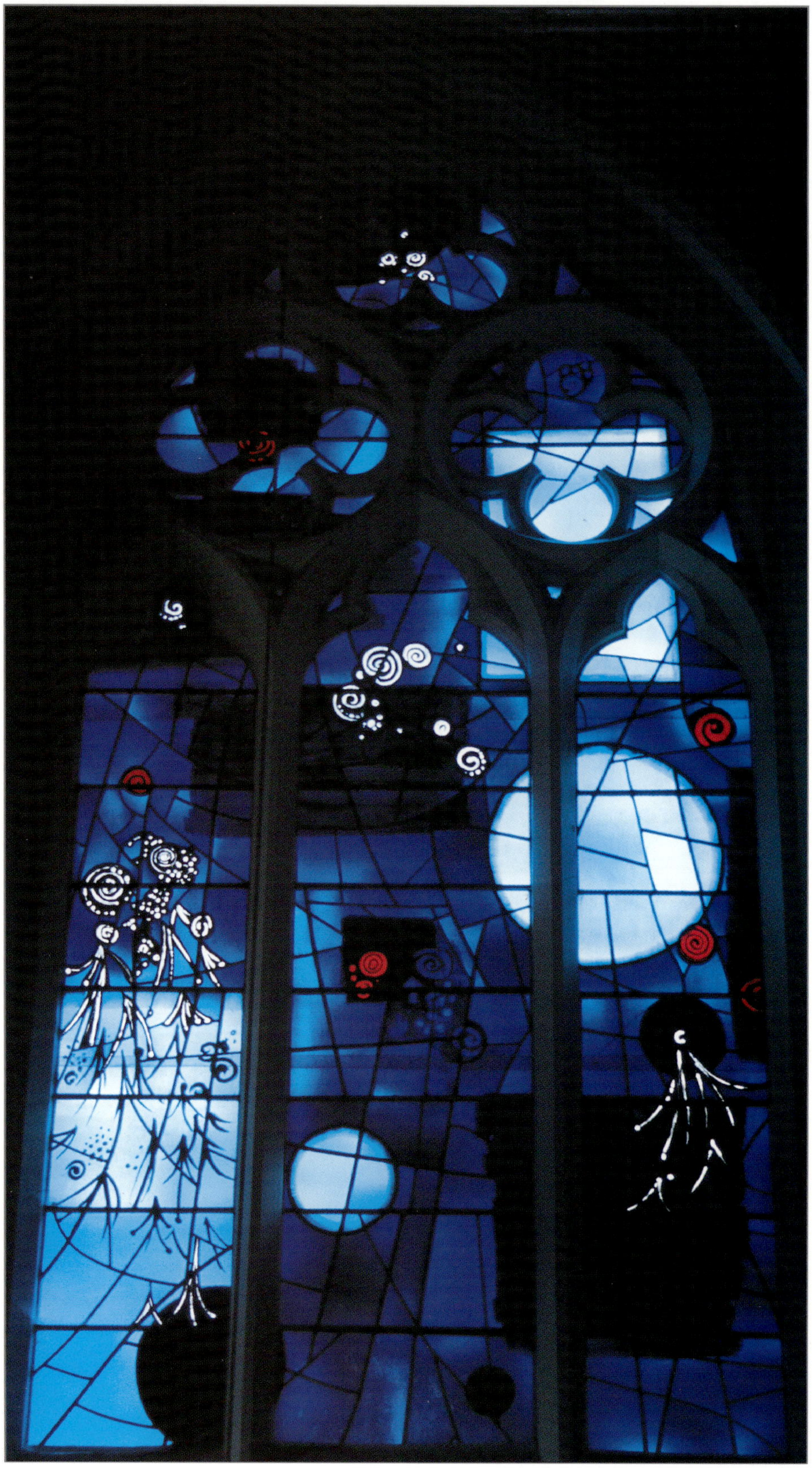

Fig. 74: Bledlow Ridge, St Paul's. West Window (see p. 100)

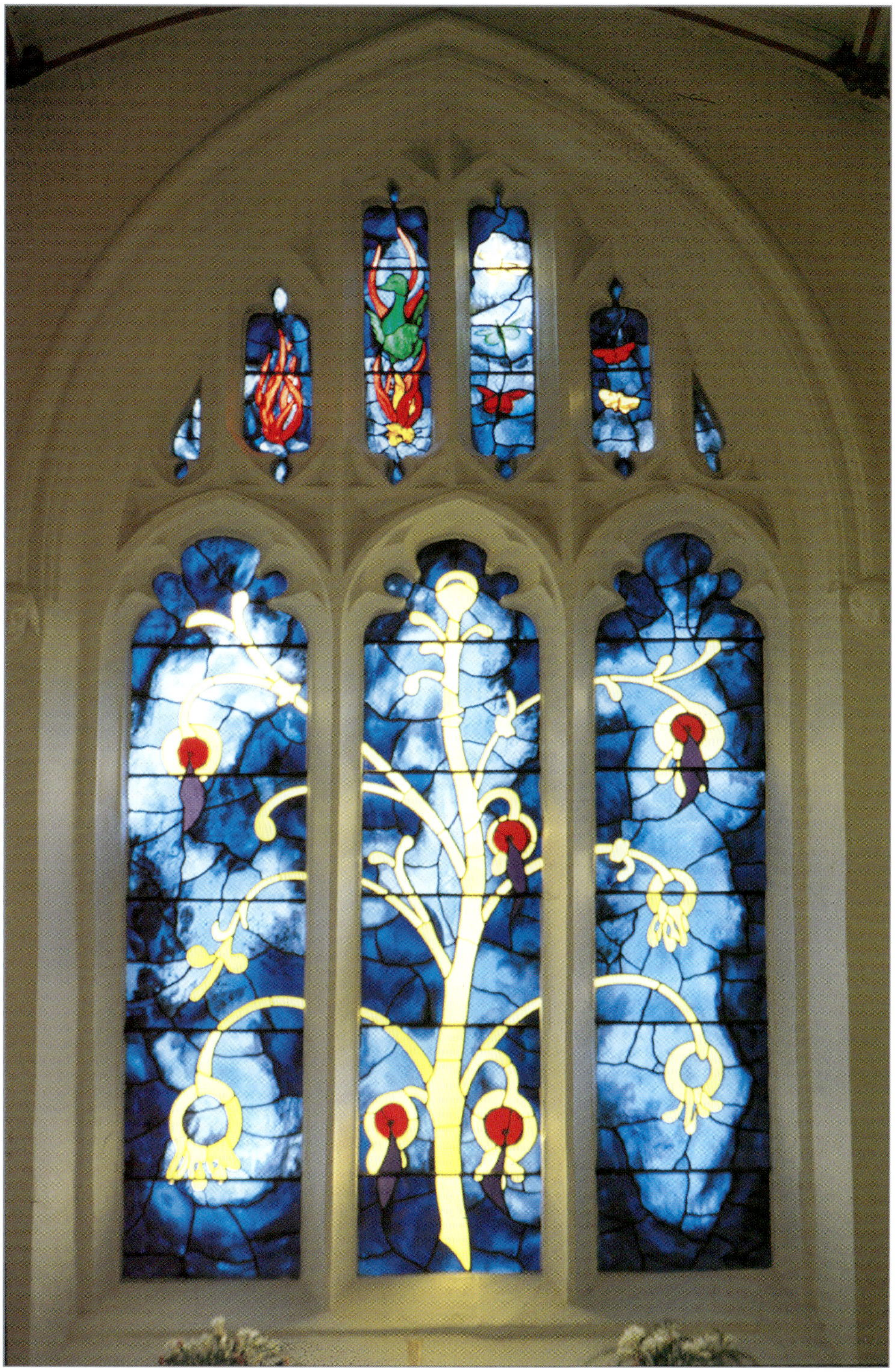

Fig. 75: Totternhoe, St Giles's. The Tree of Life (see pp. 105, 108)

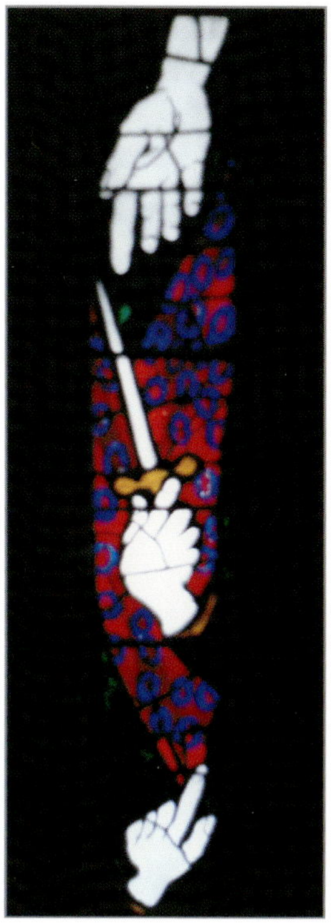

Fig. 76: Sandford St Martin. The Emblems of St Martin (see pp. 110-11)

CHAPTER TEN

THE TREE OF LIFE AND OTHER SYMBOLS: PIPER'S PERSONAL ICONOGRAPHY, 1968–77

It is extraordinary how a theme, an image, can be there in the pages of the Bible, and yet for centuries be neglected and hardly ever used. Such an image was finally taken up by John Piper, and made his own.

During the Middle Ages the subjects for stained glass, and the way in which they were depicted, were more often than not derived from the *Biblia Pauperum*, the Poor Man's Bible; themes missing from this were seldom depicted. Moreover, concepts of good and evil, of redemption and damnation, were usually portrayed in terms of narrative action. The subject of the Tree of Life does not seem to appear at all in the *Biblia Pauperum* (although its companion in Eden, the Tree of Knowledge, is there), and the River of Life is there only in its Old Testament analogy of Moses striking the rock, with the explanation 'the stone giving forth running water is the sacrament of Christ'.

The Tree of Life is referred to in both the first and the last books of the Bible, and also in the Book of Ezekiel. It is mentioned in Genesis only briefly, as growing alongside the Tree of Knowledge, and the main source for both the Tree and the River of Life is the last chapter of the last book of the Bible, the Revelation of St John, chapter 22 (vv. 1–2):

> And he shewed me a pure river of water of life, clear as crystal, proceeding out of the throne of God and of the Lamb.
>
> In the midst of the street of it, and on either side of the river, was there the tree of life, which bare twelve manner of fruits, and yielded her fruit every month: and the leaves of the tree were for the healing of the nations.

It is a vision of heaven, which continues (vv. 5, 14),

> And there shall be no night there; and they need no candle, neither light of the sun; for the Lord God giveth them light: and they shall reign for ever and ever. . . .
>
> Blessed are they that do his commandments, that they may have right to the tree of life, and may enter in through the gates into the city.

The passage in the Book of Ezekiel, chapter 47 (vv. 7–9, 12), concerns the teeming, healing waters and the fertile trees of paradise:

> Now when I had returned, behold, at the bank of the river were very many trees on the one side and on the other.
>
> Then said he unto me, These waters issue out toward the east country, and go down into the desert, and go into the sea: which being brought forth into the sea, the waters shall be healed.
>
> And it shall come to pass, that every thing that liveth, which moveth, whithersoever the rivers shall come, shall live: and there shall be a very great multitude of fish, because these waters shall come thither: for they shall be healed; and every thing shall live whether the river cometh. . . .
>
> And by the river upon the bank thereof, on this side and on that side, shall grow all trees for meat, whose leaf shall not fade, neither shall the fruit thereof be consumed: it shall bring forth new fruit according to his months . . . and the fruit thereof shall be for meat, and the leaf thereof for medicine.

The Tree and River of Life are thus emblems of transcendence, renewal and peace.

As subjects for stained glass they have been used surprisingly seldom. Wilhelmina Geddes used the Tree of Life in a memorial window of 1920,[1] stressing the aspect that 'The leaves of the Tree were for the healing of the nations'; but apart from such rare examples, it seems to have been left to John Piper to develop the theme. It is one that is appropriate in a number of different settings. The first time he used it for stained glass was for the chapel of an Anglican Theological College, Ripon College at Cuddesdon in Oxfordshire. Piper supervised the redesigning of the whole chapel interior, and his Tree of Life is in a small, roughly triangular, West Window. Four years later he returned to the theme for the chapel of a boys' boarding school, Christ's College, Christchurch, New Zealand.

The school was founded in 1850, under the Canterbury Church of England Settlement. Although Anglican in origin, the college now takes pupils of other denominations as well, and it seems fitting, therefore, that Piper should have used symbols that could be appreciated by everybody.[2]

There are two roundheaded lancets, each measuring 52 × 18 inches; the glass, dating from 1968, illustrates the Tree of Life and the River of Life. They are closely linked in colour, which is restricted to red and different shades of blue, and in treatment. The Tree, slightly serpentine, rises with red trunk and branches, blue leaves, against a paler blue area resembling water. The River of Life has a similar blue area with leaf-like forms scattered over it, and twin red streams gush either side. The forms are kept simple and dramatic, and the colours symbolic.

In the church of St Giles, Totternhoe, Bedfordshire, the Tree of Life is used again, but in much more painterly form. It is in the East Window (Fig. 75, p. 103) and dates from 1970–1.[3] Here the design of the Tree, with its curving branches and drooping fruits, is spread across the three main lights, creamy

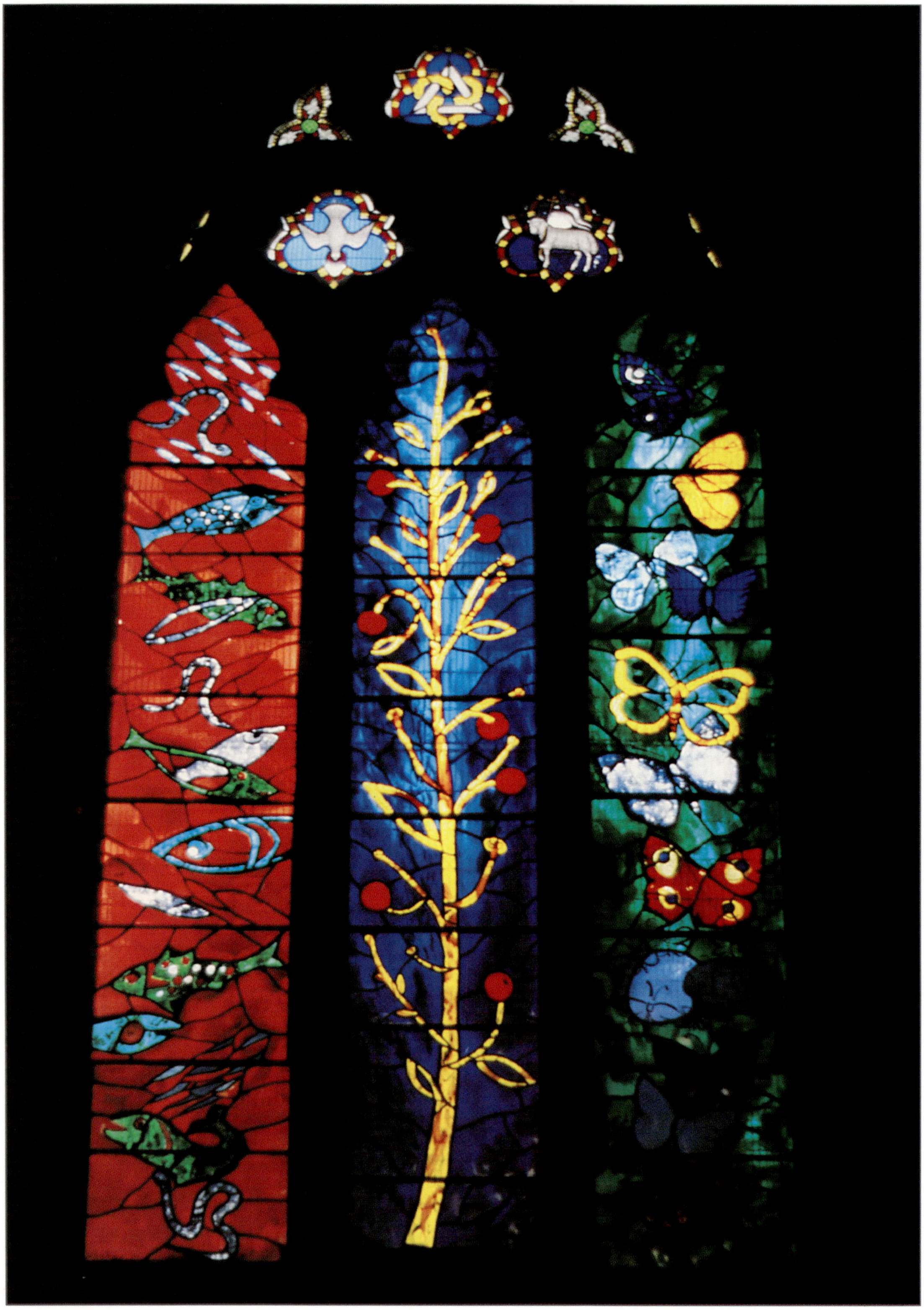

Fig. 77: Nettlebed, St Bartholomew's. East Window (see p. 108)

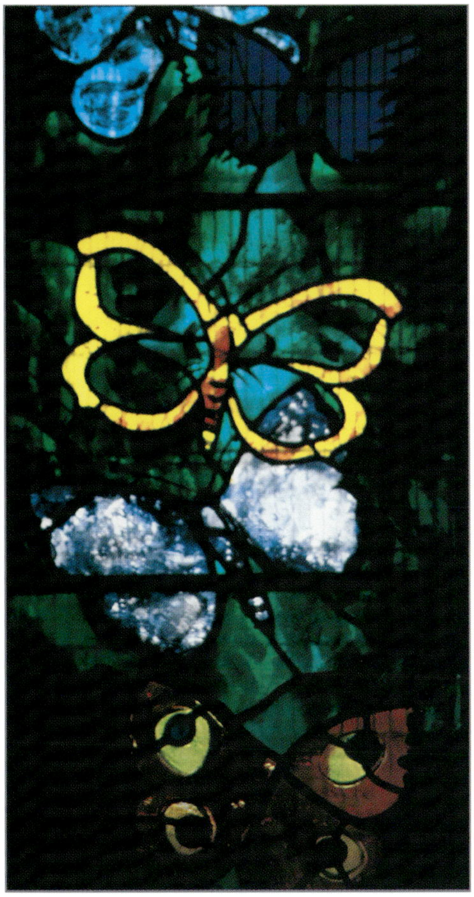

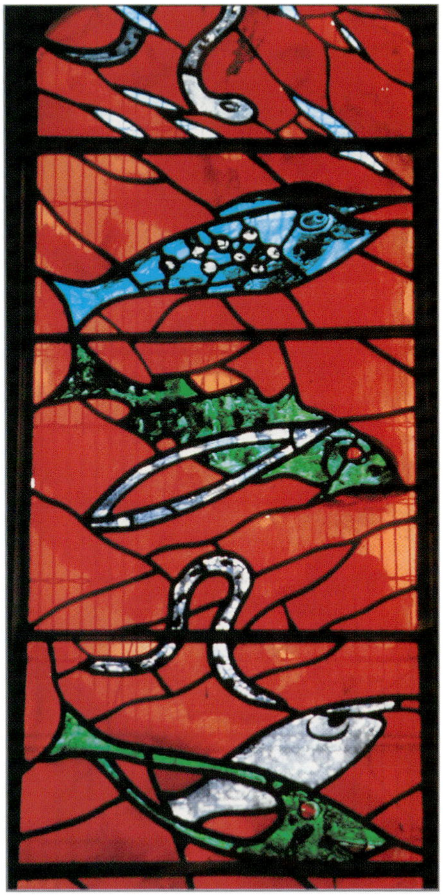

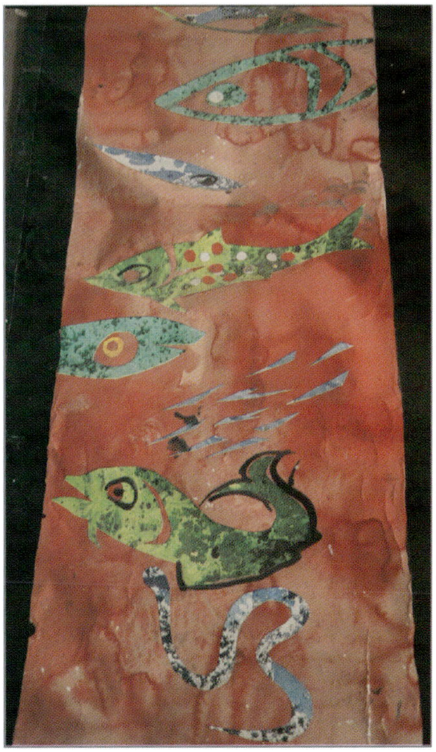

Above, left: Fig. 78: Nettlebed, St Bartholomew's. Detail of butterflies from the East Window. *Above, right:* Fig. 79: Nettlebed, St Bartholomew's. Detail of fish from the East Window. *Right:* Fig. 80: Detail from the cartoon of the fish for Nettlebed, St Bartholomew's, photographed at Fawley Bottom studio (see overleaf)

yellow against textured blue, and five of the fruits bright scarlet. Piper's cartoon for this window treats the three main lights as one; the mullions are represented as dark irregular shadows where the design fades away. Above in the tracery lights are other symbols of the Resurrection: fire, butterflies, and a fine green phoenix rising from its own funeral pyre.

The East Window of St Bartholomew's, Nettlebed, in south Oxfordshire, which Piper designed in 1970,[4] also has butterflies among its symbols of the Resurrection (Figs 77, p. 106 and 78, p. 107). As is pointed out in *Hall's Dictionary of Subjects and Symbols in Art* (Murray, 1974), the butterfly hatching out from its chrysalis was in ancient times regarded as a symbol of the soul rising from the dead body. Similarly it was taken over in Christian iconography that man's life could be represented by the caterpillar, death by the chrysalis, and the resurrected soul by the butterfly.

The Nettlebed window has three principal lights, and the butterflies take up the whole of the right-hand one. Set against a field of rich viridian, they are depicted rising from darkness into light. The lower part of the composition is very shadowy; although no chrysalis is shown, the butterflies here are in quiet colours, mainly muted blue. Then suddenly there is a red Peacock butterfly, others in shades of gold and white, and in order to unify the composition, there is just one which is ultramarine blue (Fig. 78, p. 107). There is a sense of movement throughout the entire panel.

The central light is a Tree of Life. Against a deep blue ground, which pales slightly towards the centre top, the tree is a single yellow stem with side branches terminating in buds, leaves and round red fruits. It is gently curved, but quite static compared with the butterflies, and indeed with the left-hand light. The latter has a background of red, rich carmine/vermilion; a bold and unconventional use of colour, since it represents water. It is moreover a *side* and not a central light, and red by its nature is inclined to dominate. Piper gets away with it, just, because the Tree of Life panel is invested with such serenity. The left-hand panel is busy with little fishes, green and silver (Fig. 79, p. 107). The fish is a very ancient symbol; Christian believers were known as 'pisciculi', or little fishes, and the word for a font, 'piscina', means a fishpond. The injunction to St Peter that he should become a fisher of men implies that men are fish – and indeed the symbol of the fish came to stand for Christ himself. The image in also linked to the River of Life as described in the Book of Ezekiel, chapter 47. Piper's vision has a splendid profusion of different fish, eels and darting minnows.

Piper did one full-size cartoon for the whole window of three lights. It is painted in gouache and, while making due allowance for the possibility of fading, the red against which the fishes swim is a good deal less intense than in the glass (Fig. 80, p. 107). But Piper would probably have found this difference acceptable. As he wrote in *Penrose*, 1949, (thinking then of prints, but it was also to apply to stained glass): 'When a painter's work is reproduced in colour by whatever method, he should ask for a lively parallel to his work, not an imitation of it, in colour or in any other particular.'

Six years after the East Window, Piper designed another window for this church, and again, but in a completely different way, he used the motif of the Tree of Life. It is at the west end of the south aisle, and consists of two main lights with tracery above; the glass is very subtly combined with the architecture. As the author of the *Shell Guide to Oxfordshire* (1938), he will have known well the medieval Jesse Tree window in Dorchester Abbey, where the stem and branches are sculpted masonry, and the interstices stained glass. In a similar way, Piper here used the central mullion to provide the trunk and main branches of his tree (Fig. 81, overleaf). He added golden glass to broaden it at the base, and the minor side branches, also glass, take off from this central stem. Set against a mottled blue, darker below, lighter above, is a luxuriant patterning of leaves and birds. The window was commissioned in memory of Peter Fleming, who sometimes used the nom-de-plume 'Stricks', which is a dialect word for an owl. A pinkish owl presides over the left-hand light, and below that, a bright red exotic bird; in the right light, a hawk above (Fig. 83, overleaf) and a pheasant below. In the top tracery ride the sun and moon, dodging behind the leaves. In the whole story of stained glass, there are few windows so cleverly integrated.

Designing for the other side of the Atlantic was a different matter. In 1973 came the commission to design a window for Washington National Cathedral. As usual, Piper had many other commitments, including copes for St Paul's Cathedral, a tapestry for Rothschild's Bank, and sets for opera: *Death in Venice* for the Aldeburgh Festival, and (together with Edward Piper) *Owen Wingrave* at the Royal Opera House.[5] At Washington Cathedral they wanted a window in the south-west tower as a memorial to Sir Winston Churchill. In Churchill's world broadcast on 27 April 1941, he quoted the lines of Arthur Hugh Clough (1819–61),

> And not by eastern windows only,
> When daylight comes, comes in the light;
> In front the sun climbs slow, how slowly!
> But westward, look, the land is bright.

The reasons for Churchill's choice of quotation are clear. During the darkest hours of the Second World War (1940), Britain had fought alone. Now, in April 1941, she was still alone, but there was some hope of aid from Russia in the east and the United States in the west; the Lend-Lease Bill had just been signed on behalf of the latter, promising 'all aid short of war'. (Full participation from the States came after the Japanese attack on Pearl Harbour the following December.)

'Westward, look, the land is bright' is ostensibly the theme of the window, but in fact what Piper designed is another variation on the Tree of Life. It is a very festive tree, spread across the three-light window; the main stem in the centre and curling branches either side (Fig. 82, overleaf). The whole thing glitters with light, and instead of pendant fruits there are little baubles like balls tossed in the air.

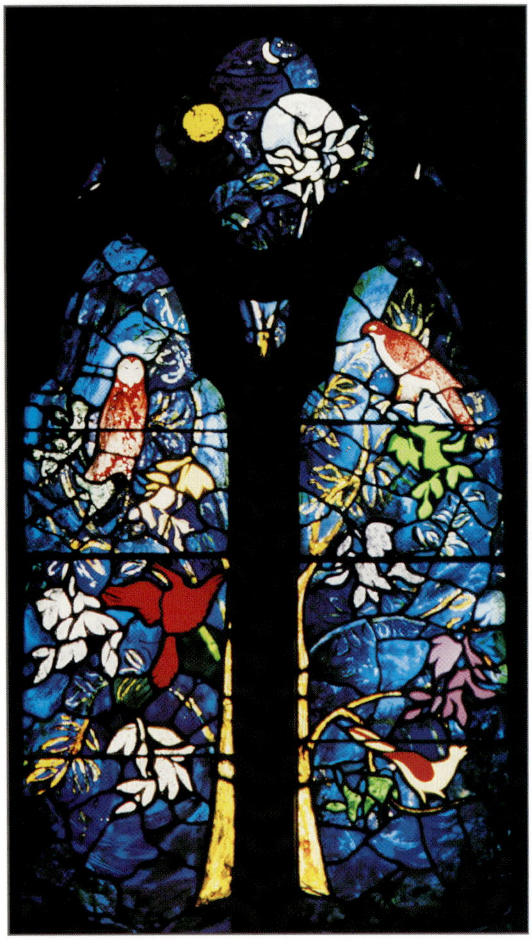

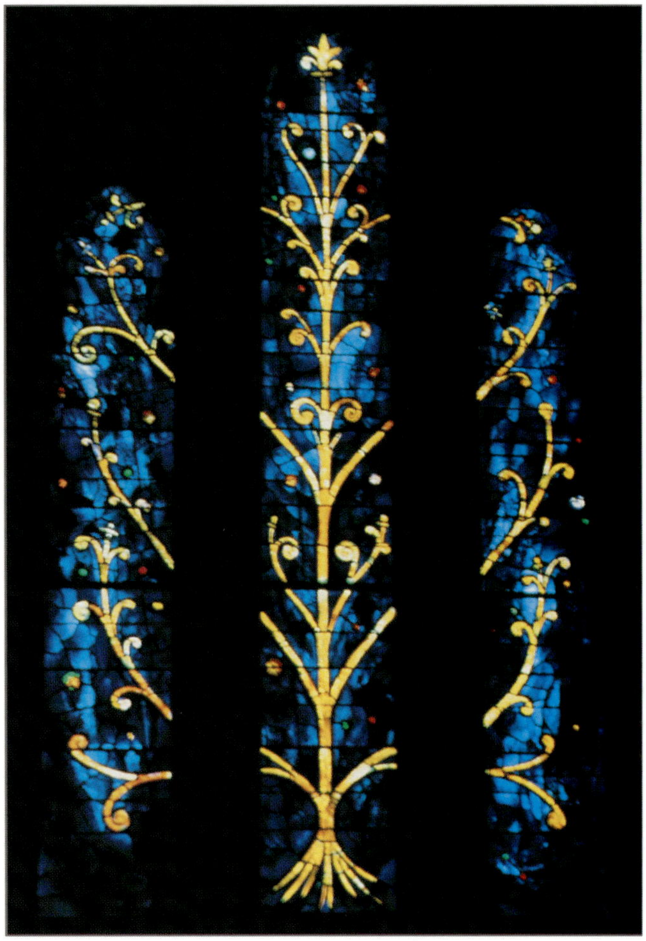

Left: Fig. 81: Nettlebed, St Bartholomew's. South window. *Right:* Fig. 82: USA, Washington Cathedral. The Tree of Life. The Churchill Memorial Window. (Photo courtesy of Washington Cathedral)

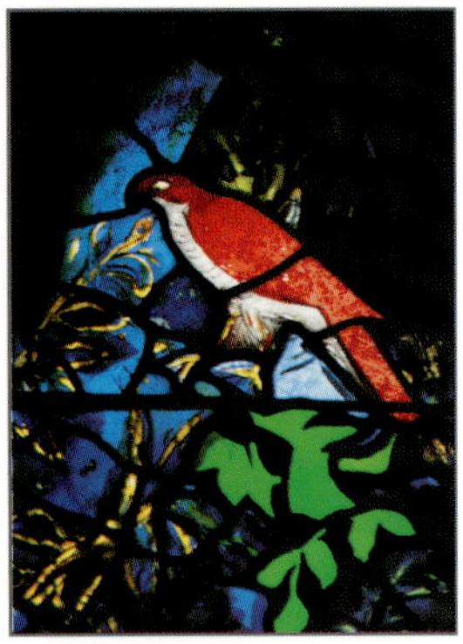

Fig. 83: Nettlebed, St Bartholomew. Detail of hawk from the south window

Piper's design for Washington Cathedral was realized, as indeed were all his windows except the last ones, by Patrick Reyntiens.

The Tree and River of Life were by no means the only symbols Piper was using. Especially where he was familiar with a particular church, he would design glass connected with its dedication.

The church in the village of Sandford St Martin, Oxfordshire, is naturally enough dedicated to St Martin of Tours. A largely medieval church, with the north and south arcades dating from the thirteenth century, it still retains a few fragments of fourteenth-century glass, including an impressive if somewhat decayed Christ in Majesty. What was required of Piper was a window relating the church to its patron saint (Fig. 76, p. 103); his window dates from 1974.

In medieval glass, for instance in the Becket Window in Christ Church Cathedral, Oxford, St Martin is customarily shown dividing his cloak to share it with a beggar. Omitting the figures of both saint and begger, Piper concentrated on the absolute essentials: the hands, the cloak and the knife. At the top of the lancet, one of St Martin's hands is holding the cloak, which is a rich crimson patterned in blue; his other hand holds the dagger to cut it; at the bottom, the hand of the beggar, larger and rougher-looking than those of the saint, reaches up to take the gift. It is a most striking window, the economical design well fitted to its elongated shape.

There is a very beautiful semi-circular window designed by Piper in 1975 for St Mary's, Turville, in Buckinghamshire. It is a set as a tympanum above a walled-up Norman doorway, and it commemorates the nearby church of St Saviour's, Turville Heath, consecrated in 1898 and deconsecrated in 1972. Piper played a large part in the restoration of St Mary's Church. The window shows in exquisite simplicity a hand holding an Easter lily; underneath are written the opening words of the Magnificat, 'My soul doth magnify the Lord' (Fig. 85). Without showing either the Virgin or Gabriel, it expresses, perfectly and lyrically, the Annunciation.

The south aisle window in St Peter's, Wolvercote, on the northern outskirts of Oxford, was designed in 1976 (Fig. 91, p. 115). The theme is Jesus's triumphant entry into Jerusalem, when he was greeted by people waving palm branches. (This account can be found in John 12: 12–13.)

There are two main lights in the window, with a cinquefoil above. Reminiscent of the way in which he treated the 'Feeding of the Five Thousand' window at Eton (Fig. 41, p. 55), Piper has shown a great number of hands reaching upwards, signifying the multitude of people on that first Palm Sunday. Above them wave the palm fronds, their tips meeting in the cinquefoil. Although nearly all the window is in blue, white yellow and green, one of the hands (otherwise deep blue) is outlined in red; a dramatic touch at the top of the left-hand light, it gives the window a 'bite' which it might otherwise lack.

In the same year (1976), Piper returned to the theme of the Tree of Life when designing a tall, narrow lancet for his own parish church, St Mary's, Fawley, in Buckinghamshire.[6] The Tree is a slender, serpentine stem meandering upwards; from the deep green at the base it bursts into a profusion of fruit and flowers, a joyful riot of colour against the rich blue ground (Fig. 84).

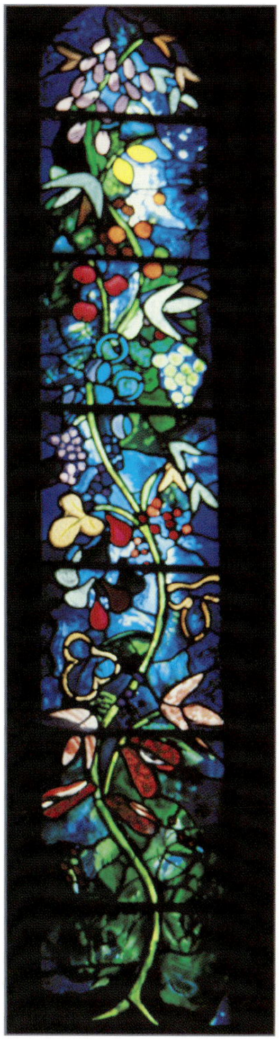

Fig. 84: Fawley, St Mary's. The Tree of Life

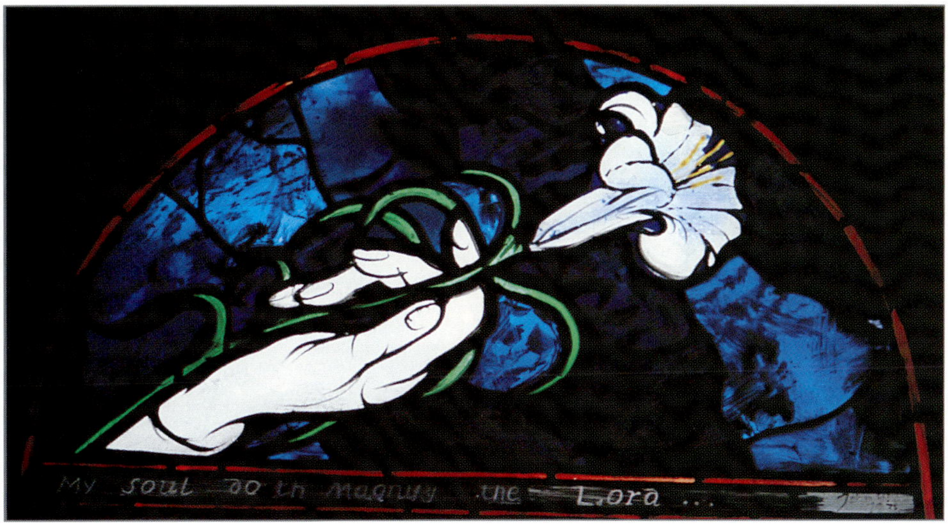

Fig. 85: Turville, St Mary's. Hand with lily

In 1977 came the commission for two windows at Charing Cross Hospital in the Fulham Road. Designing for the chapel of a big London hospital was, one might think, a very different matter. But it must be remembered that the Tree of Life and the River of Life are both subjects connected with healing, and are therefore extremely appropriate in this setting. These are simple recessed rectangular windows on either side as you enter the chapel. The Tree of Life (Fig. 86, p. 114) has, like the one at Fawley, a serpentine trunk, but it has more space to branch out at the side. It is set against a blue ground within a red border. Leaves of different shapes sprout from it, yellow and red fruits; a round-eyed pink bird of great character perches on a twig (Fig. 88, p. 114), another smaller bird below, and little yellow and green ones flutter in the upper branches. In the cartoon, executed in gouache, the birds and fruits are in *papiers collés*; some of the leaves too are in cut-out marbled paper (Fig. 89, p. 114).

The Charing Cross River of Life (Fig. 87, p. 114) is a glowing and sinuous composition. Again we find a dotted border down either side, and within this the general field is of different shades of viridian green. Towards the top is a full-bellied red pot, and from its rim gush twin streams, pale blue streaked with orange-gold. Three fish swim in them, emphasizing the downward flow of the water, and recalling the words in the Book of Ezekiel, 'there shall be a great multitude of fish, because these waters shall come thither: for they shall be healed; and everything shall live whither the river cometh'. Nowhere else is this theme so richly developed.

Perhaps the most ambitious project for stained glass during this period, and, one would guess, probably the most difficult, was for St Andrew's Church, Wolverhampton (Fig. 90, p. 115).

On Sunday 31 May 1964 the old church of St Andrew was irreparably damaged by fire. A new church, for which the architects were Richard Twentyman and Partners, was consecrated by Dr A.S. Reeve, Bishop of Lichfield, on 15 September 1967. It is a wide, spacious, modern church, obviously much used. There is little adornment except the Stations of the Cross in low relief, and a rather odd balcony with no apparent access. But what transforms the interior is the great West Window installed in 1973–4.

The first idea, suggested to Piper by the vicar, was than it should show fire and flame turned into a life-giving force (as at St Mark's, Sheffield; Fig. 50, p. 74). But the enormous width of the window and the nature of the architecture were much better suited to what Piper eventually devised.

Saint Andrew, the brother of Simon Peter, was like him a fisherman; his attributes are generally a saltire cross and a fishing-net. But individual motifs would have looked fussy in so large a window, and what Piper designed was nothing less than a vision of the whole sea. The idiom he used is similar to Bledlow Ridge (Fig. 74, p. 102) and one of the windows at Wellingborough (Fig. 51, p. 75). There are seven lights, and the window dominates the whole of the west end of the church. It was a bold idea, virtually unprecedented, to base so large an expanse of stained glass on only one colour: blue. There are, of course, variations in tone; the end panel on the right, and large parts of the first three on the left are a richly textured ultramarine; pale aquamarine occupies much of the central part of the window; there are areas, mainly horizontal shapes (apart from a half-disc like the moon), which are so dark as to appear almost black. Across the pale colours there is lively calligraphy in black, and across the dark an effusion of forms in white outline – fish, spirals, bubbles, wave-shapes, a star.

The use of just one basic colour gives the window a sense of serenity; the use of contrasting line invests it with life.

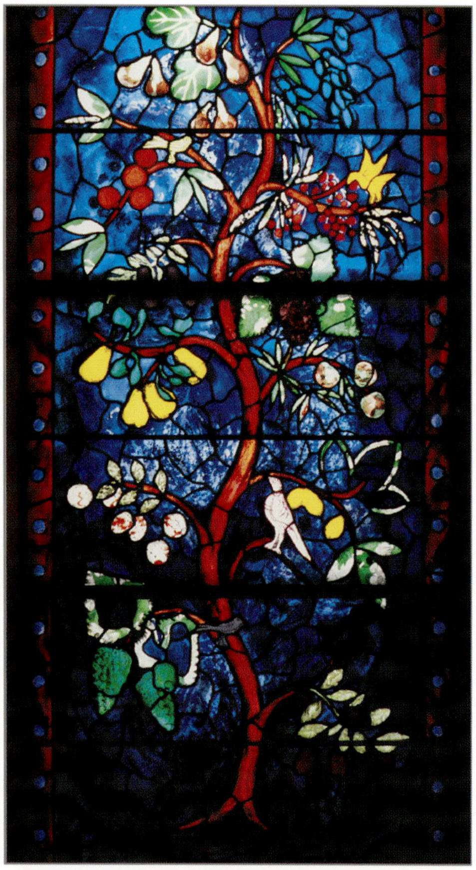

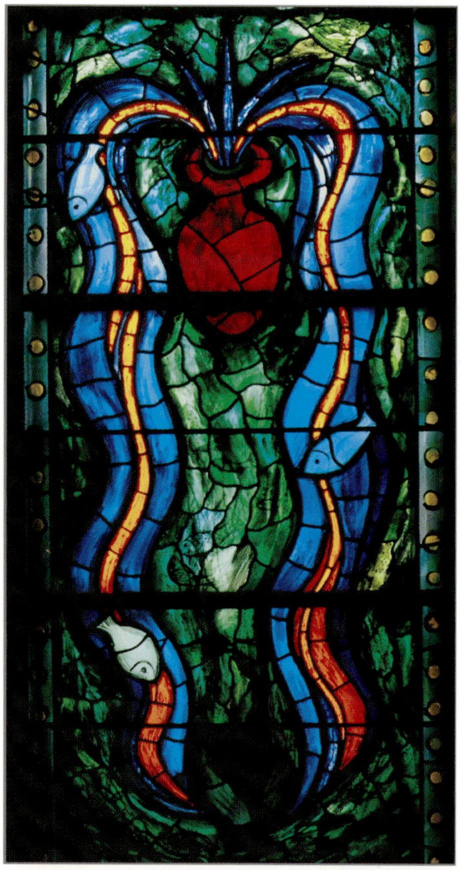

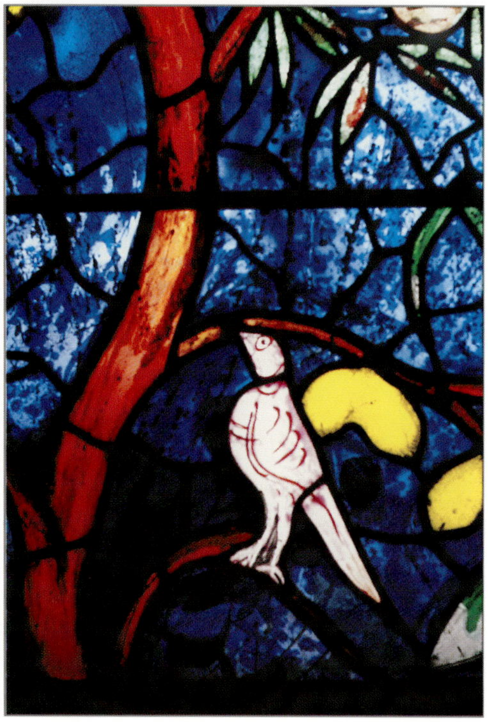

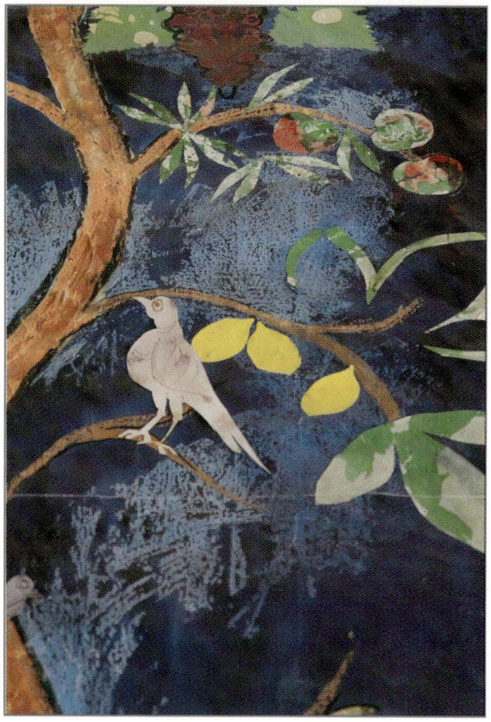

Above, left: Fig. 86: London, Charing Cross Hospital Chapel. The Tree of Life. *Above, right:* Fig. 87: London, Charing Cross Hospital Chapel. The River of Life. *Below, left:* Fig. 88: Detail from the Tree of Life. *Below, right:* Fig. 89: Detail from the cartoon for the Tree of Life (see p. 112)

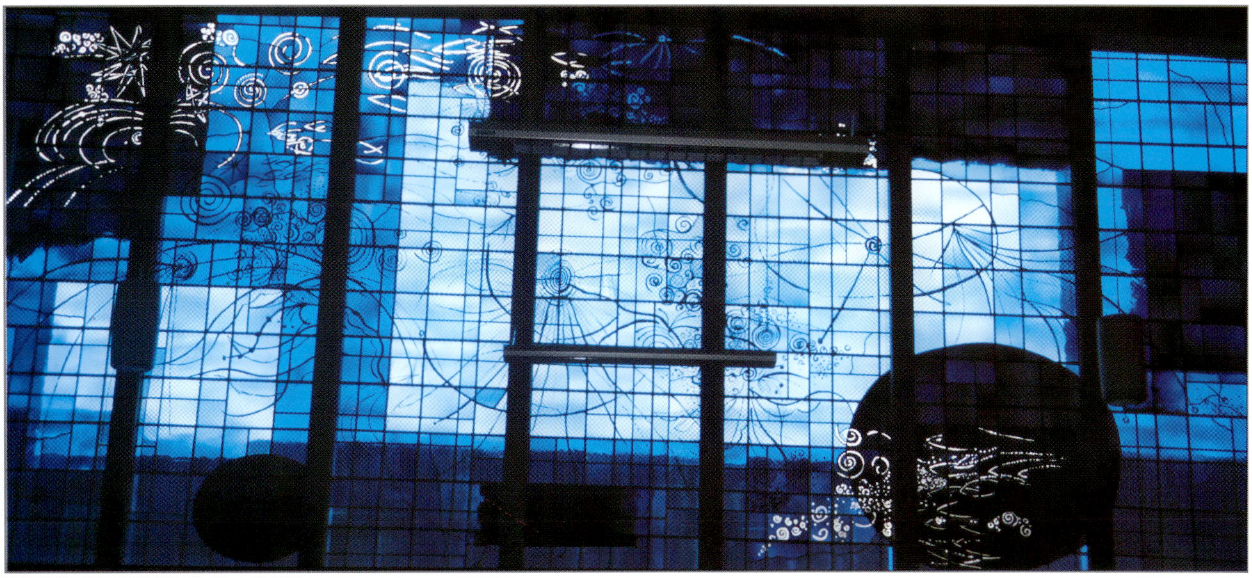

Fig. 90: Wolverhampton, St Andrew's. West Window (see p. 112)

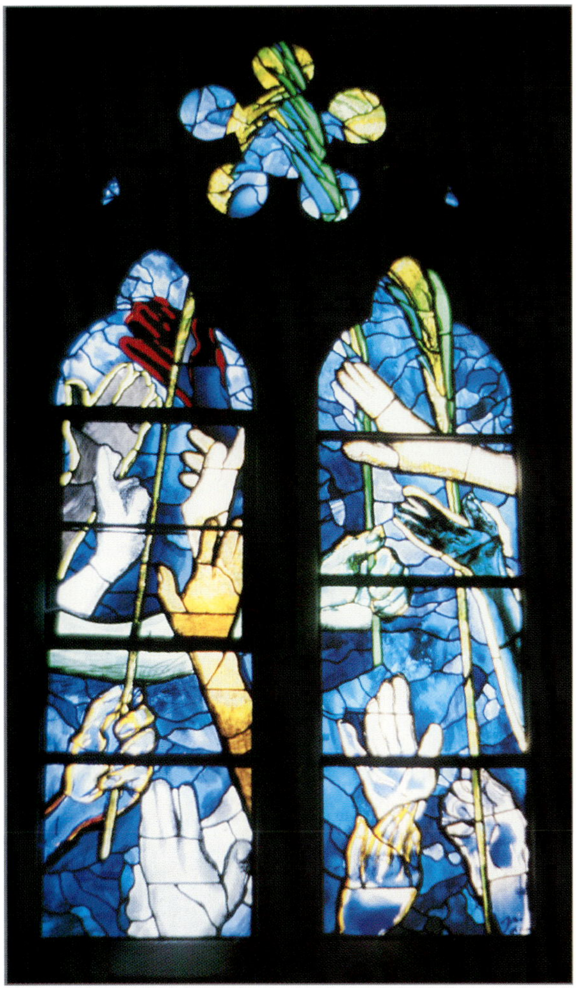

Fig. 91: Wolvercote, St Peter's. Palm Sunday Window (see p. 111)

CHAPTER ELEVEN

A FREE HAND: PIPER'S DEVELOPED STYLE

On calling an artist Romantic: 'to me the word is laudatory; its quality is warming, encouraging, enriching, and life-enhancing'.

Peter Pears[1]

If one must attach labels to artists, I suppose that which adheres most easily to John Piper is the word 'Romantic'. As he was much aware, there have been times when it has been a term of abuse. He sprang with agility to its defence by analyzing what the word actually means:

> Well, Constable may not be romantic; but if not how do you account for 'The world is wide, no two days are alike, nor even two hours, neither were there ever two leaves of a tree alike since the creation of the world' and a thousand or so remarks of the same kind?. . .
>
> To me, dreams are *not* as romantic as bits of real experience. . . . The value of abstract painting to me, and the value of Surrealist painting to me are (paradoxically if you like) that they are *classical* exercises, not romantic expressions. They are disciplines – even dreams can be disciplinarian – which open a road to one's heart – but they are not the heart itself. I doubt if under their complete domination one masterpiece will ever be created. . . . The result can be hung perhaps in Cork Street, but not hung against one's heart.[2]

Diverse as were the many fields of art in which Piper worked, he remained one and the same person. If his profoundest expressions as a painter were based on his personal perception of reality – not reality in any detached sense, but something so acutely observed that it becomes a subjective experience – then it is not surprising that sooner or later this would become also his approach to stained glass.

By the late seventies and early eighties, Piper had very much found his own voice. But just as a composer of music has to rely on instrumentalists to interpret his work (for composers are not necessarily performers), so Piper had to rely upon artist-craftsmen to translate his ideas into glass. First and foremost, it was Patrick Reyntiens. Just as Reyntiens had learnt his craft from Joseph (Eddie)

Nuttgens,[3] in his studio at Piggotts Hill, North Dean, so he in his turn was to pass these skills on to others. Together with his wife, the painter Anne Bruce, Reyntiens ran an art study centre first at Burleighfield House, Loudwater, High Wycombe, and then in 1977 he founded a new centre at Old Church School, Windsor End, Beaconsfield. This was a light and roomy building with three large halls. Two types of course were offered: a year's postgraduate course for professionals (restricted in number to six students), and a three-week basic course for beginners. As Reyntiens explained:

> Contrary to what is generally thought, the teaching of stained glass is one of considerable complexity. The craft is difficult enough, but the placing of the craft knowledge into context – so that the result will truly be art – is particularly difficult.[4]

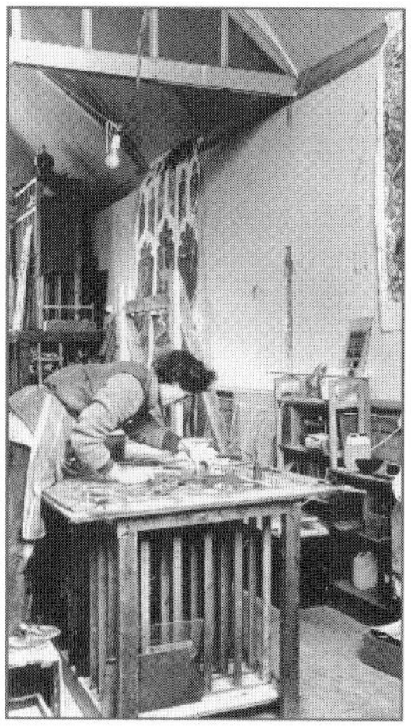

Fig. 92: Interior of Beaconsfield studio, with David Wasley. (Photo. courtesy of David Wasley)

Students may evolve into assistants, assistants may evolve into artist-craftsmen in their own right. At the centre in Beaconsfield the larger projects (such as the glass designed by Piper for Robinson College, Cambridge, Figs 111, p. 130 and 112, p. 131) would involve not only Reyntiens but a team of four skilled craftsmen, Joe Nuttgens (one of the twelve children of Eddie Nuttgens), David Wasley, Phil Kenchatt and David Williams, all of them working under Reyntiens's direction (Fig. 92). Reyntiens being much occupied with teaching (he was Head of Fine Art at the Central School of Art, London), with designing his own windows, and with writing, Joe Nuttgens took over the management of the studio. He, and to a greater extent David Wasley, both skilled artist-craftsmen in their own right, undertook the interpretation of several of the Piper windows after the Beaconsfield studio closed.[5] But whoever was entrusted with the realization of Piper's designs, especially at this stage when they were so vivid and so personal an expression, had no easy task. Reyntiens wrote of Piper: 'No painter keeps to the possibilities of stained glass better than John Piper, yet at the same time no painter stretches his executive interpreter more cruelly.'[6]

The greatest of the enterprises in this period was undoubtedly the glass for Robinson College, Cambridge, (1978–80) but it may be useful to consider some of the smaller projects first.

There was an extraordinary commission for Thorpe Tilney in Lincolnshire (Figs 93–6, overleaf). The owner of the house, F.M. Stockdale, wanted for his garden a pavilion which would double up as a small concert hall and a changing-room for the adjoining outdoor swimming pool (originally there were to be two buildings, but they were combined into one). The architect was Francis Johnson of Bridlington, and the finished pavilion, constructed from bricks from the garden wall at Leadenham Hall, was based on a temple of Castor and Pollux. It is a small square building, roofed with pantiles and crowned with an octagonal turret. Sometime between 1975 and 1977, Stockdale wrote to Piper inviting him to design glass for the four semi-circular windows in the turret, the subject to be the life of St Paul. In January 1977 Piper wrote to accept.

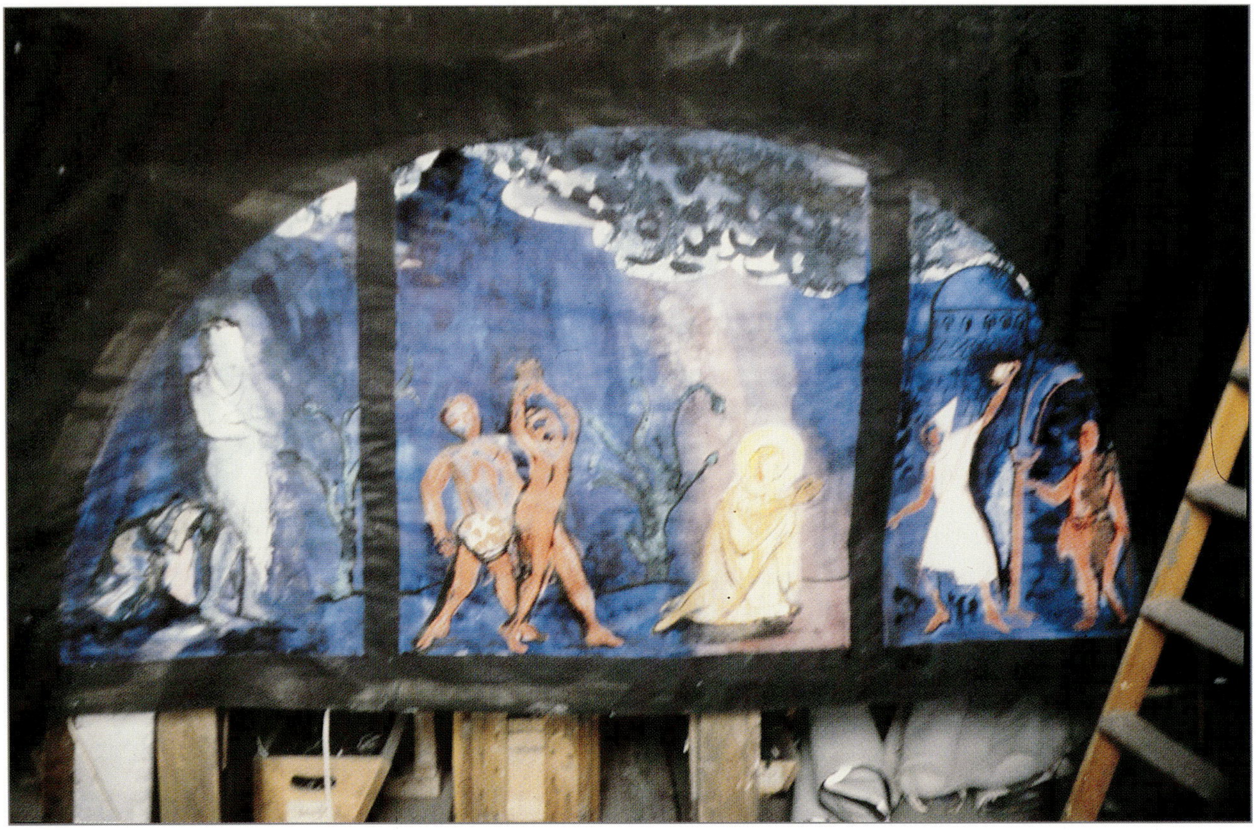

Fig. 93: Thorpe Tilney. Cartoon for the Stoning of Stephen. (Photo. courtesy of David Wasley)

Fig. 94: Thorpe Tilney. The Stoning of Stephen

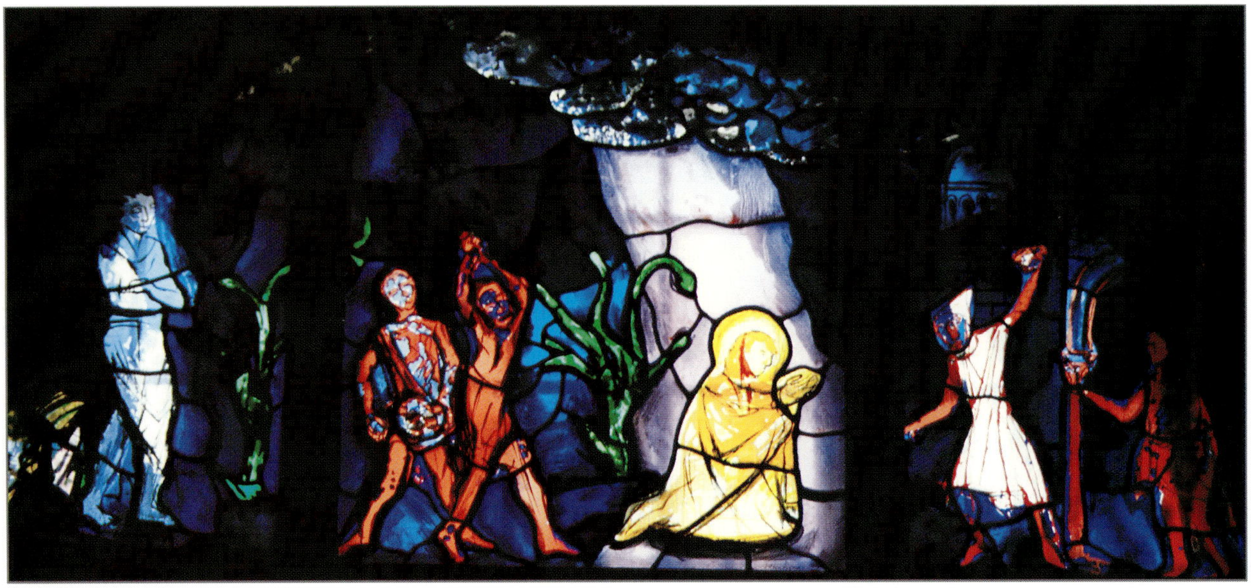

The story of St Paul begins with the stoning of St Stephen. (The reference is to Acts 7:58: 'And cast him out the city, and stoned him; and the witnesses laid down their clothes at a young man's feet, whose name was Saul.') It will be remembered how impressed Piper was with the medieval panel at Grateley depicting this scene (Fig. 2, p. 2). In his own glass, Stephen kneels, a tranquil figure with the golden mantle of sanctity about him, while lurid figures in scarlet are in the act of hurling stones. Meanwhile, Paul, then called Saul, stands nonchalantly by, a grey-blue figure with arms folded, witnessing, but unmoved by, the dreadful scene (Fig. 94).

The next window depicts the conversion of St Paul on the road to Damascus (Acts 9: 3–4: 'And as he journeyed, he came near Damascus; and suddenly there shined round about him a light from heaven: And he fell to the earth, and heard a voice saying unto him, Saul, Saul, why persecutest thou me?') Piper designed a dynamic scene in cool colours. The light from heaven descends in pointed rays, Paul's horse rears up, silhouetted against it, and Paul is thrown to the ground. The composition has a strong central focus, emphasizing the drama of the scene.

Then we come to St Paul shipwrecked on Melita or Malta (Acts 28: 1–6). Together with other prisoners, Paul was being taken to Rome, where he was to stand trial, when the boat was shipwrecked. The islanders (whom we see grouped together on the right; Fig. 96) treated him kindly and lit a bonfire. Paul, gathering sticks for it, was bitten by a snake; unharmed, he shook the creature off into the flames – convincing the credulous islanders of his divinity. Piper's interpretation has great fluidity of line. Paul crouches before the flickering bonfire; the sea is troubled and dark, the sky an ominous green, the sun engulfed in yellow cloud. A black ship is tossed on the waves. The whole scene is vibrant with movement and colour.

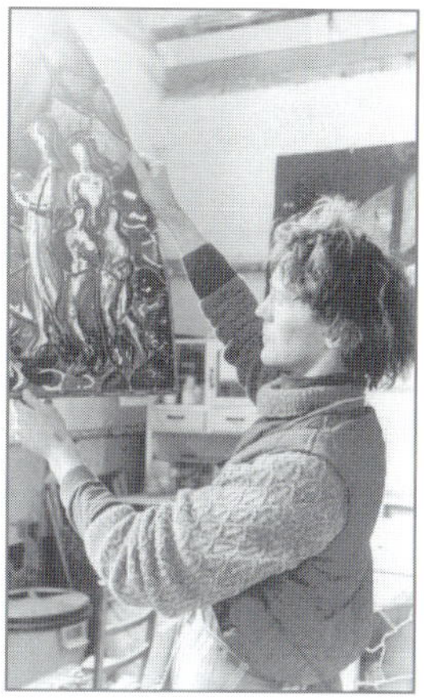

Fig. 95: David Wasley inspecting the Thorpe Tilney panel. (Photo. courtesy of David Wasley)

Fig. 96: Thorpe Tilney. St Paul shipwrecked on Malta

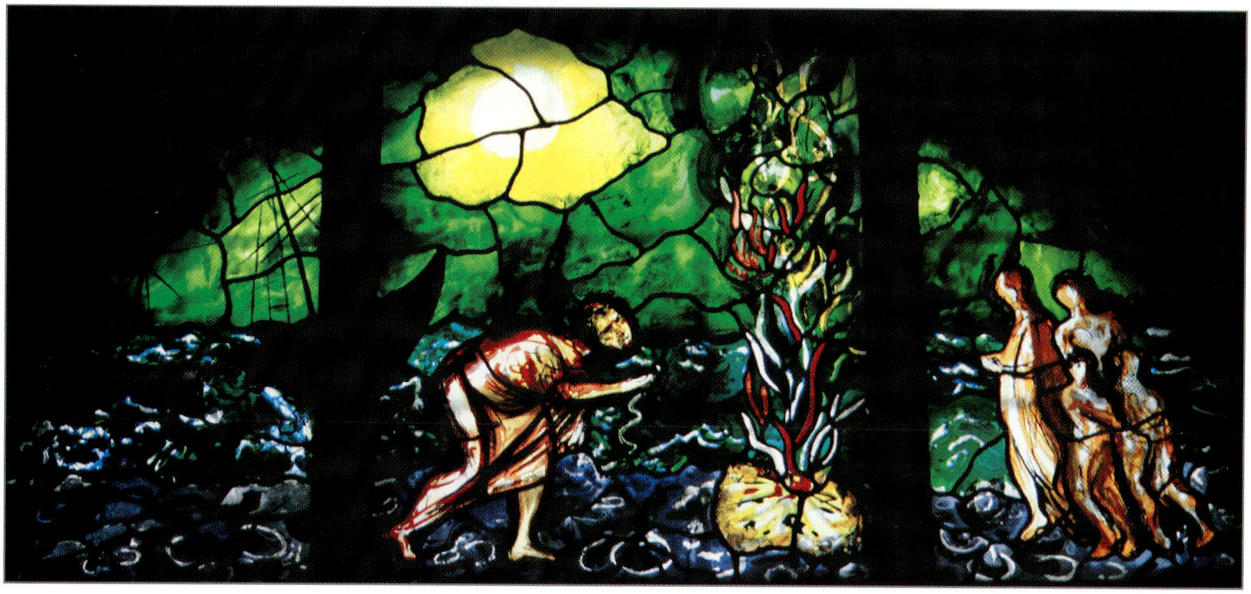

Finally we come to the beheading of St Paul. He is said to have been martyred in Rome on the same day as St Peter, but because Paul was a Roman citizen he was not crucified but executed with a sword. In Piper's window, Paul's decapitated head lies staring in a sea of red; and his blood, white not red, spurts up in three jets, which may symbolize Faith, Hope and Charity – the traditional site of his execution is called the 'Tre Fontane' (Three Fountains). Behind are black verticals, like prison bars, against blue, and pointing from above, the hand of God.

The four scenes are conceived with great drama, and beautifully executed; nevertheless it must be admitted that they are something of a surprise. 'What an extraordinary idea to have the beheading of St Paul next to your swimming pool!' exclaimed Myfanwy Piper to me.[7]

On the face of it, it may seem almost equally surprising to find opera depicted in a church, as it is in the parish church of St Peter and St Paul at Aldeburgh, Suffolk (Fig. 99, p. 122). Piper designed the window as a memorial to his good friend and fellow-collaborator for many years, Benjamin Britten. From 1947, with *The Rape of Lucretia*, he designed the sets for all Britten's operas written for stage performance; and later, beginning with *The Turn of the Screw*, Myfanwy Piper was their librettist. Britten shared with the Pipers an enthusiasm for exploring old churches, and in 1970 they, together with Peter Pears, set off for a working holiday in France – discussing their next joint project (*Death in Venice*) and admiring Romanesque sculpture.

Piper's memorial to his friend (1979) is a deeply personal and evocative work.[8] Interestingly, the three operas it features, *The Prodigal Son*, *Curlew River*, and *The Burning Fiery Furnace*, all with libretti by William Plomer, were written for church performance, so were the only ones for which Piper had not designed the sets. The window therefore fills the only gap in their working relationship.

It is composed of three main lights. In the left-hand one, we find the return of the Prodigal Son; the boy kneels at the feet of his bearded father, who embraces him. The composition is based on the left-hand half of Rembrandt's painting of the same subject, of about 1668–9, in the Hermitage in St Petersburg. Piper's cartoon is mainly in reds and purples, apart from the clothes of the Prodigal Son, which are blue-grey; in the finished window, however, there is as well as the red brick wall behind, quite a strong blue in part of the background, linking it more positively with the blue in the tracery above.

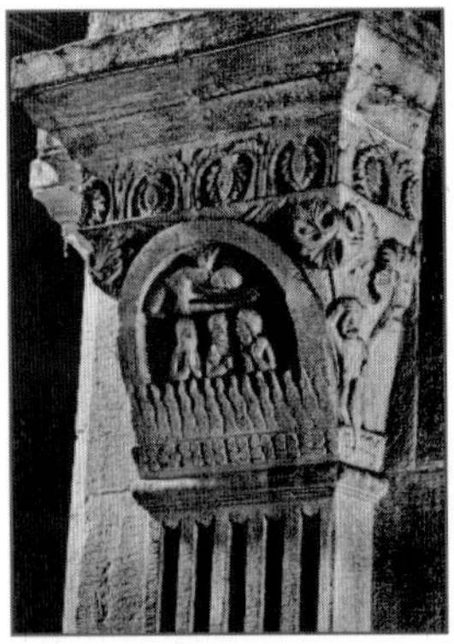

Fig. 97: Capital at Autun. Source for the Burning Fiery Furnace in the Britten Memorial Window, Aldeburgh. (Photographer unknown)

The right-hand light shows the Burning Fiery Furnace. The story is in the Book of Daniel, chapter 3; Daniel's companions, Shadrach, Mesach and Abed-Nego, were cast into the furnace for refusing to worship a golden image of King Nebuchadnezzar, but because of their faith they emerged unscathed. The three men are shown in the glow of the furnace, golden flames licking upwards. Above them hovers a protecting angel. The design is derived from a Romanesque capital, carved by Giselbertus, at Autun (Fig. 97), although Piper's figures are rather more elongated, and the flames are made part of the composition, instead of forming a sort of frieze as at Autun. Both this, and the Prodigal Son, have a red roundheaded arch above.

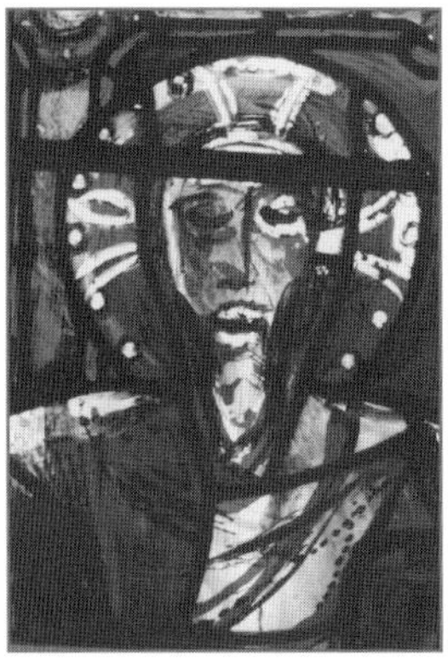

Fig. 98: Ramsgate, St Lawrence College. Detail of tracery from the East Window. (Photo. courtesy of David Wasley)

In the original design, done before the cartoon (shown in the Tate Gallery Exhibition of 1983–4), neither the Rembrandt nor the Autun reference is present. The Prodigal Son is shown kneeling sideways in front of his father, who puts one hand on his shoulder and gazes out abstractedly. The Burning Fiery Furnace has the three figures and the flames, but no angel above them.

The central light is of the Curlew River (Fig. 101, p. 123). The story is based on a Japanese Noh play, *Sumidagawa*, the plot of which involves a grief-stricken mother seeking her lost son at a river crossing. She is taken across by the ferryman, who tells the passengers of a shrine on the opposite bank. This is the grave of a young boy who died of torture in captivity the year before, and the woman realizes that this is her son. The spirit of the boy then descends and comforts her. Piper's interpretation omits any figures; he has concentrated on the shape of the river winding between green banks, seen through a lattice of bamboo branches;[9] above looms the pale shape of the spirit-bird. (In the cartoon this is a collage cut out of marbled paper; Fig. 100, p. 123.)

The glass in the tracery lights serves to link these three disparate themes. Falling leaves, a crescent moon and rising flames all set against deep blue give this wonderful window a surprising sense of unity.

The window was made in the studio of Patrick Reyntiens at Beaconsfield. In 1981 came an unusual collaboration between him and Piper. This was for the East Window of the Chapel of St Lawrence College, Ramsgate, Kent.[10] It is a window of complex symbolism. Very briefly, it is on the theme of 'Let there be Light', the Risen Christ appearing above the firmament. The main part of the window was designed, as well as made, by Patrick Reyntiens; only the Christ figure in the central tracery light was designed by Piper, and its sensitive interpretation into glass is the work of David Wasley (Fig. 98, above). Reyntiens's part of the window is in different shades of blue, much of it fairly pale, with a good deal of white and gold. Piper's section, which is based on Romanesque sculpture (in particular, it seems, on a figure at the pilgrimage church of Beaulieu, Corrèze), is much richer in tone and colour, predominantly a deep indigo.

This nature of collaboration, one artist designing one part of a window, and another another, was an experiment they did not repeat. The vision of each of them was so different that it was hard to achieve a totally balanced and unified result.

The window of the Annunciation (1982) (Fig. 102, p. 123) at the church of St Peter and St Paul, Abington, on the outskirts of Northampton, is to my mind much better integrated. Piper based his design principally on a painting attributed to Botticelli or his circle, in the Uffizi Gallery, Florence. In particular, the sinuous figure of the Virgin, in the right light of the Abington window, with the modest positioning of the hands, is very similar. Unusually, the Virgin is dressed in red. Meanwhile, other influences may be found in the urgent figure of Gabriel flying with his message. Another Annunciation in the Uffizi, by Alessio Baldovinetti, depicts the angel, like Piper's, dressed in russet red, and arriving with the same urgency. The movement of the angel is similar too to a painting by Melozzo da Forlì, also in the Uffizi.

In almost all the interpretations of the Annunciation in Early Renaissance art

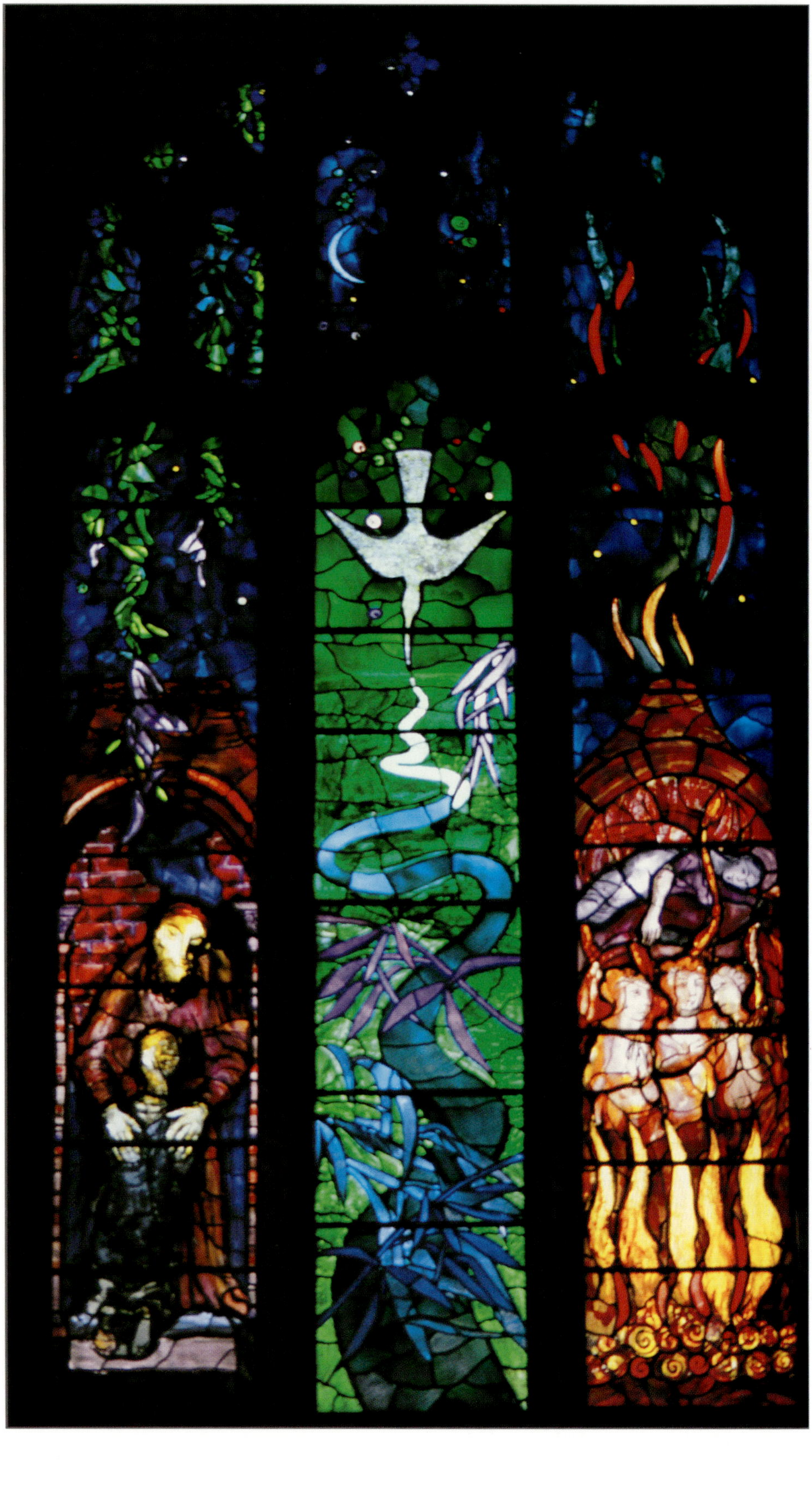

Fig. 99: Aldeburgh, St Peter and St Paul's. The Benjamin Britten Memorial Window (see pp. 120–1)

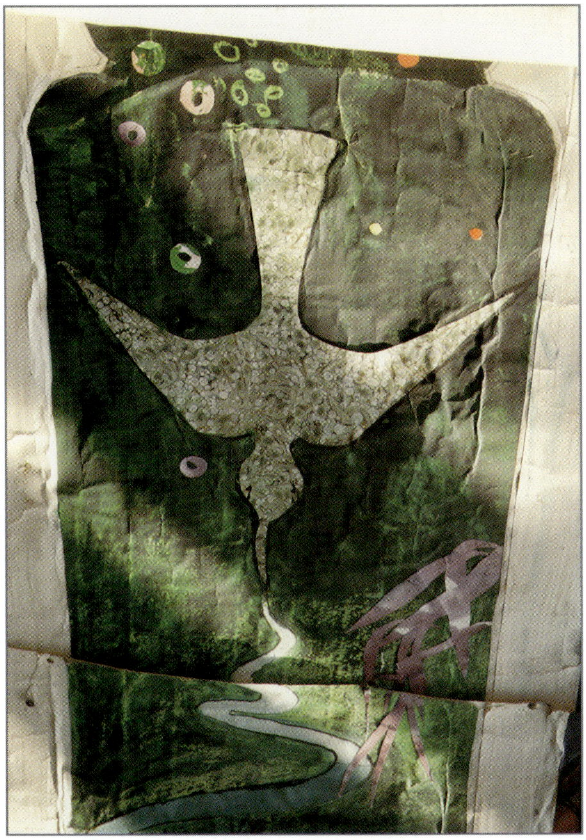

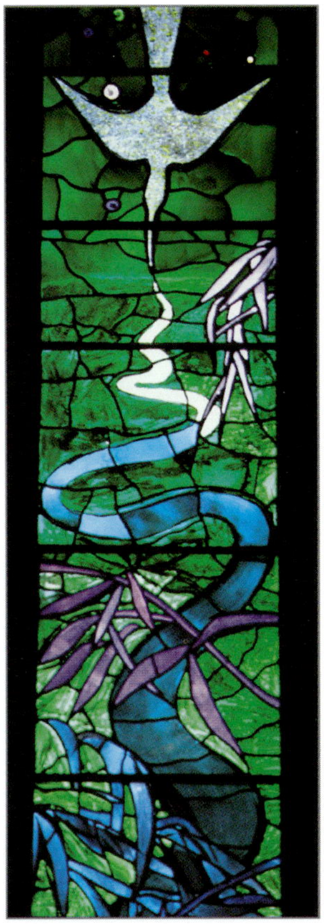

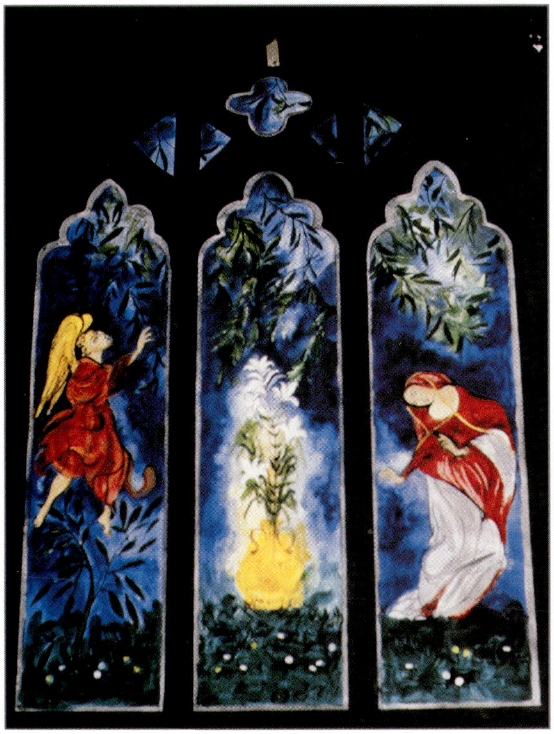

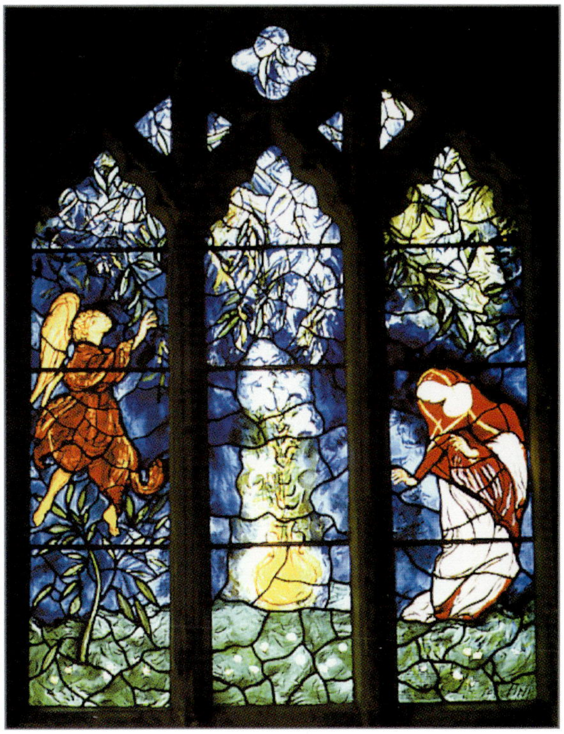

Above, left: Fig. 100: Aldeburgh. The Benjamin Britten Memorial Window. Cartoon showing detail of Curlew River. *Above, right:* Fig. 101: Aldeburgh. The Benjamin Britten Memorial Window. Detail from Curlew River. *Below, left:* .Fig. 102: Abington, St Peter and St Paul's. The Annuciation Window. *Below, right:* Fig. 103: Abington, St Peter and St Paul's. Cartoon for the Annuciation Window. (Photo. courtesy of David Wasley)

there is a gap, a distance, between the Virgin Annunciate and the Archangel Gabriel; this gap may be said to represent the gulf between the human and the divine, and it may (as in Leonardo's) be very expressive. But in stained glass to leave a gap simply would not do. Piper was at first puzzled as to how to fill it; then he decided that 'it must be a lily' – symbol of purity – and so it is: a radiant Easter lily in a golden vase. The window is full of texture and fluid lines. The way the leading is done in the central light does not correspond with the shapes of rose and lily, but suggests rather the trunk of a tree – indeed it branches out to *be* a tree when it gets to the tracery.[11]

Piper was now working with the greatest degree of fluency and individuality. This naturally applies also to his designs for secular glass. Here he was at liberty to revert to one of his favourite themes, the Green Man. He used it as an expression of the four seasons in several works: a panel for a private collection in London (Rayne House, 1981); a panel for an exhibition at Chartres (1982); and four roundels for Ipswich School Library (1981).

The panel for Rayne House (Fig. 104, p. 126) has the four seasons arranged in a horizontal row: first Winter, staring out from a red ground interlaced with a network of twigs; then Spring, divided lengthwise into dark blue and yellow; Summer is similarly divided, lips and eyes outlined in red amid a profusion of leaf forms; finally Autumn is a leaf-mask, yellow against purple.

The Chartres panel (Fig. 105, p. 126) is rather more complex.[12] It was shown in the exhibition 'New British Glass and Vitrail Français Contemporain' (20 June to 31 October 1982) in the International Stained Glass Centre at Chartres. The work was catalogued as 'The Four Seasons represented as foliate heads, symbols of fertility and the renewal of life'. Here the four seasons are arranged two and two, Spring and Summer above, Autumn and Winter below. At this time Piper's foliate heads were wider in form, more spread out, than they had been in the sixties, though three out of the four here are still divided longitudinally into different zones of colour. Spring is split into dark green and light green (but with one orange zone), with a tracery of green leaves; Summer is split into areas of dark blue and warm orange; Autumn is again a leaf-mask, delineated in yellow on a russet ground; while Winter has areas of cold, subtle colour, one merging into another, and the outlined face peering out from the midst.

For the gallery of the Library at Ipswich School (Suffolk) (Figs 106–9, p. 127), Piper designed four circular windows, one for each corner. The theme of the Green Man is used to symbolize at the same time the four seasons, the four elements, and the four ages of man.[13] The north-east window, brightest in the early morning, denotes spring, youth and the element of earth (Fig. 106); a powerful yellowish face looks out from a mass of green which round the edges merges into purple, red and black. (In the cartoon the colours are slightly more muted, olive rather than viridian as the glass is, but still the same compelling design.) The south-east window, summer, brightest in the later morning, denotes air and adulthood (Fig. 107); from the central area of rich blue a face looks out, wide-eyed and outlined in white; around this is a profusion of different flowers. Autumn, the south-west window, lit in the afternoon, signifies maturity and the element of fire (Fig. 108). It is a leaf-mask, but the leaves have become radiating flames from which the eyes gaze out determinedly but with a touch of sadness; orange, red and yellow are set against quieter tones. Winter, in the north-west corner, signifies old age and the element of water (Fig. 109). Apart from the brilliant red of the mouth, the window is nearly all blues and greens, streaked with black; the eyes look out apprehensively.

The roundels were made by or under the direction of Patrick Reyntiens, assisted by David Wasley. Comparatively few people, one imagines, have the joy of seeing them; yet what superb things they are, Piper at his most individual and expressive.

It would be wrong to forget the width of John Piper's interests. Writing in *To John Piper on his Eightieth Birthday*, his friend the archaeologist Stuart Piggott headed his piece 'A Disciple of Leland', and wrote:

> And now more recently he has executed a window for the Museum of the Wiltshire Archaeological Society in Devizes, an explicit statement of Wiltshire antiquities in a Wiltshire landscape which does indeed take us back to Aubrey and Stukeley in a vision of the past which while uniquely his own does not forget its forebears.

Piper wrote the following note about his involvement at the time: 'I have been interested in the archaeology of Wiltshire since my early teens . . . I was delighted to be given the opportunity to include some of the more evident archaeological features of this much loved area.'[14]

He had belonged to the Wiltshire Archaeological and Natural History Society for many years, and was a close friend of the chairman at that time, Bonar Sykes. The window (Fig. 110, p. 130) was financed by the museum with the help of a grant from the Victoria and Albert Museum Purchase Grant Fund. It is sited in the Picture Gallery, and dates from 1982 when this extension to the museum was made.[15]

The window may be said to epitomize the landscape and archaeology of Wiltshire. In the foreground are seen a collection of Bronze Age objects (all to be found in the museum) appearing as if they had been discovered in an excavated barrow. Paul Robinson, the Museum Curator, lists them as follows:

> The amber necklace is of Early Bronze Age (Wessex Culture) date and was excavated by William Cunnington in the barrow Upton Lovell G2e. The pots shown are of Early, Middle and Late Bronze Age date. The larger is 'the Stonehenge Urn', a Middle Bronze Age Deverel-Rimbury barrel urn from the barrow Amesbury G3, again excavated by William Cunnington. It is one of the finest Bronze Age vessels from the British Isles. The centre one is a late Bronze Age globular urn from an unknown barrow near Salisbury. That on the left – I think – is the Early Bronze Age enlarged food vessel from the barrow Wilsford G65.

In the left-hand corner of the window we find the woolly-headed thistle, peculiar to this part of the country; and running from this in a prominent

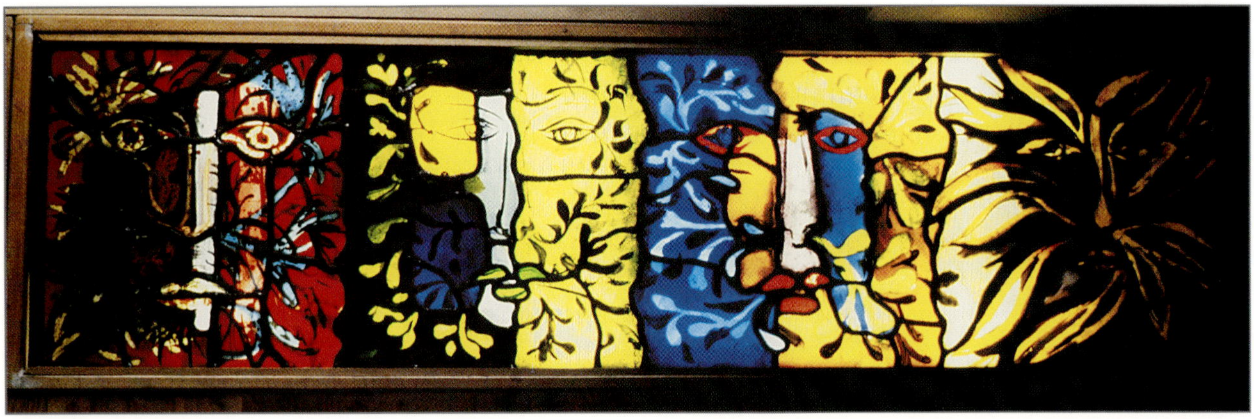

Fig. 104: London, Rayne House. The Four Seasons (see p. 124). (Photo. courtesy of David Wasley)

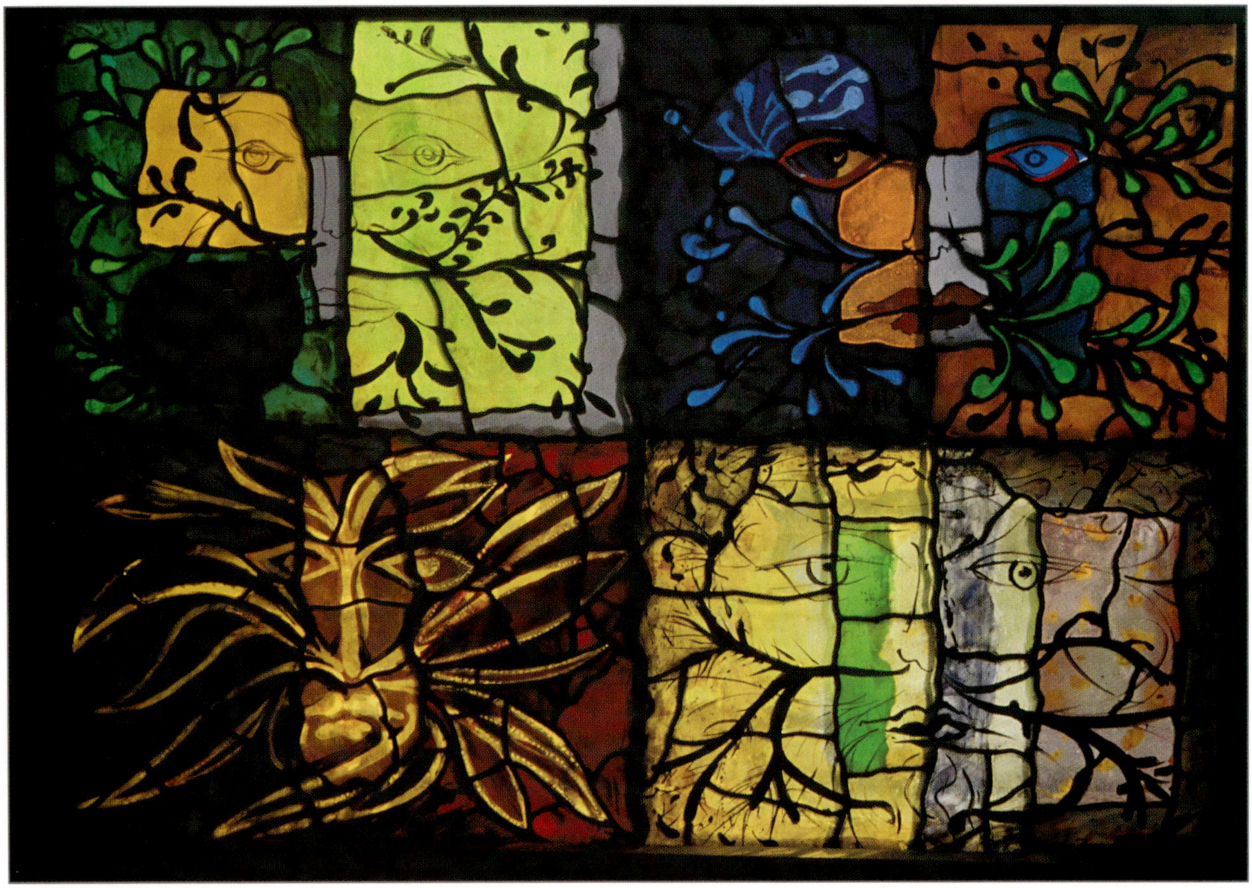

Fig. 105: Panel designed for the exhibition at Chartres. The Four Seasons (see p. 124). (Coll. Myfanwy Piper)

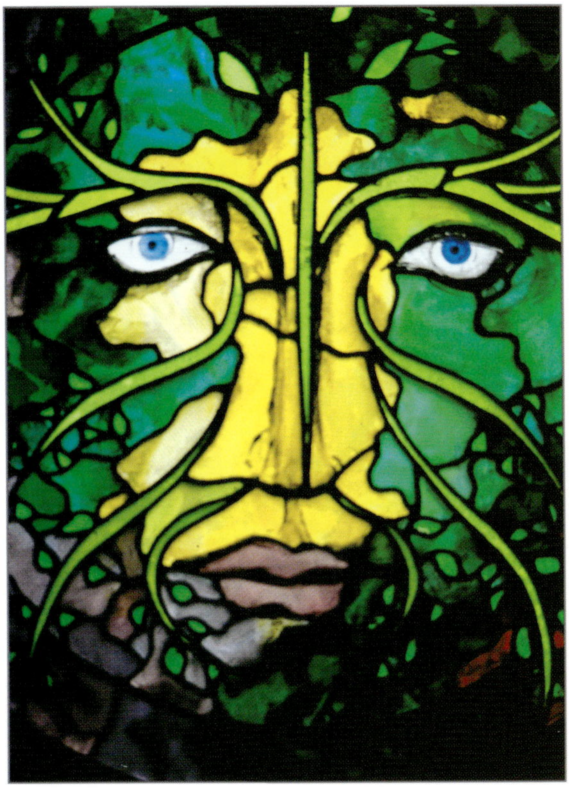

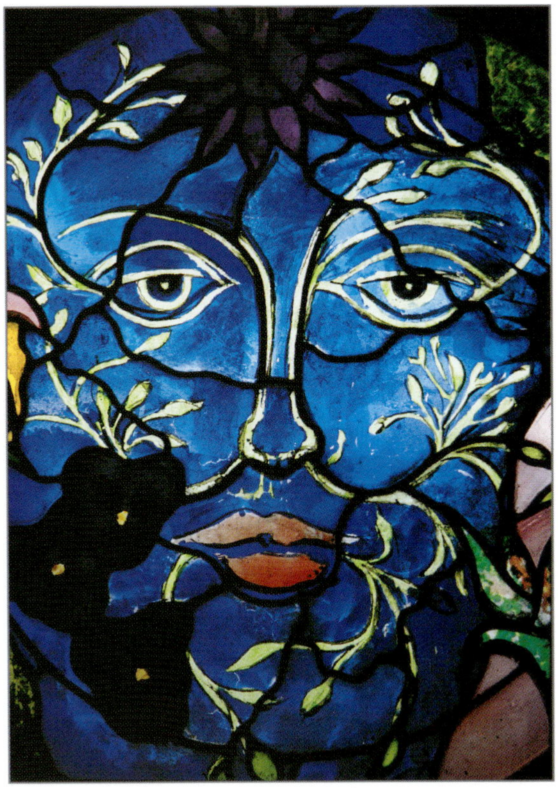

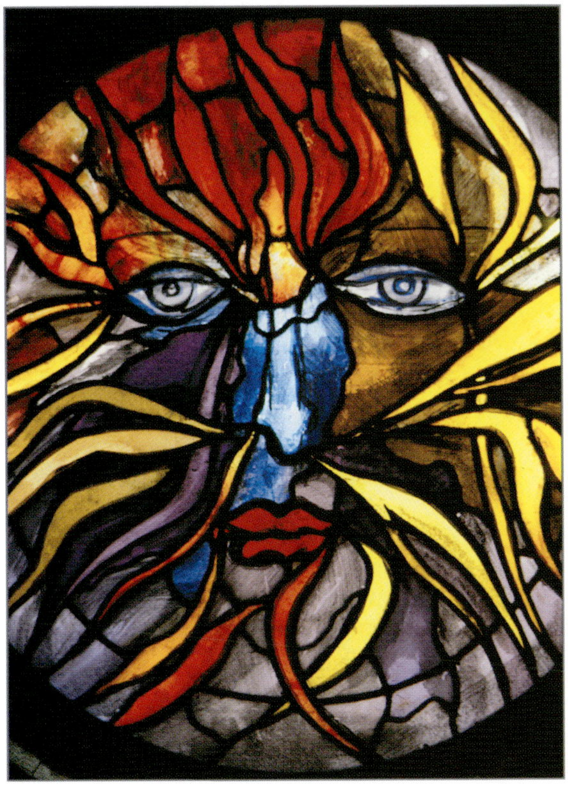

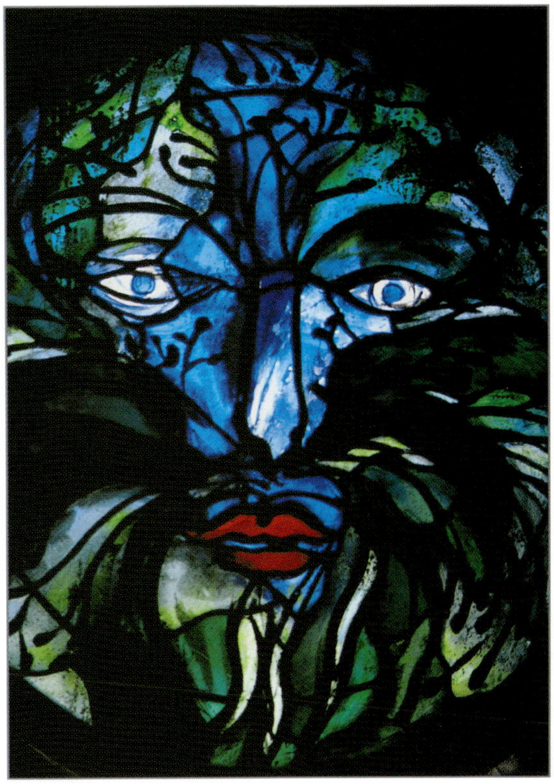

Ipswich School Library. *Above, left:* Fig. 106: North-east window: Spring, Youth, Earth. *Above, right:* Fig. 107: South-east window: Summer, Adulthood, Air. *Below, left:* Fig. 108: South-west window: Autumn, Maturity, Fire. *Below, right:* Fig. 109: North-west window: Winter, Old Age, Water (see pp. 124–5)

diagonal is the Avebury/West Kennet Avenue line of standing stones (Neolithic). In addition, Piper included other important sites on the North Wiltshire Downs: the Devil's Den, a megalithic tomb at Preshute near Marlborough; Barbury Castle, an Iron Age hillfort on the Ridgeway in the parish of Wroughton; and in the background the eighteenth-century Cherhill White Horse, cut in the chalk below the hillfort, Oldbury Castle.

A list of what it contains gives no idea of the impact of this delightful window. It is so much more than just a collection of artifacts and sites. The amber necklace glows as if new-made; the blood-red colour of two of the pots and the white, shadowed with black, of the other, give a freshness and excitement to the finds, as if they had just been dug up. The series of standing stones are touched with blue, one looming near, the rest diminishing into the distance. The flowers of the woolly thistle are like stars, the tiny white horse seems to trot over the viridian hills. In brief, the whole window pulsates with life.[16]

If, as Peter Pears observed, nature and religion were the two most dominant forces in Piper's art, nowhere is this more forcibly demonstrated than in his work for Robinson College, Cambridge. He designed two windows for the Chapel, differing greatly in style.

Robinson College was founded in 1974, through the great generosity of David Robinson. Born in Cambridge in 1904, Robinson was the third of nine children. He left school at the age of fifteen to work in his father's bicycle shop, then went into the motor industry, made his fortune in television rentals, and became one of the country's major owners of race-horses. It is not generally known what his motive was in founding the college.

The money having been donated, an architectural competition was held, and the winning scheme was that by the Glasgow firm of Gillespie, Kidd and Coia. The partner in the firm who was most closely involved with Robinson College was Isi Metzstein; the other architect connected with the project was Andrew McMillan, Professor of Architecture at the Mackintosh School of Art.

Robinson declared that he wanted the college to have a 'real chapel' with all the furnishings, including stained glass. 'Who's that man who did the Coventry Cathedral window?', he asked. 'Get him on the phone.' That was how Piper came to be involved. The original idea for the chapel was that it should simply have an apse. Obviously, stained glass would be more costly, but Robinson was very willing to cover the extra expense. (The Chapel was the only part of the building to cost more than originally estimated.)

Piper formed an excellent working relationship with Isi Metzstein, and became concerned not only with the stained glass, but with all manner of furnishings as well: the wooden cross and candlesticks, the tapestries, altar-cloths and hassocks. He advised on the tiling, the font, the altar for the side chapel (formed out of a piece of marble which came from the same source as the kitchen table-top at Fawley Bottom), and the eighty stacking chairs, stained blue. Most importantly, he designed the ceramic of the Deposition,[17] which hangs on the wall below the main window.

Piper having been consulted from at least 1977, the principal window is indissolubly part of the architecture. The whole interior is characterized by a series of step-motifs, and one of these forms the base of the window. Added to which difficulty, it is curved.[18] Remembering that the firm of architects came from Glasgow, one may detect the influence of Charles Rennie Mackintosh on some of its lines, even though others are more horizontal in style. On 11 August 1978 Piper received a letter from Yorke, Rosenberg Mardell (another firm of architects involved), promising to keep the mullions in the window as narrow as possible – Piper will not have wanted a repetition of the problem of too much masonry that he had encountered at Coventry. John Penoyre of the above firm re-drew the elevation of the window in order to show it from the inside, to make designing a little easier. David Wasley, working in Reyntiens's studio, prepared a trial panel, and Reyntiens (17 January 1978) wrote to Andrew McMillan offering to quote for the work so that a contract could be drawn up. Which done, Reyntiens assembled a team of skilled glaziers (including Wasley), and made a trip to Germany where he ordered £14,000 worth of glass.

The Chapel is non-denominational, and the main window is partially obscured from most viewpoints by a brick curtain-wall and pillar. These facts are very much bound up with Piper's use of iconography. His design is not totally abstract, and the theme of the window is 'The Light of the World' (Fig. 112, p. 131). But it is a far cry from Holman Hunt's painting of the same title in Keble College, Oxford; Piper's design is a symbolic representation. Light from a huge sun flickers through a cascade of foliage. The sun representing the glory of God, it is significant that the full form of it is hidden from human view; but it can be discerned, at least in part, through a curtain of leaves, symbolizing Nature. So not only is this stained glass fully integrated with the architecture, and an essential part of the building; it also expresses a religious conviction which may be shared by many people, regardless of denomination.

There can be few windows so texturally rich – which meant demanding in craftsmanship – as 'The Light of the World'. It took two years to make. 'Every device that was legitimately called for', wrote Patrick Reyntiens in *The Beauty of Stained Glass*, 'in the way of technical expertise was put into this commission.' Reyntiens had chosen the glass (at Hilden and Waldsassen) on the basis of slivers cut from the actual cartoon; the dominant colour of the completed window is green. The blues are confined to the lower panels; then below the pale yellow sun, off-centre to the left, there is a rich tapestry of different greens, with here and there leaves outlined in orange.

It is an astonishing and very lovely widow.

In the small side chapel, a haven of quiet, is more stained glass of Piper's design (Fig. 111, p. 130). The inspiration for this much smaller, yet very rich window was a French Romanesque tympanum (Fig. 113, p. 132). Piper wrote about it:

> In the top section of the window the Virgin and Child are receiving gifts from the Magi, flanked on each side by trumpeting angels. Beneath their feet are the Beasts of Paganism – two green, sleeping monsters. The lowest section symbolizes the beginning and the end of the Christian story with, on the left, Adam and Eve and the serpent and, on the right, the Last Supper.

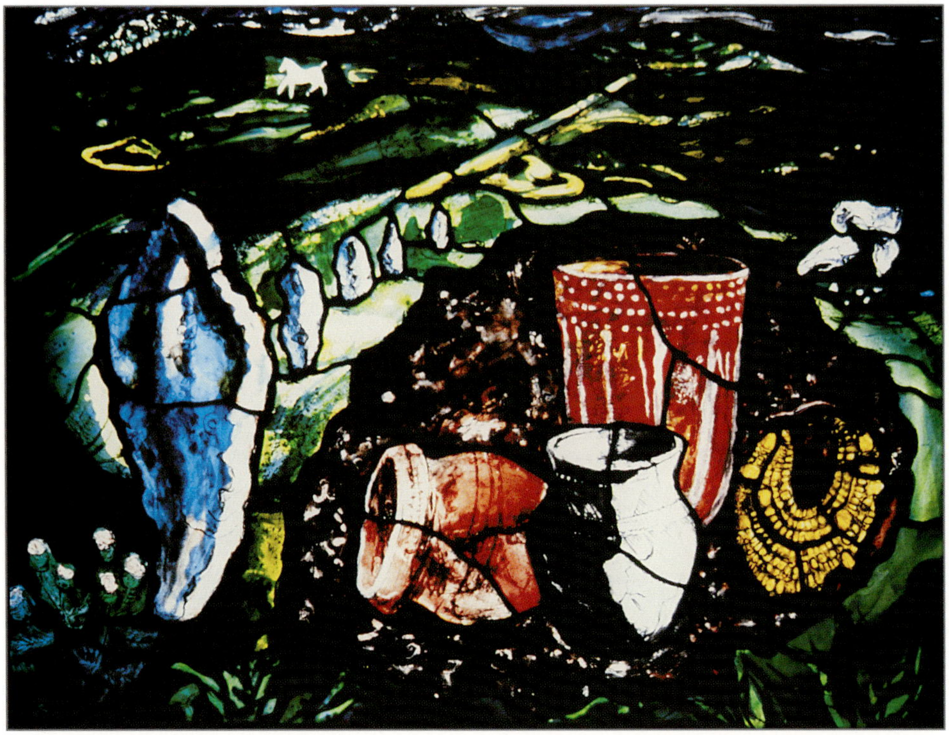

Fig. 110: Devizes Museum. Archaeological finds (see p. 125). (Photo. courtesy of David Wasley)

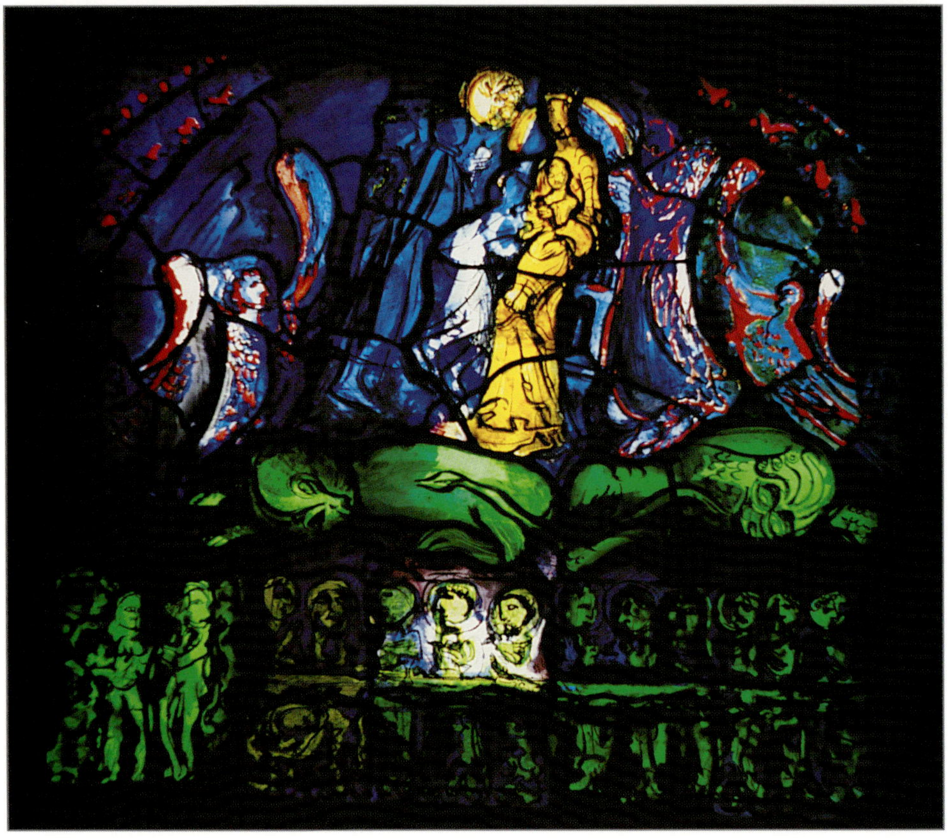

Fig. 111: Cambridge, Robinson College. Side chapel window (see p. 129)

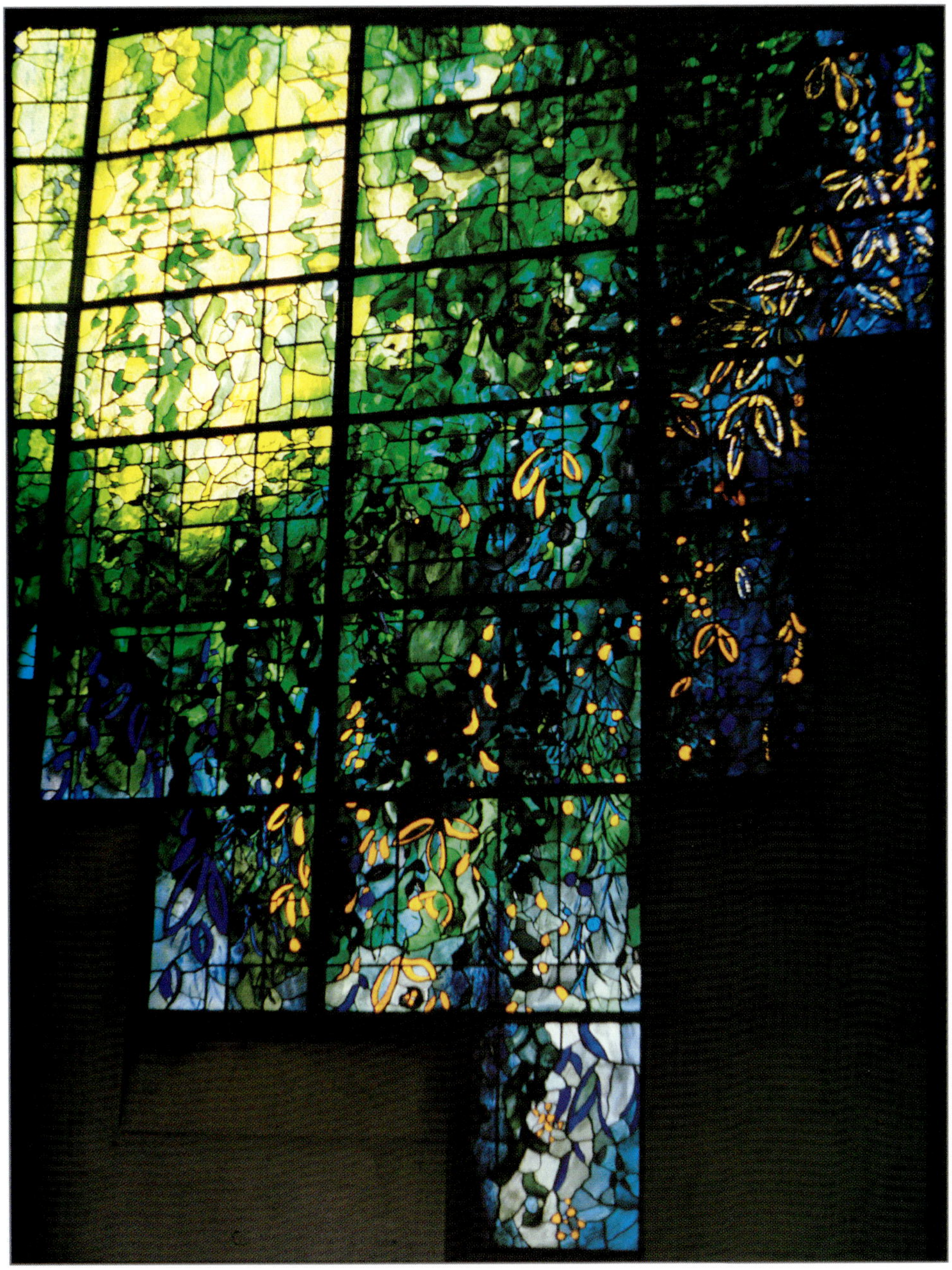

Fig. 112: Cambridge, Robinson College. The Light of the World (see p. 129)

The Romanesque stone carving which provided the stimulus for the colour invention of the window is over the west door of the village church of Neuilly-en-Donjon, Allier.

He had done a water-colour/gouache painting (Fig. 1, p. xix) of the tympanum in about 1969, and from this the cartoon was derived. It is full of subtle curves and stupendous colour; the Epiphany scene with the sinuous gold Virgin, with the flanking figures outlined in red against deep ultramarine, and then below, the

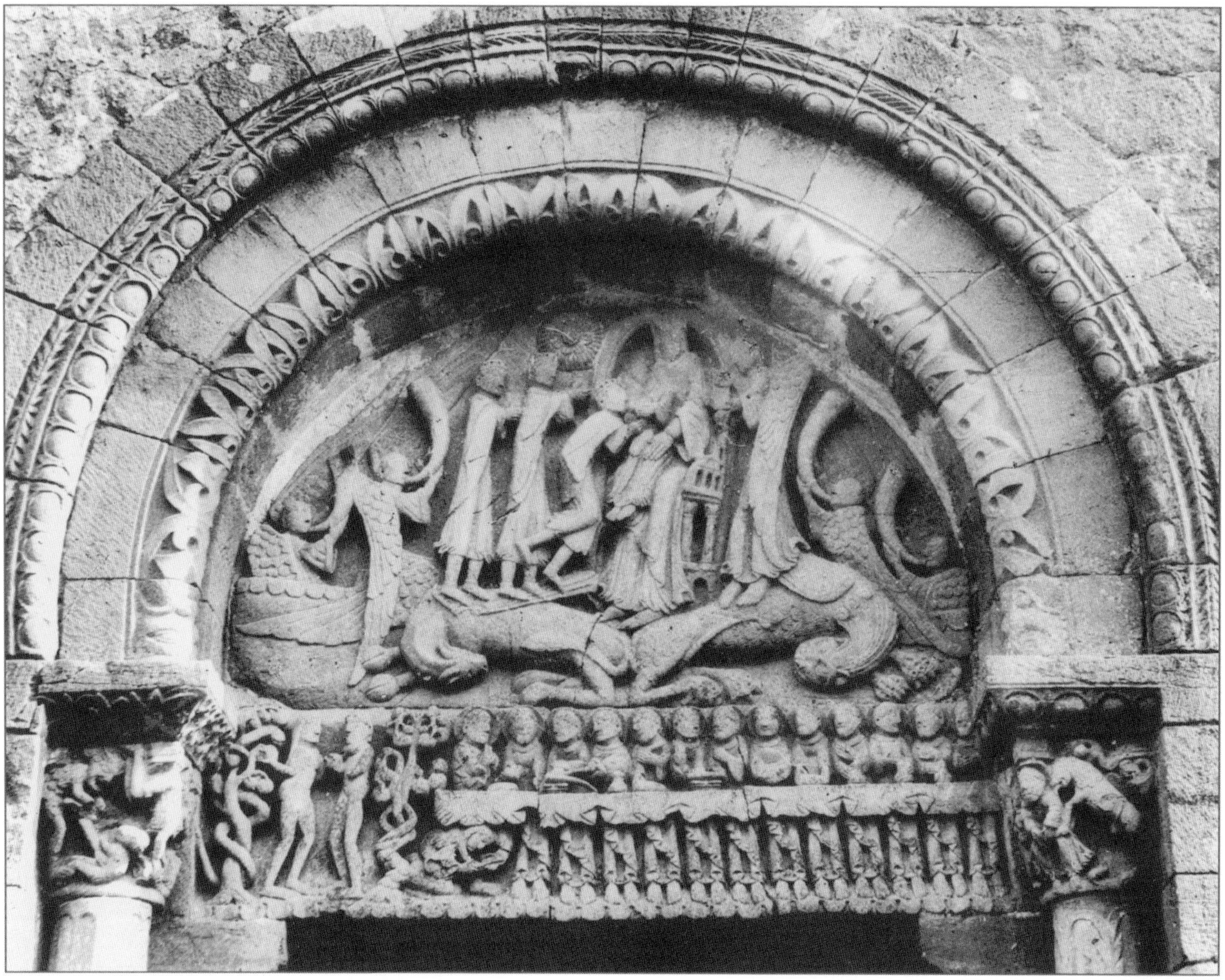

Fig. 113: Tympanum at Neuilly-en-Donjon (see Fig. 1, p. xix, and p. 129). (Photographer unknown)

sprawling green beasts and the frieze of small figures at the base. According to Reyntiens, the translation of Piper's vision into glass demanded greater expertise than any of the other windows. There are five layers of glass in it. Reyntiens wrote to Yorke, Rosenberg Mardell on 3 September 1980 confirming that the work was complete.

The surveyor in charge was Victor Bugg of Davis, Belfield and Everest. He had followed the processes with enthusiasm, and on 23 November 1979 he wrote to Piper:

> After leaving you, we went to Beaconsfield [Reyntiens's studio]. It is very exciting to see the stained-glass panels taking shape. The completed small window is a tremendous achievement – you must be very pleased.

The Chapel was dedicated on 1 November 1981. By far its best features are the windows, which represent the finest modern glass in any college, and a high watermark in the history of design.

CHAPTER TWELVE

SWAN SONGS: LATE WORKS AND A MEMORIAL

'The value of hue in all illuminations on painted glass of fine periods depends primarily on the expendients used to make the colours palpitate and fluctuate; *inequality* of brilliancy being the *condition* of brilliancy. . . . Delicacy of organization in the designer given, you will soon have all, and without it, nothing.'

John Ruskin (1819–1900)[1]

John Piper fervently believed that stained glass, of whatever period, should be judged as a work of art, and not simply recorded. Ruskin, writing a century earlier, sought to analyze the matter. He was one of the first to be aware that the medium has its own distinctive qualities, and especially important is the use of colour. 'All good colour, wrote Ruskin, is gradated:

> The first necessity of beauty in colour is gradation, as the first necessity of beauty in line is curvature. All harmonies of colour depend for their vitality on the action and helpful operation of every particle of colour they contain. No colour harmony is of high order unless it involves indescribable tints.[2]

How Ruskin would have approved of Piper's work. Indescribable tints (which I have done my best to describe) continued to characterize Piper's designs and to pose problems for their interpreters. Meanwhile, his achievements in this field had been recognized by an exhibition in Kettle's Yard Gallery, Cambridge (3 December 1982 to 9 January 1983), 'John Piper: Painting in Coloured Light'. Martin Harrison remarked in his Introduction to the Catalogue: 'One of the most remarkable aspects of John Piper's stained glass is that, as the artist is approaching his seventy-ninth birthday, he is still producing designs of a most delightful and unpredictable kind.' There were yet more to come.

Towards the end of his working life Piper designed a window (Fig. 3, p. 3) for the Saxon church of St Paul's, Jarrow, in memory of Benedict Biscop and to commemorate the 1,300th anniversary of the church in AD 685. The commission must have given him tremendous satisfaction because St Paul's is the church for which the oldest known stained glass in England was made, and it was Benedict Biscop who inspired and ordered it. So Piper was paying tribute to a great initiator of the art he so dearly loved. The window was installed in 1985, and the

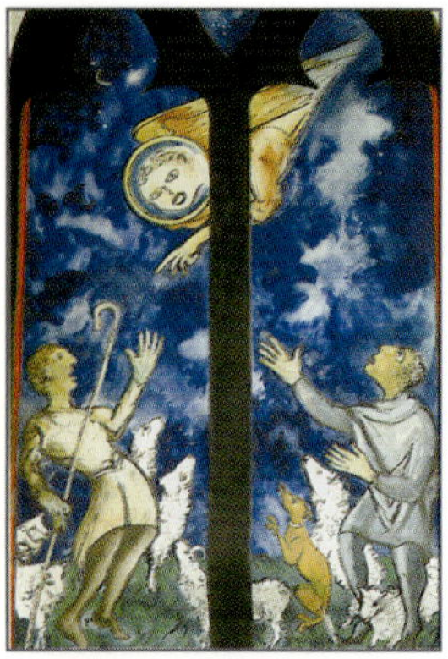

Fig. 114: Lamberhurst, St Mary's. The cartoon of the Annunciation to the Shepherds, photographed at Fawley Bottom

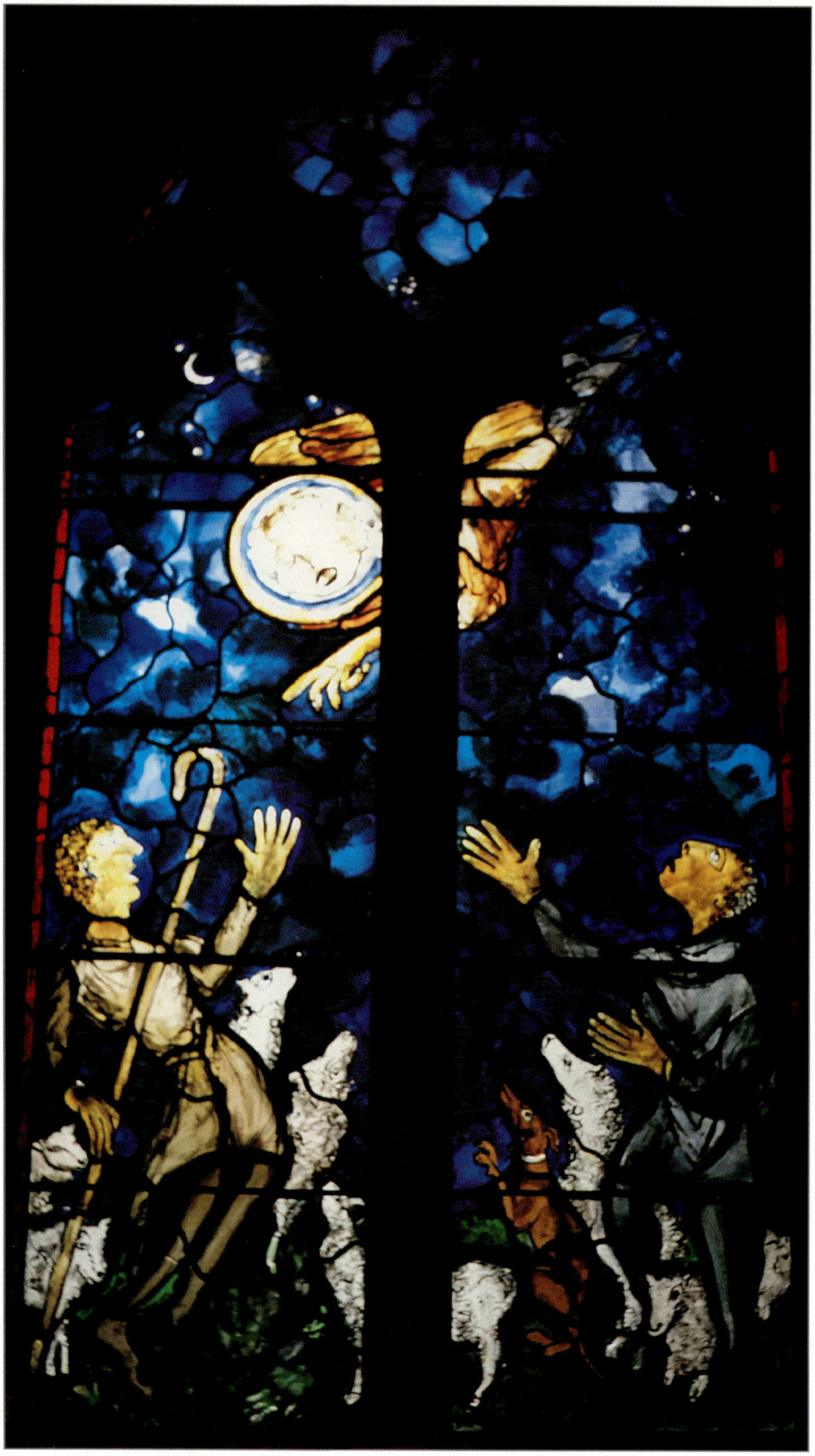

Fig. 115: Lamberhurst, St Mary's. Annunciation to the Shepherds

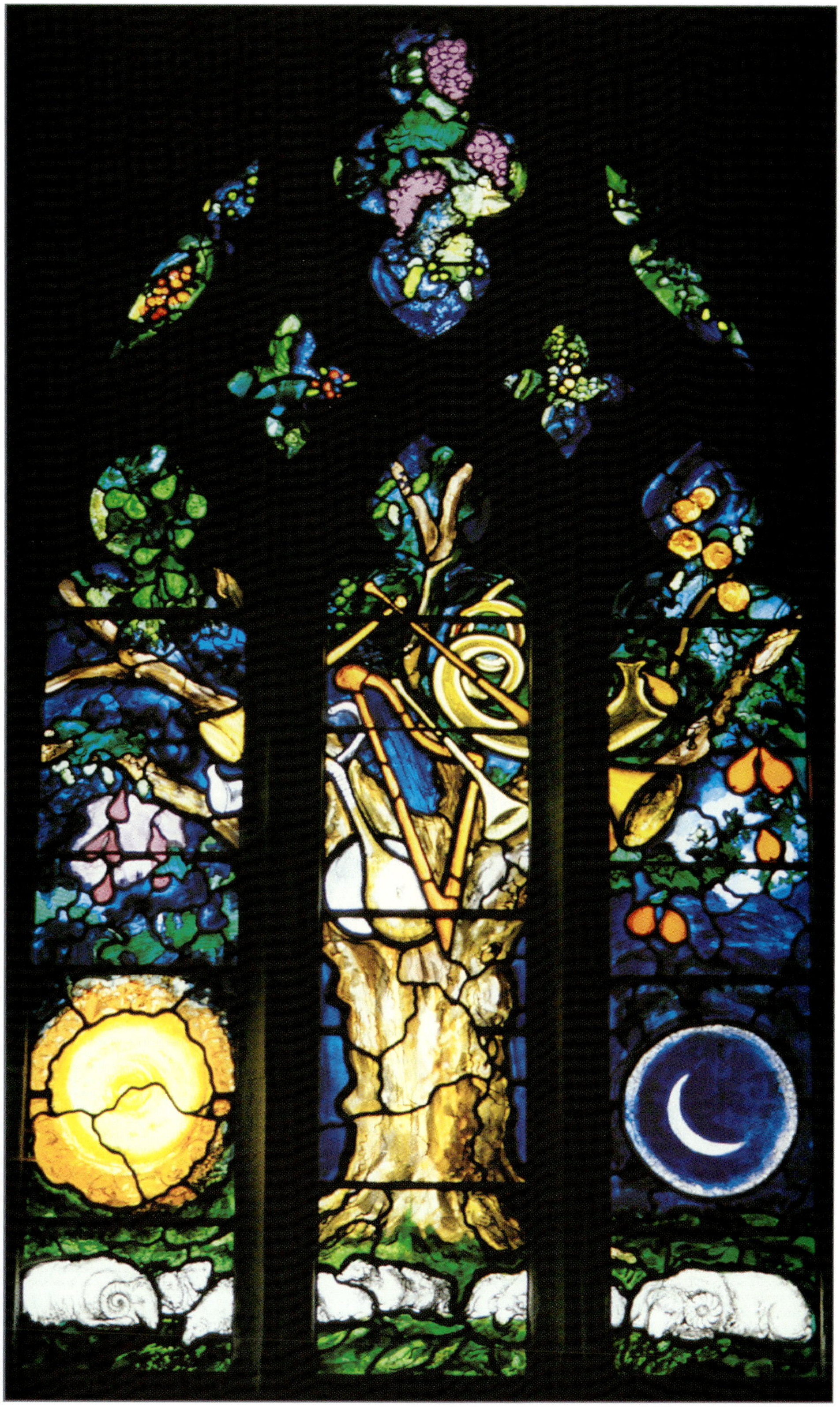

Fig. 116: Firle, St Peter's. Homage to William Blake's Book of Job. The Gage Chapel Memorial Window (see pp. 137, 140)

making was by Patrick Reyntiens. It is a simple yet satisfying design, consisting of little more than a cross and the initials BB for Benedict Biscop. The form of the cross, with its two arms (like the Cross of Lorraine, except that here the lower and not the upper arm is the shorter) is based on a stone carving known as the Jarrow Cross; and the Bs are modelled on the initial B of the Leningrad manuscript of Bede's *Ecclesiastical History*.[3]

The background of the window is blue, criss-crossed with red and yellow flames, rather in the manner of medieval diapering. The church guide-book points out the symbolic use of colour: 'The blue represents the heavens; the red and yellow, the Pentecostal Flame; and the green (which surrounds the cross), the earth. The Jarrow Cross is white through which the light of Christ always shines.' Set in a deep roundheaded embrasure, it is a design of fitting simplicity in this ancient and lovely church.

Equally right in its setting is the window which Piper designed for St Mary's, Lamberhurst, in Kent. The church, which is largely Perpendicular, stands a little apart from the rest of the village, on a knoll overlooking a rural landscape with, usually, sheep. So a window on the theme of the Annunciation to the Shepherds could hardly be more appropriate (Fig. 115, p. 134).

The cartoon for this window (Fig. 114, p. 134), which at the time of writing is on the wall of the big studio at Fawley Bottom, is a design full of life. It has something of the animation and directness of the best of folk art. Piper has depicted the moment when the angel appeared to the shepherds, as recounted in Luke 2: 8–11:

> And there were in the same country shepherds abiding in the field, keeping watch over their flock by night.
>
> And, lo, the angel of the Lord came upon them, and the glory of the Lord shone round about them: and they were sore afraid.
>
> And the angel said unto them, Fear not: for behold, I bring you good tidings of great joy, which shall be to all people.
>
> For unto you is born this day in the City of David a Saviour, which is Christ the Lord.

The design conveys vividly the astonishment and alarm of the shepherds; even the sheep and the dog are amazed. In the deep blue of the sky – a blue with that vitality and variation which would have delighted Ruskin – there suddenly appears the angel, his head ringed right round as if it were a planet, the rest of his body barely existent, a wedge of wings denoting speed. His left hand points as he delivers his message. The shepherds raise their hands in astonishment, one of them reels over backwards. The dog stands on his hind legs; four of the sheep, too, gaze up at this wonderful apparition.

It is interesting in retrospect to note that there was some controversy over this window, since the cartoon on which it was based was slightly different from the original sketch, especially in respect of the angel. Piper was challenged over this, and wrote the following conciliatory letter to the vicar, the Revd B.E.E. Marshall:

5th October 1985

Dear Mr Marshall,

As a stained glass designer who does not execute his designs himself I am well aware of the troubles and pitfalls that beset the enlarger in turning a first sketch-design into a full-size cartoon. There are always a hundred things which crop up and need adjustment, any of which can be picked on as 'differences' by anyone who wants to.

In this case there were many alterations, all of which I thought were improvements. One was to make the angel appear to be actually *speaking* to the shepherds. This has clearly caused the present trouble, and if you wish I will have the face translated back into its former silent stage. It will be a difficult thing to do at this late date, but it can be done.

I would like to add that I am very sorry to have been the unwitting cause of this little trouble which must have greatly upset the vicar and church wardens. (I am a former churchwarden here at Fawley, and am still an active member of the PCC.) I send them my apologies and sympathy, and I hope that ultimately the window may give much pleasure, as it has done to me already who helped in the making of it.

In the end the church authorities decided to leave well alone and accept the window as it stood.

The design (cartoon) was interpreted in faithful and lively spirit by David Wasley, and the window dates from 1985. Seldom has anyone, even Piper, conveyed such drama and action in a design for stained glass.

From the same year dates a fine window (Fig. 116, p. 135) at St Peter's, Firle, near Glyndebourne in Sussex, entitled 'Homage to William Blake's Book of Job'. It is based again on the Tree of Life in the Heavenly Jerusalem (Rev. 22: 2), but at the same time, as the title implies, on the work of William Blake. Piper had always been a great admirer of Blake. Many years before, he had designed a set for the ballet *Job* (music by Vaughan Williams, choreography by Ninette de Valois), which was staged at the Royal Opera House and opened on 20 May 1948. Piper's set designs were based on Blake's illustrations to the Book of Job. The ink and gouache design for his backcloth 'The Earth', in the theatre museum at the Victoria and Albert,[4] bears great similarities to the Firle window.

Most of the Book of Job deals with his trials and tribulations, but in the last chapter, 42, we read how 'The Lord blessed the latter end of Job more than his beginning. His prosperity was restored, and once again he had a family of seven sons and three daughters.

The nearest resemblance between the Firle window and Blake's work seems to be the engraving, Plate 1 of Blake's 'Book of Job', 1825,[5] though there is also the water-colour in the National Gallery of Washington, 'Job restored to prosperity', and a pen and water-colour drawing, 'Job and his family', in the Pierpont Morgan Library, New York. Piper's design omits the human figures of Job and his family, but the musical instruments (emblems of joy) are there, hung in the oak tree, the sleeping sheep in the foreground, and the sun and moon on either side.[6]

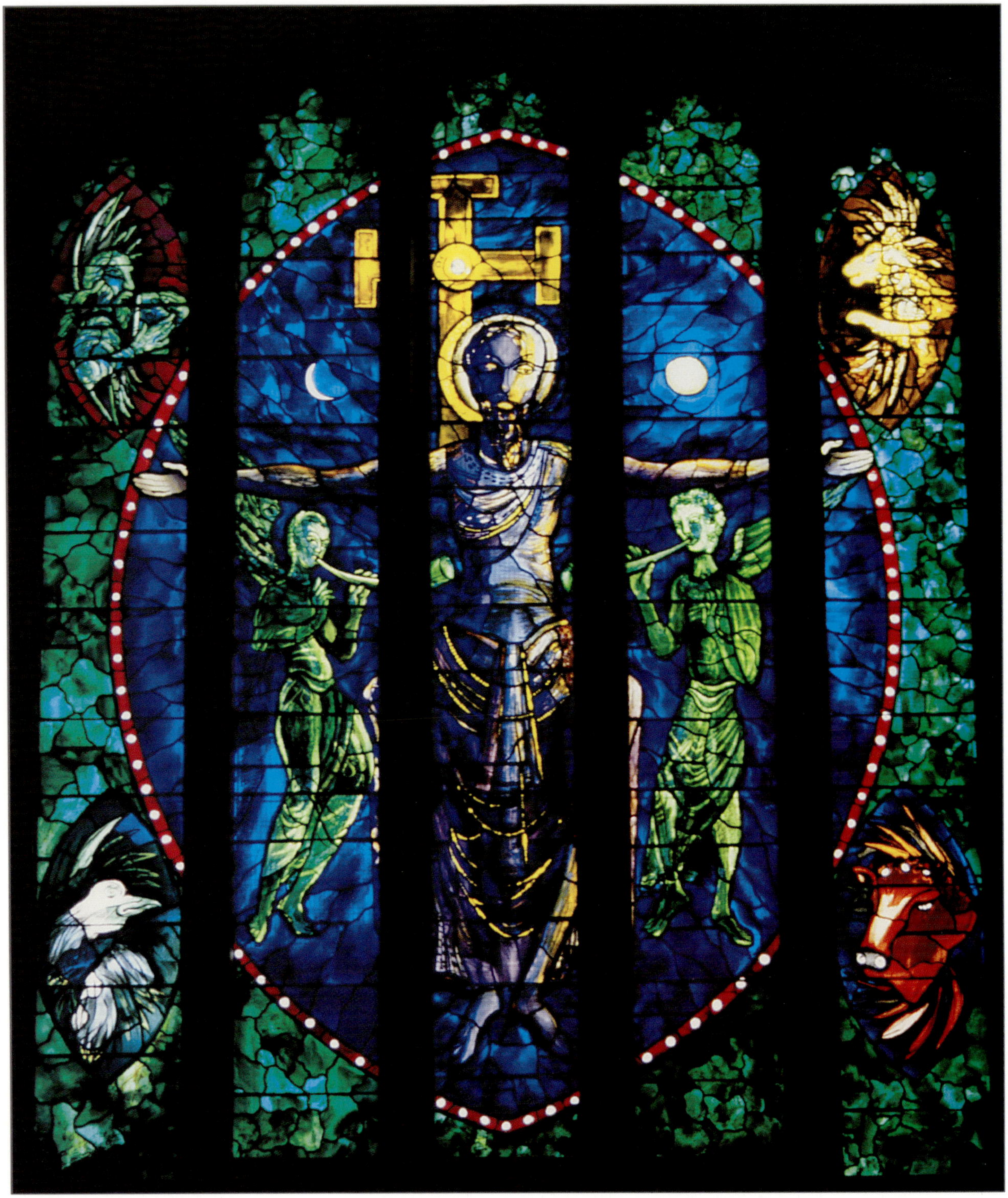

Fig. 117: Lichfield, St John's Hospital. Christ in Majesty (see pp. 140–1)

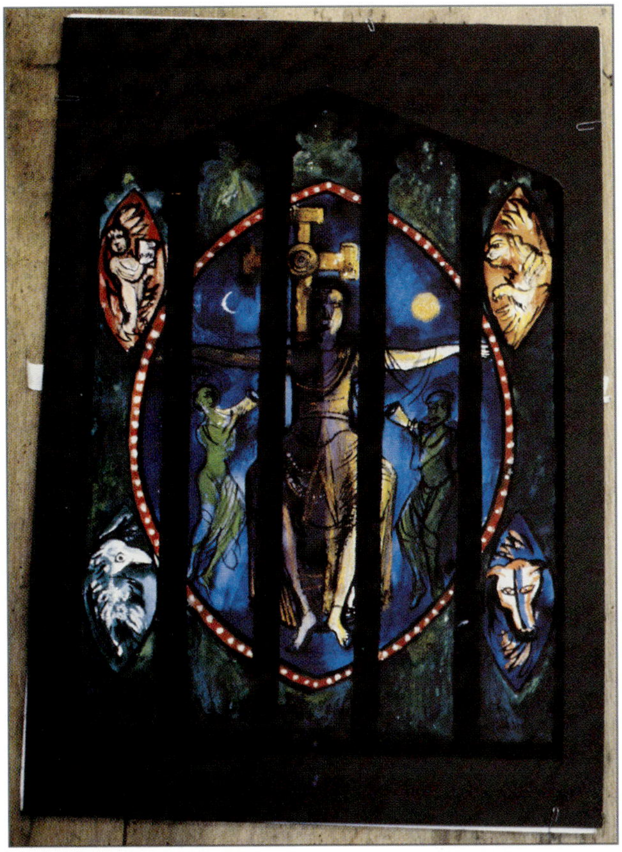

Left: Fig. 118: Lichfield, St John's Hospital. Sketch for Christ in Majesty. (Photo. courtesy of David Wasley). *Below left:* Fig. 119: Nettlebed. Dragonfly panel (see p. 144). (Coll. Mrs Betty Kelaart). *Centre and right:* Figs 120 and 121: Woodbridge. Venice panels (see p. 148). (Coll. Norman Scarfe)

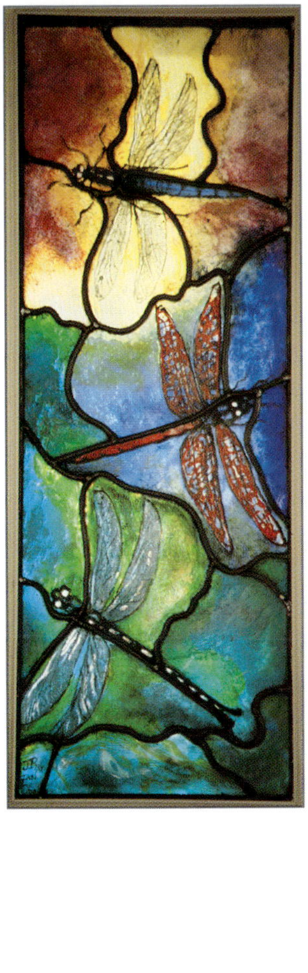

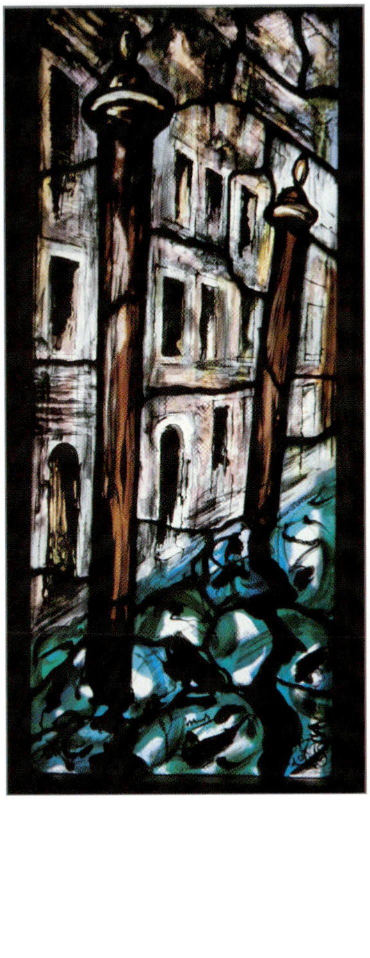

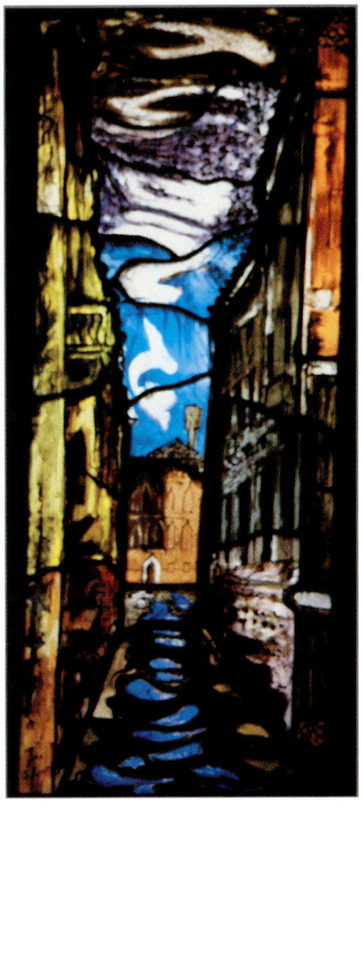

The window is the East Window of the Gage Chapel in St Peter's Church. There are three main lights. The centre is dominated by the shape of the tree trunk (there is a note in the church sayings that 'firle' or 'ferle' is an Old English word for 'oak'); on this hang the musical instruments, serpent, trumpet and harp being recognizable. In the left-hand light is the hot and crinkled sun; in the right, the crescent moon in a circle. Below on the grass are the sleeping sheep,[7] and silhouetted against a deep blue sky, the branches of the tree are rich with fruit.

The cartoon for this window is in the artist's studio. It is executed in gouache, with the fruits in collage; the masonry has been left white, rather than painted in black. Piper's design was faithfully and sensitively interpreted by David Wasley, who wrote this note (to be seen in the church):

> This window, like the Epiphany window in the ante-chapel of Robinson College, Cambridge, is elaborately made and composed of three, sometimes four, layers of glass to achieve the rich, deep atmospheric appearance which glass can offer when up high, sitting in full exposure to sunlight. Up in the window, glass is light-soaked colour becoming stained glass, the pictorial combination of harsh, difficult materials conveying the original master-stroke of the artist's picture-making.

Piper's last major undertaking (Fig. 117, p. 138) was the five-light East Window of the Chapel of St John's Hospital, Lichfield (1984). Its proper name is the Chapel of St John Baptist without the Barrs. This is not a medical hospital but a charity, founded in the Middle Ages, to accommodate 'thirteen honest poor men upon whom the inconveniences of old age and poverty, without any fault of their own, have fallen' (Statute of Bishop William Smith,[8] 3 November 1495). The men, who were given *7d* a week every Friday after dinner, were expected to be honest and devout and to attend prayers in the Chapel every day.

The Chapel, which had been a place of worship since 1135, was radically restored in 1870; the walls were heightened and a new, more highly pitched roof built. A photograph of the interior taken in about 1970 shows the east window filled with plain white quarry glass, frankly rather dull, especially when compared with the richness of the stained glass Piper designed for it.

The subject of his design is Christ in Majesty, surrounded by symbols of the Four Evangelists. Piper himself wrote about its derivation (quoted in the guidebook):

> The character of the design is influenced by a number of drawings and paintings I made of Romanesque sculptures in the Dordogne and Saintonge areas of Western France, on many visits between 1955 and 1975. The carvings are often on the large semi-circular areas above the entrance doors of churches in those parts. These churches were on, or near, the old routes to the famous shrine at Compostella, in northern Spain. The carvings have provided a stimulus, with their formal 'bigness' and grandeur, for much twentieth-century sculpture and painting.

It is a window of great solemnity and power. Against a deep blue ground, surrounded by the narrow line of a mandorla, is the figure of Christ, his thin arms outstretched as though on the Cross, but his knees bent as though seated. His head is gold shadowed with purple, a pale gold halo behind, and on either side, the sun and the moon. Behind but slightly to one side is a golden Cross, in its familiar Latin form but with barred ends. Below Christ's arms are elongated figures of angels blowing trumpets. Outside the mandorla, set in a mosaic of emerald glass, are the symbols of the Four Evangelists. The Lion of St Mark, somewhat goat-like, is set against a deep red ground and appears to grope forward. Below this is the Bull of St Luke, an impressive if saturnine animal in red. In the left-hand corner is the Eagle of St John, gazing anxiously with feathers awry. But the most unexpected of the symbols is that of St Matthew. Piper changed his mind about this. In the preliminary sketch we find the figure of an angel, leaning slightly backwards, against a red ground; in the cartoon, and again in the finished window, the young figure has turned into an old man, coloured mainly green and clasping a book with gnarled hands, green feathers behind, against a crimson ground. Perhaps in making him look old (and the eagle seems aged and balding too) Piper was thinking of the use for which the building was created. It is oddly poignant.

Fig. 122: Model for the set of *Death in Venice*, designed by John Piper (see p. 148)

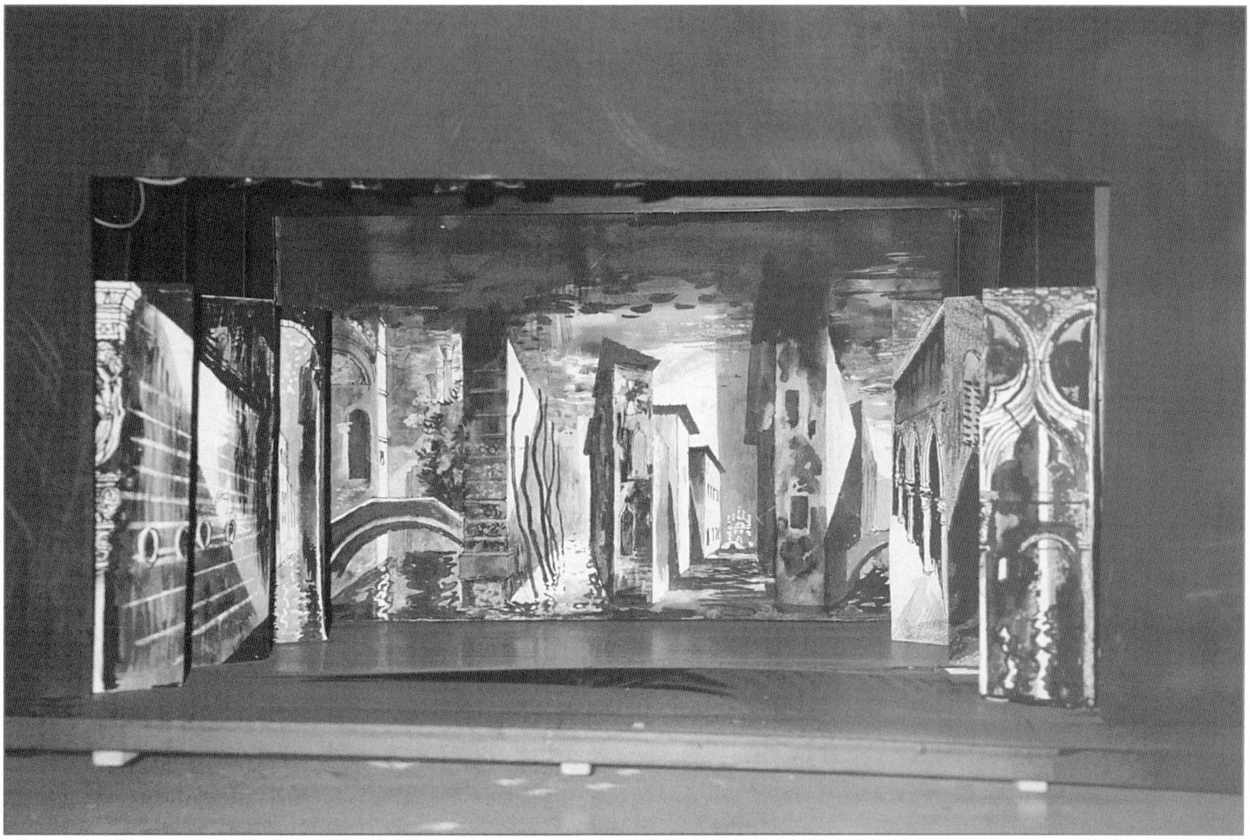

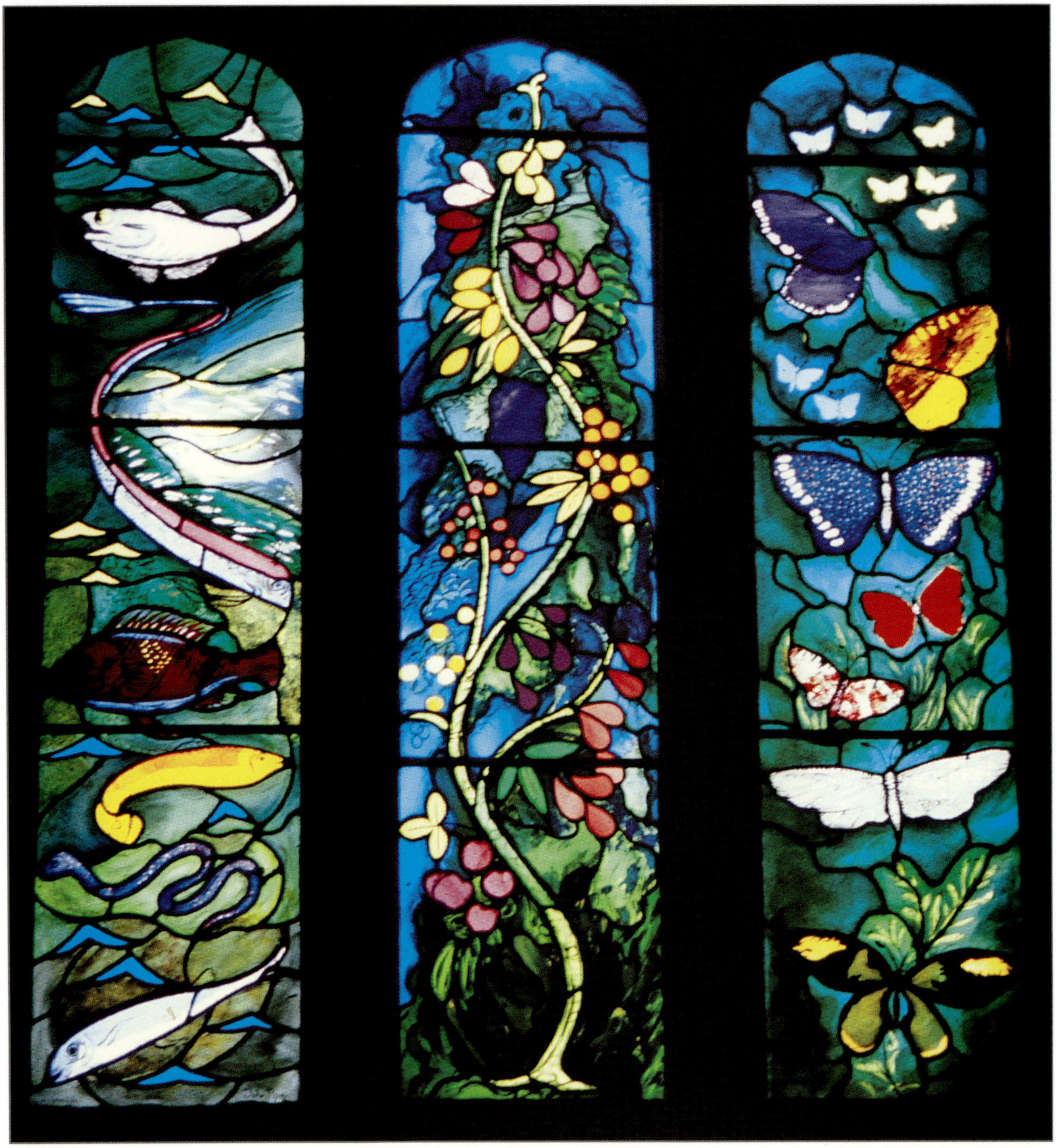

Fig. 123: Farnborough. The John Betjeman Memorial Window (see pp. 148–9)

There are a few other differences to be noticed between the sketch (Fig. 118, p. 139) and the finished window. In the former, Christ has no golden halo; but the sun is gold, whereas in the final form a halo has been added and the sun is smaller and white. The head of the Bull too has changed considerably; in the sketch it is more badger-like and looks downward instead of across. And in the finished window the lower part of Christ's body is much more shadowy, and the

Fig. 124: Farnborough. The John Betjeman Memorial Window. Detail of fishes (see pp. 148–9)

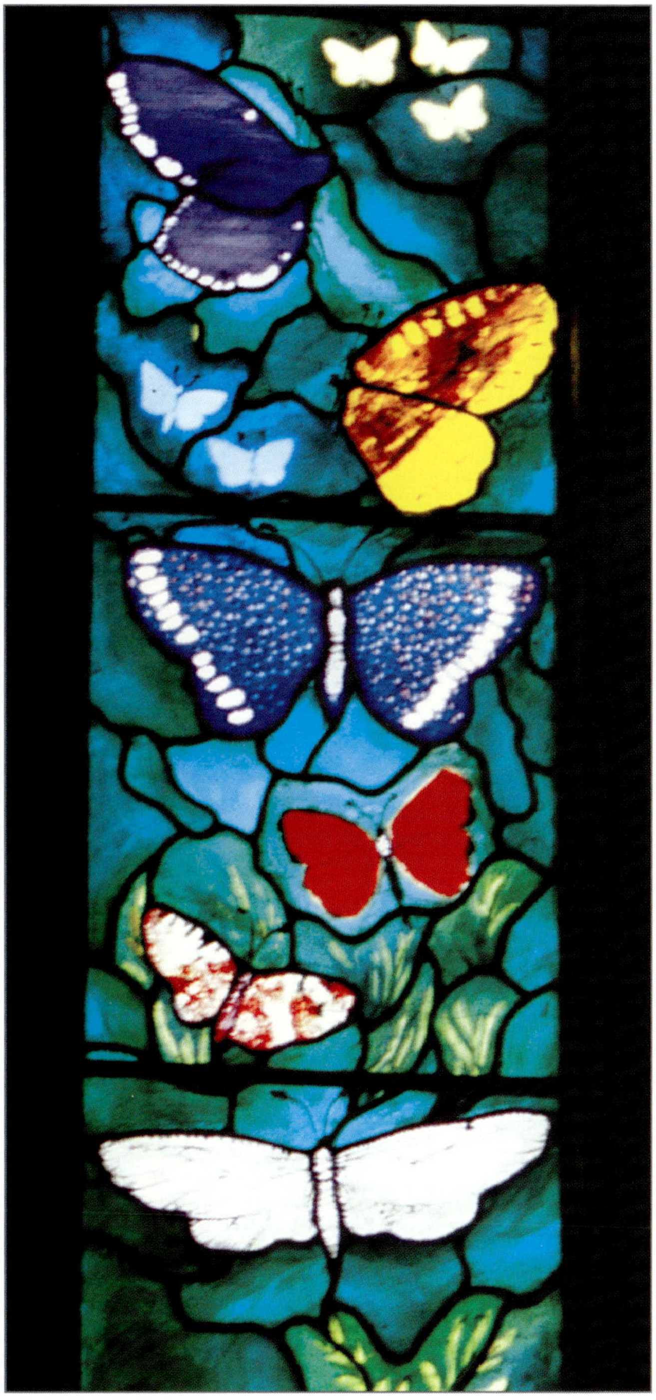

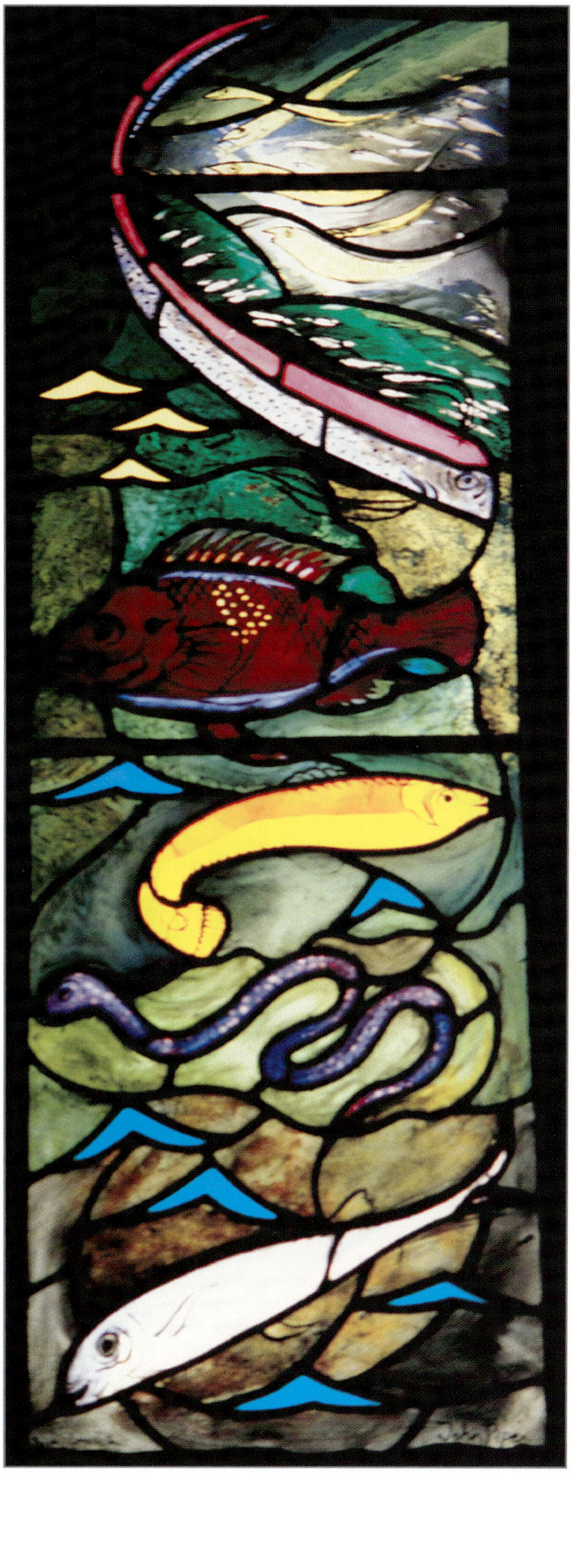

Fig. 125: Farnborough. The John Betjeman Memorial Window. Detail of butterflies (see pp. 148–9)

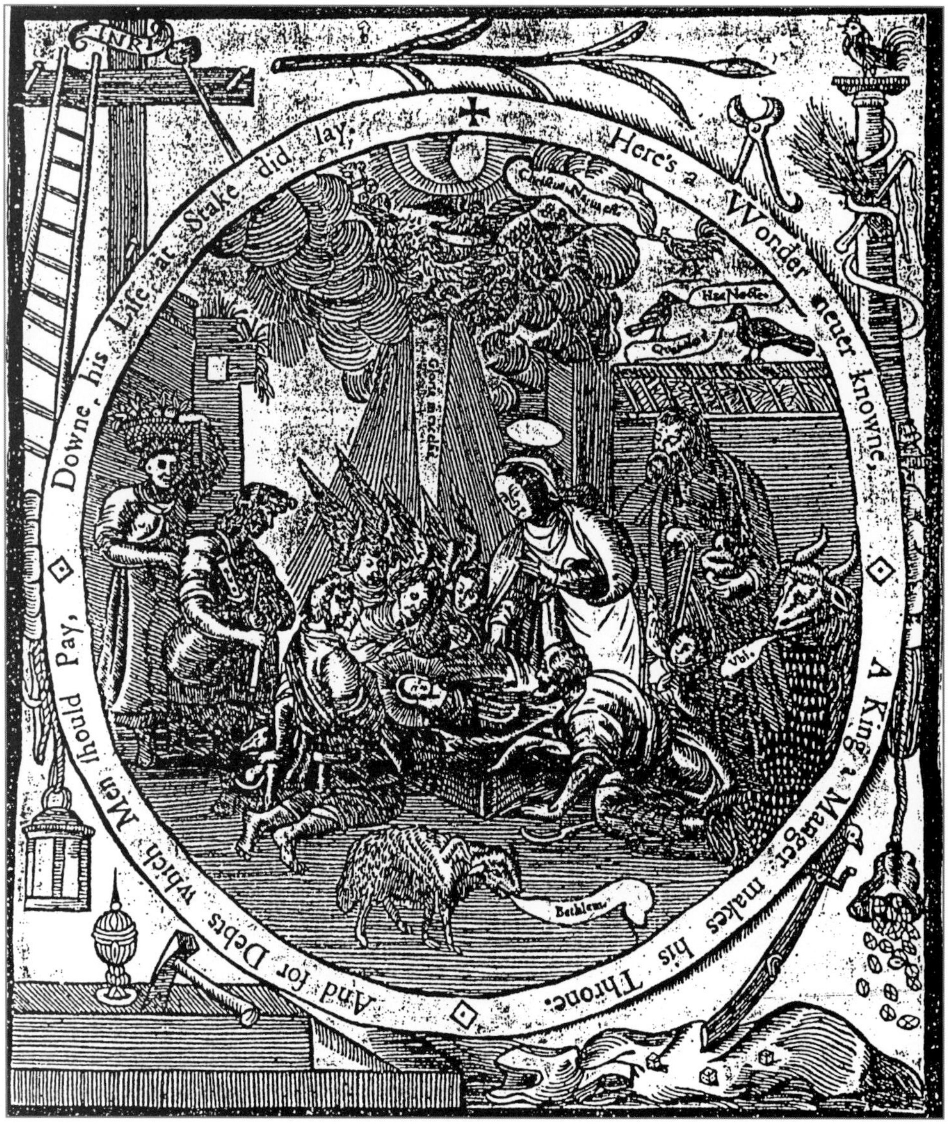

Fig. 126: The Nativity. Seventeenth-century woodcut (see p. 152)

top part streaked with brighter light; this adds to the drama and power of this most majestic window.[9]

By way of complete contrast to this large-scale work, Piper sometimes designed small windows for the houses of friends. There is an example in Nettlebed, Oxfordshire (dating from 1984), in the possession of Mrs Betty Kelaart (Fig. 119, p. 139). Her late husband Paul Kelaart, who restored furniture and loved all things well crafted, knew Piper, and commissioned a small panel depicting dragonflies to please his wife, who had a passion for them. Piper's design was realized in glass by Joe Nuttgens. The panel is set in a door. The background colours merge from green to blue to tawny, and against it are seen three dragonflies, two of them iridescent, one transparent. The cartoon, which the design faithfully and delicately interprets, is also in Mrs Kelaart's possession.

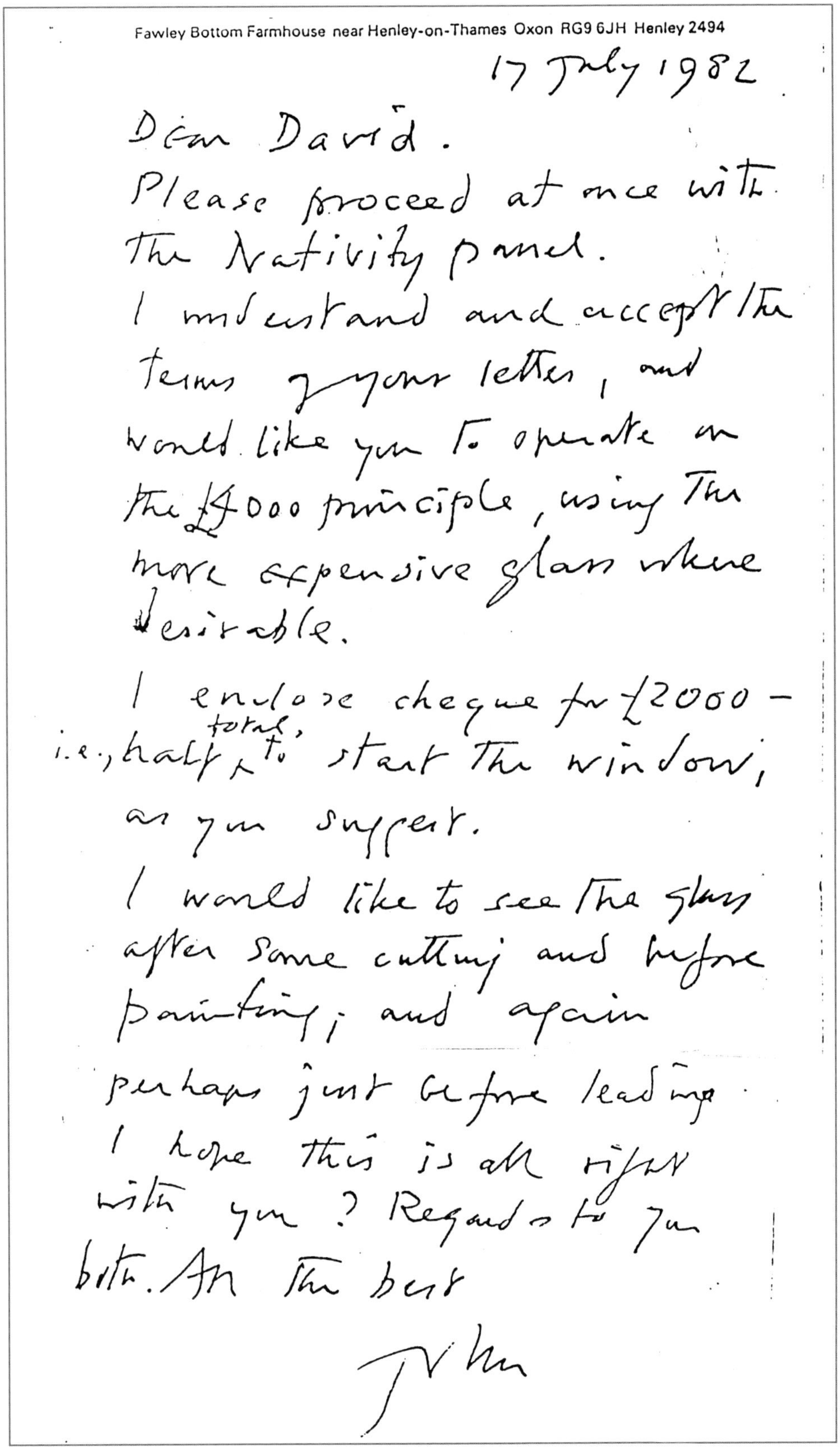

17 July 1982

Dear David.

Please proceed at once with the Nativity panel.

I understand and accept the terms of your letter, and would like you to operate on the £4000 principle, using the more expensive glass where desirable.

I enclose cheque for £2000 – i.e., half total, to start the window, as you suggest.

I would like to see the glass after some cutting and before painting; and again perhaps just before leading.

I hope this is all right with you? Regards to you both. All the best

John

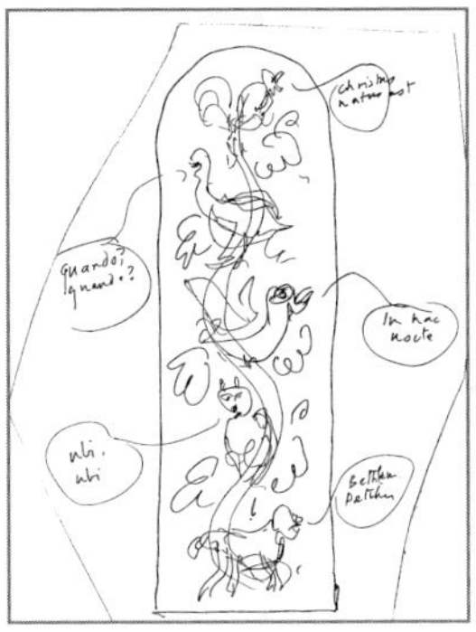

Fig. 127: Preliminary sketch for the Nativity Window (see p. 152). (Courtesy of David Wasley)

Fig. 128: Letter from John Piper to David Wasley concurring the Nativity Window, now at St Mary's Iffley (see p. 152). (Courtesy of David Wasley)

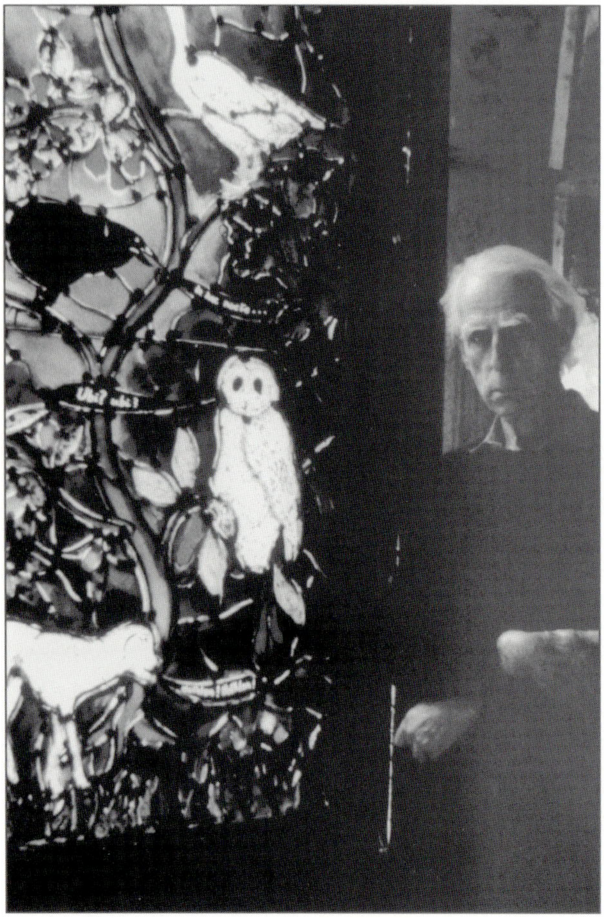

Fig. 129: John Piper with partially completed Nativity Window (see p. 152). (Photo. courtesy of David Wasley)

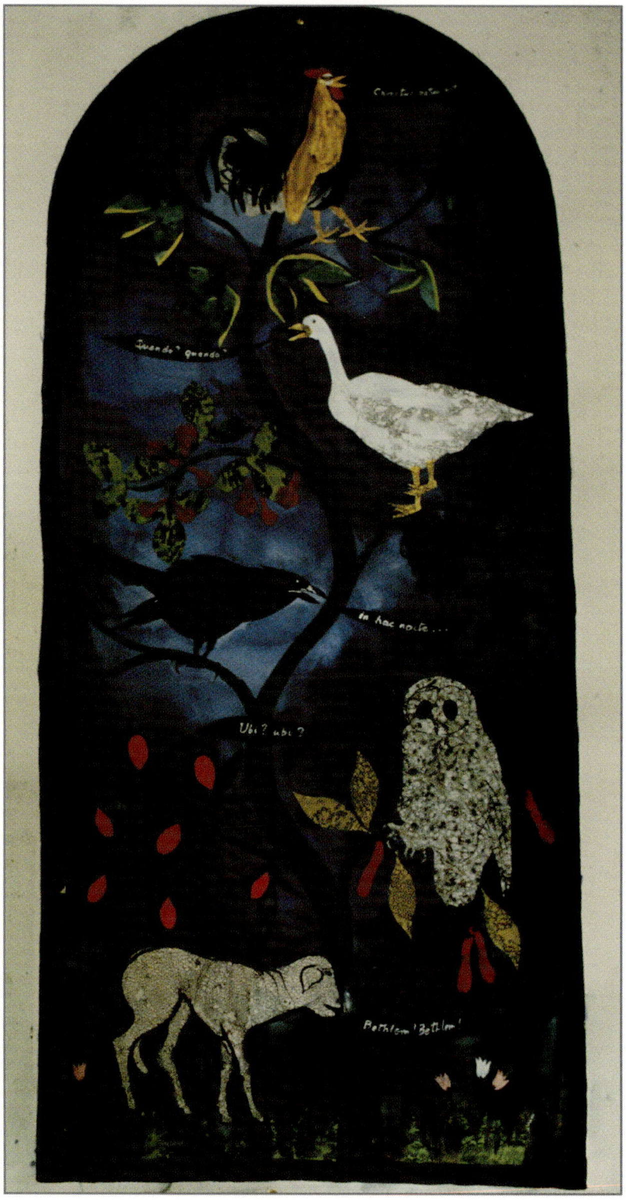

Fig. 130: Cartoon for the Nativity Window (see p. 152). (Photo. courtesy of David Wasley)

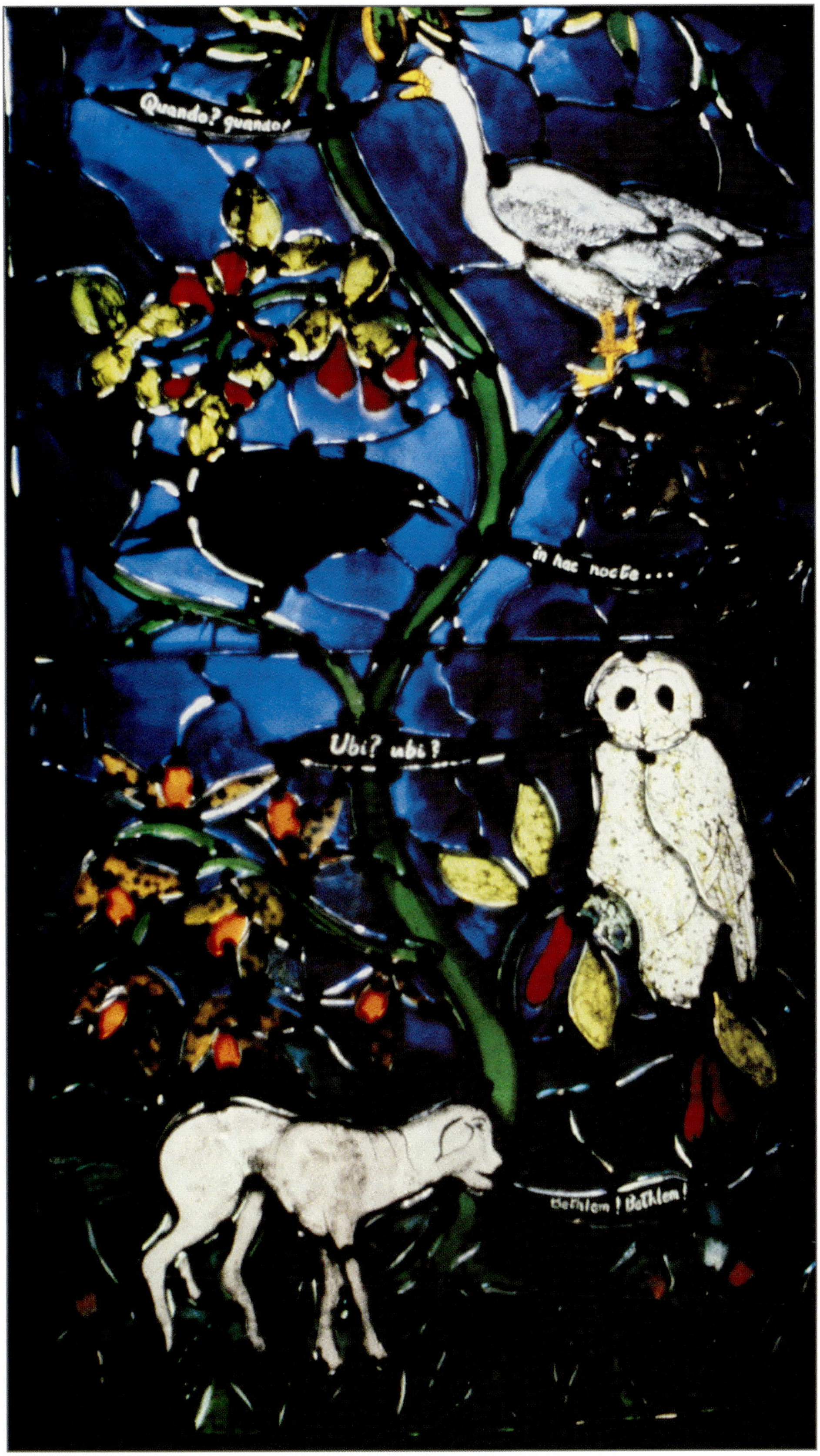

Fig. 131: Iffley, St Mary's. Nativity Window, work in progress (see p. 152). (Photo. courtesy of David Wasley)

Norman Scarfe, the writer, came to know John Piper through the writing of Shell Guides (it will be remembered that Piper had been involved with these since the *Oxfordshire* volume, 1938), beginning with the guide to Suffolk in 1960 which Piper called 'a model of compression'. Scarfe lived in Suffolk, and frequently met the Pipers at the Aldeburgh Festival. On one occasion, when Piper was visiting his house in Woodbridge, Scarfe complained about the view from the two windows on either side of the fireplace in his sitting-room, from which could be seen nothing more interesting than the garage. Piper offered to design some stained glass, and asked Norman Scarfe if he had any ideas as to content. He immediately suggested 'Venice' and Piper, delighted at the choice, designed not only for those two windows (Figs 120 and 121, p. 139) but for three others as well. They date from 1986. Some are based on water-colours that Piper had made in the city (he did a number of paintings there in 1959 and 1960), and the one to the right of the fireplace (Fig. 121) on his set for the opera *Death in Venice* (1973; Fig. 122, p. 141). The windows by the fireplace are rich in tone and colour, while those upstairs tend to be more muted. Realized in glass by David Wasley, they all have a truly Venetian quality of fluidity.

Of all Piper's friends the closest and most valued was almost certainly Sir John Betjeman; and after he died in 1984, there was no doubt who should design his memorial window (Fig. 123, p. 142).[10] It was completed in 1986, and is situated in the west wall of All Saints, Farnborough, on the Berkshire Downs. Betjeman lived for some time in this tiny village, and used to attend the church of All Saints. He wrote in a letter to Oliver Stoner, dated 7 August 1948:

> I well understand what you feel about your church. The clergy are often saints, the congregation devils. Here the clergyman is lazy and good-natured, woolly-minded and useless and I go on going to church because I know that however awful my church is, it is Christ's body in this village and I can't rend it apart by leaving it.[11]

Whatever misgivings he may have had about the incumbent at the time, it seems right that Betjeman should be commemorated here, and he would surely have been delighted with the window Piper designed for him.

Like the East Window at Nettlebed (Fig. 77, p. 106), the Farnborough window is composed of three lights, their themes symbolic of the Resurrection: in the centre light, the Tree of Life; to the left, fishes; and to the right, butterflies. (See p. 108 for an analysis of the symbolism.) But here there is far greater unity than in the Nettlebed window. There are subtle transitions of colour, greens and blues in the backgrounds; they are shaded and varied with an 'inequality of brilliancy' that would have delighted Ruskin. Here too we find the curvature of line that he advocated. The Tree of Life, with its varied fruits, rises in a series of S-bends. The fish have their own rhythm, which is not entirely regular, but note how the curve of the fierce-looking fish at the top is mirrored by the form of the tranquil golden one below the bottom saddlebar (Fig. 124, p. 143). The butterflies in the right-hand light flutter upwards, the flock of little ones at the top, compared with the big heavy-winged ones below, suggesting a flurry of movement (Fig. 125, p. 143).

The cartoon is in the collection of Mrs Myfanwy Piper. It is mainly in gouache, but the features that contrast most vividly with the background, such as the fruit and most of the butterflies, are picked out in collage. The mullions between the lights are indicated in black.

The interpretation into glass was done by Joe Nuttgens. He had, it will be remembered, worked under Reyntiens and was entrusted with the running of the studio. On the death of Nuttgens's father, Eddie (under whom Reyntiens had trained), Joe took over *his* studio, where, decades earlier, the very first panel Piper designed had been made. Nuttgens told me that interpreting the Betjeman cartoon was no easy task. Piper was very clear about the effects he wanted. He had used brilliant colours that Nuttgens said were theoretically impossible, but he was able to interpret them by using a variable number of layers of glass (this is apparent if the window is inspected from the back). Nuttgens thought the design for the butterfly window was somewhat nebulous, but tried to emphasize the spiral in this, and to vary the green by using yellow stain over it. Piper remarked on his logical approach to the problems involved; and Nuttgens was both sensitive and painstaking in interpreting his ideas. The whole effect is a triumph of colour and subtlety, quite the most cheerful memorial window ever created.

Finally, we come to the window that now stands as a memorial to Piper himself (Fig. 137, p. 151). The subject is the Nativity, symbolized by animals; Piper designed it in 1982.

There is a very old legend that the night before Christmas, animals have the gift of human speech, so that they may announce the birth of Christ. The earliest records of such an idea date from the fourth–fifth century, in the lines of the greatest of early Christian Latin poets, Prudentius:[12]

> Vacca 'puer natus' clamabat nocte sub ipsa,
> Qua Christus pura Virgine natus Homo est;
> Sed, quia dicenti numquam bene creditur uni,
> Addebat facti testis asellus: 'Ita',
> Dum aiebat 'Ubi?' clamoso gutture gallus:
> 'In Betlem, Betlem' vox geminabat ovis.
> Felices nimium pecudes, pecorumque magistri,
> Qui norunt Dominum concelebrare Suum.

A cow cried 'A child is born' on the very night on which Christ was born man from a pure Virgin.
But because real credence is never given to what a single speaker says,
A little donkey, acting as witness to what had happened, added 'yes'.
While a cock said 'Where?' from its clamorous throat.
A sheep's voice doubled this with the words 'In Bethlehem, Bethlehem'.
Fortunate indeed the beasts, and the masters of beasts, who know how to glorify their Lord together.

The legend persisted and became widespread; we find evidence of it in France, Italy, Portugal, Maderia, Switzerland, as well as in Britain. It is referred to by

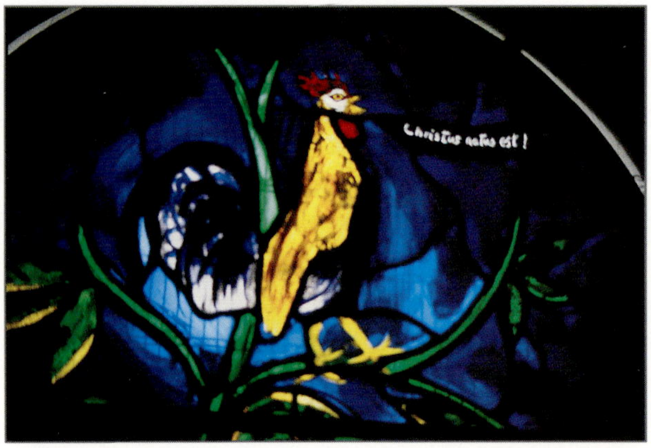

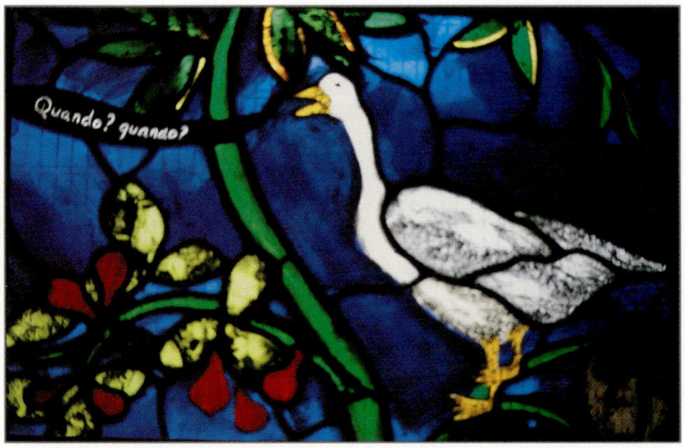

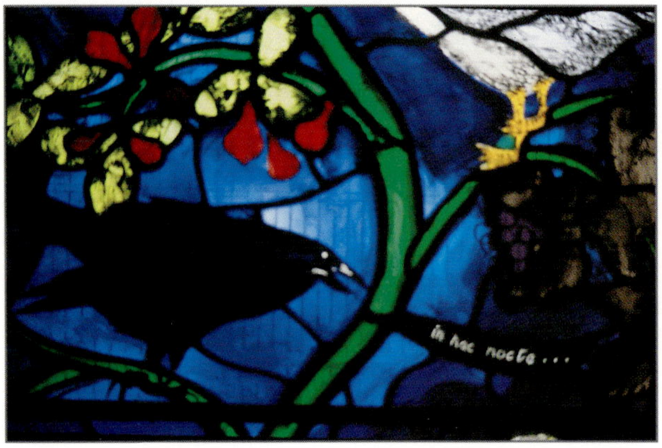

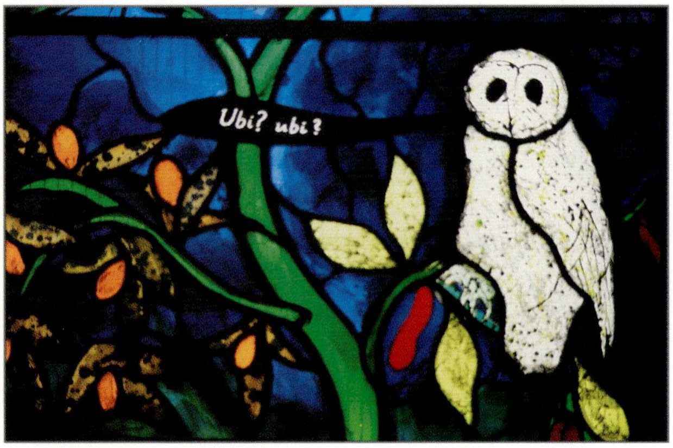

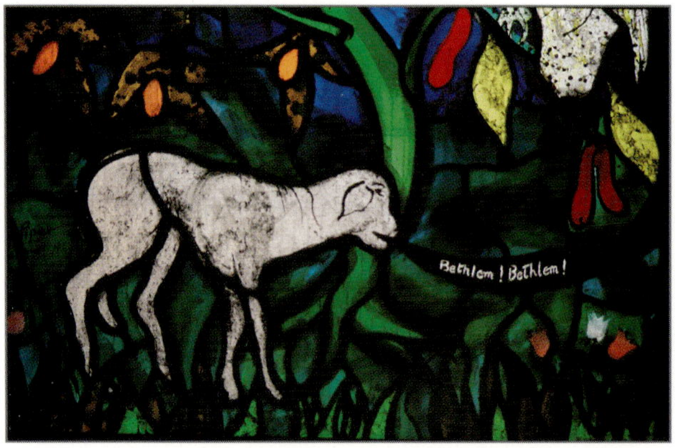

Iffley, St Mary's. Details from the Nativity Window. *Top, left:* Fig. 132: the Cock; *top, right:* Fig. 133: the Goose. *Middle, left:* Fig. 134: the Crow; *middle, right:* Fig. 135: the Owl. *Bottom, centre:* Fig. 136: the Lamb (see pp. 152–4).

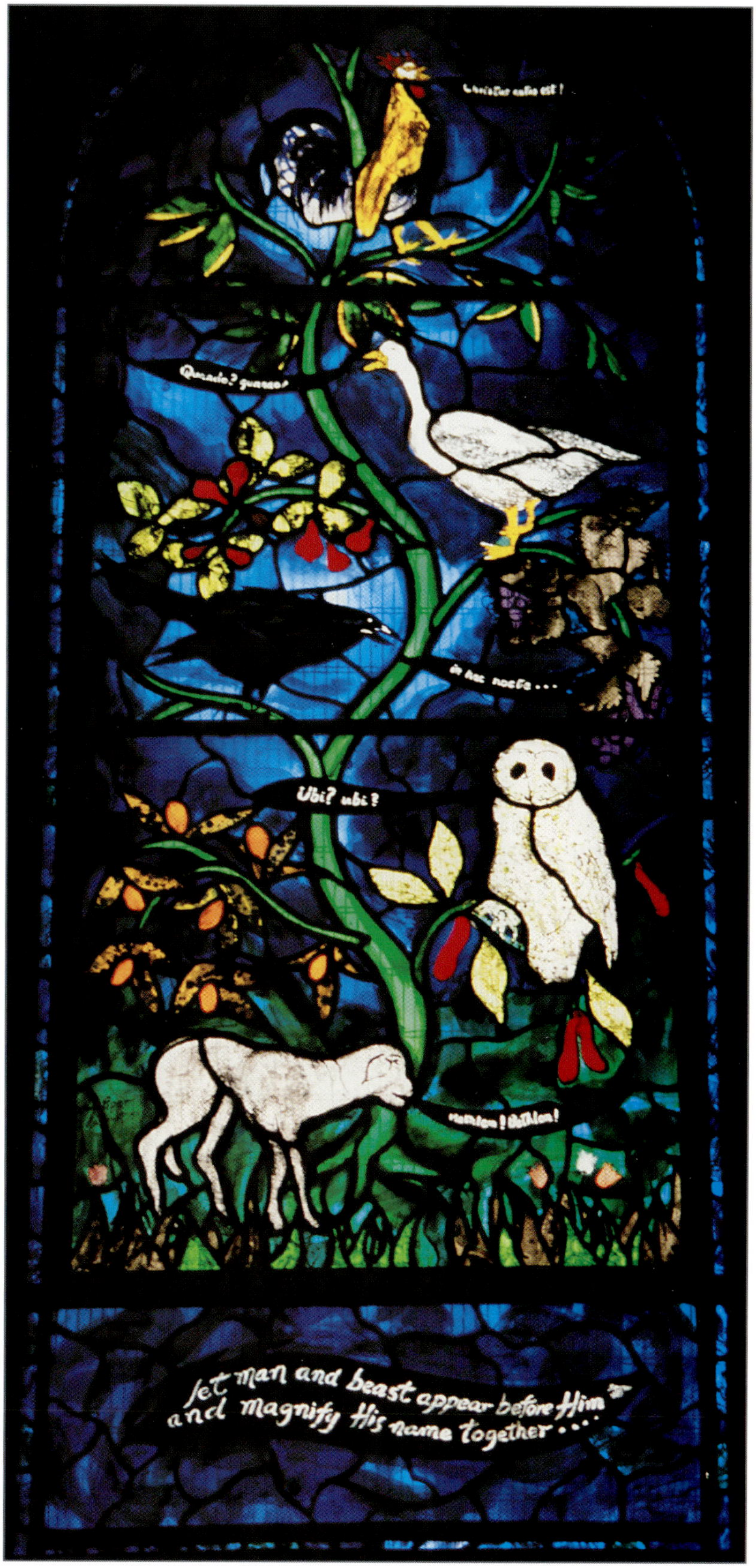

Fig. 137: Iffley, St Mary's. The completed Nativity Window

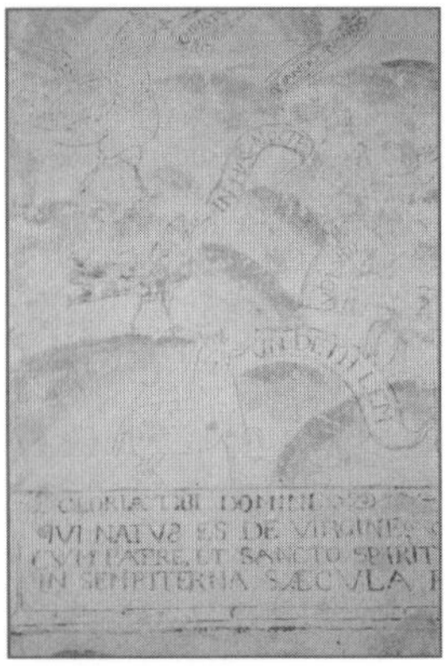

Fig. 138: Shulbrede Priory. Detail from sixteenth-century wall painting

Shakespeare (*Hamlet*) and Voltaire, in Beatrix Potter's *The Tailor of Gloucester*, and the idea of animals worshipping is suggested in Thomas Hardy's poem 'The Oxen'. In recent times it has been the subject of a poem by Charles Causley ('The Animals' Carol') and a carol 'In Hac Nocte' with words by Christopher Wood and music by John Baird (Camden Music, 1992).

In visual terms, there is a wall-painting, dating from *c.* 1550, in Shulbrede Priory, Lynchmere, near Haslemere, on the West Sussex/Surrey border (Fig. 138).[13] This is now very faded, but still discernible are the cock, crowing 'Christus natus est' ('Christ is born'); the goose, saying 'Quando, Quando?' ('When, when?'); the crow, replying 'In hac nocte' ('This night'); the ox or cow, asking 'Ubi, ubi?' ('Where, where?'), and the sheep or lamb, declaring 'In Bethlem'.

Above, the Latin tells simply that the Virgin conceived and bore a Son and His name shall be called Emmanuel; below we find the doxology 'Glory be to Thee O Lord who was born of a Virgin, with the Father and the Holy Spirit, for ever and ever, Amen'.

Although Piper knew of the Shulbrede Priory painting, a more direct influence is probably a seventeenth-century woodcut (Fig. 125, p. 144). Together with a Nativity scene with adoring shepherds, we find the cock, the crow, the goose, and the lamb, all with their appropriate dialogue. The lamb in the foreground, bleating 'Bethlem', is a sad, sacrificial-looking animal. This aspect is emphasized by the inscription '. . . And for Debts which Men should Pay, Downe his Life at Stake did lay'.

Piper's panel was made in the first place for an exhibition in Bristol, 'Prophecy and Vision'. The exhibition was organized by the Bristol Museums and Art Gallery, and was spread between three venues, the main Art Gallery in Queen's Road, the Arnolfini Galleries, and the University's Van Dyck Gallery. It was in the latter that the stained glass was exhibited; the cartoon for the Chartres Four Seasons was also shown (Fig. 105, p. 126).

The interpreter of the Nativity design was David Wasley.[14] Piper sent him a letter and preliminary sketch (Figs 127 and 128, p. 145), asking him to go ahead with the making, and telling him at which stages he would like to inspect the panel (Fig. 129, p. 146).

Although the Nativity panel was completed for the Bristol exhibition, this will hardly have been Piper's main motive. For it is not simply a decorative piece; it is rich in symbolism. The animals and bird are placed not among the rolling hills of the Shulbrede Priory painting, but in the setting of a Tree of Life. So instead of an ox or cow (which could hardly perch among the branches), he put in an owl. 'Ubi, ubi' sounds at least as much like the hoot of an owl as it does the lowing of a cow. The choice of beasts he could have included was very wide indeed, as it evidenced by Charles Causley's poem; the significance of those he did include I have attempted to analyze:

> Some say, that ever 'gainst that Season comes
> Wherein our Saviour's Birth is celebrated,
> The Bird of Dawning singeth all night long:
> And then (they say) no Spirit can walk abroad,

> The nights are wholesome, then no planets strike,
> No Fairy talks, nor Witch hath power to charm;
> So hallow'd, and so gracious is the time.
>
> *Hamlet*, I, i

The Cock is of course the 'bird of dawning' mentioned above. In classical mythology it was dedicated to Apollo because it greets the rising sun. It is a very ancient symbol of vigilance. The belief was that when the cock ceases to crow, the Day of Judgement will be at hand. Additionally, there is the connection with St Peter.

The Goose is linked with the Archangel Gabriel – the honking of wild geese was likened to the baying of Gabriel's hounds. There were consecrated geese on the Capitol in ancient Rome. The goose is connected with Michelmas (goose-fairs), and also with Martinmas, being the symbol of St Martin of Tours, whose feast-day is 11 November. 'Goose-weather' or 'the old woman is plucking her geese' means that it is snowing. The goose is, of course, a symbol of stupidity as well as the main dish eaten at Christmas.

The Crow has very mixed meanings; it may symbolize discord, strife, darkness, or it may mean longevity. At the same time, it may be regarded as the attribute of *Hope*; the bird was associated with Hope in Roman mythology because it calls 'Cras, cras' – tomorrow, tomorrow.

The Owl is an ancient symbol of wisdom, and also of night. 'They say the owl was a baker's daughter' (Hamlet, IV, v) refers to a legend that a baker's daughter reproved her father for giving bread to Christ, crying 'Heugh, heugh!' in derision, and was punished by being transmogrified to an owl.

The Lamb, who points the way to Bethlehem, is the most Christian of all these symbols. In early (Byzantine) art, the Twelve Disciples were often shown as lambs, and Christ in their midst as the Good Shepherd. The symbol of St John the Baptist is the Lamb (and flag). There is the tradition that a lamb was brought as the shepherds' gift at Christ's Nativity. Above all, it is the embodiment of gentleness and sacrifice, hence the emblem of the Redeemer (John 1: 29).

The Nativity panel remained in the artist's studio for many years until Myfanwy Piper decided to donate it to the diocese of Oxford as a memorial to John. Of all the churches in the diocese the choice finally fell on St Mary's, Iffley.[15] The church is a wonderful example of Norman or Romanesque architecture (almost certainly Piper's favourite period). It dates from 1170–80 and was a gift of the St Remy family. It is very well preserved except for the absence of original stained glass; indeed the one thing it lacked was really good stained glass of any period with that intensity of colour which would tell in such a setting. It was finally decided to put the panel in an original window embrasure enriched with Norman zigzag and roll mouldings, at the west end of the south wall of the nave. It looks so right in this setting that one might think it had been made for it; but inevitably the dimensions were not quite the same. So David Wasley made a small fillet of blue glass to go round the edge, and a panel, also blue, at the bottom, with a quotation from Christopher Smart's 'Jubilate Agno' (Rejoice in the Lamb):

Let Man and beast appear before Him,
and magnify His name together. . . .

At the head of the window, that is at the top of the tree, is a cock (Fig. 132, p. 150) crowing 'Christus natus est!': naturally a good deal smaller than the splendid cock at Babraham, it has similar verve, largely coloured gold with bright red comb and wattles. Below the cock, the goose (Fig. 133, p. 150) asking 'Quando, quando?'; then the crow (Fig. 134, p. 150), a black shape under a branch of red and yellow fruits, answers 'In hac nocte'. Lower down, the owl (Fig. 135, p. 150; comparable with the owl in the Peter Fleming window at Nettlebed) hoots 'Ubi, ubi?' The owl is almost entirely white, just flecked a little with iron-oxide paint and yellow stain. Then finally the lamb (Fig. 136, p. 150) bleating 'Bethlem! Bethlem!' It is a shorn lamb, rather than the shaggy animal of the woodcut, but its stance is similar, as it steps across the spiky grass. The main colour of the window is a richly varied blue, deeper behind the near-white of goose and owl, paler behind the black of the crow. The flowers and fruits (picked out in collage on the cartoon (see Fig. 130, p. 146)) glow with so much light that they appear to be on a different plane from the rest.

When the panel was in the studio, propped up against the window, against so much white light it always seemed a little dark. But now (since December 1995) it is so sympathetically installed in St Mary's, Iffley, the Nativity pulsates with new life. A fitting memorial to John Christmas Piper, a man of rare talents and one of the greatest names in the story of stained glass. For what other designer of the twentieth century has left so rich and varied a legacy?

APPENDIX A

THE TEXT OF JOHN PIPER'S STAINED GLASS: ART OR ANTI-ART?[1]

> . . . nobody takes in all the details of the windows at Chartres (except with binoculars and a guide, which are not indispensable accessories of the Christian). But the subject is 'there' all the same, and what sinks in to the faithful is not just an empty play of lines and colours, nor is it the stories themselves, it is in the emotion of the artist who dealt with these stories, the sum total of the love they aroused in him. A credo of Bach does not represent faith as such but it is all the same a moving equivalent for it, turned upside down in the soul of a man of genius. As in any age in which men struggle hard to find a form in which to embody themselves, painting today can perhaps give this same faith some vitality in the form of revelation of the exterior world through more intense interior vision, a moment of truth in which the rhythms of life naturally assume a form of meditation.
>
> *Le Vitrail Français*, Jean Bazaine (Edition Deux Mondes, 1958).

Will good stained glass continue to exist? Has really good stained glass ever existed? The depressing answer to both these questions is 'yes, but very little'. Books on the subject are listed in booksellers' catalogues among 'the minor arts'. The art is minor when it is mediocre: when it is first class it is major, like any other art. But major or minor, it always, all the time, involves a *craft* as well: which is what the booksellers really mean.

As craft it is in constant need of direction and control and nourishment of all kinds from art: from painting, sculpture and architecture. It seldom gets it. When it does, fine stained glass can happen; when it doesn't, ordinary 'commercial glass' – just another window – is added to the ghastly, vast, existing stock.

The average stained glass designer-craftsman of our own day was apprenticed, when he was a beginner, to an artist craftsman, or he was at an art school which had a stained glass department. When young, in any case, he was in direct touch with art in some way, if only studying it 'in the museum', as directed by Degas, or doing some life drawings in the evenings. If he is successful in his career however, he cannot go on being in direct touch with art after a few years unless he struggles hard in his spare time. He will be influenced, gradually and inevitably, by the job in hand, trimming his original gift. And he will probably be lost before he realizes his situation, for the 'good' man is always in demand, and the money is useful. But before he gets finally lost, if we search him out we find that he *dare* not get in touch with art again – the art he began to know as an apprentice or art student – because he would lose his acquired 'vision', which is delivering the required goods. And if he lost that he would do the job that had come to be expected of him badly; he would be 'experimenting', and looking for new ways of 'seeing', and once he starts that he is no longer the good, ordinary man.

There is a gulf fixed between any craft and art. It can be leaped, but anyone leaping it must do so with a clear vision and a stout heart.

Stained glass is a great leader-astray for anyone who works at it – designer and craftsman alike. In terms of colour and form it is eccentric. Colour is abnormally bright, since the light *comes through* the material instead of being reflected from the surface; tone is usually dictated by bounding leads or area joints of some kind. The whole thing is imprisoned within glazing bars that form an inexorable grid and are structurally necessary. This is its proper splendid, discipline. But constant reference back to painting as a source and norm is essential – it is the staff of the glass-maker's life, however much this gets forgotten. The stained glass studio can provide a marvellous life of communal work and camaraderie – and has clearly done so since the 12th century – but the big problems of painting and sculpture are still best tackled in isolation. The undiluted practice of a craft purely as a craft prejudices even the most innocent eyes.

This situation bears on the whole history of stained glass. But for the moment, think again of the position of our young craftsman, who has now emerged from the stained glass department of his art school, or apprenticeship in a studio, and has had a commission of his own. He has been drawing and painting in the life class or studying 'basic-form' and has some personal ideas about colour and shape which need to crystallize and cohere. He is influenced by some admired painter, or by some influential student, and his painting is forming itself in this way at the moment. In order to keep going he seizes the job with enthusiasm. If he is exceptionally talented and lucky, he gets another. For the time being he has to do all the work himself, making as well as designing. The making – cutting, painting, firing, leading – is demanding, for it must be precise, and is extremely time-taking and pre-occupying. The craftsman has already begun to take over from the artist. If he still draws and paints his vision will be influenced, however little, by practice of the craft. The way stained glass falls into 'right' patterns in relation to lead lines – right for stained glass – influences vision and painting practice. If he does not keep the two things going side by side, or at least on equal terms, he is lost. His painting will cease and his stained glass will become stereotyped.

In the fairly recent history of stained glass the Pre-Raphaelites came nearer to success, for longer than any other groups or individuals; because they believed in thorough, sound craftsmanship and because their inspiration came from painting, and served architecture. The same processes were no doubt at work in the Middle Ages, though I suppose it would take a dedicated mediaevalist to prove it. What all of us can see easily is that not all old glass is good glass, contrary to the ordinary archaeologist's view. Archaeologists say, in effect, 'There is no bad stained glass, but some (like beer) is better than others'. In fact, as in painting and sculpture, there always were a few men of genius, and 'the rest'. Without trying to trace the personal development of individuals of genius, (difficult anyway, before the 16th century) it is easy enough to isolate the work of gifted men – the innovators, who in fact were the people who kept glass alive and in the main stream. Self-expression then was considerably more restrained than it is expected to be today. The drawing of an original position of a head, or the outline of a personalized profile, was as far as anyone without genius was expected to go. The pattern of the window, the assembly of figures and decorative features in a panel, was usually pre-determined by habit and tradition anyway, as it is in run-of-the-mill commercial work at any time. And presumably the innovator's big chances came when the master masons and architect-designers made changes in the scale and arrangement of wall openings, in the creation of a new style.

When I first started to look at stained glass, all 13th-century glass looked somewhat alike to me. In those days I was interested in identifying it and dating it, in being a good amateur archaeologist and topographer about it. Then I became gradually a looker rather than a cataloguer, and now that I have eyes for nothing but its particular impact I am struck by the great *differences* in early glass – not the similarities – in the various buildings in which one finds it. The 'Charlemagne' window in Strasbourg is unique in its odd, squarish components and the similarity in size, shape and tone of the *pieces* of glass that add up to a composition resembling an early Mondrian in abstract feeling. It is a work of a primitive compared with almost anything else of this quality in France, though Germany may have nearer parallels. The glass at Chartres is very different in feeling from the glass at Bourges, which is so much more mauve and pinkish-purple in effect, so much more feminine, more suitable to the feminine, flying-buttressed, crinolined architecture of the east end. But then Le Mans, more flying-buttressed than either, has such masculine glass that yet seems totally appropriate in its clear apposition of reds, blues and yellows. Lincoln is different in feeling from Canterbury, also. It must be that a different genius in each case was responsible, through his personality and the power of his art, for the local characteristics. We may never get any further with naming these early artists or the artists of manuscripts – the 'art' from which most of the traditional and original features of stained glass design came – but because we cannot name them (or any but a few) it does not mean we should not be grateful for them and celebrate them. 'Villard de Honnecourt (active about 1250) greets you and begs all who will use the devices found in this book to pray for his soul and remember him. . . .' It is a pity more of his fellow artists did not leave such clear traces behind them.

'There were no builders of "Romanesque" cathedrals or "Gothic" cathedrals, no more than there were Romanesque or Gothic workshops. There were only some builders who created and others who copied them, relying on older techniques.' (*The Cathedral Builders*, Jean Gimpel.) There were no stained glass 'designers' per se, either – there were only some artists who created and others who copied them. The fact that there were, clearly, workshops in Oxford, York, Canterbury, Lincoln, Chichester and other places, glass from which is often found in panels and fragments in neighbouring churches, is usually accepted as of creative, not simply as of quantitive, interest. We know for instance that there was a man named Osbernus Vitrarius of exceptional ability who was a friend of King Stephen and who died in 1153. We know bits about a good many others, and we know some other names; but seldom as much as about Villard de Honnecourt, who was an innovator and inventor, a 'universal man', artist and architect, who not only formulated stone masonry principles, and systemized building practices, but on his travels sketched all sort of things that interested him – grasshoppers, bees, snails, as well as imaginary dragons, which served as models for his own designs as well as for the people who worked under him. That we cannot actually name stained glass artists of great talent, as we can often name painters, does not matter at all. It is easy enough to recognize really original work. In France for instance, the Ascension at Le Mans; the Crucifixion at Poitiers; the 'Belle Verrière' at Chartres; the extraordinary attenuated Virgin and Child at Vendôme – here are four which are not only 'the best', the gems, the prizes of their period; they are masterpieces in their own right, and by obvious leaders.

On the whole, the stained glass lover is not looking for art history, or even for masterpieces – though it is good to have a clear eye for recognizing one when you see it – but for the glow and the glory, and the general pattern of the art. The 'climate' has certainly been favourable during recent years, because some of the most consistent preoccupations of modern art do concern stained glass, especially early glass.

Among them are texture, the glow of rich colour, drama of tone and rectilinear or symmetrical arrangement of design. As to texture, it is an acquired characteristic, and a very important one; because its present condition was no part of its designer's intention. A close examination of any fragment of early glass (such as the head at Wilton) shows that a great deal of its present day effect is accidental, the result of a number of small accidents that build up to a total falsification of the original. There is always pitting of the glass which can be seen best outside; minute depressions – and sometimes bigger ones – have been made in the surface and have filled with dirt, so that the characteristic shading is produced, giving each piece a quality and a character; a *patin*. This modifies the drawing of details, making them seem often more sensitive, often again more dramatic and full of bravura. In any case this influences our half unconscious, automatic apprehension of the old and the weatherworn and the valuable, our sentimental feeling for 'pleasing decay'. It can give unity to fragments and coherence, especially coherence of tone, to assemblages of 'bits'. It can even give unoriginal, copyist work – just ordinary colour and drawing – a modern-looking abstract slant that jerks us into exaggerated approval.

Texture acquired over the years should put restorers on their guard. It is the irreplaceable quality in old stained glass, as in old buildings. Renew the facing stonework of a third-rate building and you are left with a third-rate piece of architecture that has lost its first-rate picturesque effect. Restore glass and you have removed what only age can provide. York Minster glass has in our lifetime lost immeasurably, to my eye, in over-all effect. There was a glimmering richness about the glass thirty years ago that all the zealous and loving attention it has received since has greatly marred. It has indeed been carefully handled – preserved, re-leaded, heads have been replaced, whole areas of nonsense made into sense iconographically – but this has not been done by the eyes and hands of rebellious artists, who would have resisted doing much of it anyway, but by careful craftsmen and zealous scholars, and some of the flavour has gone out of the gorgeous food. Only another five hundred years of rain, dirt, frost and sunshine can put it back. Re-leading may be essential: cleaning and restoration may not be!

There is one panel of 13th-century stained glass which is very much a part of my life. It is one of the nave windows of the small nave-and-chancel church of Grateley in Hampshire. I have known it since I was in my early twenties, when I did a copy of it in water-colours.

On the whole I learnt more about using colours doing this copy than I have ever learned before or since. The panel is at a convenient height from the window-sill – about head height if you stand on a hassock on the sill. (It is rare to find glass to study at head height without trouble or a scaffolding, though opera glasses can be a great help.) It is not a particularly distinguished piece of 13th-century English stained glass – but it *is* convenient, and has never been much interfered with or restored.

The church at Grateley is on the upland plain between Andover and Salisbury, on the old main line from Waterloo to Salisbury. The village is small and remote. It possesses the panel because when Salisbury Cathedral was restored by Wyatt in 1815 he 'Georgianized' it getting rid, among other things, of the remains of the mediaeval glass which, to do him justice, must have been pretty damaged and fragmentary already. The glass he got rid of was 'thrown in the town ditch'. Many bits of it have been recovered, and Canon Baker in the 1930s had a whole window re-leaded for the Cathedral. The incumbent of Grateley in 1815 recovered this whole panel, and took it back to his church, where it has remained ever since, along with some bits of 13th-century border work, which are in the east window. The panel represents the death of Saint Stephen: the Saint, having been driven out of the temple into the open air, is stoned to death as he prays. The 'open air' is represented by a small roll of clouds at the top of the composition, that looks like white hair done up in curlers after washing, and also a tree that, like all 13th-century trees, looks to our equally prejudiced eyes like a garden vegetable. The hireling stone-throwers are clearly meant to be Jewish in facial profile, reflecting the contemporary anti-Jewish feeling which raises its head elsewhere around 1250. Saint Stephen's head is represented on a piece of red 'flashed' glass shaded in deepening red in an abstract impression of his bleeding to death as he kneels. 'Stephenus orans expirat' – Stephen prays as he dies – reads the inscription.

The subject is a common one. The Jerusalem Chamber in Westminster Abbey has a panel of 13th-century glass that represents it too, and there are plenty of others in England and in France. Now this panel has much more 'presence' and 'romance' today than it can have had when it was new. It was part of a 'programme' of panels and was to some extent done by rote, according to the pattern books: in other words it is not a wholly original masterpiece, or anything of the kind. But owing to time, place and circumstances, which in this case have been more chancy even than usual, it has a life and personality that is rare and fragile, and beyond price for those that feel its presence. Nobody has described this life better than Ruskin. In *Modern Painters* he speaks of the old tower of Calais Church – 'The grey peak of it seen far across the sea, principal of the three that rise above the waste of surf and sand and hillocked shore. . . . I cannot tell the half of the strange pleasures and thoughts that come about me at the sight of that old tower; for, in some sort, it is the epitome of all that makes the continent of Europe interesting, as opposed to new countries; and above all, it completely expresses that agedness in the midst of active life which binds the old and the new into harmony. We, in England, have our new street, our new inn, our green shaven lawn, and our piece of ruin emergent from it – a mere specimen of the middle ages put on a bit of velvet carpet to be shown, which, but for its size, might as well be on a museum shelf at once, under cover. But, on the continent, the links are unbroken between the past and the present, and, in such use as they can serve for, the grey-headed wrecks are suffered to stay with men. . . .'

Here in England mediaeval stained glass panels and fragments are to be found in quantity, small symbols of man's unforced relationship with the past, as Calais tower was to Ruskin. Restoration is their great enemy. Preservation, maybe re-leading, is all that they need: no other interference! There are not so many as there used to be that have not been cleaned and re-arranged. The precious character that belongs to the panel at Grateley is not lost *en masse*. When it was in Salisbury Cathedral it was one element in a geometrical organization of panels in a big window; in other words a small piece of a symmetrically-planned kaleidoscope of colour that transformed the whole interior envelope of the Cathedral, so that 'the light of day never came to disturb our own interior light', in El Greco's phrase. The achievement of the 13th century in creating this transforming effect has never been equalled since. Later there was to be a much clearer and cleverer manipulation of light, and relation of detail to architecture, and relation of interior to exterior, but the transformation action was never so complete again. And of course the style 'gets' the present age. We are still fairly new and fervent converts to Romanesque. The brightness and the primary colour-contrasts; the geometrical arrangements of not *completely* geometrical forms, within bold, black glazing bars; the absence of desire in the makers to achieve any formal recession in drawing or colour – these have provided a sympathetic appeal to the eyes of the many in our two thirds of the 20th century. Nobody has described the 12th- and 13th-century transformation scene as well as Proust, an early convert to Romanesque. 'There was one among them which was a tall panel composed of a hundred little rectangular windows, of blue principally, like a great game of patience of the kind planned to beguile King Charles VI; but either because a ray of sunlight had gleamed through it or because my own shifting vision had drawn across the window, whose colours died away and were rekindled by turns, a rare and a transient fire – the next instant it had taken on all the iridescence of a peacock's tail, then shook and wavered in a flaming and fantastic shower, distilled and dropping from the groin of the dark and rocky vault down the moist walls, as though it were along the bed of some rainbow grotto of sinuous stalactites that I was following my parents, who marched before me, their prayer books clasped in their hands; a moment later the little lozenge windows had put on the deep transparence, the unbreakable hardness of sapphires clustered on some enormous breastplate; but beyond which could be distinguished, dearer than all such treasures, a fleeting smile from the sun, which could be seen and felt as well here, in the blue and gentle flood in which it washed the masonry, as on the pavement of the Square or the straw of the market place; and even on our first Sundays, when we came down before Easter, it would console me for the blackness and bareness of the earth outside by making burst into blossom, as in some springtime in old history among the heirs of Saint Louis, this dazzling and gilded carpet of forget-me-nots in glass.'

Romantic richness and gloom, the glow of gorgeous colour in dark surroundings, the glow of controlled fire, this is the basis of the appeal. What we admire at Chartres today is the overall effect of iridescence, flame and fantasy coruscating in the near darkness: not the message. What we see there now must amount to a gross misreading of the original effect. We should no doubt have disliked that intensely, and would have found it impossibly bright, brash and aggressive, and (like the most abused Victorian windows) not only destructive of worship but against all decent canons of art. I was in the Cathedral lately on a February morning; two of us were alone there except for the ever-present old lady with the postcard stall in the north-west corner. It was cold and very dark – there was a wind blowing heavy clouds across the channel from England, and a feeling of snow in the air. One had to grope one's way up the nave, and the total effect was of a more stunning beauty of colour than I have ever known in brighter weather. The predominant blues blazed deeply out of what seemed like great areas of black in the windows; the black looked scrawled or poured, apparently at random. Figures, and the geometrical patterns of panels in the whole design, even at close range, looked purely incidental. Reds gashed themselves across the blue like wounds, and the mollifying yellows and greens and whites trilled and piped and warbled in between, but there were very few of them, and they seemed very small in the area of rich, but barely illuminated, wall. One felt surrounded by cliffs of stone with coloured perforations: the windows seemed to give onto tunnels with light only at the far end of them.

Time and the action of weather surely give unity and this look of purpose and organization to stained glass, good or bad, as they do to building good or bad. The glass at Chartres in its old and weathered age gains a new and glorious unity through the drama of spots and spillings of choked light barely illuminating bright colours – a unity of a sort we have become used to in the paintings of Jackson Pollock, Soulages, Dubuffet and others. After a visit, you may well not be able to recall a single detail of Chartres glass a week later. It is not what it is *about* that matters to us: what matters is that it creates another little world within the world.

The Renaissance proved to be the undoing of stained glass. It was undone because, instead of being animated, inspired and nourished by painting and trying to serve architecture, it began to imitate painting and dictate to the architects. By the second half of the 14th century the signs were there, though some of the most beautiful and even original of all English glass painting was being done at the time, and many further beauties were to come. Herbert Read, talking of the east window in Gloucester Cathedral, once said: 'this wide radiant triptych, gleaming rather like crystals of snow than flames of fire, is one of the most convincing of all the monuments of English art'. He rightly added: 'from all appearances it seems that the glass-design has determined the window design', and he quotes G. McN. Rushforth in a footnote: 'In principle, though the form is somewhat different, the subject and its treatment is the same as that of such well-known pictures as the almost contemporary triptych in the National Gallery, which goes under the name of Orcagna, and the later versions of the theme by Fra Angelico in the Louvre and Fra Filippo Lippi in the Accademia at Florence, not to speak of many other works'.* Danger signals!

Pictures were being imitated. Growing naturalism, the new ideal of nature as a standard of truth, the appeal of the growing hordes of the admirers of Saint Francis and his attitude to materialism and the physical world – these were the animating forces. Architecture was developing light, spacious structures of stone, and becoming so full of virtuosity that it could afford to be sympathetic to its agreeable and decorative little sister, stained glass. 15th-century windows begin to be unashamedly pictorial. The pieces of glass become bigger as the details become smaller and more delicate, the scenes depicted more like easel pictures. The churches in the wool countries such as Suffolk and the Cotswolds glow with gold and light from yellow-stained windows with delicately-drawn angels with outspread wings.

It is silly to get solemn about pictorial representation in stained glass. Where would King's College Chapel, Cambridge, and the choir at Lichfield, and many other splendid buildings be without it? It is colour and glow and 'interest': it is what the architects expected and wanted. It is what saucy revue promoters call their productions: 'naughty, but nice'. When artists such as Dürer and Holbein provided designs for windows, which they did – the drawings exist – the craft

* Read, London

was now so well developed and agile that the designs could be executed just as they came, with very little adaptation or interpretation. The west window in All Souls' Chapel at Oxford is painted on glass after Sir Joshua Reynolds' originals. This kind of pictorial glass got such a bad name from the archaeological folk of the following generations that *even after the last war* there was a barely victorious fight to get it replaced where it belonged; though of course it would be most sadly missed, as would be the old boys on the stone pillars round the Sheldonian Theatre, if it, or they, disappeared. But things had certainly got out of hand a bit with these virtuoso performances by the makers. The best of the English glass artists – the Gyles, Pryces and Pecketts, and Rowell of Wycombe – made windows that have dramatic excitement, and look appropriate in Georgian churches and College chapels that have box pews, classical monuments and plasterwork. Classical borders surrounding pictures in framed panels; coats of arms, Royal and otherwise; Moorish canopies over nude figures in Adam and Eve – they are all precious and they have survived into an age when, thank goodness, they are preserved instead of being ruthlessly destroyed by late Gothic Revival 'restorers' or Edwardian tidiers. They are beautiful, and right for their settings as well as being (what everyone is at long last conceding) 'interesting' manifestations of their own age.

All the same, looking at stained glass one can easily see why the Gothic Revival happened, and what inspired Pugin to such volcanic zeal and fury. (What is surprising is that his own work looks so mild.) As far as stained glass is concerned the whole Revival for forty or fifty years from its serious beginning described a miniature arc, like the bright inner arc of a double rainbow, in relation to the great dim arc of real Gothic. Gothic glass began majestically and ended by imitating pictures; Gothic Revival glass began revolutionally and dramatically and ended by conforming utterly. The great early 19th-century designers, David Evans of Shrewsbury, Eginton of Birmingham, Hedgeland, Willement and the rest, began as pioneers and reformers, and they or their immediate successors all became *con*formers. In the next generation, the early work of Hardman is far more original and convinced than his later work. The same is true of Wailes, Warrington and O'Conner. These stained glass men became flourishing later Victorian institutions, providing good conventional windows which, in the end, lacked all original creative power and all connection with contemporary painting, while the firms they founded flourished. And flourished, on the whole, in inverse ratio to the beauty of their goods. The same story continues. John Keble writing to J.C. Coleridge in 1861 about church architects, says: 'Instead of Butterfield it might be as well to consult Woodyer . . . Is not our dear friend Butterfield getting, to the general, rather grotesque in his ornamentation? . . . (As for stained glass) it is the fashion now to go to Clayton and Bell, or rather Bell'. And windows of that time by Clayton and Bell have indeed much thoughtful beauty. Twenty years later, though still decent, their products are stereotyped – good, recognizable 'establishment' products. The destructive process was at work, added to the effect of the usual commercial progress of the 19th century, the new materialism, which killed bits of genuine art – the little gift, the personal vision, the individual creative impulse – in stained glass designers as in everyone else. This was where the Pre-Raphaelites came in. They soon pulled a brand or two from the burning. Early glass by William Morris, 'period' as it is, has a touching and haunting quality – like wild flowers or birdsong – that could never be recaptured. It is significant that the glass is not fully fledged, from the craft point of view. There is a small piece of glass of this unfledged kind over the entrance to the dining hall in Bradfield College (Berkshire), said to be the first glass designed by Rossetti, which stays in the mind for its direct appeal. And Madox Brown's design, executed by Morris, at Brightwalton (also Berkshire) of Christ suffering little children to come unto Him is another moving composition. But the windows just *after* the earliest by Morris, Rossetti and Burne-Jones are remarkable for freshness and beauty. More so than the later, more developed ones, though it is true they kept it up pretty well until Morris and Co's built-in designers had to cope with too many orders, and became conventional and depressed in the early 1900s.

It seems likely that future generations will find that the Pre-Raphaelites' most useful and original contributions were not to painting but to the crafts, printing, book production and stained glass. Morris was a real reformer and a real prophet: reformer because he went against the stream of commerce and the conventional satisfaction of a demand, and prophet because he led the way back to Mother Art, who had been out of sight behind the imitations of imitations by the later Gothic Revivalists and who has never been completely lost sight of since. The windows the Pre-Raphaelites produced soon became sound and well-made, and unassailable from the craft point of view, and they were not designed by the official built-in designers but by the best contemporary artists Morris could find. (In the end, usually Burne-Jones.) They kept the way open – as it still is *just* open – for the stained glass craftsman to sense the current of contemporary sensibility, which is probably against his nature and certainly against his tradition. To some extent they also conditioned the public and the clergy to this habit, too.

Morris was very careful about what churches he would make windows for. As a rule he would not work for medieval churches, because the new work would not 'rightly harmonize'. The difficult, self-denying moral stands that were made by him have been of profit ever since. He was a precedent, to act on and to quote. To this day it is quite common for artists and designers to be asked to provide one window for a church that may well be better without it; a church perhaps that needs all the light it can get, or that has plenty of stained glass already. Churches can so easily become imitation art galleries, with odd and hopelessly divergent examples of different personalities in the windows – not placed as a gallery is hung, in helpful relation one to another, but arbitrarily, in the mere order of commissioning. Alfred Manessier has recently said: 'I believe less and less in the stained glass window and only in the creation, at one "go", of a light-filled architectural whole, considered and produced by a painter as a single unit'. Well, Morris also said it, a hundred years ago. This is the sign that an artist has got the hang of the medium!

If the story of modern art in relation to glass begins with William Morris, it leads on from him through strange, devious channels – through the Arts and Crafts movement, certainly, and the pink and green curlicues of Art Nouveau glass, and the Paris Exhibition of 1900. But it also pressed on strongly against the tide of the browns and mauves and plentiful dirty whites, and the demoralized Gothic, of establishment Edwardian windows. In 1912 Alfred Wolmark's west window at Saint Mary's, Slough, is a landmark, because it is an artist's window clearly related to a contemporary movement. It shows how fragments of the 'idea' – in this case Vorticism – could begin to infiltrate in odd places; which is really all that the church even now allows it to do, fifty years later. Brangwyn did a window or two, reflecting his own painterly mannerisms too strongly for the glass to be finally agreeable, or influential; but it was through the sympathetic influences of Harry Clarke, Wilhelmina Geddes and Evie Hone that positive constructive relations were again established between stained glass and painting. Ireland had a strong influence at this time.

In France, the reinforced concrete church at Le Raincy, (a Paris suburb), by Auguste Perret, finished in 1922, has glass by Marguerite Huré which is completely abstract, and an inspired answer to the tricky problem of adding a lot of colour to this splendid church. It is the first modern parallel to the Romanesque transformation scene. (It incorporates some figure groups by Maurice Denis, which were clearly a sop to the priesthood, but are insignificant in the overall effect, though Denis had been a strong influence for good in other places.)

Herbert Read prophesied forty years ago that 'the only hope of any reform would seem to lie in the final triumph of those principles for which William Morris stood. For these principles are not altogether dead: they have merely migrated, and on the continent, especially in Germany, there is a school of glass-painting which is not only modern in intention, but is inspired by all that is vital and significant in modern art.' And he mentions Jan Thorn-Prikker and Carl Schmidt-Rottluff, and Thorn-Prikker's 'fine modern glass' at Hagen railway station.

There were signs before the second world war, though they were pretty isolated signs, that modern art might really do more than nod occasionally at stained glass: that it might break in as it had broken into the theatre, especially the ballet through Diaghilev. Sophie Taueber-Arp and Theo van Doesburg made windows related to the de Stijl and Constructivist movements in the early 1920s. Joseph Albers made panels with fragments at the Bauhaus. Marcel Gromaire and other modern painters were designing windows when the war began. Evie Hone, who had studied with Léger and Gleizes, was at work in Ireland making painter's windows conceived in terms of glass. But it was not until the war ended that the modern revival really got on the move. The list of artist-interpreter, double-harness, designer-makers of the last twenty years is a long one. It includes Matisse/Paul Bony, Léger/Jean Barillet, Braque/Bony, and Chagall/Charles Marq.

New churches with money to spare, that is what are needed! Good artists can be trusted: so clergy, be bolder! Until you become so, I can only end as I began:

there *is* good stained glass, *but only a little*. The great windows of modern times are all the work of artists working with collaborative craftsmen. They could be seen to represent an eleventh-hour rescue for a lowered and degraded medium, with its back to the wall – held to ransom on the one hand by its own conscience in relation to art, on the other by the conservatism of patrons and the clergy. But looking back over the whole performance for the past hundred years it may be that the few great modern windows are more justly interpreted as the expected hillocks in a generally flat and dismal prospect. Such interest and excitement as they have is, anyway, a direct reflection of the interest and excitement of the art contemporary with them.

The windows by Matisse at Vence are the pure expression of a painter who thought deeply about the stained glass medium and used it for his own entirely honest ends. They are a kind of free adaptation of his very original late *papiers collés*, and are cut from clear-coloured glass without any 'painted design or modification added, they are thought of as light-transmitting from the beginning. And the way their image is doubled on the floor of the chapel in sunshine is one of their prime beauties.

The Léger windows in the small suburban church at Audincourt (a suburb of Montbéliard, where Peugeot cars are made) are masterpieces of a different kind, symbolic and heraldic; designed by a man of such conviction and strength that they are, as it were, 'signed all over'. And this in spite of the fact that they were executed by another man (Jean Barillet) in that most difficult medium *dalle de verre* – especially difficult on this rather small scale where every piece of glass bonded in concrete counts in the total effect.

These two examples deny every precept laid down for the medium, in principle or practice, before they happened just as Picasso's designs for *Tricorne* disobeyed all the stage design rules in 1919. (It was aggressively simple, unmysterious and self-assertive.) By themselves they have opened up infinite possibilities, though it is most unlikely that these possibilities will be pursued and developed. Nobody can move the body of stained glass practice and *expertise* at a faster rate than it wishes to be moved; and it is the servant of a very slow-moving tradition. It is the traction-engine of the crafts.

Now that we have a window by Marc Chagall in England, at Tudeley near Tonbridge in Kent, his message may become more real and urgent, and acceptable. Chagall himself paints on the glass. Charles Marq, his collaborator, obviously has a strong influence in many ways – on the choice of glass, placing of leads and so on – but Chagall's technique makes a convincing overall statement. He works with an adaptation and not a repetition of his painting technique, and the windows he produces are a real contribution to the medium, not a mere extension of painting.

The glazing of the church at Hempempont near Rubaix in northern France by Alfred Manessier was executed in *dalle de verre* by Barillet. This profited by being done on the early wave of *dalle de verre* enthusiasm, and used most of the medium's real assets – its capacity for hardening an already bold design, for giving full point to white areas among rich colours, and so on – and it is therefore original and influential. Manessier has also done designs for traditional glass: but notice his remarks about designing glass for churches in general.

Among other interesting post-last-war experiments in France and Germany, apart from those illustrated or referred to elsewhere, are the windows at St Rémy, Baccarat, in north-eastern France, when there are sculptured windows as well as a high-level rectangular grid with different obscurations of the elements of it, suggestive of the work of Vasarely; the painter Léon Zak's successful windows at Issy les Moulineaux near Paris, and the impressive glazing of the church at Maria Königin in Cologne (Marienburg), done in the traditional technique entirely in whites, greens and grey-greens of different densities and textures, by the architect of the church, Dominiku Böhm, and Heinz Bienefeld.

METHODS

This is not a book on technique, but there are things that people who look more than superficially at stained glass, old or new, want to know almost at once. The craft has always had a powerful influence on the art it is expressing. This, as I have tried to say, is its burden as well as its glory, but without knowing a smattering about the technique it is difficult to see why.

Normally, every change of colour in a window indicates a different piece of glass, cut to a specific shape and set in a lead, which separates it from its neighbours. This has been so from the earliest times, and still is so; and it must be clear that the consciousness of these interrupting leads for colour changes soon becomes ingrown in the designer, and deeply affects the character of his design. It gives the present-day worker an immediate bond with the past, also, which is very dangerous unless he uses the technique properly, which means skilfully and ruthlessly. The general character of the procedure has remained extraordinarily static: only details have changed. The early makers fired in kilns with wood and charcoal; today's kilns use electricity. They had no large sheets of paper to draw their cartoons on, and no large sheets of glass to use as mounting frames, which are so necessary to us, for assembling the pieces of glass in order to try out one piece against another, to alter and adjust, and to see the design as a whole before completion. For a traditional window has two design elements – the coloured glass itself and the painting on it. Today we stick all the coloured pieces onto a plate-glass window in a jig-saw of colour, and then draw in line or tone on it – in broad sweeps, or fine detail, just as we fancy. It was not so easy before the days of plate-glass. We are told exactly what they did instead in Theophilus' 10th-century treatise (translated and quoted at length in Charles Winston's *Hints*, 1847). They whitened smooth boards with chalk dissolved in water, and when they were dry drew the design on them; then cut all the glass and placed it in position, and the design showed through. If the colour in the glass itself was too obscuring they substituted white glass and painted on that, then cut the dense glass to the same size and held both up to the light, transferring each section of painting to the relevant coloured piece.

Glass-makers are not the same people as window-makers. There is an enormous range of coloured glass available in sheets (they average about two feet square), including plain, bubbled and streaky glass, in all colours. It is cut with a diamond and if necessary chipped into sometimes intricate shapes, and the colour and texture are – when all assembled – modified by painting in black or yellow, in lines, tones or stipples. In black and yellow *only*. Iron oxide mixed with powdered glass and diluted with water, painted onto glass and fired in a kiln, becomes indelible because it fuses with the glass and is unassailable by the weather. This method was used from the earliest times. At the beginning of the 14th century, 'yellow stain' was discovered: silver nitrate painted onto the surface, as iron oxide had been for many years. This, applied in different densities fired at different temperatures, was found to produce any tint of the range from pale yellow to rich dark yellow, or even burnt sienna.

This discovery caused a sort of revolution, used (as it came to be) with more and more delicate and naturalistic line work, and it prompted most of the later developments of the craft; especially as it allowed the use of two colours on the same piece of glass, without an intervening lead. No other general principle so far-reaching has since been discovered, and only one real principle of any kind: the etching of 'flashed' glass by hydrofluoric acid, used since the late 19th century. Flashed glass is clear glass with a skin of coloured glass on one side. White lines and areas can be etched away if the piece of glass is painted with an acid resistant except where the etching is required, and the whole piece immersed in hydrofluoric until the coloured 'flash' is eaten through, so that in those areas (or lines) only the white glass remains.

When all the preliminary work has been done – the glass cut, assembled like a finished jig-saw, painted, fired in the kiln (with each piece numbered for correct replacement in the jig-saw after firing) – after all this there begins the laborious business of joining the pieces with H-sectioned lead and soldering of all the joints, until a panel of pre-determined size can be lifted in one piece. Putty and cement are forced into all the joints between the lead and the face of the glass on both sides of the panel, to keep out the weather and to strengthen the panel physically – it is remarkable, incidentally, how it also strengthens the sense of the design. Windows are made up of such separate panels, attached to the thick horizontal glazing bars let into the stonework on both sides of each lancet.

During the last thirty years or so other methods of colour-glazing windows have been explored. The French began to use *dalle de verre* in the 1930s, and it has become widely used in Europe and America since the last war. The lantern of the new Liverpool Roman Catholic Cathedral is glazed in this way. Slabs or 'sets' resembling pavement lights are the *dalles*, and they are bonded in concrete or epoxy resin (threaded with reinforcing wire) which forms the joints between the pieces of glass, in the place of the traditional leads. Large sections are cast in this way. They are, of course, very heavy, but they have the functional character of a weight-bearing building material and so can be costed by architects as essential parts of a building. For this reason they are often used where traditional glass – an unfunctional decorative addition – would not be. The slabs of glass are used 'neat': they cannot be modified with paint to carry any design. Being about an inch thick – each one weighs about 10 lbs. – they are difficult to cut into any but very simple angular, or rectangular, shapes. They are naturally somewhat intractable as elements in any but a broad, large-scale design. The Léger-Barillet windows at Audincourt (1952) are masterpieces in this medium.

Coloured glass of the conventional thickness has also been bonded in polyester or epoxy resin, and of course glass can be bonded to glass in a kiln that fires at high temperatures. This has been done a good deal in England in recent years, but as a medium it lacks a built-in discipline. Coloured resin is also used, without glass, poured onto glass fibre sheets to form a translucent substance that can be cast in quite large sections without leads, even for colours changes. There is prejudice against it at present: it is thought to look too synthetic or 'plastic', at any rate for churches. But as good artists use the medium more and more there is no doubt it will gain ground. In view of the richness of colour and variety, there is probably quite a future for it.

APPENDIX B

LIST OF WORKS IN STAINED GLASS DESIGNED BY JOHN PIPER

Unless otherwise stated, the designs were interpreted in glass by Patrick Reyntiens.

Date	Setting	Notes on Composition, Setting and Theme
1954	Myfanwy Piper Collection	'Two Heads'. Experimental panel, preparatory to Oundle windows. Exhibited at Aldeburgh Festival 1955. Made by Reyntiens in Eddie Nuttgens's studio.
1954–6	Oundle School, Northamptonshire	Three 3-light windows in apse of School Chapel, for 400th anniversary of School's foundation. Nine figures of the different aspects of Christ: the Way, the Truth, the Life; the Vine, the Bread, the Water of Life; the Judge, the Teacher, the Good Shepherd.
1957–68	Parish Church of St Andrew, Plymouth	Six windows:
		Astor Memorial, 5-light window in tower. Symbols of the Passion, and Cross of St Andrew. 1957–62
		6-light window in Chancel to commemorate Lady Nancy Astor, Britain's first woman MP. The Four Elements: Earth, Air, Fire and Water. 1963
		5-light East Window of Lady Chapel. Symbols of the Virgin (based on the Litany of Loreto). 1965–6

Date	Setting	Notes on Composition, Setting and Theme
		5-light window, St Catherine's Chapel, south aisle. St Catherine's Wheel, with symbols of the Four Evangelists. 1965–6
		Dr Harry Moreton Memorial Window, north transept. Two harps; on a gold ground executed in silver-nitrate stain. 1968
		3-light south transept window. Creation and Trinity: Hand of God with doves and fishes. 1968
1959–64	Eton College Chapel, Berkshire	Eight large windows, divided by a transom, the lower half of each window shows the problem or proposition, the upper half the resolution.
		North side: Four miracles, from East to West: The Raising of Lazarus; The Stilling of the Waters; The Feeding of the Five Thousand; The Miraculous Draught of Fishes.
		South side: Four parables, from East to West: The Light under a Bushel; The House built on Rock, and The House built on Sand; The Lost Sheep; The Wheat and the Tares.
		(The two earliest to be completed were The Raising of Lazarus and The Light under a Bushel.)
1959–60	London. Showrooms formerly belonging to Arthur Sanderson & Sons, 52 Berners Street.	Large window beside main staircase. Abstract composition with plant forms.
1959–62	Coventry Cathedral, W. Midlands	Baptistry Window. Near-abstract composition, symbolic of the Holy Spirit.
1961	Victoria & Albert Museum, London	Brittany Beach Scene.

Date	Setting	Notes on Composition, Setting and Theme
1960–9	All Hallows Church, Wellingborough, Northamptonshire	Three windows: Helen Wells Chapman Memorial Window. The Four Evangelists and their Old Testament antecedents. 1960–1 Rose Window, the Tower. Rose and star composition. 1963 Constance Elizabeth Chapman Memorial Window. 'All Things Bright and Beautiful'. 1969
1961–2	Llandaff Cathedral, Llandaff (Cardiff) S. Glamorgan	Window in Chancel arch. The Supper at Emmaus.
1963–4	St Mark's Church, Broomhill, Sheffield S. Yorks.	West Window. Flames.
1964	St Woolo's Cathedral, Newport, Gwent	Rose Window set in Chancel reredos. Abstract composition within double cross tracery; interpreted in yellow stain.
1964	The Chapel, Ripon College, Cuddesdon, Oxfordshire	West Window. Tree of Life.
1964	Wessex Hotel, Winchester, Hampshire	Interior screen divided into panels with twelve foliate heads.
1965–6	St Mary's Church, Swansea, W. Glamorgan	In Lady Chapel, two abstract windows flanking the altar.
1965–6	The Chapel, Nuffield College, Oxford, Oxfordshire	Five windows: window in (liturgical) west of The Five Wounds of Christ, the other four windows abstract.

Date	Setting	Notes on Composition, Setting and Theme
1965–7	Metropolitan Cathedral of Christ the King, Mountpleasant, Liverpool, Merseyside	Tower lantern, of *dalles-de-verre*, 16 bays, each nearly 70 feet high. The Holy Trinity, symbolized by zones of the three primary colours. Designed in conjunction with Patrick Reyntiens, assisted in the construction by David Kirby.
1966	All Saints, Misterton, Nottinghamshire	East Window of north aisle. Symbols of the Stigmata set on a foliate Cross.
1966	St Peter's Church, Babraham, Cambridgeshire	East Window (Adeane Memorial Window) of 3 main lights. Emblems of St Peter: the crowing cock; the fishing boat; and the keys. In the tracery: anchor; fish; chains; and a keyhole above.
1966–7	The Chapel, Malsis School, Cross Hills, Nr Keighley, N. Yorkshire	Seventeen memorial windows ranged on north and south sides of Chapel, commemorating former pupils and one master killed in the Second World War. Mainly abstract, with insignia of the services.
1967	All Saints Church, Clifton, Bristol	Integral fibreglass windows, made by David Gillespie Associates. Baptistry windows of the Tree and River of Life, and blue side windows.
1967–8	St Margaret's Church, Westminster, London SW1	Eight windows in Nave. Abstract designs in green, yellow, grey-green and white.
1968	Bledlow Ridge. St Paul's Church, Bledlow Ridge, Buckinghamshire	West Window. Near-abstract window symbolizing Heaven.
1968	The Chapel, Christ's College, Rolleston Avenue, Christchurch, NZ	Two lancets of red and blue glass. River of Life and Tree of Life.
1968	St Matthew's Church, Southcote, Reading, Berkshire	Two diamond-shaped fibreglass windows, made by David Gillespie Associates. Abstract designs, suggestive of wings.

Date	Setting	Notes on Composition, Setting and Theme
1969	St Paul's Church, Pishill, Oxfordshire	Memorial window to Philip James Hall. Emblems of St Paul: hands holding a book, set against the Cross-shape of a red sword.
1968–9	Bakers' Hall, Harp Lane, London EC3	Three windows in Hall. Windows commemorate the three times the Bakers' Hall in Harp Lane was destroyed by fire: 1666, Great Fire of London; 1715, Fire in Thames Street; 1940, Blitz in Second World War.
1969	George VI Memorial Chapel, St George's Chapel, Windsor Castle, Berkshire	Two windows. Abstract compositions, largely in blue.
1970	The Chapel, Churchill College, Cambridge, Cambridgeshire	Eight windows of abstract compositions, integrated into the architecture.
1970–1	St Giles's Church, Totternhoe, Bedfordshire	East Window of Chancel. Tree of Life; in the tracery lights, fire, butterflies and phoenix.
	Mayfair Theatre, Stratton Street, London W1	Revolving light in theatre foyer, called 'Dorephos sixty four'. *This has unaccountably disappeared.*
1970, 1976	St Bartholomew's Church, Nettlebed, Oxfordshire	Two windows: 3-light East Window of Chancel, Dr Williamson Memorial Window. Symbols of the Resurrection (Tree of Life, butterflies and fish). 1970 Peter Fleming Memorial Window, 2 lights, south aisle. Tree of Life with birds including owl. Sun and moon above. 1976
1973–4	St Andrew's Church, Wolverhampton, W. Midlands	Large West Window, of 7 lights. Seascape, almost entirely blue, symbolizing the life of St Andrew, a fisherman.

Date	Setting	Notes on Composition, Setting and Theme
1974	St Martin's Church, Sandford St Martin, Oxfordshire	1 lancet window. Symbols of St Martin: hands; cloak; and knife.
1973–4	The Cathedral, Washington DC, USA	Tower window. Churchill Memorial Window, 'Westward, look, the land is bright'. A Tree of Life.
1975	St Mary's Church, Turville, Buckinghamshire	Semi-circular window in tympanum of walled-up door. A hand holding a white lily, symbolizing the Magnificat of the Virgin Mary.
1976	St Peter's Church, Wolvercote, Oxfordshire	2-light window, south wall. Bellamy Memorial Window, on the theme of Palm Sunday, hands and waving branches.
1976	St Mary's Church, Fawley, Buckinghamshire (Piper's own parish church)	One lancet window. (Anthony Hartley Memorial Window.) A Tree of Life.
1977	Charing Cross Hospital, Fulham Palace Road, London SW7	Two windows at entrance to Chapel. Tree of Life, with birds; River of Life, with fish.
1977	Garden Pavilion, Thorpe Tilney Hall, Lincolnshire	Four semi-circular windows in base of turret. Episodes from the life of St Paul: the Stoning of St Stephen; the Conversion of St Paul; St Paul shipwrecked on Malta; the Beheading of St Paul.
1978–80	The Chapel, Robinson College, Cambridge, Cambridgeshire	Two windows: Very large East Window of main chapel, integrated in architecture; The Light of the World. Side Chapel, Epiphany Window, based on Romanesque tympanum at Neuilly-en-Donjon, Allier.
1979	Church of St Peter and St Paul, Aldeburgh, Suffolk	One window of 3 main lights. Benjamin Britten Memorial Window. Inspired by Britten's three operas for church performance: *The Prodigal Son*; *Curlew River*; and *The Burning Fiery Furnace*.

Date	Setting	Notes on Composition, Setting and Theme
1981	St Lawrence College, Ramsgate, Kent	East Window of Chapel, designed in collaboration with Patrick Reyntiens. Piper designed Risen Christ (in tracery lights) – made by David Wasley. The rest of the window, The Firmament, designed and made by Patrick Reyntiens.
1981	Rayne House, Kensington, London	Panel of the Four Seasons, symbolized by foliate heads.
1981	Ipswich School, Ipswich, Suffolk	Four circular windows in gallery of School Library. Foliate heads, each symbolizing the Four Seasons, the Four Elements, and the Four Ages of Man.
1982	Church of St Peter and St Paul, Abington, Northampton, Northamptonshire	3-light East Window. The Annunciation based on painting of the school of Botticelli (Uffizi, Florence).
1982	The Wiltshire Archaeological and Natural History Society, The Museum, Long Street, Devizes, Wiltshire	One window in Picture Gallery. Illustrating the landscape and archaeology of Wiltshire.
1982	Myfanwy Piper Collection	Panel of the Four Seasons, symbolized by foliate heads. Made for Exhibition 'New British Glass & Vitrail Français Contemporain' at Chartres, International Stained Glass Centre, 1982.
1982		Nativity Panel: see 1995, Iffley.
1984	Mrs Betty Kelaart, Nettlebed, Oxfordshire	Dragonfly panel. Made by Joseph Nuttgens.

Date	Setting	Notes on Composition, Setting and Theme
1984	The Chapel, St John's Hospital, Lichfield, Staffordshire	East Window. Christ in Majesty, with symbols of the Evangelists.
1985	St Mary's Church, Lamberhurst, Kent	2-light window in south wall. Annunciation to the Shepherds. Made by David Wasley.
1985	St Paul's Church, Jarrow, Tyne & Wear	1-light window. Benedict Biscop Window, to commemorate 1,300th anniversary of the church. Jarrow Cross and the initials BB.
1985	St Peter's Church, Firle, near Glyndebourne, East Sussex	East Window of Gage Chapel. Memorial to Henry Rainald Gage. Version of Tree of Life, entitled 'Homage to William Blake's Book of Job'. Made by David Wasley.
1986	Norman Scarfe, Woodbridge, Suffolk	Five windows on themes of Venetian architecture. Made by David Wasley.
1986	Church of All Saints, Farnborough, near Wantage, Berkshire	3-light West Window. Memorial to Sir John Betjeman. Symbols of the Resurrection: Tree of Life; Fishes; Butterflies. Made by Joseph Nuttgens.
Installed December 1995	St Mary's Church, Iffley, Oxford, Oxfordshire	Window created in 1982, shown in Bristol 'Prophecy and Vision' Exhibition. Given by Myfanwy Piper as a memorial to her husband, installed in a south nave window December 1995, and dedicated in June 1996. Nativity,* symbolized by animals speaking with human voices. Made by David Wasley, who also designed and made the panel with Christopher Smart quotation underneath.

* There is another smaller version of the panel in a private collection.

Other works in the collection of Mrs Myfanwy Piper
Christ between St Peter and St Paul, *c.* 1955
Small panel with dark and light forms (musicians?)
Two Brittany Beach scenes, 1961

Still life with candle
Small version of 1985 Jarrow Benedict Biscop window
Small abstract panel (gold, red, green, orange)

Other works in the collection of the Victoria & Albert Museum, London
(not normally on view)
Scale model and trial panel for Coventry Cathedral Baptistry Window. 1959
Christ between St Peter and St Paul, *c.* 1958

In compiling this list I have been greatly assisted by Martin Harrison's list made for the Catalogue of the exhibition '*John Piper: Painting in Coloured Light*' at the Kettle's Yard Gallery, Cambridge, 3 December 1982 to 9 January 1983.

NOTES

Introduction

1. The centre part, or bullion, being unsuitable for stained glass, was sold off cheaply for domestic use. Nowadays it is rather fashionable to have bullions set in front doors.
2. The bubble could also be blown into a metal cylinder or 'muff'. For a detailed account of these and other processes see Patrick Reyntiens *The Technique of Stained Glass* (Batsford, 1967, 1977).
3. Ervin Bossanyi, 1891–1971. A Hungarian-born artist, Bossanyi studied in Budapest, Paris, London and Rome. He worked in Britain from 1934.
4. I am much indebted to David Wasley (who worked seven years in Patrick Reyntiens's studio) for the information he gave me on this subject.
5. 'Flashed' glass. This is glass where the colour does not go right the way through (as in pot metal), but where a layer of colour is superimposed, in the liquid state, on a layer of white or clear glass. In the case of red derived from copper, this was a necessity, as red alone would be so dense as to be virtually opaque. Medieval red glass was often made in a 'jam sandwich' of several layers; and, astutely used, a number of different shades of red could be obtained.
6. John Betjeman, *Letters*, Vol. II, 1951–84 (edited by Candida Lycett Green, Methuen, 1995). This letter was written from The Mead, Wantage, Berkshire, and dated 22 May, 1954.

Chapter One

1. Stephen Spender, 'A talk with John Piper', *Encounter*, May 1963.
2. John Piper, *Stained Glass: Art or Anti-Art?* (Studio Vista, 1968).
3. There is a memorial window to Benedict Biscop, designed by John Piper and dating from 1985, in St Paul's Church, Jarrow.
4. In soda glass the alkaline element necessary to its manufacture is supplied by the addition of burnt seaweed or wood-ash to the basic component, which is sand.
5. *The Age of Bede* (Penguin Classics), Chapter 6, 'Bede's *Lives of the Abbots of Wearmouth and Jarrow*' (translated by D.F. Farmer).
6. The only exception was in the case of 'grisaille' (greyish), non-representational glass.
7. *The Book of Suger*, XXIII.

8. There were very close links between England and northern France at this time. Henry I ruled Normandy as well as England, Stephen was Count of Blois, Henry II was born at Le Mans, and his wife not only came from Aquitaine, but before divorce, was queen of Louis VII of France. Professor Madeline Caviness suggests that the Poitiers Crucifixion *may* have been the work of English glaziers (see *Catalogue to English Romanesque Art Exhibition*, Hayward Gallery, 1984 [Arts Council]).
9. It seems genuinely old; that is to say, it was re-examined in 1927 and held to date from the first century AD. See Jean Favier, *The World of Chartres* (Thames & Hudson, 1990).

Chapter Two

1. Piper, *Stained Glass: Art or Anti-Art?*
2. Ibid.
3. Ibid.
4. Ibid., p. 31.
5. Designed by Burne-Jones for Powell & Sons, 1859.
6. Over the years since Piper wrote his book (1968), attributions have altered. He ascribed the Bradfield College glass to Rossetti, and said that the Brightwalton window was designed by Ford Madox Brown and executed by Morris.
7. Reluctantly, Morris had been forced for health reasons to sell the Red House, and in Queen's Square he lived 'over the shop'.
8. Letter to the Revd F.B. Guy, 1861.
9. Piper, *Stained Glass: Art or Anti-Art?*, p. 34.
10. By Charles Harvey and Jon Press in their excellent book *William Morris: Design and Enterprise in Victorian Britain* (Manchester University Press, 1991).

Chapter Three

1. Piper, *Stained Glass: Art or Anti-Art?*
2. Ibid.
3. Report to the Royal Commission of Art in Ireland, quoted in *The Irish Builder*, 1906.
4. 1859–1923. Co-founder of the Abbey Theatre, Martyn did much to promote the arts and the Irish language.
5. The window is a memorial to the organist, who died at the organ after evensong on 4 January 1925.
6. Clarke's dates are 1889–1931. For an exemplary study of this artist, see Nicola Gordon Bowe, *The Life and Works of Harry Clarke* (Irish Academic Press, 1989). Among the illustrations in the book, Figs 27 and 28 are from photographs by John Piper.
7. The panel was exhibited in the 'Glass/Light' Exhibition at the Royal Exchange, London, in 1978.
8. By Nicola Gordon Bowe, David Caron and Michael Wynne. Irish Academic Press, 1988.

9. Again in Piper, *Stained Glass: Art or Anti-Art?*
10. From *Le Vitrail Français*.
11. Later Chagall was to design windows for the rest of this church, and also a window for Chichester Cathedral.
12. Patrick Reyntiens, *The Beauty of Stained Glass* (Herbert Press, 1990).

Chapter Four

1. Piper, *Stained Glass: Art or Anti-Art?*
2. *Sixty-three: not out*, 1925, illustrated by John Piper. Piper's father was Charles Alfred Piper, and the book was published by Curwen Press.
3. In *The Architect & Building News*, 9 May 1941, p. 85.
4. Admittedly when Piper wrote his book, it was shortly before the parlous state of Canterbury's glass was discovered.
5. Media he was later to use for his stained-glass cartoons.
6. Letter to Leslie Waddington, December 1993, published in the catalogue to the John Piper Retrospective Exhibition at the Waddington Galleries, 1994.
7. In this contribution to *John Piper on his Eightieth Birthday* (Stourton Press, London, 1983). Oddly, they were not related.
8. Eddie Nuttgens died, aged ninety, in 1983; he had twelve children. One of them, Joseph, became a stained-glass artist; he worked some years with Reyntiens, and is now established in his father's old studio.
9. The subject of foliate heads/green men is discussed on p. 80.
10. This was true at the time of writing (1996), but subsequent to Myfanwy's death, it may well be moved.
11. Goldilegz: Betjeman's nickname for Myfanway Piper. John he always called 'Mr Piper', or sometimes Mr Pahpah, both in writing and when they discussed architecture in fake northern accents.

Chapter Five

1. Letter to the Provost of Eton College, 14 March 1957. Unless otherwise stated, all quotations about the Eton windows are from correspondence in the College Library (coll/P9/25b) and are reproduced by the kind permission of the Provost and Fellows of Eton College.
2. Letter of 20 October 1955.
3. Letter of 14 November 1955.
4. Harry Stammers's best work is probably the Lady Chapel glass in St Mary Redcliffe, Bristol, *c.* 1960.
5. 22 March 1958.
6. Reyntiens was asking £13 per square foot including transport and insurance, but excluding fixing, scaffolding, labour, saddlebars or Piper's fee. Although it was pointed out that Evie Hone's glass had been a good deal cheaper, working out at just over £11 15*s* per square foot, Reyntiens in the end got what he asked.
7. Headmaster of Eton College, 1949–63.

8. It is interesting to note how much this one window cost.

No. 8 window	Design	£1,000
	Making	£3,216 2*s*
	Fixing and fees	£ 177 10*s*
	Scaffolding	£ 102
	Architect	£ 163 19*s* 6*d*
	Quantity Surveyor	£ 104 17*s* 5*d*
	Total	£4,764 8*s* 11*d*

Chapter Six

1. *Vingtième Siècle*, 1 July 1938, p. 41.
2. Also in London's West End, there used to be a revolving foyer light, designed by Piper, in the Mayfair Theatre, Stratton Street. It was said to be an abstract geometric design, entitled 'Dorephos sixty-four'. It seems to have disappeared without trace, and the staff of the Mayfair Theatre and Hotel disclaim all knowledge of it.
3. The painting is in the Herbert Art Gallery, Coventry. Both this and the picture now in Manchester were first exhibited in 'War Pictures' at the National Gallery, in October 1941.
4. In his book *Ruined and Rebuilt* (Council of Coventry Cathedral, 1962).
5. Under the Chairmanship of Lord Harlech, the members were the Very Revd H.A. Jones, Provost of Leicester Cathedral; Sir Philip Morris, Vice-Chancellor of Bristol University; the Right Revd L.D. Hammond, Suffragan Bishop of Stafford; Sir Percy Thomas, Past President of the RIBA, and the Revd E. Benson Perkins, of the Methodist Church.
6. I am greatly indebted to the staff of Coventry Cathedral, in particular the archivists, for making it possible for me to see, and (with discretion) quote from, correspondence concerning the Baptistry Window.
7. He never failed to acknowledge his monthly cheque.
8. Now in the Victoria & Albert Museum.

Chapter Seven

1. Extract from a letter to Paul Nash, 12 January 1943.
2. In his contribution to *To John Piper on his Eightieth Birthday* (Stourton Press, 1983).
3. St John's Gospel opens 'In the beginning was the Word', so the emphasis is on knowledge as well as faith.
4. Compare this with the Dr Harry Moreton Memorial Window at St Andrew's, Plymouth (Fig. 33, p. 47).
5. Later, in 1978–80, stained glass for another Oxford college, for the Hall of Jesus College, was under consideration. Piper did some designs, but the project was abandoned.
6. Harper Collins, 1990.

7. Second to third century AD. I am grateful to Dr Martin Henig for pointing this out to me.

Chapter Eight

1. Report to Cardinal Heenan, Archbishop of Liverpool, 1962.
2. Artists who designed glass for these include Ceri Richards and Margaret Traherne.
3. According to Reyntiens, they taper 1 foot in 70 feet.
4. I am most grateful to the Cathedral archivists for helping me sort out information on this commission; and also to the staff of Cathedral House for sending me a copy of the video 'Crown of Glass', made at the time for the Shell Petroleum Company, and directed by Michael Heckford.
5. In recent years (1990s) there has been discovered a conservation problem, on which it is reported: 'The vertical joints between the glazing panels and the structure which are sealed with a mastic are leaking, but at the moment the water penetration is finding its way back out of the structure at various points possibly left to cope with condensation. As this is such an awkward position, it is possibly best left until the main roof is tackled when inspection of the whole of the glazing etc. can be carried out, and any other repairs completed. Investigation would have to be made as to whether scaffolding was necessary or whether it could be done from impromptu cradles from roof level, the latter being by far the cheaper.' The cost was estimated as being between £10,000 and £50,000, according to the method of operation.

Chapter Nine

1. *John Piper* (Martin, Secker & Warburg, 1979).
2. See Fig. 111, p. 129.
3. This account is dated 28 April 1980.
4. The East Window was given by Sir Robert Adeane in memory of his father and mother, Charles Robert Whorwood and Madeline Pamela Constance Blanche Adeane.
5. The first Hall is said to have been in Dowgate; the Company moved to Harp Lane in 1506.
6. The window is a memorial to Philip James Hall, 1886–1967.

Chapter Ten

1. St John's (C of I), Malone Road, Belfast.
2. The windows were commissioned in memory of Canon E.C. Cross, Headmaster and Chaplain, 1921–30.
3. It was donated by William Pratt in memory of his wife, Rosina, and his parents, Walter John and Hannah Pratt of Church End Farm, Totternhoe, and dedicated by the Bishop of Bedford, 9 May 1971. The donor was delighted, and said to Piper, 'You have made an old man happy by helping him make a quiet wish reality.'

4. In memory of Dr Williamson.
5. Both of these operas have music by Benjamin Britten and libretto by Myfanwy Piper.
6. Anthony Hartley memorial window.

Chapter Eleven

1. In his contribution to *To John Piper on his Eightieth Birthday*.
2. Extracts from a letter to Paul Nash, 12 January 1943.
3. Nuttgens, a fine glazier in the Arts and Crafts tradition, died in 1982, aged ninety. His son Joe (see p. 149) took over the studio.
4. In an interview with the *Bucks Free Press*, May 1979.
5. For a full account of the Reyntiens Centre at Beaconsfield, See *Bucks and Berks*, vol. 20, no. 157 (Countryside), article by Norman Coomer, 'Exciting new Future for Beaconsfield School'.
6. *The Beauty of Stained Glass* (Herbert Press, 1990).
7. January 1996.
8. Dedicated by the Bishop of St Edmundsbury and Ipswich, 6 June 1980.
9. The bamboo branches are absent in the preliminary design.
10. In memory of Canon R. Perfect, Headmaster 1938–69. It was dedicated on 29 June 1981.
11. This is not so apparent in the cartoon. In the latter there is a slightly different colour balance, the green in the foreground being a good deal darker, the Lily very luminous.
12. In the collection of Mrs Myfanwy Piper.
13. The dedications, made retrospectively, are: Spring, to Roger Cooper, an old boy of the School; Summer, to Allan Leggett, Governor and benefactor of the School; Autumn, to Patrick Bills, former pupil who died in the Rocky Mountains; no dedication, as yet, for Winter.
14. Much earlier, in the 1930s, Paul Nash had done a somewhat similar painting of a Wiltshire archaeological landscape; he also made a print, an example of which can be seen in the Archaeological Institute in Oxford. Nash's colour is cooler, and the foreground artifacts are missing; but the treatment of the Avebury/West Kennet Avenue is akin to Piper's. Paul Nash was, of course, a friend of his.
15. I am indebted to Paul Robinson, Curator of Devizes Museum, for supplying me with information on this window.
16. The cartoon, which is also in the Devizes Museum, is quieter in colour, the stones grey rather than blue, the pot lying on its side a good deal less red, the greens more muted. Piper made an oil painting, of the subject in 1983 (exhibited in 'Works from the Artist's Studio' at the Waddington Galleries, London, in 1994), where the colours are more akin to those in the stained glass.
17. The ceramic, based on a twelfth-century carving from Exernsteine in West Germany, shows Nicodemus and Joseph of Arimathea taking down the body of Christ from the Cross, in the presence of the Virgin and St John.

Above is the half-figure of God the Father; below, Adam and Eve in the coils of the Serpent.

18. Stephen Games described it, rather unkindly, in an article in the *Guardian* (8 December 1980): 'The Chapel, looking rather like a thirties cinema, has a bulging wall of stained glass designed by John Piper, which seems to burst through its brick container like an over-fed stomach through a zip-up sweater.'

Chapter Twelve

1. 'The Two Paths', Appendix V.
2. Ibid.
3. I am very grateful to Fr Paul Baker, team vicar of St Paul's, Jarrow, for supplying information on this window, which was a donation to the church by the Juno Charity Trust.
4. Illustrated in the catalogue of the Tate John Piper Exhibition of 1983–4.
5. Fig. 168 in David Bindman's *Blake as an Artist*, Phaidon, 1977. The Washington water-colour is also illustrated, fig. 173.
6. The reference to musical instruments is in Job 21: 'They send forth their little ones like a flock, and their children dance./They take the timbrel and the harp, and rejoice at the sound of the organ.' The reference to the sun and moon is in Job 31:26. The window was made in memory of Henry Rainald Gage, 6th Viscount Gage, who died in 1982.
7. Southdown sheep, a breed developed in the eighteenth century. The Gage coat of arms has a ram crest.
8. Smith had been Chancellor of the University of Oxford and was the founder of Brazenose College.
9. The window was paid for partly from a bequest from Mr Samuel Hayes, who had been a resident at St John's, and partly from the funds of the Trustees.
10. Indeed, it seems that Piper would not even accept a fee for it. I am told this by Jennifer Patten, whose father Ivor Bulwer-Thomas was at that time Director of the Friends of Friendless Churches. A subsidiary trust of this, the Cottam Will Trust, funded the making of the window.
11. John Betjeman *Letters*, Vol. I, ed. Candida Lycett Green (Methuen, 1995).
12. Aurelius Clemens Prudentius 348–after AD 405. Born in Spain, he first practised law and rose to a high position in the Imperial court. He left public office to take up a religious life. He wrote seven groups of religious poems, including the *Cathemerinon liber*, hymns for the canonical hours and the Christian festivals.
13. I am most grateful to Ian Russell and his wife, owners of Shulbrede Priory, for allowing me to see and photograph the wall-painting, and for supplying further information about the legend.
14. There is another, smaller, version of the Nativity (also made by David Wasley) in a private collection.
15. The window was dedicated on 23 June 1996 by Rt Revd Richard Harries,

Bishop of Oxford, during the course of a very special service of Holy Communion, attended by the Piper family and many of their friends and associates. Especially for this occasion, John Rutter had composed a wonderful anthem, 'Canticle of the Holy City', on the theme of the Tree and River of Life, and he conducted it himself. After the Communion, the animal carol 'Christus Natus Est', composed by Sue Edwards, was sung by a choir of children.

Appendix A

1. John Piper, *Stained Glass: Art or Anti-Art?* (Studio Vista, 1968).

BIBLIOGRAPHY

BOOKS

Anderson, W. *Green Man*, Harper Collins, 1990

Angus, M. *Modern Stained Glass in British Churches*, 1984

Bede *The Age of Bede*, Penguin Classics, 1965 & 1983

Betjeman, J. *John Piper*, Penguin Books, 1944

Betjeman, J. *Letters* 2 vols, ed. Candida Lycett Green, Methuen, 1995

Bindman, D. *Blake as an Artist*, Phaidon, 1977

Bowe, N.G. *The Life and Works of Harry Clarke*, Irish Academic Press, 1989

Bowe, N.G., Caron, D., and Wynne, M. *Gazetteer of Irish Stained Glass*, Irish Academic Press, 1988

Cowen, P. *A Guide to Stained Glass in Britain*, Michael Joseph, 1985

Day, L. *Windows*, Batsford, 1909

Favier, J. *The World of Chartres*, Thames & Hudson, 1990

Grodecki, L., and Brisac, C. *Gothic Stained Glass*, Cornell UP, 1985

Grodecki, L. *Le Vitrail Roman*, Fribourg, 1977

Hall, J. *Dictionary of Subjects and Symbols in Art*, Murray, 1974

Harrison, M. *Victorian Stained Glass*, Barrie Jenkins, 1980

Harvey, C., and Press, J. *Williams Morris, Design and Enterprise in Victorian Britain*, Manchester UP, 1991

Heckford, M. (dir.) 'Crown of Glass' [video recording], Shell Petroleum, Company, *c.* 1965

Howard, R.T. *Ruined and Rebuilt, the Story of Coventry Cathedral*, Coventry Cathedral, 1968

Ingrams, R. *Piper's Places*, Chatto and Windus, 1983

John Piper on his Eightieth Birthday, Stourton Press, 1983

Piper, J. *A Painter's Camera*, Tate Gallery, 1987

Piper, J. *Stained Glass, Art or Anti-Art?*, Studio Vista, 1968

Piper, J. *Romney Marsh*, Penguin, 1960

Osborne, J. *Stained Glass in England* (2nd edn), Alan Sutton, 1993

Reyntiens, P. *The Beauty of Stained Glass*, Herbert Press, 1990

Reyntiens, P. *Technique of Stained Glass*, Batsford, 1987

Rousel, R. *Bourgoyne Romane*, Zodiaque, 1974

Ruskin, J. *The Two Paths*, Cassell & Co., 1908

Sewter, A.C. *The Stained Glass of William Morris and his Circle*, Yale UP, 1975
Winston, C. *An Inquiry into the Difference of Style observable in Ancient Glass Paintings*, Oxford & London, 1867
West, A. *John Piper*, Martin, Secker & Warburg, 1979

CATALOGUES

'Glass Light' Catalogue of exhibition at the Royal Exchange, London, 1978
'John Piper: A Retrospective' Catalogue of exhibition at the Waddington Galleries, 1994
'John Piper' exhibition at the Tate Gallery, 1983: a most useful catalogue
'John Piper' exhibition at the Ashmolean Museum, Oxford, 1992
'Painting in Coloured Light', exhibition at Kettle's Yard Gallery, Cambridge, 1982–3. Catalogue has introduction by Martin Harrison, and a list of glass designed by Piper up to that date
'New British Glass & Vitrail Français Contemporain', exhibition at Chartres, 1982 (Centre International du Vitrail)
'Prophecy and Vision' exhibition at Bristol City Art Galleries, 1982

GUIDEBOOKS

The guidebooks to many churches and cathedrals, too numerous to list here, are an invaluable aid to the study of this subject.

INDEX

For illustrations see List of Illustrations, pp. vii–ix.

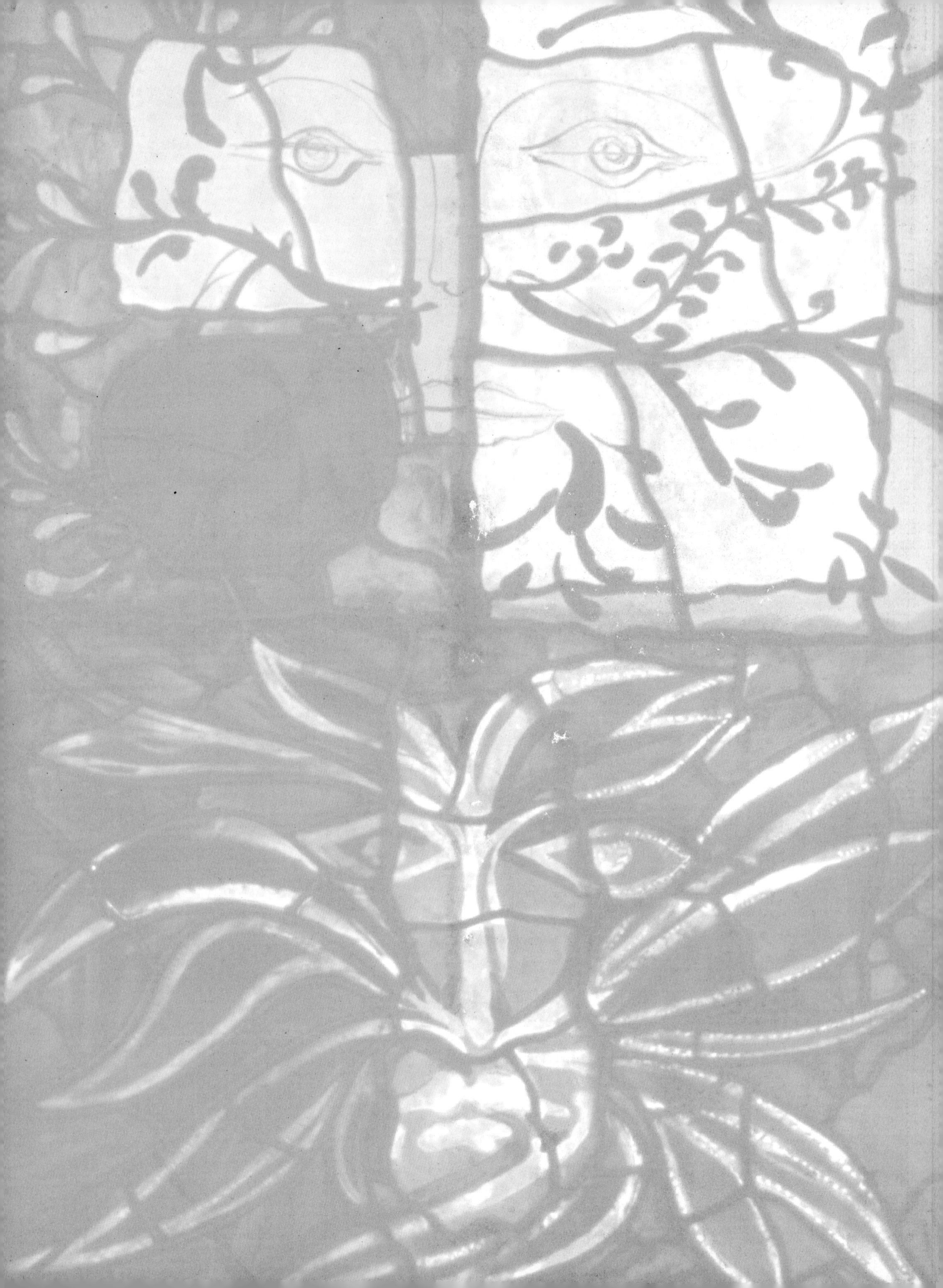